INTERNATIONAL BEARINGS
OF
AMERICAN POLICY

LONDON: HUMPHREY MILFORD
OXFORD UNIVERSITY PRESS

International Bearings OF American Policy

BY

ALBERT SHAW

BALTIMORE
THE JOHNS HOPKINS PRESS
1943

PRINTED IN THE UNITED STATES OF AMERICA
BY J. H. FURST COMPANY, BALTIMORE, MARYLAND

TO

VIRGINIA SHAW

FOREWORD

The unity of the present volume is to be found in its central idea. The several chapters array themselves around the main theme without strict regard to chronology. Although written in the order in which they appear, they deal for the most part with distinct topics, are not much affected by any logical sequence, and might be read in reverse order.

Furthermore, since the book is essentially one of reminiscence, there is no attempt to avoid the expression of personal views, whether regarding things immediately current, somewhat recent, or more remote. Judgments and conclusions, in such a review of diplomatic and political episodes, cannot be expected to assume a judicial character. Indeed, they may at certain points seem injudicious and biased. While not meant to be partisan or unduly assertive, the point of view is always frankly personal.

But for the encouragement of Dr. Isaiah Bowman, President of The Johns Hopkins University, this medley of statement, opinion, quotation and recollection would never have been undertaken. While, therefore, his tolerance and unfailing kindness are acknowledged, it must be made clear that neither he nor the University is in the slightest degree responsible for any of the author's attitudes or avowals.

It is suitable to absolve Dr. Bowman in this way, because he should not be under the necessity of explaining that he is not committed in any manner to the views or verdicts of an alumnus of President Gilman's period, merely because such views find outlet under the auspices of the Johns Hopkins Press.

Dr. Bowman once made a sage remark about the League of Nations, referring to its broad purposes rather than to its mechanism in detail. It was, he said, "intended to promote the idea that a desire to have things work well often makes them work well." Loyalty to the ideals of right and justice sets a standard by which things may be judged. Dr. Henry M. Wriston, President of Brown University, has well observed in his admirable brochure *Prepare for Peace*: "The need is to have a sense of direction, then take one step at a time to realize the potentialities of our faith." In some of the chapters of the present book it is shown that it often requires long years of vexing delay to bring a particular situation to a right and therefore permanent ending.

But the sense of right direction is what saves us from hopeless bewilderment. Thus the announcement on October 13th of a plan for untrammeled democratic government in Italy is an instance of a high ideal and a true sense of direction. The object may conceivably be realized in the near future, or it may be long deferred by reason of internal conflicts and struggles. But the pattern has been set; and there must be faith that it can be realized, since the purpose is proclaimed and the promise given. As for American policy, in spite of waverings and wobblings, it has always found its bearings in the national devotion to ideals of justice, order and peace; and this is true of external as well as internal affairs of political relationship.

ALBERT SHAW.

Hastings-on-Hudson, N. Y.
October 18, 1943.

TABLE OF CONTENTS

CHAPTER I

AN INTRODUCTORY SURVEY

THIS BOOK is presented in support of a thesis, but it has no controversial purpose and is not meant to challenge well-informed opinion in any direction. Neither does it attempt to offer a competing solution for problems that will be faced as Americans, along with other men of good will, seek to establish a more permanent basis for just and peaceful world relationships.

Its appeal is to the logic of historical facts rather than to syllogisms or formulations; and its review of American experiences may, I hope, assist some readers to clarify their mental attitudes. This would not affect them in a practical sense as they are confronted with the stern necessities of wartime, but it might help them to proceed with more confidence, and perhaps with more optimism, upon a course to which we are committed as a nation.

Motives and objects have a tendency to become confused in the toil and din of unprecedented conflict. The present war began with a series of detached aggressions; for example, those of Hitler's seizure of Austria, disintegration of Czechoslavakia, and assault on Poland, with England and France at once involved, followed by Germany's rapid occupation of the Low Countries, Norway and France.

Italy had entered upon a program of imperial expansion that had been too feebly reproached by world opinion and too mildly condemned by the League of Nations. At length, however, the valor of invaded Greece made the world ashamed of its previous indifference to Mussolini's brigandage. Japan's assaults upon China by land and by sea had been steadily gaining in momentum and audacity, although the "Chinese incident" was treated as second-page news by a lethargic American public.

These unrelated wars in Europe, Asia and Africa had found American sympathies generally on the side of the victims of aggression; yet it was not until Great Britain and France declared war, on September 3, 1939, that the Europeans themselves were aware that a second conflict of rival coalitions was to involve the world. Our government declared its neutrality; but for the first time in the history of American policy there was no official pretense of asserting neutral rights impartially. Anglo-American collaboration became at once extensive, and was undisguised.

If opinion in this country had been free from the partisan influences of an impending electoral campaign in 1940, with unusual domestic issues at stake, the pro-Ally attitude of the Roosevelt administration might have been more fairly and reasonably discussed. The debates and the election results, however, showed clearly enough that questions of right and wrong in the European war situations could not be ignored by the United States. International law doctrines relating to neutral impartiality in conduct, if not in thought, had been outgrown and superseded. We might not have to fight, but we could recognize and assist the better cause. The measure of our assistance was to be determined by facts, as in 1917–18.

There had once been peculiar bonds of friendship between the American and Japanese peoples, and there was a tolerance on the part of our government toward Japan's program of imperial expansion that friends of China in this country found it impossible to understand. It is enough to say that conditions in Eastern Asia had been baffling and complex for more than twenty years; and, with pressure upon us to intervene in Europe, it was hoped at Washington that through delay and appeasement—especially in view of our lack of a two-ocean navy—we might somehow avoid a war in the Pacific.

But when the aggressors achieved actual integration of their several programs of conquest, it became plain enough that war was not far from our own doors. No policies of neutrality or appeasement would have afforded us protection. We had allowed the Japanese to purchase enormous quantities of war material in exchange for raw silk and other exports. Part of these supplies they had used in their aggressions against China, but the greater part had been held in accumulated reserves by them for the war against us that they regarded as inevitable. An abrupt curtailment of export-import trade, followed by an uncompromising declaration of American policy made to Japanese envoys by Secretary Hull, were preludes to the attack upon Pearl Harbor.

This attack was by virtue of pre-arrangement with Hitler and Mussolini. Germany and Italy were also at war with us immediately. To keep in mind the sequence of dates, Prime Minister Neville Chamberlain, with English and French associates, had conferred with Hitler at Munich in September, 1938. It had been agreed that if a German-speaking slice of Czechoslovakia were transferred to Germany, Austria having already been annexed, Hitler would make no further territorial claims. This pledge was violated by the invasion of Poland, and Great Britain at once declared war. I was in Great Britain at the time, and had been recently in Holland and France. It was not hard to discover that there was general reliance in these countries upon American support in case of war.

It is to be remembered that Americans—certainly not less cordially than others—at the Peace Conference of 1919 had upheld the establishment of an independent Czechoslavakia and the creation of a reunited Poland. Masaryk had gained enthusiastic support in America for the cause of his fellow-countrymen, and Paderewski had attained the stature of a statesman through devotion to the undying aspirations of his people, with general American sympathy and the encouragement of President Wilson.

With the attack upon Pearl Harbor we were awakened, with deep chagrin, to the mortifying fact that the Japanese since the First World War had become second only to militarized Germany as a land-power, and superior to Great Britain and America combined, in naval and air power in the Pacific. We were also to learn that the Japanese, in their passionate insistence upon treatment as racial equals, had grown in arrogant self-appreciation until they had adopted the theory that they were supermen, destined not only to expel white intruders from Eastern Asia and the Pacific, but to avenge past grievances by conquering the United States.

I have no thought of summarizing the story of the Second World War, in its beginnings or in its further stages. Rather, I am intent upon expressing an underlying view of the character of the war in its larger bearings. With Russia, it has of necessity been a war to turn back the most formidable invasion in modern history. In Britain's case for two years or more it was a war of stubborn defense. With the growth of American war industry, and with a group of United Nations signing the revised Atlantic Charter, it was to become a war of purposes beyond the defeat of aggressors and the restoration of occupied countries. There was to be a new order in the world, not merely of abstinence from international conflict, but also of political freedom, economic advancement, and recognition of the common interests of civilization.

II.

Thus the war on the part of the United Nations becomes in fact *a legal process*, to break down organized brigandage and piracy. Furthermore, the United Nations have given it their recognition as possessing that character, and have agreed to go forward after the war upon constructive lines of improved relationship.

In the chapters that follow I have attempted to show the international bearings of American policy as illustrated in many episodes that have arisen in the course of our national expansion. Even our wars that have been least understood have had certain results of a constructive character. The War of 1812 confirmed our position as a rising member of the family of nations, and established the permanent peace—that has been further cultivated to good effect—between the United States and Canada. The Mexican War gave strength to the principle of self-determination, as resolute pioneers of American stock became predominant in Texas and afterwards in California.

I have given attention to the causes of the Spanish-American War and to its consequences, both in the West Indies and across the Pacific, since I was exceptionally familiar not only with circumstances of wide range, but also with the motives of men who directed our policies. This statement applies to the diplomacy of Cuban independence, the Panama Canal, and the Philippine occupation.

More than any other country, the United States has urged the settlement by arbitration, or other peaceful methods, of disputes between nations, and has taken consistently advanced positions in the development of international law. It is the background of more than a century of notable experience that gives us our best reasons to hope for great further progress, within the lifetime of the present generation. We have met many dangerous situations in the past, and in numerous instances we have arrived at solutions destined to have permanence, because they are based upon methods of reason and justice, and not upon appeals to force.

International law was ceasing by degrees to recognize belligerents as entitled to set the stage for a legitimate duello, that is to say, for a contest requiring fair play and non-interference, as under medieval rules of chivalry. To abandon that view of war as a status of two-sided legality is not to abrogate international law, but to modernize its character. Rules to humanize war had been adopted, but aggressors would observe no rules. The end, in their code of might-makes-right, justifies the means. Gangsters have no scruples, acknowledge no rights, deserve no consideration.

It is to the credit of President Wilson that after two years of the First World War he had revised his conceptions, and had begun to recognize the fact that war was no longer a duel, a tourney, or a regulated prize fight, but an assault against modern life and civilization. Mr. Wilson "kept us out of war"; Mr. Wilson led us into war; and I am convinced that his conduct was neither vacillating nor insincere. The character of the First World War was not obvious in its origins, so far as popular comprehension was concerned in this country. At the outset Theodore Roosevelt, William Howard Taft, and other leading Republicans were as definitely committed as President Wilson and the Cabinet to the doctrines and practices of neutrality.

Mr. Wilson in declaring the neutrality of the United States in 1914 had abjured us to be neutral in thought as well as deed. For two or three years our State Department was engaged in controversies with the British Foreign Office in assertion of our trading rights. We were fighting over again in verbal broadsides the battles for neutral rights that had led to the War of 1812, and to the Geneva arbitration after our Civil War. The Germans were always quick to reply that they would act decently and legally if the reluctant and misbehaving English would do the same. From the British standpoint, it was very much as if Chicago racketeers and gangsters had said that their gunmen would be restrained if the police were confined to night-sticks and were never allowed to carry revolvers.

Yet our government was both intelligent and right-minded, and the American people were conducting themselves as a nation with admirable propriety. It seemed to us that Europe was engaged, after a long period of comparative peace, in a readjustment of the balance of power. The invasion of Belgium, indeed, met with American disapproval; but this was neutralized to some extent by the forgeries and fakes that invented Belgian atrocities for American propaganda purposes.

Early in the war there came into my hands a collection of

British war posters. They had not been prepared to influence Americans, and had not been seen in this country. They were intended to stimulate British resistance, voluntary enlistment, and general war activity. They represented some unaccountable, spontaneous outburst of artistic genius. Nothing like them had ever been seen before, or has ever been produced since that time. I was president of a New York club previously composed largely of people concerned with the producing of books and periodicals; but—at the time to which I refer—a majority of the members were midtown business and professional men of various callings. The club had in its large dining-room ample expanses of wall space, and I hung the posters, with the thought that the members would appreciate a temporary art exhibit of such unique character and merit.

To my surprise I was waited upon by a committee of members who told me that the posters must come down to prevent a disruption of the club. In our membership were many excellent men of German origin, and their sympathies in 1914-15 were not with the Anglo-French-Russian combination. They thought I was violating an unwritten rule of impartiality. They were courteous, and did not accuse me of acting as an agent of British propaganda. The club servants obeyed my orders swiftly, and the posters came down. This incident is recalled to illustrate the unsettled state of mind that prevailed among us in the early period of the First World War. Opinions were changing in the East when Mr. Hughes ran against Mr. Wilson in the campaign of 1916, but in the Far West they voted again for Wilson because he had " kept us out of war."

When in April, 1917, Congress supported Mr. Wilson's recommendation, and voted to enter the war, public opinion was prepared for this momentous step. And there were no men more loyal to the United States, as the country took up arms, than those businessmen of German descent who had objected to my exhibition of the British war posters. The President could cite such atrocities as the sinking of passenger ships without warning by German submarines; but the real motive that led the country to war lay in our general recognition of the struggle as deliberately aggressive on one side, and as defensive of established rights on the other.

III.

Without challenging anyone of contrary views, since I think there should be no serious ground for disagreement, I am calling attention to President Wilson's Fourteen Points, as, in plain fact, the most advanced formulation of international principles ever effectively agreed upon in the history of the world. It should be remembered that this series of numbered provisos was presented to Congress on January 8, 1918, as a statement of our war aims and of the conditions upon which we would willingly negotiate peace. It was incorporated in a careful speech that interpreted and elaborated the summarized points.

This speech was studied throughout the world, and was as familiar to the political and military leaders of the Central Powers as to those of England and France. When the Armistice terms were in preparation, Wilson's Fourteen Points supplied the broad program which the Germans accepted as basic and of permanent validity. The military details of the Armistice agreement were technical and elaborate, as was necessary in the case of a capitulation affecting such wide areas. But the fundamental character of the truce—which it was believed was also to be that of the final peace treaty—was supplied by President Wilson.

I am presenting the text of the Fourteen Points in an appendix, because the first five and the fourteenth are statements of general principles that still hold good and are not to be disregarded. I was in England while the Armistice terms were under careful consideration by the Allied governments. Along with certain other Americans I was directly informed by the Prime Minister that the truce would be based upon Wilsonian principles. That the Germans had studied the Fourteen Points even more carefully than anybody else might have been assumed in the nature of the case.

Since Franklin D. Roosevelt as Assistant Secretary of the Navy was then an active member of an administration that supported Mr. Wilson with rare loyalty, it cannot be supposed that he has ever doubted the permanent validity of the six points in Wilson's declaration that embodied enduring principles. The other eight numbered points related to particular countries, and had to do with states of fact then existent. Yet even these are surprisingly pertinent today; and one readily reads into Point 6, relating to Russia, the circumstances that exist in 1943. It should be remembered that the British took up arms in 1939 to support Mr. Wilson's 13th Point, that demanded an independent Polish state "which should include the territories inhabited by indisputably Polish populations."

Mr. Wilson's last point called for a general association of nations, and the first one forbade secret diplomacy and hidden understandings. As I was made aware at the time by long conversations with him, Mr. Wilson resented with intense displeasure the network of secret understandings in which the Allied governments had entangled themselves, having to do with the distribution of conquered territories.

I have given much attention, in the chapters that follow, to the League of Nations because Mr. Wilson regarded its establishment as the fulfillment of all his hopes. I have been guilty also of an impertinent paradox by intimating that the United States—far from being antagonistic in declining to occupy its place at Geneva—was the only major power that ever really belonged to the League in the full sense of sympathy, understanding, and cooperative spirit.

The League was so constituted—not through any fault of Mr. Wilson's, but perhaps through the influence of post-war elections in Great Britain and France—that it could not in practical experience accomplish any of those major purposes that the President had in mind. I should be less willing to make such a statement if it were not so generally admitted by the most competent authorities, and especially by candid and straightforward English critics.

The chapters that follow in this book make no pretense of dealing by research methods with the several topics that they discuss as illustrations of American policy. Recent historical scholarship has answered most questions that called for accurate study. I am simply endeavoring to show that our Federal Government in its very nature has always partaken of an international character. We have gone forward progressively, and in the main consistently, in our external policies, both as regards our immediate neighbors and also as related to what may be called the legal and political remedies for the evils of war.

There is no reason to believe that we have reached a status of accepted advancement which would justify our neglect of any past experiences. Many things that were done in the right way were done " for keeps," and are fixed land-marks, or foundation-stones (to change the simile), that will serve post-war purposes. If we study the past for the encouragement we derive from successes, we must also study it to become aware of actual failures or of narrow escapes from disaster.

There are accomplished students of international law and diplomatic procedure in half a hundred nations; but, without undue claims for the United States, I think it may be said that we have a greater number than any other country of men and women who have studied foreign affairs, and are versed in the history of world relationships.

If we were seeking for men of the highest qualifications to become members of a Parliament of Mankind, we would doubtless find a greater number of them connected with our universities and colleges (including law schools and post-graduate departments of political science) than anywhere else, although the American Bar Association, the Council on Foreign Relations, the Foreign Policy Association, the peace societies, and certain bodies of clergymen could supply lists of remarkably well-qualified Americans.

I have not hesitated to give this volume a certain aspect of association with the Johns Hopkins University, because it was there that I first studied international law, and became an unpretentious follower of able and statesmanlike thinkers who believed that legal methods could be made to supersede force, not only in local and national groupings of mankind but also in the larger society of nations. In reminiscent mood, with nothing in the performance to justify a suggestion of egotism, I am republishing (as a chapter) an essay that I wrote while a post-graduate student entitled " The Growth of Internationalism." I was endeavoring to show how the law of nations had evolved, as civilized life had been broadened through commerce and intercourse, and how the nations were moving toward the creation of distinct institutions of higher government.

In that period I was studying institutional history in daily association with Woodrow Wilson; and the views that I expressed in that long-forgotten essay were also entertained by him in 1883, thirty-five years before he formulated his Fourteen Points. We had no thought at Baltimore of superior wisdom in our studies of political science. We were fully aware of the eminent positions of Francis Lieber and his successors at Columbia, of Andrew D. White at Cornell, of President Angell at Ann Arbor, of authoritative scholars at Harvard and Yale, and of men of like standing in many other institutions. If I have written more especially about the institution that Dr. Gilman created, it is simply because one naturally proceeds from the place where he finds himself.

It would be presumptuous for me to make proposals; but I have long wished that there might be created a new society, with a classified membership, made up of those persons who can think with what Dr. Nicholas Murray Butler has always called "the international mind." This would properly include in a smaller class the members of international-law societies, the university scholars, and those people (several thousand in number) whose studies or whose official experiences have made them experts in foreign affairs. The next class would include several million people—many of them in ministerial associations, women's clubs, chambers of commerce, labor unions or fraternal bodies—who have given intelligent thought to the establishment of peace, and are willing to support the experts.

Many years ago in an address at Cleveland I made a plea for a new kind of citizenship which would not impair any one of three existing loyalties. Every public-spirited person in Ohio could at the same time be an active citizen of his town or locality, of his proud Buckeye Commonwealth, and of the Federal Union. But I held that a fourth loyalty could be entertained at least in theory, namely, that of world citizenship; and I thought that institutions might in the future give a framework and a tangible form to this international conception.

IV.

The League of Nations made for itself a useful place as a focal point for various activities. It created a suitable habitat at Geneva, and it was not to be undervalued, certainly not to be disparaged or scorned. Yet as an organization for revising the treaties of 1919 it was wholly ineffective. For purposes of improving and strengthening international law, its representative structure was not suitably devised. As an agency for stern intervention when war was threatened, it had no capacity for swift decision, and none at all for initiating action. It had no personal head—no executive leadership. It is because we know all these things about it, however, that it would now seem so feasible to return to Geneva, and to make the Covenant a more sincere and straightforward document, giving to the League such ranges of authority as a new constituency of open-minded and disinterested statesmen might choose to confer upon it.

The high point in all the history of American diplomacy was not the subsequent embodiment of the Covenant of the League of Nations in the Versailles treaty with Germany, but the universal acceptance in 1918 of the Fourteen Points. At the most critical juncture of the World War, President Wilson laid this program for peace, in its complete and definite form, before both houses of Congress; and it did not escape the attention of any intelligent citizen of the United States from Maine to California.

Its general principles could not be refuted, because they were in accord with the historic spirit of American political development. They interpreted the doctrines of Jefferson as regards the relationships of federalized states, and they confirmed the faith of Lincoln, in his unflinching support of the principle that strength lies in union. In the background of the address of January, 1918, there lay years of consistent study and thought, and also much consultation that had been a continuing process for more than three years.

The two authors to whom we are most indebted for understanding studies of Wilsonian diplomacy are Ray Stannard Baker and Charles Seymour. Mr. Baker's *Woodrow Wilson and World Settlements*, in three volumes (with much documentary material), appeared in 1922, and his authorized biography of Woodrow Wilson in eight volumes was completed in 1939. In editing the so-called *Intimate Papers of Colonel House* (in four volumes, completed in 1928) Professor Seymour, now President of Yale University, made such wisely selective use of materials, with the added interpretations of his own trained historical scholarship, as to have created a standard work in the field of American diplomacy.

But the most convenient, and now most applicable, contribution by President Seymour is his volume on *American Diplomacy during the World War.* It was published by the Johns Hopkins Press in 1934, and consists of lectures given by Dr. Seymour in the previous year in the series known as *The Albert Shaw Lectures on Diplomatic History.* Nowhere else have I found any account of our preliminary American efforts to negotiate peace that can compare with Dr. Seymour's chapters, in their appreciation of facts, and their understanding of difficulties. We are allowed to know the objections that had to be overcome in persuading the English, French and Italians to accept the Fourteen Points substantially unimpaired, after the Germans had agreed to sign an armistice based upon the Wilson program. During these pre-Armistice negotiations, the President was in Washington. Colonel House was acting for him in Europe, and Generals Tasker Bliss and Pershing were in consultation on technical points.

Like a wise historian, Dr. Seymour holds himself strictly to his topic. He is informing us of progressive steps in our diplomacy *during* the war. Post-war diplomacy, beginning with the negotiation of peace treaties in 1919, is accounted for, from President Wilson's standpoint, in Ray Stannard Baker's volumes, and also in an ever-rising and broadening flood of historical volumes in all languages, and in official documents so numerous as to baffle many librarians. It is to be hoped that the Geneva collection will be kept intact and again become available for students from all countries, as the Library of the League of Nations resumes its interrupted functions.

By way of deliberate emphasis, I should like to repeat—even with some assertiveness of tone—that President Wilson achieved a great victory for American ideals when through firmness and skill at a critical juncture he secured the acceptance of the Fourteen Points as a basis for actual peace in November, 1918. What member of the large group of countries now known as the United Nations would deliberately seek to withdraw from the commitments that were accepted alike by friends and foes twenty-five years ago?

If the attempt to give practical effect to the Fourteen Points was disappointing, the nations nevertheless stand committed to the principle; and in point of fact the United Nations are already regarding their war alliance as an association for those permanent objects that President Wilson outlined, and that were accepted in 1918, although not completely embodied in the peace treaties of the following year. Views of this kind are finding expression on all hands in the year 1943 (as the chapters of the present volume are written).

But, with great respect for the intelligence of certain thinkers and writers who have been advancing projects for world organization, I might offer a word of caution as applicable to some of their proposals. A single sentence will suffice to express the criticism: These hopeful and right-minded thinkers detach themselves too much from the past, with its achievements and mistakes, and seem to regard the present and future as constituting a wholly new era.

As a corrective, and as a sobering exercise, I should recommend a study of definite phases of American policy as related to particular countries or to continuing problems. No better example of the results of such study could be found than Professor James Morton Callahan's elaborate work entitled *American Foreign Policy in Canadian Relations.* This volume appeared in 1937, and its thoroughness as an instance of historical research gives presumption of validity to its inferences and conclusions. To read it is to know that many critical situations must arise, even between neighboring states that have every good reason to live together in harmony. Dr. Callahan carries us through a hundred and sixty years of boundary experience with such accuracy of detail that while we gain confidence in the achievements of American policy, we also learn the nature of difficulties that have often required the passage of an entire generation for final adjustment.

V.

If it has required so much patience and such continuous effort, first to maintain peace along an American border-line, and then to develop the merely negative absence of conflict into positive relations of cooperative friendship, we must learn to view Europe's complex of national entities with some sense of the flight of historic time. The rivalries and conflicting ambitions that the peoples of the Continent have indulged, since the Napoleonic wars, have dimmed their sense of the values that inhere in Europe's common civilization. In one of my earlier chapters I have discussed the war-provoking tendencies of ill-adjusted nationalism in Europe.

A study in contrasts was made in 1936 by Professor James T. Shotwell of Columbia University. Its title *On the Rim of the Abyss* seemed to superficial readers a warning of imminent danger; but that was not Dr. Shotwell's meaning when he selected the phrase. No student of world politics has ever been more sober-minded, and less inclined to be sensational than Dr. Shotwell. He was active at Paris in the peace-making months of 1919, and made proposals, in March of that year, for changes in the Covenant of the League of Nations that would have brought it into better conformity with the contrasting conditions of Europe and America.

He proposed to provide for Associate Memberships in the League, and for stated periodic conferences in which the associate members would participate. As Dr. Shotwell puts it, the purpose of his proposal was "to erect a League of Conferences, rather than a League for judicial settlement and peace enforcement." It was the common-sense of regional situations that Dr. Shotwell kept in mind. The "Abyss," with which in fact the peace conference was dealing at Paris, was that of war-torn Europe. We might not escape involvement in a second European cataclysm, but at least we were in a situation quite unlike that of the members of the so-called European system. Says Dr. Shotwell in his careful and convincing argument:

"The place of the United States in such a system is clear. It is a place dictated by its position on the *outer rim*—but not outside—of the danger of war. We are relatively safe from the vortex in which other nations may be engulfed, and our first impulse, when war threatens others, is to play with the hope that we can escape from the dangers and responsibilities in which our position in the world involves us."

I am aware of no book that deals as reasonably with the actual work of the League of Nations, in the face of the great variety of post-war problems that confronted it, as this volume by Dr. Shotwell—who is not a special pleader but a profound historical scholar. His last chapter, which discusses the relations of the League and the United States, opens with sentences that did not presuppose the suspension of the League during a war period that was to begin three years after the book was written. Nevertheless, I think that Dr. Shotwell would re-affirm his predictions, and I will quote herewith a sentence or two:

"Anyone who knows the history of this country can have no doubt of the ultimate answer to the central problem of the preceding chapters. It is that the United States will find a way to rectify its relations with the League of Nations, either by joining it upon terms which will effectively safeguard its interests, or by making some arrangement with the League which will prevent a repetition of the sad story of misunderstandings and maladjustments in times of crisis." The subject is not left by our author without further discussion of the kind of League to which the United States might give adherence with a clear understanding of its obligations in all their bearings.

The distinctions that Dr. Shotwell made in his memorandum of 1919 had been further tested and sharpened by sixteen years of experience in observing the League of Nations as it functioned, when he wrote the book from which I have quoted. The League was amassing data, building up precedents, and exerting valuable influence in many directions, even with the embarrassments of operating behind a false front. Dr. Shotwell does it no injustice; and also he gives full credit to Mr. Hughes, Mr. Hoover, Mr. Kellogg and other Americans for the wide range of their efforts to advance the common ends of peace and justice in association with the League.

Frank Simonds, in his lectures on *American Foreign Policy in the Post-war Years* (The Johns Hopkins Press, 1935), taking American public opinion as he found it, assumed that the Wilsonian theory was permanently rejected. But I think that Mr. Simonds had in mind what I have called the "false front." He thought the League of Nations valuable for many purposes, but hopelessly ineffective as a system for checking aggression and eliminating militarism. He regarded the Hoover-Stimson doctrine as applied to Manchuria provocative rather than useful. To quote his own language: "Japan is in Manchuria to stay. Great Britain and France, with far greater material interests in Asia than the United States, have tacitly accepted the *fait accompli*, thus reestablishing friendly relations with Japan. We should follow their example, frankly renouncing the Hoover-Stimson policy which was at once provocative and without practical effect."

I have deep regrets that Mr. Simonds is no longer with us, to write of the Second World War as he wrote so brilliantly of the First. His view of the situation in the Far East, as he expressed himself in 1935 with his wonted frankness, was realistic and was then widely held, especially in Europe. But it was the futile inquiry instituted by the League of Nations that most infuriated the Japanese. When the Assembly of the League finally adopted a resolution that condemned the Japanese as aggressors in Manchuria, they withdrew from the League in high dudgeon and thenceforth pursued their imperial policies openly and defiantly. One violation after another of treaty clauses relating to Europe further exposed the League's utter inability to give effect to its seeming authority as vested in Articles 10 and 16 of the Covenant.

As Mr. Willkie has discovered, the peoples of the world have multiplied their inter-relationships, and will either fight or learn to cooperate. But also they are finding that regional situations seem to call for some degree of separate consideration. Dr. Shotwell would presumably continue to regard the Geneva League as an organization to be reconstructed in order to deal primarily with European, Mediterranean and Near East situations. The American republics and the British dominions could well be Associate Members, joining the European powers in periodic and frequent world conferences. The Washington naval conference of 1921-22, which forms the subject of one of my chapters, affords an illustration of actual achievement through a conference held for definite purposes.

VI.

The two earlier conferences at The Hague in 1899 and 1907, in which American delegations took the most active part, resulted in bringing many subjects of international law to the point of better expression and wider agreement. Elihu Root who was Secretary of State, and was associated with President Theodore Roosevelt in calling the second Hague conference, referred in 1908 to its various conventions and agreements as presenting the "greatest advance ever made at any single time toward the reasonable and peaceful regulation of international conduct, unless it be the advance at the Hague conference of 1899."

These were gatherings of such importance that they must always stand as landmarks, in their adoption of a wide variety of rules and regulations. When the present world war is ended, and institutions of international character are established, it will be found that much of the spade-work in the preparation of codes of law was accomplished in those two conferences. I might fairly claim to have been deeply interested (although not in attendance at either conference), because I was allowed some influence in preparing the instructions for the American delegation in 1899, and some part in the selection of delegates in 1907.

Realizing the difficulties that lay before the nations Mr. Root remarked, "The greater the reform proposed, the longer must be the process required to bring many nations differing widely in their laws, customs, traditions, interests, prejudices, into agreement. Each necessary step in the process is as useful as the final act which crowns the work and is received with public celebration." Forty-four states were represented at the Hague conference of 1907, and perhaps the most important agreement was one for the pacific solution of international conflicts.

The late Dr. James Brown Scott, who compiled the texts of both Hague Peace Conferences, elucidates their proceedings and results in a scholarly introduction that adds a worthy chapter to the history of internationalism. Dr. Scott's earlier approach to his position as a publicist and legal authority was academic (by way of Harvard, Berlin, Heidelberg and Paris). He was afterward for several years Solicitor of the Department of State. For a third of a century (1910-43) he was an officer of the Carnegie Endowment for International Peace, serving meanwhile upon a great number of commissions of conciliation, Pan-American committees of jurists, and as law adviser in conferences, notably at Paris in 1919. Dr. Scott has regarded the development of the common law of nations as following a course singularly like that of the common law of England.

The American delegation at the conference of 1907 urged and secured the adoption of a plan for a third conference, and for further reunions at intervals of about eight years. The third conference was to be held under broad international auspices in 1915. But the world was then at war, and the next effort to deal with world problems in a large way was at Paris in 1919.

Writing in 1908 Dr. Scott[1] remarked that "it may be contended that international law lacks an essential element of law because there is no international sheriff." It was, of course, intended by Mr. Wilson to confer administrative powers upon

[1] Dr. Scott died in the summer of 1943 while still engaged in active service.

the League of Nations that would enable it to proceed against law violators with authority akin to that of a sheriff in local jurisdictions; but at this point the project failed to realize the Wilsonian ideal. Students of international relations are not likely to begin their proposals for post-war adjustment by suggesting a glorified sheriff, or a Chief of World Police for global peace-keeping. Such authorities as Dr. Scott and Dr. Shotwell would be more likely to proceed from recognized regional spheres of achievement, opportunity, or necessity.

What has already been accomplished in the Western Hemisphere stands for *achievement.* All those high authorities who are studying European problems recognize *need.* They will propose solutions through an improved League of Nations, or in some other way. The demand for freedom of the seas has never been fully met, and in that sphere lies what I regard as the greatest and the most concrete *opportunity.* I have devoted Chapter XVII to the consideration of a possible government of seas and islands, vested with sovereign authority, and exercising control by means of its own naval and air forces.

The pattern of the world as we now see it has greatly changed within the past quarter-century. The most impressive change has taken place in Russia. Occupying the eastern half of Europe, spreading across the northern parts of Asia, and reaching far into Central Asia, the Union of Soviet Socialist Republics has a vast regional domain about three times that of the continental United States, and a growing population of approximately two hundred millions.

Almost a hundred years ago we were beginning to subdivide the two-thirds of our continental area lying west of the Mississippi, and preparing for what is now the completed series of forty-eight self-governing states. With that process in mind, we can better understand what has been taking place in Russia since drastic revolutions have swept away the autocratic Czardom and the landed nobility that dominated the country when the First World War brought Russia into conflict with Germany.

Throughout the Russian domains there is taking form a series of autonomous federated republics, comprising inhabitants of many races and languages. The basic principles of Russia are personal equality and social cooperation. Because private capital was no longer existent, industrial development had to be achieved and controlled by collective authority, that is to say, by the government.

Our own institutions being what they are, we are conscious that aggression could have no real place in our national ambitions. This experience of life in a country that is locally democratic, while federally representative, helps us to understand what is taking place in Russia. No other country, unless it be China, will have better reason than Russia to seek the ways of peace and pursue them, when at liberty again to restore the areas that have been devastated by hostile armies. Thus the Union of Soviet Republics represents a distinct regional interest that promises well for the hopes and aims of the United Nations.

Those who know best about changing conditions within the inhabited areas that belong rightfully to the Chinese people, are the persons who seem most inclined to express confidence in the political future. They find China working towards an efficient republic, with capacity for central control, together with local and provincial institutions destined to have a democratic basis. The discipline of long struggle since 1931 has affected the Chinese people more profoundly, according to our best authorities, than could have been thought possible in the nineteenth century. The rights and the well-being of China have been the object of American diplomacy for a long time, especially since John Hay as Secretary of State was defending Chinese commercial equality in his so-called " Open-Door Policy " more than forty years ago.

Dr. W. W. Willoughby, for many years professor of political science at the Johns Hopkins University, and (like several other Johns Hopkins men from time to time) a political adviser of the Chinese government, has contributed much to our knowledge of China's diplomatic relations, especially as brought to light in the arraignment of Japan by China before the League of Nations in 1931. His well-documented volume on that controversy (published by the Johns Hopkins Press in 1935) is encyclopedic in its authoritative information upon Japanese aggressions. In the political sense, as we may believe with good reason, China is to experience " a new birth of freedom."

So much has happened to disturb the tranquillity of nations that it is hard to believe that the great Monetary and Economic

Conference, attended by all the world, was in session at London only ten years ago. It could not achieve the practical results that were too eagerly expected by the Prime Minister, yet it was not a failure when set in its place as an historic event.

VII.

In the concluding chapter of this series I have given space to a memorandum that I prepared ten years ago, as an onlooker at the impressive London scene. It has not been published hitherto, and it has some advantage for the purposes of this book because it reflects more accurately the hopes and the disappointments of that unprecedented gathering than any account of similar brevity that I might write from my general memory of the occasion, or from League of Nations documents. The initial steps had been taken by the Hoover administration in friendly conference with the British Government, and in cooperation with the Geneva League. With the change of administration at Washington a delegation was appointed by President Roosevelt and was ably headed by Secretary Cordell Hull and the Honorable James M. Cox.

So serious and so universal were the economic disturbances of that period that it seemed necessary at the beginning of the Conference for all the leading nations to declare a Truce of a wholly unprecedented character. This was not a truce to end fighting, because at that moment the world was comparatively peaceful. It was a truce that was to preclude any further erection of trade barriers during the conference period, or at least for two months. If the conference was to reach certain broad agreements, it would base them upon the *status quo* as existing when the delegates assembled.

The very fact that such a truce could have been proposed and could have been agreed to by all the leading nations, shows how far governments had gone in their bristling and shifting arrangements for economic self-defense. In one of his opening conference speeches Mr. Hull made clear the reasons for such a truce when he said: "Economic nationalism as practised since the war has expressed itself by every known method of obstructing international capital and trade, such as high tariffs, quotas, embargos, exchange restrictions and depreciated currencies. The reaction upon production, employment, prices and distribution within every nation has been disastrous." The following year saw the beginning of our system of bi-lateral trade agreements, negotiated through the Department of State, but aided by an expert Tariff Commission, and approved as a method by periodic renewals of legislative authority.

The London Conference was entertaining hopeful proposals looking toward a tentative formula for stabilizing the principal currencies of the world. President Roosevelt's adverse decision made it necessary for Treasury departments to pursue such *ad interim* schemes as have actually been employed to keep the American dollar and the British pound sterling at a fairly balanced rate of exchange. The added experience of further kaleideoscopic changes has now given the monetary problem a widely different character. It will have to be dealt with on new terms; and the accumulated stocks of gold and silver owned by the American government will have some part in the solution of a problem upon which the prosperity of the world's future trade is essentially conditioned.

As a general policy American tariffs for promotion of domestic industry, from the days of Alexander Hamilton to those of William McKinley and later, can be defended in view of their results. Ninety-five per cent of our commerce was domestic, and it accounted for the largest experiment in free trade that the world has ever known. Of the remaining five per cent, all of our exports were tax-free, and a large part—perhaps half—of our imports were on the free list. But there must henceforth be a new era of economic freedom and international distribution, both of raw materials and of finished products.

A large proportion of the men who studied all these subjects as members of economic committees at the London Conference are in active life today, and should resume their studies of concrete topics. Provision for post-war life on levels of decency, and freedom from want and fear, were not considered during the four years that preceded the Armistice of 1918. Under Herbert Hoover's direction, arrangements on an immense scale were improvised for relief and rehabilitation in Europe after the Armistice. But Mr. Hoover had to contend with food blockades that continued for almost a year longer.

Of the present situation it can at least be said that we are reversing the old adage that bade us in peace prepare for war, and are believing it both possible and necessary while in war to prepare for peace. We shall not escape altogether from the recurrence of depressions and bad times when the war tension ceases; but plans to avoid some of the peacetime disasters that followed the First World War were taking form in 1943 in the United States, in England, and in some other countries.

VIII.

The title of this book, *International Bearings of American Policy*, is chosen with a more precise sense of the meaning of each word than some readers might suppose. In a small but weighty brochure entitled *The United States in the Far East*, Mr. Stanley K. Hornbeck uses as a sub-title the phrase "Certain Fundamentals of Policy." He defines our foreign policy as a "product and expression of the political concepts from which stems the American democratic way of life."

Proceeding with distinctions and definitions Mr. Hornbeck, who has been for a long time a valued member of the State Department's advisory expert group, explains that our Far Eastern policy is "in no manner separate and peculiar, but is a part of the general and consistent foreign policy of the country that has been rooted in the history of the settling of a continent." Several terse sentences follow the affirmation that our foreign policy "rests upon, resides in, and flows from principles and precedents."

Let me quote the following sentences from a statement made by this clear thinker before the American Historical Association, several weeks after the attack at Pearl Harbor. Referring to the foreign policy of the United States, Mr. Hornbeck says: "It is not the work of one man or of one department or one agency of the Government. It is not a product of secret decisions secretly arrived at. It is not a thing created in a vacuum. It is not a creation of a moment. It is the product of the concepts, the thoughts, the beliefs, the aspirations, the decisions, the acts—through the years and the decades and the generations—of the American people."

The volume from which I make the foregoing quotation proceeds to recount, with explicit facts and with appended documents, the history of our relationships with Japan and the Pacific regions. But at this point I am referring not to the disappointing breakdown of our friendship with Japan, but to Mr. Hornbeck's remarks upon American policy. There is implied in his definition the further statement that our foreign or external policy has always kept step with our internal policy, and has in fact been an inseparable part of our application of judicial principles to the dual-sovereignty system of our federal union.

When Jefferson expressed the view that our type of federal government could be extended indefinitely, he believed that our own union would spread across the continent, and he foresaw the possibility that it might project itself across our northern and our southern boundary lines. But he was making speculative rather than practical forecasts and had no thought of urging premature consummations. American policy, as he envisaged it, embraced operations that were sometimes domestic and sometimes foreign but were fundamentally unified.

To acquire the great unsettled areas included in the Louisiana Purchase was an operation in foreign policy, with no motive except the extension of our domestic system of dual sovereignty. The annexation of Texas involved us in a foreign war; but the principles upon which our policy was based were thought to accord with the Declaration of Independence and the Constitution adopted in 1788.

There were later developments north of our national boundary that resulted in the creation of a neigboring federation on the dual-sovereignty plan. Proposals to give political unity to these two systems have been rejected from time to time, for convincing reasons. If Canada had not been able to form and maintain a continental system of its own, annexation to the United States might have come about piece-meal, so to speak, as in the case of Texas. But in the practical working of American policy it was found that the central administration was carrying all the load it could well bear, in view of diverse territorial conditions. Thus cooperative relations with the Dominion of Canada became a natural outgrowth of the same American policy that had resulted in associations of comparative harmony among our forty-eight sister states.

Thus our relations with Canada, Mexico, South America, and in due time with Great Britain, the British Dominions, France, Russia, the Scandinavian countries, and also—as we hoped and believed for a long time with an over-ambitious Germany—were simply the out-working, beyond our national boundaries, of the principles that had given stability to our federal system. To meet the final test of our ability to maintain this American system, we had been obliged to fight a war between opposing groups of our own states. In the historic sense, the justification of that war lies both in the previous experiences that had given completeness to the federal domain, and in subsequent events that have illustrated the need of national unity and strength.

IX.

Abraham Lincoln was true to the Jeffersonian conception as he contended for the permanence of the United States in its continental sweep. When, therefore, I prepare chapters recounting incidents that have historic place in the course of our external relations, I think of them not as separate phases of foreign policy, but as episodes that illustrate the external *bearings* of what has always been our American federative policy.

* * *

At the center of our American system, as umpire in questions that have arisen and may yet arise between the states, is the Supreme Court. Its position and its functions, in the theory of our coordinate branches of government, are familiar to all intelligent citizens. But in one particular aspect of its historical position its achievements have been so efficient and so conclusive that the average person takes them as a matter of course, or is wholly unaware of them. I refer to the settlement of actual and serious disputes that have arisen from time to time between two or more of our commonwealths.

No state would seek to escape from the verdict of the Court, and no case has arisen for which the Court has not been able to find a solution. The most impressive statement of such cases that I have ever seen was made by Mr. Charles Warren, an eminent legal authority of Boston and Washington, in an article that was published by *World Affairs* in December, 1940, and reprinted in the following month by the Carnegie Endowment for International Peace.

No autonomous entities have ever existed side by side in a better atmosphere of harmony than our forty-eight states. Yet questions involving far-reaching differences among them have arisen, and if we had not established a well-conceived system for their adjudication these differences might have led to outbreaks of violence. In his presentation of many cases, Mr. Warren keeps before his readers the analogy between our settlement of interstate disputes and the possibility of efficient adjustment of disputes between nations by a World Court. Having explained the issues in a number of these interstate disputes, Mr. Warren refers to the skepticism that was wide-spread a century or more ago about the durability of our higher system of justice, and he summarizes the bearings of some recent decisions of our great tribunal in the following paragraph:

" Men say that a World Court is an impractical dream. Well, statesmen one hundred years ago, in the days of rigid State-rights views, would have said that it was a wild, a fantastic dream, if it had been suggested to them that in later years the Supreme Court would take judicial action depriving a sovereign State of 2,400 square miles of its territory, or would deprive a sovereign State of 200 square miles of its oil resources, or would limit a sovereign State in diverting the waters of one of its own rivers, or would cut down by one-third the use by another sovereign State of its river waters, or could require another sovereign State to establish at great expense a new sewerage disposal system, or would deprive a sovereign State of the right to control its natural gas, or would force a sovereign State to pay many millions of dollars on account of a debt to another State. All these things would, in 1832, have been regarded as a wild dream. But the dream came true."

Regardless of its relationship to a League of Nations organized upon an ill-constructed constitution, American jurists and legal authorities have had unbroken faith in the value of the Permanent Court of International Justice established at The Hague. Our own interstate relations have become increasingly complicated, as many regional interests have a tendency to ignore boundary lines. The Supreme Court has shown itself capable of applying broad principles to these new situations. In like manner, as any well-informed person can foresee, there will be far more questions at issue among the numerous sovereignties of Europe in the next quarter-century than in the last one. It must be an important part of the business of the Supreme Council of the United Nations to see that disputes are referred to the World Court and that the tribunal's decisions are upheld.

There stand unrepealed, and still valid, the pledges given in the Kellogg-Briand Pact, also called the Pact of Paris. It was signed in the form of a multilateral treaty on August 27, 1928, and became a World Statute—International Law in its highest expression. The first of its two short articles reads as follows: "The High Contracting Parties solemnly declare in the names of their respective peoples that they condemn recourse to war for the solution of international controversies, and renounce it as an instrument of national policy in their relations with one another." The second article, also of one short sentence, states the same idea on its positive or constructive side: "The High Contracting Parties agree that the settlement or solution of all disputes or conflicts of whatever nature or of whatever origin they may be, which may arise among them, shall never be sought except by pacific means."

This agreement was signed for Germany by the Prime Minister of the Republic, Gustav Stresemann, and for Italy and Japan by high officials. These three countries, while pursuing separate courses for a number of years after their adherence to the Pact of Paris, soon entered upon programs that violated the Pact in spirit and in letter. In each case their policies took deliberate form as imperialistic adventure on the large scale. Until 1939 their actions were tolerated with a complacency on the part of other governments, notably those of Great Britain and France, that must now be recalled not so much for reproach as for warning.

In their useful and timely volume on the *Problems of Lasting Peace*, Herbert Hoover and Hugh Gibson summarize with dates and details the circumstances and conditions that led to the present conflict. It would, indeed, be a pitiable failure of good sense and sound judgment to attempt in war-time to ease the burden of guilt resting upon the three principal aggressors by distributing some blame to peace-keeping nations that failed to act in time. There was needed a collective authority powerful enough to uphold the pledges given in the Pact of Paris.

A Japanese scholar, who was also a high official and a leading member of the Japan Peace Society, once wrote of the prevalence of wars and of measures for their prevention in a book to which I make reference in a subsequent chapter. He remarked (writing in 1915) that "Europe in the last 300 years has had 266 wars." His statistical summary included the statement that "there was warfare in 3,131 years, and there were only 227 years of peace" in a specified period beginning about the year 1496 B. C. Such statistics, although they cannot be regarded as having any character of historical accuracy, are meant to convey the impression that the human race has somehow survived through long epochs during which, in one place or another, masses of men were constantly contending against other masses of men, with lethal weapons.

Far more significant than these crude summaries is such a study of war as the University of Chicago undertook in 1926, two years before the Pact of Paris was signed, and brought to completion in 1942, after sixteen years of continuous research. This study was conducted with the help of many colleagues and associates by Quincy Wright, professor of international law in the University of Chicago. Merely to characterize its method and scope would require a number of pages. The results of this *Study of War* are embodied in two massive volumes of about 1600 pages. Faint hearts might be discouraged as the chapters of this great work reveal the prolific causes of war, and the futile efforts of the past to prevent calamitous appeals to force.

But nations that can unite in such colossal efforts as those of the present struggle to uphold the right and to defeat aggression, must also be capable of applying their energies not merely to ending a world war but to the establishment of peace. Hitherto there has been no effort to put organized world authority behind such an agreement as the Kellogg-Briand Pact. In so far as the people of the United States are concerned, they have only to proceed along the lines of their past experience and their present convictions. Professor Quincy Wright concludes his foreword to the *Study of War* with the following observations:

"Continuous thought and study, closely integrated with practical effort by our own and successive generations, is the price that must be paid for a less violent world. But neither thought nor action can be effective without a clear and widespread vision of the world as a whole, of the interactions of its past and its present, of the interrelations of its regions, and of the interdependence of its peoples."

Although the merging of separate wars in Europe, Asia, Africa, the Pacific, and the outer fringes of North America has resulted in the most stupendous conflict of all historic time, we may regard it as fortunate that there is less confusion of issues than in many previous wars. The aggressors having pooled their assets and coordinated their strategies, it became necessary for the United Nations also to reach understandings. These go beyond the combination of resources for war, and envisage the legal, political, economic, social and moral aspects of peace-making and peace-keeping.

When practical adjustments begin to take form, it will be discovered that in spite of past mistakes much has been accomplished that has been worthy of endurance. I have tried in some of the chapters that follow to give an account of certain achievements that will remain as landmarks, or as structural fragments, when the revised pattern of the world that is to come assumes more definite outlines.

Chapter II

NEUTRALITY COLLAPSES IN A GENERAL WAR

In the course of a half century including and following the American conflict, international law recognized War as a legal institution, and sought to diminish its terrors and brutalities by improved rules and regulations, embodied in general treaties. During our Civil War the European nations not only laid chief emphasis upon the rights of neutrals, but they expanded the scope of international law in practical ways, to limit the interference of belligerents with the normal pursuits of commercial nations.

In earlier periods wars were the rule rather than the exception; and international law was concerned with efforts to make such appeals to force less destructive of the common fabric of European Christendom. The wars of the Seventies (notably the Franco-Prussian and the Russo-Turkish) found America, like other non-combatant governments, observing the obligations and performing the duties of neutrals. When war came again in 1914, we had that same conception of our rights and duties. But as the First World War progressed, both groups of belligerents not only disregarded our neutral rights, but tore to shreds the rules of blockade and contraband that we had regarded as sacred and inviolable.

International law, however, had not been repealed or discarded. It had made developments that we failed at first to recognize. Public opinion had been moving in the direction of the outlawry of war. The fabric of internationalism—that is to say of human relationships across political borders—had become too valuable to endure the furies and ravages of war between Christian nations. We began to discover—in spite of contradictions and confusions—the reason underlying the loss of influence on the part of neutrals.

We found that the doctrine of neutrality as we had asserted it could avail neither to protect our alleged rights, nor to secure respect for our offers of mediation. This was because War had ceased to be a protected public institution. One side or the other, in motive or in methods or both, was aggressive and defiant, using force to seek its own objectives. This relationship of object and method, that gave one side a better cause than the other side, was what weakened the position of non-belligerents. Their sympathies were bound to discover that one belligerent or one group had provoked war for conquest and gain, while the other side was resisting, and was therefore representing the higher law of justice and safety, in a world that had outgrown the crudeness of militarism.

I had spent much time in Europe, making repeated visits during more than half a century, and returning from the last one in September, 1939, just after the beginning of the present war. I had known Europe in a far happier period of prosperity and hopeful social advancement. I had become aware of alarming changes, which culminated in the First World War. More clearly now than at the time, I can understand in retrospect why our attitude of neutrality failed, and why in 1917 it became necessary for us to join the Allies in their support of what was plainly the better cause. The present chapter deals with some of these changes and contrasts.

WE DID NOT think of it as the approach to World War No. 1 when in 1914 Germany joined Austria, and France joined Russia, in the mobilization of conscript armies. We were expecting to stand aside as a neutral power and observe the greatest military duel that Europe had witnessed since the Napoleonic Wars. It seemed a strictly European struggle on the old-time balance-of-power theory, and it had relation to the changing conditions of the new Balkan states and of the Turkish Empire. Germany and Austria sought domination in order to expand their empires to the Bosphorus and the Black Sea, and to assure themselves of opportunity to undertake and control economic development all the way to Mesopotamia.

Russia on her part had for half a century assumed the role of guardian and protector of the South Slav states, which, with her assistance and with the encouragement of the Gladstonian Liberals of England, had won their independence and set up their institutions of recognized nationality. Pressing southward at the eastern end of the Black Sea and along the Caspian, Russia was hoping at some opportune moment to turn westward through Anatolia, following the southern shore of the Black Sea, and to acquire Constantinople by encirclement.

In view of what most Americans, in accord with Mr. Gladstone and his Liberal followers, then thought of the "unspeakable Turk" (having in mind the despotic but crumbling empire of Abdul Hamid), the aspirations of Russia seemed beneficent rather than sinister. The Congress of Berlin had not been forgotten; and historians of our own times thought of Bismarck as having outwitted the courtly Gortchakoff, Russia's foreign minister and leading delegate. Russia's treaty of San Stefano, after the justified defeat of the Turks, was virtually abrogated under compulsion by a group of powers " ganging up " under German leadership, each of these seeking some selfish object of its own. Unquestionably American sympathies were with Russia rather than with Germany in 1914, although England's gallantry in taking arms in defense of Belgium surprised some neutral states, even as it enraged Germany and gave joy to France and Russia.

A British fleet had checked the Russian armies at San Stefano in sight of the dome of St. Sophia. There had followed in 1878 the great European Congress of Berlin, dominated by Bismarck and Disraeli (Lord Beaconsfield). Turkey had met with deserved defeat in the Russo-Turkish War, and Russia could not be deprived altogether of certain advantages. But England and Germany were more subtle and more skillful than Russia at the council table.

It is enough, perhaps, to recall the state of opinion in the United States at the time. I was near completion of my college course, and intensely interested in the liberation of the Balkans. Russia's championship of the oppressed Christian races had won for her our sympathy and approval. The Czar, as Americans thought, had been unjustly assailed by France and England on behalf of Turkey in the unhappy adventure known as the Crimean War. Alexander II had liberated millions of Russian serfs, and, as we understood, he had refused to join the Emperor Louis Napoleon in a coalition against Lincoln and the Union cause in our Civil War. Without too profound a knowledge of the intricate and mysterious game of European diplomacy and " power politics," we applauded the disintegration of the Turkish Empire. We thought of Russia as having been more consistently friendly to the United States in our crisis of the early Sixties than the governments of Lord Palmerston and Louis Napoleon.

When in 1870 this French Emperor had led his army against Prussia, American sympathy turned distinctly to the German side. The old Emperor William had made goodwill for the Hohenzollerns; and " Unser Fritz," who had married the daughter of Queen Victoria, was an American favorite. Bismarck's statesmanship after Sedan, in creating the German Empire on the federal plan, seemed to us a tribute to the success of federalism in our own republic, although this was a fallacious idea.

On the other hand, when Thiers rose so completely to the situation, and other patriotic Frenchmen joined him in creating the Third Republic, while the whole French nation responded to the call of their country and paid the German indemnity without a murmur, there was the return in America of a feeling more than cordial toward the gallant nation that had shared in the struggle for our national independence.

At the outset of the Franco-Prussian War the British government had taken a remarkable step in vindication of the principles of international law and justice. In 1831, when the previous political union between Belgium and Holland was dissolved by mutual consent, the divorce had been approved by the neighbors. It had been the clear purpose of the major powers to guarantee the smaller countries bordering on the Baltic and the North Sea, against interference or attack. Not only was the future immunity of Belgium declared a part of the public law of Europe, but it was specifically guaranteed by England, France, and Prussia.

When, however, the duel of 1870 between France and Germany had become inevitable, there was danger that the armies of one or the other of these two powers might be tempted to violate Belgian soil for obvious reasons of military strategy. Britain then addressed the two governments in identical terms. If they both agreed to respect the neutrality of Belgium, England would take no part. If either France or Germany violated Belgian rights, England would enter the war in support of the other.

Thus Belgium escaped damage, England remained impartial, and the clash of arms was brief though decisive. The two major political events that followed were regarded as distinctly in the line of political progress and European stability. These, as I have said, were (1) the establishment of the Third French Republic on the wreckage of Louis Napoleon's empire, and (2) the successful adoption of a federal system in Germany that was (as we mistakenly thought) free and representative, rather than arbitrary, dictatorial, or dangerously centralized.

There followed a period of peace among the major powers of Central and Western Europe that lasted for forty-four years. A few years earlier, Garibaldi had become a hero in American eyes, and Cavour's statesmanship had won enthusiastic plaudits.

United Italy had taken her rightful place as a European power, under a liberal constitution.

Russia's war against Turkey, occurring a few years after the Franco-Prussian War, was regarded by America and by Liberal England rather as an intervention for the rescue of Bulgaria and Serbia than as an appeal to force through motives of imperial aggrandizement or rapacity. Turkish atrocities in Bulgaria had been denounced by Gladstone in terms that resounded throughout Christendom. Since this war had a constructive and humanitrian aspect, it left no dark stain upon the picture of European peace for the better part of half a century.

During this period of peace, Europe, America, and the world at large had made an astonishing record of material and intellectual advancement. Germany had claimed credit for leadership in the application of scientific research to the arts and industries that were multiplying in quantity and variety the products that supplied human wants. Hundreds of millions of people were lifted an appreciable distance above the poverty line that had formerly prevailed. German universities were acclaimed, and their methods were imitated in the United States, as our older Eastern colleges and the State institutions of the West were adopting higher standards and offering advanced instruction.

It seemed to hopeful and optimistic minds that the nations were actually moving toward the early realization of some form of international society that could prolong indefinitely that epoch of comparative harmony. As I remember that period—and the whole of it lies within the range of my recollections—optimism was justified. I spent much time in European countries, my sojourns beginning at the middle point of that long interval of peace that stretched from 1870 to 1914. I was studying politics and government, methods of administration, public-health measures, and social conditions at large, in a number of countries. Everywhere I found myself breathing a generous atmosphere of kindliness and of international good-will on the part of officials, publicists, professors, and journalists. I experienced no more need of passports in Europe than within the United States. I used indifferently the money of at least half a dozen countries as I happened to have it. It was accepted everywhere, willingly and without discount.

II.

Differences of language were the principal barriers, but they were far less formidable than I had expected to find them. The English, French, and German languages were widely known. Hotel waiters were trained to speak at least four languages quite fluently. The obstacle of language did not at all baffle scientists or administrators. Reforms were proceeding all over Europe under the leadership of men of science. Bacteriology was abolishing epidemics and uniting mankind. Among the leaders of that day were Pasteur in Paris; Koch and his associates in Berlin; Pettenkofer in his laboratory at Munich; British collaborators who followed Lord Lister; contemporaries in Vienna and Budapest, who were applying the results of laboratory research to actual administration in the field of public health.

All these, and many others in more or less related fields of investigation, were creating a type of internationalism that seemed to me to foreshadow clearly some plan of improved cooperation in the political world that would insure peace among the European peoples throughout the Twentieth Century.

It would be easy to expand this general picture of conditions, and to supply particulars; for I was studying at first-hand these very matters. Even in Egypt and parts of Asiatic Turkey there were hopeful signs of social and political reform. As for Greece, Bulgaria, and Serbia, their enthusiasm for self-government and modern progress, as I knew them more than fifty years ago, suggested the optimism if not the boastfulness of some of our new Western states. Their high hopes and anticipations were infectious, and I shared them confidently. The Bulgarian leaders had been trained in Robert College at Constantinople, spoke American English, and cherished our ideals of liberty and progress. I felt at home among them, and I was satisfied that their feet were on the ground as they were applying sound judgment to the problems of a new state.

This chapter is preliminary to a description of the changes that had begun to appear in Europe as the yeasty ferment in the Balkans gave pretext for the major struggle that opened in 1914. There had been disturbances elsewhere that reacted unfavorably upon the picture of the prolonged epoch of friendliness and peace that I have tried to sketch in foregoing paragraphs.

Undoubtedly Great Britain's conquest of the Soudan, her war for imperial extension in South Africa, and the American war against Spain in the West Indies and the Far East, had greatly stimulated the ambitions that were taking form and direction at Berlin. These so-called "Anglo-Saxon" exhibitions of power and acquisitions of territorial authority had been misinterpreted in several countries, but especially in Germany. England and America, charitably judged, would have been found engaged in extending the principles of liberty and self-government to new areas. But this amiable purpose was not clearly apparent even in France, and much less was it thus interpreted and appreciated in Germany and Austria.

In the chapter that follows I have endeavored to show the German Empire entering upon its new policy of economic exploitation in the Near and Middle East. The Young Turks were setting up a parliament at Constantinople, and offering representation to Bosnia. But the Congress of Berlin had granted Austria a mandate to administer Bosnia in order to bring order and peace to a turbulent province. I remember the situation well, because it had claimed my especial interest.

Bosnia was nominally a part of the Turkish Empire. It was actually administered by Austria, with conspicuously good results. Its most eager and determined claimant, however, was Serbia, because the Bosnians, though mainly Mohammedan, spoke a Serbian dialect and offered the small kingdom its one future opportunity to realize what was called the "Great Serbian Idea." To forestall Turkey, and to preclude the vain hopes of Serbia, Austria-Hungary in 1908 announced its annexation of Bosnia and Herzegovina.

Balkan history thereupon wrote further chapters of its restless and unstable course. The well-meaning heir to the Austrian succession, the Archduke Francis Ferdinand, visited Bosnia with his wife in June 1914 and they were both assassinated at Sarajevo on the 28th of that month by an agent of an irreconcilable Serbian secret society. Austria issued a harsh ultimatum, and a month later declared war on Serbia. In this interval of weeks it was well known that Russia was mobilizing to intervene. It was equally evident that Germany could have restrained Austria, in order to give Serbia time and opportunity to make any reparation that an arbitral authority might have decided upon.

But within a week after Austria declared war, the German troops had crossed the border into France and Russian troops had crossed the border into Germany. On August 7, ten days after Austria's war declaration, the German troops were in Belgium on their way to Paris. Germany and Austria were in war alliance, and so were Russia and France. An understanding had been reached between England and France known in diplomatic circles as an "*entente cordiale.*" It did not require England to fight with France and Russia, but it had smoothed the way for British cooperation in dire emergencies.

Home Rule for Ireland as enacted by the Liberals under Asquith, with Mr. Lloyd George as the most prominent member of the Cabinet, had caused disaffection in the high ranks of the British Army. The Germans had been convinced that England could not take part in the war—certainly not without weeks or months of delay. Mr. Asquith might in July have acted upon the diplomatic precedent of 1870 and asked from both sides a pledge to respect the neutrality of Belgium. If Germany and France had replied affirmatively, England—in view of her military unpreparedness, and the evident reluctance of the nation to enter upon a Continental war—might have declared neutrality as in 1870.

No one knows what bearing that course might have had upon the war. It is enough to say that the Germans entered Belgium on a certain day in August 1917, and the British Expeditionary Force landed in France nine days afterwards and four days before the Germans had occupied Brussels. The guaranteed neutrality of Belgium had been violated, and the British had acted with amazing promptness in view of the swiftness with which the conscripted armies of four great European powers had entered upon a colossal war.

III.

Wars cause inconvenience and loss even to the countries that are not belligerents. Although the United States did not regard the ultimatum to Serbia as justified, and could not look with bland indifference upon the invasion of Belgium, we were not prepared to pronounce judgment, much less were we ready to align ourselves with either side. Some among us thought of the war as one of those periodic struggles that had in former generations involved nothing more than a shifting and readjustment of the balance of power in Europe. It had obviously some relation to rivalries for external trade and colonial possessions in Asia and Africa. But there were at first no convincing voices raised to declare that this was also our war. President Wilson proclaimed our Neutrality, and insisted upon its sincere and impartial observance.

International law in earlier periods had recognized the hard fact that wars were usual and peace was exceptional. Statesmen and legal authorities had sought to mitigate the savagery of war and its blighting effects. Rules had been formulated for the better protection of non-combatants and their property. The care of prisoners, and the immunity of hospital and relief agencies, had been subjects of theoretical discussion and of practical agreement.

Thus while war was deplored and peace was extolled by doctrinaires, international law seemed to deal with war as an institution to be legalized and regulated, rather than a hideous plague to be outlawed—an accursed thing to be exorcised. Belligerents were disposed to regard themselves as favored by the rules of the game while neutrals were expected to stand well aside, under penalty of being hurt. The red lights were turned on for the duration. There were no green lights or safety zones for the non-fighters. Neutral nations found themselves in constant peril, even on the common highways of the sea.

But international law in its earlier developments was an outgrowth exclusively of European experience. The wars with which Grotius, Pufendorf and the other early internationalists concerned themselves, were those that involved Catholic and Protestant Christendom. These mentors of the war-lords were doubtless affected in their thinking by the customs of the age of chivalry, and the more or less romantic ethics of knighthood. Their rules were not considered applicable to the methods of imperial conquest employed in America, in Asia, and in the Dark Continent.

However, with the rise of the United States to a position of influence and power in the family of nations, new emphasis began to be placed upon those doctrines of international law that were concerned with the rights of neutrals. In the earlier period, when our maritime interests were paramount, our commerce had been swept from the seas in total disregard of neutral rights, alike by England and by France. We had fought the War of 1812 to assert the new doctrine that the oceans belonged to all peoples for peaceful commerce, and were not to be regarded solely as a theater of hostilities for the navies of belligerent powers.

When forty years later, by a turn of fortune's wheel, our position was that of a belligerent in the War between the States, European governments changed their emphasis upon such rules as were applicable. They proclaimed their adherence and devotion to what had been the American view of neutral rights and belligerent obligations. We could not close Southern ports by Northern edict. We must maintain an effective and rigid blockade. We must not practice Europe's time-honored methods of visit, search and seizure at sea, but must conform to what had been the previous American doctrine. Mr. Lincoln was quick to learn wisdom, and conformed quite scrupulously to those interpretations. They were actually a triumph of American principles, and they were to bring forth the peaceable fruits of right action.

The United States met all the obligations upon which the European neutrals placed new emphasis. She respected the rule that had abolished privateering. She did not raid peaceful commerce upon the high seas. She yielded to the British ultimatum in the Trent affair, and thereby won a first-class moral victory, for Britain was at last, with some hypocrisy, reversing her former position and standing upon American ground.

America as a belligerent had observed the rules of international law with fidelity. England and France, as professed neutrals, had been less scrupulous. England afterwards made handsome acknowledgment of error, in accepting the verdict of the Geneva Board of Arbitration and paying the award. France had her proper humiliation at the bar of public opinion when she met disastrous failure in Louis Napoleon's ill-starred Mexican adventure.

It will not be necessary to dwell at greater length upon these concrete instances. They illustrate the increased emphasis upon the rights and duties of neutral countries, when faced by the facts of a major war. Let us turn again to the position of the United States in 1914.

IV.

President Wilson's view was not essentially that of a narrow neutralist or isolationist. Even England, close to the scene of action, had hesitated at first. She might have remained a neutral, but for (1) the proximity of Belgium to the British Coast, and (2) her still valid guarantee of Belgian neutrality.

When President Wilson on August 19 issued his Proclamation of Neutrality, he enjoined upon Americans the obligation to maintain " the spirit of impartiality, and of fairness and friendliness to all concerned." He reminded the people of the United States that it was " natural and inevitable that there should be the utmost variety of sympathy and desire among them with regard to the issues and circumstances of the conflict." But he proceeded to warn us against fighting the European war among ourselves in " camps of hostile opinion, hot against each other."

He proceeded as follows:

> Such divisions among us would be fatal to our peace of mind and might seriously stand in the way of the proper performance of our duty as the one great nation at peace, the one people holding itself ready to play a part of impartial mediation and speak the counsels of peace and accommodation, not as a partisan, but as a friend.

In concluding the Proclamation, he declared it to be

> the earnest wish and purpose of every thoughtful American that this great country of ours should show herself in this time of peculiar trial a nation fit beyond others to exhibit the fine poise of undistributed judgment, the dignity of self-control, the efficiency of dispassionate action; a nation that neither sits in judgment upon others nor is disturbed in her own counsels, and which keeps herself fit and free to do what is honest and disinterested and truly serviceable for the peace of the world.
>
> Shall we not resolve [he concluded] to put upon ourselves the restraints which will bring to our people the happiness and the great and lasting influence for peace we covet for them?

I am taking some pains to make it clear that Mr. Wilson thought of our neutrality not merely as affording us a sequestered place so that we might escape the disasters of warfare, but also as a position that might prove serviceable for the peace of the world. Except for Spain, Switzerland, Holland, and the Scandinavian countries, virtually the whole of Europe was already involved in the war. And these exceptions to the rule were so situated on the fringes of the war zones that they could not assert their rights as neutrals either with separate boldness or in association with one another. The nations of the Western Hemisphere, on the other hand, led by the United States, could act with sympathetic agreement in upholding the doctrine that peace is to be regarded as the aim and object of civilization in the Twentieth Century, and that all wars are in violation of accepted principles.

The Dominion of Canada presented the only exception to the rule of Western-Hemisphere neutrality. When Canada assumed of her own accord a belligerent status in a European conflict, the war was brought to our very borders, in legal principle. If Canada in arms could attack Germany, the Monroe Doctrine could not be interposed to protect Canada from counter-attack. There was nothing in the political relation of Canada to England that precluded freedom of decision at Ottawa.

It seemed at the time that Canada was proceeding without full consideration, and that it might have been more statesmanlike to have abstained from actual belligerency, while not subscribing to Wilson's credo of impartiality. What was regarded at Washington and also at Quebec as an immature verdict on the part of the Canadian Government at Ottawa, did not prove ill-judged in the light of further events.

Mr. Wilson's theory of neutral rights and duties, as a starting point from which to restore the ruptured fabric of peace and international order, had its merit. It seemed to fit our American circumstances. But from the very start the sheer mass of war-force greatly outweighed the mass of neutral influence and power. If we could not uphold and protect our own rights as a neutral under established rules of international law, we could hardly expect to impress the belligerents when we advised them to cease fighting and accept our mediation.

Mr. Wilson was demanding a negotiated peace—a "peace without victory"; but neither side would admit that Mr. Wilson's voice carried international authority. The Vatican also sought to bring about a truce and a settlement by negotiation and compromise; and the Pope had a traditional place in European councils that an American President could not then expect to occupy.

If I seem to dwell upon this well-intended effort of ours to employ the leverage of neutrality as an instrument by which to lift the world out of the predicament of destructive warfare, my purpose is to throw some light upon the otherwise puzzling story of our diplomatic record during the years 1914-16. The efforts of Mr. Wilson and the State Department were mainly devoted to protests and demands relating to the violation of our rights on the sea. The British had thrown to the winds the established doctrine of blockade. They had enlarged the definition of contraband of war to include anything whatsoever that might serve the needs of people in enemy countries. They had calmly repudiated all their former principles and doctrines regarding search and detention of unarmed neutral vessels engaged in trade between neutral ports.

Germany's violations of neutral rights were not greatly different from those of England in the earliest stages of the war. It is true, moreover, that Germany was more prompt in professing her readiness to comply with the rules of international law affecting neutral trade, if England would also agree. The English Foreign Office, however, either persistently ignored American protests or else greatly delayed answering them. When the answers came, they were regarded at Washington as evasive, equivocal, and tediously discursive. The Washington protests against British practices were far more indignant and severe than those which were made by the State Department in its exchange of dispatches with Germany.

V.

There was a tone of asperity in some of the diplomatic dispatches emanating from Washington that seems almost incredible as we read them now, almost thirty years later. They were signed by William J. Bryan as Secretary of State previous to his resignation on June 9, 1915. Afterwards, and more notably, they were signed by Mr. Bryan's successor, Robert Lansing. But when several years later I was responsible for publishing in two volumes the *Messages and Papers of Woodrow Wilson*, some of the more important of these Bryan-Lansing dispatches were included. Since my compilation was made with Mr. Wilson's authority, and included nothing but materials authenticated by the White House, it must be understood that the President himself was the author of these dispatches.

Having taken his stand upon the American doctrines of neutrality, he was proceeding to uphold them with tenacity in protest and argument. He seemed to be establishing a basis for some future claims before an arbitration tribunal. The belligerents were charged with tearing to shreds the rules and agreements that had resulted from the two Hague Conferences of 1899 and 1907, followed by the Declaration of London.

This London Declaration was in effect a code of maritime international law. It prescribed the rules that were to govern the signatory nations whenever engaged in war, in whatever concerned blockade, definitions of contraband, rights of neutral shipping, and other related matters. It was signed at London on February 26, 1909, by the United States, Great Britain, Germany, Austria-Hungary, France, Russia, Italy, Japan, Holland, and Spain.

It may be said that the Declaration of London touched the high point in the tendencies that were giving priority in international law to the rights of neutrals. Promptly in the first week of August, 1914, our government urged upon the belligerents the advisability of their agreeing "that the laws of naval warfare as laid down by the Declaration of London of 1909 shall be applicable to naval warfare during the present conflict in Europe." To state the results in summary terms without needless detail, it may be noted that within a few days Austria-Hungary and Germany replied in the affirmative without qualification. Great Britain replied that she would adopt "generally the rules of the Declaration, subject to certain modifications."

The British and French governments thereafter issued steadily enlarging definitions and lists of contraband, and in other respects made such radical modifications of the Declaration of London that the United States in October withdrew its suggestion of August 6. The belligerents were notified that the United States would stand strictly upon its own views of neutral rights. It would reserve the right " to enter a protest or demand in every case in which the rights and duties so defined are violated, or their free exercise interfered with by the authorities of the belligerent governments."

Within two weeks after this American assertion of neutral rights, Great Britain declared (November 3) the entire North Sea a war-zone. Germany in retaliation on February 14, 1915, declared the waters surrounding the British Isles and the whole English Channel a war-zone, and announced that, in return for Great Britain's violations of the maritime rules of war, all enemy merchant vessels found in the war-zone would be destroyed after February 18. Navigation in the waters north of the Shetland Islands, and in the eastern part of the North Sea, was outside of this German war-zone. Neutral shipping was to be allowed (for Germany's advantage) in a zone thirty miles wide along the Dutch Coast.

Neutral vessels were warned that although German submarine commanders had orders to refrain from violence against shipping under non-enemy flags, the conditions were dangerous, because Great Britain was violating international law by running up neutral flags as a deceptive and illegal subterfuge. When, under instructions, Ambassador Page at London took up the question of the illegal use of the American flag to safeguard British ships, no satisfactory response was elicited.

This phase of our relation to the First World War was reaching a conclusion that we had not shaped or invited. The war had assumed an extent and a character that made our protests and claims seem absurdly feeble, even as they were altogether futile in effect. To fight both groups of belligerents at once, in vindication of our commercial rights at sea, would have been fantastic and preposterous.

The British said in effect that things so much more important were at stake that they really could not be diverted from their war policies to consider our grievances, which they thought were relatively trifling. Their national existence was at stake, while ours was secure.

Thus the doctrine of neutrality, failing to secure the deference of belligerents in a major war, was but a broken reed as regards the claims to immunity of American commerce. Neither was the doctrine of neutrality conferring upon the United States a position favorable for mediation between the belligerent groups.

Early in 1915 our government had specified in precise terms certain principles in conformity with which it asked Germany and Great Britain to adjust their maritime policies. At the same time it asked Germany to agree upon a suggested plan for the importation of food from the United States, and its restricted distribution to German non-combatants. Finally, as a part of the same memorandum, Great Britain was asked to revise its contraband list, and further requested to abstain from interference with shipments of food to Germany for distribution by American agents to the non-combatant population.

One of the three points set down for joint acceptance by Germany and Great Britain was in the following words: "That neither will use submarines to attack merchant vessels of any nationality, except to enforce the right of visit and search." Germany's reply was favorable in the main, certain provisos regarding food for civilians being stated. Great Britain, however waited two weeks longer and then declared that it did not understand from the German reply that submarine practices would be abandoned. The British note also recited other German offenses against humanity, and declined to modify the British blockade. This was not a blockade in fact, but rather a prohibition of trade with Germany.

Gradually disputes took on a different aspect, and American public opinion began to think less of legal rights and to think more deeply about the methods and realities of the Great War. In a relatively isolated conflict between two nations (such as the former war between Japan and Russia), it had not been difficult for Great Britain, the United States, France, and Germany to uphold the maritime rights of neutrals; and in that historic instance the offer by President Theodore Roosevelt of American mediation was influential enough to secure the acceptance of friendly counsel and to result in a treaty of peace.

But in the circumstances of the "First World War" as the struggle had proceeded and had continued for more than two years, we were confronted with unprecedented conditions. Neutrality had lost standing as a principle upon which to build up a structure of security and peace. The war was not destined to end in a deadlock or a compromise. One side or the other would be victorious. The side that prevailed would write the future code of international law in its own way.

Furthermore, the side that already had the better cause would, if successful, be more likely than its opponent to prove a beneficent law-giver. At the end of the year 1916 we were changing our attitude for reasons more profound and of farther reach than were set forth at the time. They are clearer now in perspective than they were when on April 2, 1917, President Wilson addressed a joint session of the newly-elected Congress and recommended that Germany's course be treated as war against the United States. In a succeeding chapter I shall review this change of attitude on the part of the United States from the standpoint of its causes, its consequences, and its bearing upon the future security of nations.

Chapter III

RIVAL EMPIRES AND GERMAN MILITARISM

In this chapter I am noting changes and contrasts in Europe as I observed them in the quarter-century before the First World War. Much that we had once praised as evidences of unprecedented progress was contributing to the support of false ideals and ill-considered ambitions. There had been no real attempt to frame a political organization of Europe that could reconcile rivalries by making provision for the common good. Although trade expansion had intensified the need of secure markets, there had been little effort to equalize economic advantages, and to make Europe a prosperous commercial and industrial unit.

The lack of a secure control of the sea-lanes for the free and equal use of all nations engaged in foreign trade had led to a dangerous rivalry in naval construction. England's conquest of the Sudan, and especially the adventure in South Africa, had been bitterly denounced throughout Continental Europe. It had stimulated Germany's determination to create an empire of her own by encroachments in Africa, in the Far East, in the South Seas, and especially by economic and political penetration of the Near and Middle East. The imperialists of Britain had made serious mistakes, but these had been largely corrected by the verdict of public opinion at home. Thus conquered South Africa had been given back to the Boers, who were helped to create an autonomous federated Union of South Africa. Egypt had been treated with consideration, and the Sudan had been placed under an administration that gave justice and security to its Arab peoples, who were encouraged to live in their own manner. But these essential facts had not lessened the jealousy or changed the ambitious programs of the German military caste.

Germany at an earlier day had produced eminent thinkers and scholars who were intent upon economic, social and cultural progress, not merely for their own country but for a more unified world of civilized men. It was the home of philosophers, humanitarians, leaders in scientific research, apostles of international order and the higher interests of human society. But their voices were suppressed in the rise of militarism and imperial ambition, impelled by a new racial doctrine of superiority, glorifying national power and the appeal to force.

Thus Germany's leaders were inoculated with the virus of an all-embracing nationalism. They were learning how to divert the total energies of the country to the achievement of the foremost place in Europe and the world through relentless war, scorning all scruples and ignoring the rights of other peoples. The military group that had gained mastery over German policies also won full control over the mind of a vainglorious emperor. This restless William II lacked the cosmopolitan character of his admired Father, who would have done his best to resist the military clique if he had lived. Nor did William possess the prudence and balanced judgment of his grandfather, whose achievement in the federation of Germany had been regarded as a notable instance of statesmanship, not detrimental to the stability of what men in those days called the "Concert of Europe."

Germany was waiting for the opportune moment. It came with the dispute between Austria and Serbia. The immediate object of the war, as I explain in the present chapter, was to crush Russia before the Czar's armies became too well equipped. To enter Paris in triumph by a surprise march through Belgium seemed little more than a holiday excursion to the enthusiastic German strategists as they welcomed their unexampled opportunity.

AT THE BASIS of the upheavals that produced the American and French revolutions are to be found the new movements in navigation and trade that followed the discovery and colonization of undeveloped parts of the world. And also in the background lies the breakdown of feudalism, with the spread of the new doctrines of human rights and universal liberty. The economic and political changes following that intense period at the end of the eighteenth and the beginning of the nineteenth century have been so extensive in their areas, and so vast in their statistical aggregates, that they baffle analysis and computation.

Out of that intense period of change there came the typical representative democracy that was destined within a century or more to become the most favored form of political association among men. There emerged the modern ideals of local, national, and international life, as swayed by the intelligence of the masses. "Public opinion" became an established institution, so that its necessary instruments—the right of public assembly and the liberty of the press—were safeguarded in constitutions and laws. Invention and discovery also became recognized agents of social progress; and through these agents, within a century, the civilized nations had achieved an economic emancipation that was giving to the many what had been available to the privileged few alone in the eighteenth century.

It has been true, however, of historical progress that conflicting influences are always present and that forward movements must fight their way, sometimes suffering temporary defeat. The leading minds of the American and French revolutions had a conception not merely of the rights of man as related to the government and growth of separate nations, but they also contemplated the establishment of universal peace through a federation of states and through a subjection of purely national ambitions to the larger aims of civilization as a whole. It was believed that these great conceptions might be realized through their strong appeal to the growing intelligence of mankind.

It was thought that the common man, acquiring enough education to read and think and take part in the government of communities and states, would firmly renounce so barbaric a thing as the use of force in the settlement of differences between nations. It was believed that those ideas and methods which had triumphed in the establishment of the United States would in due time have the effect of democratizing and unifying the peoples of Europe. Thomas Jefferson, George Washington, and other Americans believed that the Western Hemisphere should, in so far as possible, keep aloof and develop the principles of democracy and confederation until Europe, influenced by American success, might also adopt democratic methods in the government of states and nations, and might substitute some form of confederation for the military alliances and the "balance of power" principle that must inevitably lead to periodic wars.

Unfortunately, however, several great forces of human progress that were stimulated in that period of revolutions had set forth upon their careers at unequal rates of movement. Universal education, as one of these forces, intensified popular devotion to the language, the history, the ideals, and the aspirations of particular nations. Thus national unity and progress became a passionate object of endeavor—in Germany, for instance, then in Italy, then in Russia, and in many of the smaller principalities and racial and political entities. Hungary had awakened to an intense national consciousness; Poland was demanding restoration and unity; and the people of the Balkan regions in particular had experienced an almost unprecedented evolution of political and racial ambition.

This exaggerated nationalism could be ascribed above all else to the methods of universal education. The rapid forming of the reading and writing habit within a period of two or three generations was so directed by schools and by the popular newspapers as to promote nationalism and strengthen language barriers. Thus, for a time at least, the spread of intelligence was to weaken the larger cause of unity and harmony among nations.

Furthermore, the great forces of invention and scientific discovery were producing many consequences that could not have been foreseen. In some decades they encouraged vast migration, while in others they produced conditions that checked the export of men and promoted the export of commodities. These discoveries reduced the ravages of epidemic disease, and aided in the increase of the population of civilized countries by from one hundred per cent to two hundred per cent in a very short period. The application of science to industry had enabled this expanding population to produce vastly increased supplies of the necessities and luxuries of life.

In the industrialized nations which possessed or could secure supplies of iron and coal, and which could make and use machinery while having the technical ability to produce cloths of cotton, wool, silk, and linen on a large scale, the output of manufactured articles increased in something like geometrical ratio. But, on the other hand, the production of articles of food necessary to sustain the industrial population went forward at an arithmetical rate of gain. The inevitable consequence of these two major facts in the conditions of Europe's economic production was an enormous growth of foreign trade. Regions that less than a hundred years earlier had been almost wholly agricultural, except for the local and household industries that had supplied shelter, clothing, and the ordinary utensils and implements, had now become so transformed that more than three-quarters of the people were engaged in commerce and manufactures.

II.

The products of their industry were sold throughout the world, and the question of markets had become vital. They were obliged to study the customs and wants of Asia and Africa, as well as of North and South America and the various parts of

Europe, and to awaken new wants and help form new habits and customs, for the sake of enlarged markets. They were obliged in return to import vast supplies of raw material to supply their factories, and increasing quantities of food materials from the temperate zones and the tropics to provide the workers with bread and meat, fruits and spices, tea, coffee, and cocoa.

This had necessitated a correspondingly large increase in the tonnage of merchant shipping. It had transformed the aspiring nationalism that resulted from popular education into a nationalism of trade rivalry that extended to the remote parts of the earth. The growth of overseas commerce, and the increase in the number and tonnage of merchant ships, made the freedom of the ocean highways a matter of anxious concern to governments. The doctrine of naval expansion and power was proclaimed and justified on the ground of commercial necessity.

Let us take the growth of Germany as an illustration. At the end of the Napoleonic wars, the entities that afterwards became the German Empire had a population of less than 25,000,000. A hundred years later, at the outbreak of the Great War of 1914, this population had grown to nearly 70,000,000. As recently as the Franco-Prussian War of 1870-71, the German population was only a little more than 40,000,000. At that time German industry was not highly developed as compared with that of England or France. But it became the policy of the new German Empire to promote scientific and technical education and to stimulate the growth of German manufactures of all kinds. The success of this policy was so great that Germany became increasingly able to compete everywhere with the manufactures of other countries.

German migration to America practically ceased because there was ample employment in the home country. This meant, in simple terms, that besides an average improvement in the standards of living and the conditions of German communities, which absorbed much of the new production of goods, there had come to be a population of many millions on German soil who were wholly dependent in normal times upon trade with the outside world.

What was so true of Germany was in greater or less measure true of other industrial nations. That is to say, an increasing percentage of their population was engaged in the production of articles which required international markets in contrast with domestic markets.

The period of discovery, in the sixteenth century and later, had been followed by the growth of commercial or trading empires, notably those of Spain, England, France, Portugal, and Holland. One of the aims of the revolutionary period of the eighteenth and early nineteenth centuries had been to break up these empires and create a series of democracies. Thus the United States was created out of great strips of British, French, and Spanish colonial domain. The Latin-American republics in due time deprived Spain and Portugal of most of their acquisitions of the earlier period.

Great Britain, as an island nation, and as the earliest of the countries to attain modern industrial development and large export trade, had been driven to the policy of naval supremacy. This unwavering devotion to the idea of a vastly superior navy, conjoined with Great Britain's acceptance of the principle of colonial self-government and democracy, had been effective in keeping the British Empire from falling apart, and in adding greatly to its extent when Africa came to be subdivided among the European powers.

After the American Revolution, Great Britain gave up the old idea of the commercial or trading empire, which meant the exploiting of colonies to their own detriment and to the exclusion of the trade of other countries. England in due time gave to her own colonies full liberty of commerce and industry; and she also opened her home trade and the trade of her colonies to the competing trade of her European rivals. Nevertheless, the industries and commerce of England doubtless derived a certain measure of advantage from the political relations between the mother country and the outlying parts of the empire.

This position of the British Empire, viewed with just and temperate judgment, did not greatly menace the peace and harmony of the world, and it did not obstruct either the process of democratic evolution or that of the internationalization of trade and commerce. But it made the British Empire so ubiquitous, as it were—so omnipresent at every point of international rivalry or of local transition—that the danger of serious clashes with other growing empires was illustrated by one incident after another.

Thus, for a period of years, there was misunderstanding between England and Russia, because of Russia's vast territorial expansions in Central Asia that seemed to threaten England's control of India. There were also differences between England and France, over respective spheres of influence in Africa.

Precisely as England's historic position had tempted her to adhere to the policy of naval supremacy, so Germany's historic position in the heart of Europe had led her to the maintenance of a policy of militarism. The conception of a nation which could at will turn all its energies and forces from the pursuits of peace to the achievement of victory in war had doubtless been entertained by a certain number of minds in different countries. But Germany was the only modern country which had so ordered her affairs as to be the stronger for war by reason of every access of strength in the pursuits of peace. It would be useless for us to consider whether Germany originally adopted the military ideal through fear of powerful neighbors and the need of self-defence, or whether the German race is inherently militant and aggressive. It had usually been thought that the Germans were naturally peace-loving and contented; and the world had been disposed to praise them greatly for their educational and scientific progress and their many contributions to culture and civilization.

After the unification of Germany, following the war with France and the smaller wars of the Bismarckian period, there came the rapid growth of industry and commerce to which I have referred. Germany began to assume the role of the leading power within the European system. France strove for recuperation and formed an alliance with Russia. Germany secured Austria and Italy as allies, but relied mainly upon her own military prowess for protection against the Gallo-Slavic combination.

III.

In a country like England, military ideals were obsolete, and the army was considered an emergency police force, somewhat necessary but an expensive adjunct of government. The island boundaries of the United Kingdom were fixed by nature, and were not to be changed. The relations of the United Kingdom with Canada, Australia, New Zealand, and South Africa, were increasingly those of mutual helpfulness and voluntary cooperation. The future of India was to be determined by the developing capacity of the Indian peoples for mutual tolerance and for maintaining just and beneficent political institutions. Speaking generally, the British people conceived of their empire as a thing in harmony with world progress, and not as a thing that was blocking the rightful progress of any other nation or race.

But if the British Empire on its part was a finished affair, subject to peaceful decentralization through the growth of the oversea dominions, it was quite otherwise with the German Empire. The British army was a small, professionalized body of soldiers. "Tommy Atkins," the English private, was in no sense a civilian or an ordinary citizen. But the German army was in an almost complete sense the nation itself. There was an exception, however, which was fraught with a danger that was not wholly understood when we entered the First World War. This exception lay in the great body of highly trained German officers. These army officers were soldiers and not civilians. Their training, for every grade and rank of commissioned military service, was serious, intense, extremely intelligent.

This permanent military caste was imbued with the doctrine of sheer force for the advancement of a nation's ends; and the progress and dominance of the nation was for them the supreme ethical law. Comprised within this great body of permanent officers was a vast system or mechanism for training all the young men of the nation, as they reached the suitable age, to serve the country as soldiers. The system was carefully adjusted to promote rather than injure industrial and commercial advancement. Well-educated young men could be returned to civil life within a year, while intensive training for two or three years made the country bumpkin or the village boy a more valuable civilian than he otherwise would have been.

Thus while German militarism employed this twofold system, one for the development of the great body of professional officers, and the other for the disciplining of young civilians, there were also the specialized groups under the Great General Staff, such as the engineering and technical corps and those concerned with international military intelligence. Through these specialists all the progress of Germany and of other countries in mechanical, electrical, and chemical engineering was so adapted as to be available for military purposes.

At the time of the Franco-Prussian War, the population of Germany and France was almost equal, being about 40,000,000 each. That of the United Kingdom was somewhat more than 30,000,000. In a period of forty years following that war, the population of France had remained almost unchanged, while Great Britain had surpassed France and contained about 45,000,000 inhabitants. Germany on her part had increased in numbers to a total somewhat less than 70,000,000. German industry meanwhile had made a far more rapid relative development than had the population, so that Germany was not only able to throw the nation quickly upon a war footing with 10,000,000 trained men under arms, but her great workshops could supply vast quantities of guns and munitions, while her chemical industries could provide new kinds of explosives and war materials, and her railroads, which had been built from the strategic as well as the commercial standpoint, were ready to serve ends and objects that had been carefully planned in advance.

France, Russia, Italy, and Austria were also on the basis of general military training and service; but in no other country were the collective resources of the nation so readily convertible into terms of immediate military efficiency as in Germany. There were relatively few men in Europe, and still fewer in America, who could understand in advance what this convertibility of national power into terms of immediate military efficiency might mean in case of the sudden outbreak of a general war. It was not until the war had continued for three years that there came to be any wide understanding of the nature and extent of Germany's stupendous superiority, at the outset, in military efficiency.

This adaptability of the nation's resources of men and of industry to the purposes of war had been created, in the first instance, because of Germany's geographical position amidst the conflicting tribes and races of Europe. Russia occupied vast territories. Her population seemed to be approaching the 200,000,000 mark. She also had a system of general military service and a large body of professional officers; but her industrial resources were comparatively undeveloped. While Russia was dreaming her Pan-Slavic dream, Germany was looking forward to what she deemed her inevitable conflict with the Franco-Russian alliance. France also was highly militarized, but the Germans, weighing all military resources in the aggregate, regarded their own efficiency as at least twice as great as that of the French.

Thus as Germany grew in a sense of military primacy, her body of professional officers also grew in the conviction that a blow should be struck before Russian resources of science and industry were developed enough to enable Russia to maintain large armies over considerable periods of time. Furthermore, as Germany's foreign commerce increased, her ambitions expanded and she began to conceive of her destiny as something more than that of leadership within the continent of Europe.

England, with 45,000,000 people in the home islands, controlled a vast empire in all continents and in all seas. Germany, with 70,000,000 was now outstripping England in quantity and variety of industrial products and was rapidly contesting England's primacy in merchant marine. Germany began to demand her " place in the sun." As her sense of military and commercial power increased, her national pride assumed aggressive and arrogant forms. Although Germany accused John Bull of a traditional arrogance, the facts show that in the main there was a surprising readiness on England's part to recognize Germany's progress and to admit German merchants everywhere on equal terms.

Fear, rather than arrogance, however, is at the root of much discord and conflict between nations, as between individuals. Germany feared that the great merchant fleet needful to carry her expanding commerce might at some critical time be driven from the seas unless protected by a great navy. England, on the other hand, feared lest Germany, already dominant on land by reason of her superior army, might at some juncture destroy the British Empire, if to Germany's military machine there was also added the power of a German navy approaching that of England in extent. Thus Britain was led to lay aside all differences with France and then with Russia, and to arrange for the combined use of the English and French fleets, while England also began to construct new warships and to revolutionize the world's navies in size and character.

IV.

During the first year or two of the war—that is to say throughout 1914-15—German propagandists came to the United States and enjoyed as much freedom of intercourse as their rivals from England and France. Of the Germans who came, the most influential was Dr. Bernhard Dernburg. He arrived in New York as a special representative of his government only two or three months after the war began. His mission was ostensibly on behalf of the German Red Cross. I was invited to meet him at a small private luncheon of perhaps ten men in the Faculty Club of Columbia University.

Taking him aside after the luncheon, I found him willing to talk to me with remarkable frankness, on the understanding that he was not then to be quoted. He did not contradict me when I charged that Germany could have prevented the war, even if she had not planned it. He explained that Germany's program of expansion could be blocked only by the might of Russia. The Czar's government had entered upon an armament policy that could not be completed for several years. In 1914 Germany's military equipment was five or six times greater than that of Russia. The Czar's armies could not fight very long, without more guns and military supplies. Dr. Dernburg's statements were the more impressive because Germany had already taken about 100,000 Russian prisoners in the battle of Tannenburg, and he was confident that Russia would collapse sooner or later. Also Germany was already exploiting the resources of Belgium, and expected to hold Antwerp permanently as a German port through which to obtain supplies from abroad.

Dr. Dernburg had written a statement for the American press, published first in the *New York Sun*, endeavoring to show that Germany was not merely adopting the doctrines of General Von Bernhardi (whose gospel of German militarism, along with the teachings of Treitschke, bore the same relation to the First World War as Hitler's *Mein Kampf* to the present conflict). He was replying to an article by Ambassador Bryce (who was about to return to England to accept a peerage and enter the House of Lords). In the course of his article, however, Dr. Dernburg was hardly less emphatic than the Prussian militarists in pleading

Germany's claims for empire as against the alleged rapacity of Great Britain and France.

This plausible German emissary wrote an article for me (published in the *Review of Reviews* for November, 1914) in which he set forth with great detail the arrangements that had been made to provide Germany with an ample food supply for at least two years, and probably for all future time. He had been for four years the Emperor's Minister of Colonies, was now one of Berlin's leading bankers, and was a member of the Upper House of the Prussian Parliament. He had perfect command of the English language, and disclosed a vast range of European and international knowledge. He might have been one of the most useful and influential leaders of a movement for economic cooperation and harmony, as a substitute for the European rivalries that had led to destructive warfare. Dr. Dernburg was only one of many able men of affairs in Germany who did not like war and would have preferred a system providing equal advantages for all nations. But these men could not withstand the alluring arguments of the war-lords.

What impressed me most, and therefore remains most clearly in my memory, was Dr. Dernburg's frank admission that Germany had forced the war in order to crush Russia's growing power before it might be too late. This has some significance as we consider Hitler's rash conclusions in 1941 that his conquest of Europe could not be safe until he had broken the strength of the Red armies and acquired permanent control of the Ukraine.

The growth of international commerce had created countless ties and relationships across the boundary lines of states. Science and education had found many ways to communicate and to cooperate. But whereas there had been developing a network of voluntary association and intercourse among the peoples of different nations, there had been a failure to secure the harmony and cooperation of governments, which was the one thing supremely needful. Powerful states had intensified the danger arising from unregulated nationalism by entering belatedly upon programs of imperialism in rivalry with one another.

If two great nations like the United States and Great Britain, possessing a common language and many bonds of unity and agreement, had at times found it hard to avoid conflict and to reconcile differences arising from policies of expansion or empire or trade, how much harder must it have been for Russia and Austria-Hungary to avoid conflict and reconcile differences. For, in addition to national dissimilarities of language and tradition, there were added the rivalries of imperial policy between two great governments, each of which was seeking overlordship of the lands that had once constituted European Turkey.

V.

The Turkish Empire at the time of its greatest extent had held in subjection various lands and nationalities of southeastern Europe, western Asia, and northern Africa. The forces of progress that became so sharply accelerated with the revolutionary period at the end of the eighteenth century came to the aid of the western nations as against the decayed despotism of Turkey. Greece, Serbia, Roumania, and Bulgaria emerged as European peoples and began to struggle for boundaries, for seaports, for future security, as their people became intelligent and infused with an intense spirit of national ambition.

Inevitably Turkish authority was superseded in Egypt and the Barbary States, through the commercial and colonizing energy of the western European powers. Germany and Austria-Hungary were increasingly convinced that in the further disintegration of the Turkish Empire they must be recognized in an exceptional way, and must be allowed by Russia, Great Britain, and France to acquire an undisputed influence from the Adriatic to the Black Sea and the Persian Gulf.

Not only was Turkey collapsing, but Persia had become subject to the commercial energy and political influence of the European empires, Russia and England having substituted spheres of Persian influence for what at one time had seemed a dangerous competition. Germany's capacity, meanwhile, for taking a large part in the commercial and economic development of the world, was increasing more rapidly than that of any other European nation. With this growth of capacity, as I have already explained, came the increasing need of markets. German advance agents saw in the undeveloped regions of Asiatic Turkey, and beyond, a great opportunity for obtaining many products and materials needed in Germany, with the prospective opportunity of creating in those regions a large and permanent market for German wares. The Baghdad Railroad was projected as a part of a much larger scheme of eastward expansion.

In furtherance of this ambition for an economic and political confederation extending from the North Sea to the Persian Gulf, German diplomatic and military influence had for a long time been at work in Constantinople to gain a dominating place in the councils of the Turkish Government. The alliance with Austria-Hungary was a necessary part of the great project. It was further needful for Germany that Austrian rather than Russian influences should guide the destinies of the smaller Balkan states which lay between the Teutonic empires and the Turkish domains and suzerainties.

The importance of the Balkan and Turkish struggles of those years, and of the bitter feud between Austria and Serbia over the annexation of Bosnia by the Vienna government, can only be understood when one has in mind the great projects upon which German policy was embarked. Austria had made a bitter enemy of Serbia when she had destroyed that dream of a "greater Serbia" which required Bosnia and a part of the Adriatic coast for its principal fulfillment. The assassination of the heir to the Hapsburg throne gave Austria her pretext for an attack that was expected to secure control of necessary river and rail routes to Turkey. Russia, on the other hand, saw her dream of control at Constantinople endangered, together with her plans for further "peaceful penetration" of Persia and of the Turkish provinces south of the Black Sea.

Germany was prepared to support Austria to the utmost, while Russia felt herself compelled to take the field on behalf of Serbia. It was fully realized by Germany that France must support Russia. It was not believed in Germany that Great Britain would be involved, and it was expected that Italy would remain neutral while perhaps rendering a certain amount of material and moral aid to her allies, Germany and Austria.

The British on their part had not foreseen the danger and were quite unprepared. The critical condition of the Irish question rendered it the more certain, from Germany's standpoint, that England could not bring military aid to France. Russia, as I have explained, had entered upon large plans of military preparation, but these were not to culminate for three or more years. Germany, on the other hand, had immensely increased and strengthened her war machine.

From the German standpoint, the fateful hour had arrived. Germany had full equipment for at least five times as large an army as Russia could supply with arms and munitions. Austria-Hungary might be regarded as almost, if not quite, able to cope with Russia, while Germany, moving swiftly against France, could bring the entire war to an end within a few weeks—probably by October and certainly before Christmas, 1914.

The boundary-line between Germany and France was barely two hundred miles long, extending from Belgium to Switzerland along the border of Alsace-Lorraine. This stretch of boundary was strongly fortified on both sides. The easiest way to France from the southern parts of Germany and from Austria was through the edge of Switzerland. The easiest way to France from central and northern Germany was across Belgium. But Belgium had, for the greater part of a century, been under the protection of a solemn guaranty of neutrality signed in successive treaties, Germany, France, and Great Britain being parties to the agreement. France was not prepared for an attack by way of Belgium and the German law of "military necessity" prescribed an attack upon your enemy, despite treaties, by the path which your enemy has left unguarded.

In choosing this path, Germany failed to understand the Belgians themselves. It was known that they would protest, but it was not expected that they could make war. Germany had planned to use Belgian railways and highways so swiftly as to make it certain that there could be no advance of the French forces to offer formidable resistance until the German armies were moving upon Paris. Belgium was to be indemnified and rewarded for having suffered under duress the passage of the German forces.

An even greater mistake of calculation was Germany's confidence in the inability of the government and people of Great Britain to drop the Irish question and unite in supporting a declaration of war. Belgium's resistance had delayed the movement of the great German war machine, and had given the

French time to save Paris while the Russians were invading East Prussia. The British, meanwhile, were coming resolutely to the aid of the French army; and what was to have been a short war was inevitably changed to a long one. What was to have been a single brilliant campaign, with peace terms based upon unqualified victory, had been of necessity transformed into a supreme struggle of years, destined to involve the whole world for reasons not so much of sheer material force as of moral conviction.

I am dealing with underlying causes of the conflict and with some of the principles involved as bearing not only upon the conditions that I have already endeavored to describe, but also upon the further progress of human society. It was not at first so clearly a war of principles. Opposing doctrines were not so sharply in conflict as to be clearly seen through all the complicated factors that had entered into the struggle in such fashion as to confuse the underlying issues.

VI.

Gradually it was seen that this was a war to bring harmony into the world on principles of justice and freedom, and to create an organization of the world's public opinion that should be stronger for peace and order than any single empire or alliance could be for attaining its ends through military power.

The Austrian ultimatum to Serbia had been harsh and peremptory beyond all modern precedents. Its principal objects and aims were prescribed at Berlin, regardless of the details. The thing intended was to bring Serbia under the sway of the allied Teutonic powers. Not only must Austria's annexation of Bosnia no longer be questioned, but Serbia herself must become a vassal state, or ultimately a portion of a South-Slav member of the Austro-Hungarian confederation.

If the terms of the ultimatum had been accepted in full, Serbia would have yielded up certain attributes of independence and sovereignty that Austrian and German policy would never have allowed her to recover. Her answer had to be made very quickly by the terms of the ultimatum. She must yield without resistance, or she must make a stand for her own distinct future and for the rights of small nationalities.

If Serbia had yielded, the pretexts for an immediate war would have been removed; the projects of political and economic assimilation throughout the Balkans and Turkey would have been pressed forward by the Teutonic Empires. Tremendous preparations would have been made on both sides for the postponed European war, that should determine whether Russian or German influences were to become predominant in southeastern Europe and western Asia.

If under England's leadership the issues between Austria and Serbia could have been referred to the Hague Tribunal for settlement, the immediate peace might have been preserved. Furthermore, it was the hope of the friends of peace throughout the world that with every postponement of war the influences and forces that were trying to build up international methods for preventing conflict would gain strength, so that the truce maintained by the "balance of power" might by degrees become transformed into an assured and constructive peace based upon world organization.

This desired transition, however, was not destined to come about. Even the non-aggressive nations were reluctant to trust their destinies to an untried kind of world union for peace-keeping and common humanitarian ends. They were living in a world which had been transformed by modern science, industry, commerce, and education, but which had remained dangerously obsolete in its political structure.

Germany had not become formidable through her martial spirit and prowess alone, nor through her expansion of industry at home and of trade abroad. Her power had been developed through the marvellous union of all these things. With the growth of her power, her world ambition had become more far-reaching and more daring. And she had come to believe that she was being deprived by other nations and races of opportunities in the world justly commensurate with her extraordinary attainments in education, science, industry, and social order.

Nations and races that thought they could make better use of lands, resources, and facilities than others in possession, have in all recorded time persuaded themselves that they were justified in using power to attain their ends, believing that ultimate results would give historic vindication. Thus the European colonists dispossessed the aboriginal races of North and South America. And thus the European governments partitioned Africa among themselves, while menacing the integrity of China and laying hands upon whatsoever portions of Asia they could secure by one means or another.

Germany's excuses and pretexts for precipitating the World War in 1914 had no validity whatsoever. History will not condone her employment of military power, with the frightful sacrifice of millions of lives and the devastation, impoverishment, starvation and disease that swept Europe from the English Channel to the Black Sea. The opening years of the twentieth century should have been signalized by the abolition of these barbaric contests between civilized nations.

It was true enough that other empires had been guilty of aggressions, and their own men of liberal mind and spirit would not try to condone them. But no other government was threatening aggression against Germany in 1914. There must come a time when freedom of thought and speech has been recovered by the German people, so that historical truth may be told without evasion. When European nations become rivals only in seeking to exceed one another in neighborliness, they can readily find prosperity in combining their efforts.

But how does the present condition of European turmoil and devastating strife concern the future of American policy? The answer to that question should no longer be in dispute. Since experience proves that we cannot avoid intervening in Europe's wars, it becomes evident that we cannot afford to withhold our support from Europe's efforts to find permanent methods of reformation, regional order, and democratic freedom. The fact that such an attitude on our part comports with generous ideals should not condemn it as "unprofitable altruism." Wars are expensive; and to escape them requires a hard-headed kind of intelligence in public policy, no less than a religious spirit of good-will.

It has become necessary to understand the extent of our past commitments and the true nature of our further vital interests. We belong to the group of nations that must maintain common security in the North Atlantic basin and also in the South Atlantic. Our future safety is not disconnected with that of Great Britain and western Europe; and the destruction of German military policies and ambitions demands on our part a continued interest in the reorganization of Europe. No statement of our position henceforth, as regards external commitments and responsibilities, has been more lucid and convincing than that which is made by Mr. Walter Lippmann in his recent volume entitled *U. S. Foreign Policy: Shield of the Republic.* This experienced student defends the thesis that a nation's *power* must fully balance its accepted *responsibilities.* He is meeting the remnant of isolationists on their own ground, and proving the necessity of certain "nuclear" alliances, and of continued Anglo-American naval agreement.

The stronger the democracies prove themselves in developed capacity to maintain their own freedom, the better able they will be to encourage the philanthropists, and to support the effort to create a new spirit of accord in Europe. We can believe that history reaches turning points that mark a fresh beginning. So we may hope that the German people—chastened by retributive justice for their repeated misdeeds of the first half of the twentieth century—can resolve to devote the second half to the re-building of their national fortunes upon the principles of justice and liberty.

CHAPTER IV

THE KELLOGG-BRIAND PACT AND THE HOOVER POLICIES

At the half-way point of the twenty-year interval between wars there was a brief period when the American view of peace through universal goodwill seemed likely to prevail. This high-water mark of American initiative took form in the Kellogg-Briand Pact, adopted in 1928 while Mr. Coolidge was President, but not fully ratified for a year. President Hoover gave it effect with impressive ceremonies in the summer of 1929, in the presence of representatives of forty-six signatory nations, including Germany, Austria, Italy, and Japan.

President Hoover through long years of professional and official experience had become more widely acquainted with conditions in Europe and Asia, as well as the Americas, than any other public man of his day. Yet he seemed to personify the American doctrines of compassion and relief as fundamental remedies for world disorder, and he believed in disarmament, while Europe still distrusted such optimism and believed that security demanded reliance upon force. In proclaiming the Kellogg-Briand Pact, however, the President gave it a new significance looking to the future.

He referred to it as a " Platform " from which to appeal to the moral opinion of the nations " regarding specific acts and deeds." Thus he and his Secretary of State, Henry L. Stimson, soon afterwards acted on that principle when they refused to recognize Japan's forcible invasion and control of Manchuria, treating it as in violation of the Kellogg-Briand Pact.

This so-called Pact of Paris did not provide for force to check aggression, but it eliminated from the status of neutrality all the former presumptions of an impartial attitude. It was the further development of this Stimson-Hoover doctrine that led the United States, under the Presidency of Franklin D. Roosevelt, to show steadily increasing disapproval of Germany's aggressions, as the military machine came into the open again and supported Hitler's Nazi dictatorship.

Through preparatory stages the Second World War, involving the whole of Europe in 1939, revealed itself plainly as a renewal of the former struggle, after a truce of twenty years. Germany's military structure had been rebuilt, with more complete application of national resources to war purposes than in 1914, and with more ambitious objectives. There could be no remedy but the destruction of this military power, and the organization of a democratic Europe.

TWENTY YEARS in the flight of historic time—when we have usually characterized past ages by centuries rather than decades—seems too short an interval for profound changes in prevailing states of mind. Yet mental attitudes, acquiescent or ardently approving, do in fact shape the destiny of nations when competent leadership asserts itself. The Peace Treaty of Versailles was signed in 1919, and in 1939 virtually all the nations that signed it were engaged again in warfare that became world-wide, excepting only the United States.

Many things internal and external had affected the nations in the course of those two decades. Contemporary volumes that are concerned with these events already form an immense library of official and unofficial documents, and of more or less ephemeral but highly significant news reports. It becomes essential to have the unadorned facts brought into the open. No honest effort to relate or interpret them can be frowned upon or denied. Freedom to think, to find reasons, to express opinions, has not yet made its unhampered way beyond a few favored areas. Yet freedom of thought and speech is one of the things at stake in the pending struggle.

Just midway between the dictated peace of 1919 and Mr. Chamberlain's declaration of war following Germany's attack on Poland, the better hopes of mankind found encouragement for a few brief months. The era of peace and good will had actually arrived, as wishful men made themselves believe, and America was taking credit for the initiative in starting the round-robin that every government in the world was ready to sign with alacrity, and with the semblance of sincerity. Frank B. Kellogg was Secretary of State and President Coolidge was in his last official year when our government proposed that the nations should bind themselves by firm agreement to "condemn recourse to war for the solution of international controversies and renounce it as an instrument of national policy in their relations with one another." They were further to pledge themselves that the settlement of disputes by other than pacific means should never be sought.

Aristide Briand was at that time the French Minister of Foreign Affairs, and he was not only ready to sign such an agreement with the United States, but was prepared to join his name with

Mr. Kellogg's in seeking the adherence of all other nations. At first M. Briand had proposed a Franco-American pact to mark the tenth anniversary of America's war declaration (April 6, 1917). Mr. Kellogg took his time and elaborated the suggestion. What was to have been a mere expression of sentiment between two friendly nations at length took form in a multilateral compact.

The care with which this agreement was prepared and presented singly to the governments of leading nations for their consideration gave it much more significance than a polite lip-service assent to the doctrine that peace is an appropriate status, other things being equal. The pact was not to supersede provisions in the covenant of the League of Nations or other existing treaties or agreements that had the force of international law.

In volumes of the *Review of Reviews* for the years 1928 and 1929, I discussed the Kellogg-Briand Pact in its formative phases and its final acceptance. The most searching analysis then made of it was published by me in the issue for September, 1928, and it was written by Frank H. Simonds under the title "America's Second Peace Adventure." Mr. Simonds regarded Secretary Kellogg's views as not differing in fundamental conception from those of President Wilson. No American writer of our time has ever scrutinized discordant European policies—in which the United States had sought to exercise beneficent influence—with such penetrating insight as the late Frank Simonds. In 1935 he gave the annual course of lectures at the Johns Hopkins University in the series known as *The Albert Shaw Lectures on Diplomatic History*, his topic being "American Foreign Policy in the Post-War Years." While these lectures (as published in that year by the Johns Hopkins Press) are not comforting to any American illusions, they throw highlights upon many situations with which American policy was concerned.

In his analysis of the Kellogg-Briand Pact in 1928, Mr. Simonds explained that before it had been put in final form and signed it had been subtly transformed by certain changes and reservations. America believed that the basis of peace must be the common sense of mankind joining in a determination to outlaw the scourge of war. Europe in contrast held to the conception that peace could be preserved only by the application of force. When the Kellogg proposal was pushed to its conclusion and accepted by all the powers, it seemed a natural view in Europe that America must be sidestepping its policy of isolation and planning closer cooperation with the League of Nations.

As for Mr. Simonds' own opinion, he thought it "desirable to recognize that, to Europe, the treaty constitutes a moral commitment, on our part." He proceeded as follows: "It comes then to this: that after a full decade our second peace adventure in Europe brings us once more face to face with the fundamental difference between American and European conceptions of how peace is to be established." I quote further paragraphs, as follows:

At bottom this fundamental difference turns upon the fact that for the bulk of the people of the United States the problem of peace in Europe seems ethical, and therefore simple. This judgment is disclosed in the fact that American endeavor to promote peace has largely taken the form of missionary campaigns to establish the crime of war, educational drives to emphasize the waste of conflict, and international negotiations to bring about formal renunciation of war.

These American efforts proceed from the assumption that the situation which exists is peace, that peace itself is the mere absence of war. Such a conception is not only natural but inevitable for the American mind, because in our own experience peace and the existing situation are identical. Possessing as we do liberty, unity, and security to the greatest conceivable extent, we can see in war only a mad adventure or a criminal undertaking. That any American statesman, political party, or sectional group should advocate war as an extension of national policy, would seem to indicate depravity or imbecility.

No error among all the misconceptions which characterize American opinions of Europe is at once so common and so complete as this. On the basis of American conditions, we mistake the European status quo for actual peace, and assume the acceptance of existing conditions by all right-minded people in every country as the point of departure for pacific endeavor. In this assumption lies the basic American misapprehension of the problem of peace in Europe.

In reality, from the collapse of the Roman Empire to the present hour, neither Europe collectively nor any Continental nation individually has known peace in the American sense. On the contrary each of the rapidly succeeding wars has been followed by a status quo tolerable only for the victors. Each of these situations, too, has been accepted on every hand as no more than a truce imposed by the might of the victor and the exhaustion of the vanquished—destined to endure only until its fortuitous balance of forces was destroyed.

Thus while American thought is directed toward discovering the means to preserve a peace actually possessed, European effort is concentrated upon the attempt to transform a transient truce into an enduring system of order. Americans are seeking to preserve peace; Europeans are striving to find it.

Mr. Simonds proceeds through a number of pages to develop these views that show contrasts, and the reasons for them, between European and American conceptions. I had been closely associated with Mr. Simonds, who dedicated the volume of 1935 to me, "gratefully recalling [as he wrote] twenty years of association on the *Review of Reviews* which remain one of the pleasantest memories of my life as a journalist." As a student of military history he was unsurpassed, and at my request he wrote in five volumes a History of the World War. His position as an eminent authority was widely recognized on both sides of the Atlantic.

While I regarded his knowledge of military history, and particularly his detailed acquaintance with European affairs in the first twenty years of the present century, as more extensive and thorough than my own, it was not temperamentally possible for me to accept in full his severely realistic views. My typical American optimism could not be suppressed, and I held to my belief in the early triumph of reasonableness and good will throughout the civilized world. The Peace Pact was signed at Paris by the foreign ministers of the fifteen leading powers with whom negotiations had been carried on, and it was at once submitted to thirty-one additional governments, by all of whom it was accepted.

Beside Mr. Kellogg, the most conspicuous foreign ministers who signed the Pact of Paris were Aristide Briand of France, Gustav Stresemann of Germany, and Austen Chamberlain of Great Britain. I was so anxious to have the treaty derive value from the force of universal public opinion that I advised ministers and religious leaders of all creeds and faiths to read it to their congregations, and called upon superintendents of education to have it featured in public school assemblies. I believed that the signing of the treaty was one of the majestic occurrences in world history, and thought that it would give more promise of permanence if we showed faith in its influential character. Since I was publishing the elaborate Simonds article in the same issue with my own editorial panegyrics, I tried to soften the blow of his more skeptical analysis by the following paragraph of comment:

> Mr. Simonds does not wish us to be cynical or pessimistic. He would not dampen our enthusiasm, but he would like to temper it with intelligence and understanding. He is right in advising us not to attach to the signing of this treaty the kind of significance that the facts do not warrant. But he would not deny the value of the treaty as a wholesome influence, cooperating with a hundred other things to make war an obsolete institution. Our modern activities in commerce, travel, communication, science, public health, literature, art, sport, and entertainment, will not submit to arbitrary national barriers. Our civilization makes for the strengthening of international ties, and the lessening of the old-time arrogance and self-sufficiency of nationalism.

II.

Now that we train great armies of specialists, build the supreme navy of all history, and seek with grim calculation to surpass both Germany and Japan in air power, there are literally millions of Americans who are asking why this war has happened, and what we can do when it ends to give the next generation some assurance of peace. Our students of foreign policy are not all of them profoundly wise or deeply informed; but speaking in terms of "intelligence tests," we now have a vastly greater number of men and women who would make the higher grades than we had in 1929 or 1919. Americans still believe that good will is the basis of peace, that the Golden Rule is sound international doctrine, that extreme nationalism is dangerous and delusive, and that something must be done about it.

But they also believe, as Americans never believed before, that we cannot henceforth step aside and leave the rest of the world trying to discover for itself the basis of those motives and methods that have made North America harmonious, and that are stabilizing relationships throughout the Western Hemisphere. In the next chapter I shall revert again to the Wilson policies and the American verdicts of 1919-20. Meanwhile, I am prepared to admit that I still believe completely in the Kellogg-

Briand Pact as it stands on the record, and in the value of the approving public opinion that was called forth in many countries by its adoption. It was not, indeed, enough to have expressed those sentiments. Much was left undone that should have been done to give them effect at moments of danger. But the world has been at war most of the time through thousands of years, and new forms of organization for peace may well require the experience of a half-century at least to give them a fair chance of survival.

Relatively valuable foundations have been built in North America, and this is true, if in lesser degree, in some other parts of the world. The only object of this book, as I shall remind readers from time to time, is to show that peace is not a dream, an illusion, or a mirage, but something that can be established in plain reality, with many of the elements already fabricated and ready to enter into the feasible structure. Visions that men see in times when their minds are free from clouds of fear and doubt are worth preserving, because they may be realized if not discarded or forgotten.

Mr. Simonds in 1935 declared: "The Kellogg Pact was the high-water mark of American endeavors for world peace, which consisted in undertaking to combine the idea of political and military isolation with that of moral and material involvement." We were not committed (he adds) to any contract which might compel us to send our boys abroad to fight again. "We were not bound to share in any military campaign to prevent aggression, but only to serve on a jury which would pronounce judgment."

This was an instance of the keenness of perception that characterized Mr. Simond's thinking. If war should come, we should hardly fail to test it by the ethical standards of the Kellogg Pact. As a "jury" we should discern relative war guilt and pronounce an ethical verdict. We should be drawn by virtue of that peace pact to lend our moral support to the better cause. We would refrain from active belligerency while we could, but would adopt measures one after another "short of war" to aid those who were resisting a dangerous and powerful aggressor.

Back of it all, and underlying this approach, were the principles upon which the United States had created its own institutions and had proceeded in its international relations. It is true that the Pact of 1929 had no enforcement clauses; but it stands today as a moral expression which cannot be disregarded. I still hold the views that I expressed in 1928 in the following paragraphs:

There is nobody living today who can give a trustworthy guarantee that his great-grandchildren will not commit crimes, cheat their creditors, or mistreat their wives and children. Yet we all know that citizens may set standards of public and private conduct, faithfully observed in their own day, that will influence posterity unto the third and fourth generation, and longer still. Whether or not our forefathers were altogether consistent in their practices, they laid the foundations of our Government upon plans that have achieved permanent peace in this hemisphere. They saw world harmony in hopeful visions, as they considered the spread of enlightenment and of popular self-government to other parts of the world. Our forefathers could not indeed give pledges that we, one hundred and fifty years afterwards, would be true to their principles. But far from ignoring or disregarding their principles and practices, we are endeavoring, with the momentum of our accumulated prestige and power, to make their ideals and aspirations the heritage of many other nations besides our own.

It is quite true that the Hon. Frank B. Kellogg and the high commissioners of some fourteen other nations meeting at Paris on August 27 cannot give enforceable pledges that the treaty which they have agreed to sign will be observed in spirit and in letter by mankind in ages to come. Many a private contract is broken, and many an agreement between nations has been sacrificed to the exigencies of an unforeseen occasion. Germany, France, and Great Britain had signed a treaty guaranteeing the neutrality of Belgium and the inviolability of its territory. Germany tore the agreement to shreds in 1914, on the pretext that if she failed to "do it first," France, in connivance with the Belgian authorities, would march against Germany by that open route. But private contracts continue to be made, and under usual conditions there is just reason to suppose that there is good faith on both sides, and that agreements will be faithfully observed. In like manner treaties are made between nations.

And, since nowadays secret clauses are frowned upon and diplomacy is an open book with treaties previously tested in the sphere of public opinion, there is ground for feeling that agreements have more validity now than ever before, and that their binding hold upon the men and women of the future is destined to be more seriously regarded than in times past. Especially when individuals or nations enter into compacts that are praiseworthy in themselves, and that involve no sacrifice or humiliation on either side, there may be ground for believing that unborn generations will not trample such deeds of trust or public conventions under foot.

When, therefore, Mr. Briand, Mr. Chamberlain, Mr. Kellogg, Mr. Stresemann—and all the other eminent statesmen representing the peoples as well as the governments of fifteen countries—unite in signing the agreement relegating war to the limbo of discarded remedies for disputes between nations, we have good reason to hope that the impression made upon the minds of a thousand million men, women, and children now living, will be so profound that they must transmit it as a heritage to two thousand million people to follow them. To pretend that we can pledge those unborn people to live in relations of fidelity, even within their own narrow spheres of action, would be obviously presumptuous. To assume that men now holding office in the administrations of great countries can control the political and international conduct of those who are to come after them, would be futile and vain.

But it is not necessary to believe in the perfectability of mankind to become convinced that we are changing for the better our type of civilization. The sort of nationalism that hitherto has relied upon the principle of force, planning the development of armaments and superiority in the art of war, is undergoing modification. To seek the accomplishment of objects held to be advantageous at the expense of some other nationality by fire and sword, is not to be tolerated henceforth. Just as in the smaller areas we have established recourse to laws and tribunals, and have insisted upon outlawing the *lex talionis* as well as the vigilance committee and the "lynching bee" of a more immature society, even so the community of nations can no longer endure the easy resort to foreign war.

Europeans aspire under difficulties to gain the sort of benefits and advantages that are our lot in the family of forty-eight American States. They will have to overcome obstacles that we can hardly comprehend before they can arrive at our enviable status. The circumstances are so different that we ought not to be blinded to the reasons why Europe has come to this point of signing the so-called Kellogg treaty after some months of misgiving and hesitation. In view of these reasons there is, in our opinion, an unprecedented gain for the cause of peace and good will in the mere fact that they are actually coming together and putting their names on the paper that commits them all to the notable declarations set forth in the multilateral treaty.

As I have already remarked, the fifteen governments whose foreign ministers met at Paris in August, 1928, and signed the pact renouncing war had not treated the affair as a bit of diplomatic showmanship, but had taken it seriously. They had spent several months testing opinion in their respective countries and taking counsel with one another. Signing the pact, however, was only the beginning; because in many if not in all countries it had to be submitted to some parliamentary authority for ratification.

The same course had to be observed by many additional governments which were invited to adhere to the agreement, and so it happened that almost a year had elapsed after the fifteen signatures at Paris in early August of 1928 before the treaty could be proclaimed as having been generally ratified and therefore in effect as public law.

Meanwhile Herbert Hoover had been elected President of the United States, and had been inaugurated on March 4, 1929. The Pact was proclaimed by him on July 24 as having been ratified by the original fifteen signatory nations, with an additional thirty-one countries, making a total of forty-six. Several others were soon to deposit at Washington their instructions of adherence to the treaty. Mr. Coolidge and Mr. Kellogg returned to Washington as President Hoover's guests, and they stood on either side of him as he made a brief address in the presence of representatives of all the signatory countries.

III.

Few public men then in active life were as widely acquainted with the world and its peoples as Herbert Hoover. Graduating at Stanford University in 1895, he spent some time in the West as an expert minerologist and mining engineer, after which he went to Australia to pursue that same profession. Next he became head of China's new Department of Mines, and then spent some fourteen years in the line of his professional and business activities in Russia, Burma, Turkestan, South and Central America, Korea, Alaska, Egypt, Mexico, Ceylon, and Italy (to quote this remarkable list of countries from standard authorities). As head of widespread enterprises, he maintained offices in New York, San Francisco, and London. Although absent so much from this country, his business interests brought him home at frequent intervals and kept him in touch with the course of public affairs.

Mr. Hoover was well known in the circles of his own profession and also in the business world; but my own first definite knowledge of his qualities and capacities was acquired in the summer of 1914 when the outbreak of war found several hundred thousand Americans stranded in Europe, many of them cut off from their bank accounts, and unable to secure shipping accommodations. They poured into London by the scores of thousands. Mr. Hoover happened to be there and he took control of the situation, and saw that relief was provided for at least a hundred thousand and perhaps twice as many.

Refugee Belgians were also flocking to England by the thousands; but the main task of Belgian relief was in their own small but densely populated country. England and France provided the funds (supplemented by voluntary contributions from the United States) and the Germans in occupation of Belgium permitted a system of distribution under the direction of some acceptable citizen of a neutral country. Herbert Hoover was so obviously the man for the place that no one else was considered. For nearly three years in charge of that particular field (including also Northern France) Hoover familiarized himself with all the problems of food supply and distribution, not only as they affected the Belgian people but Europe at large.

During those years Mr. Hoover enjoyed the confidence of the British and French governments while maintaining relations with the occupying German authorities. When the United States entered the war in April, 1917, his functions in Belgium were transferred to a European neutral, and he himself returned to the United States with confidential information from the British authorities. Arriving in New York, he caught a train for Washington without delay, to confer with leaders of the government. On less than an hour's notice Cabinet officers who could be reached, and several others of official standing, were invited by a California senator to dine at his house and hear Mr. Hoover's story. I happened to be at the home of a Cabinet officer, and, since I was also a friend of Senator Phelan, I was invited to the dinner as the only unofficial guest.

It was the darkest hour of the war for England, because the submarine campaign against ships carrying food and supplies had reached a climax of intensity and destructiveness. The full truth had not been disclosed to the President or our naval authorities. Mr. Hoover, whose gift of silence is well known, can also speak, when occasion offers, with fluency and convincing power. For several hours at Senator Phelan's dinner he described the situation as they knew it in London, and as he alone in America comprehended it on that particular day.

Mr. Hoover's news was gloomy, but his energy and capacity for dealing with difficult situations gave him an immediate and commanding influence. His work as Food Administrator secured the cooperation of all the housewives of America, and made possible a movement of wheat and other supplies to Europe that saved millions from starvation. His work as conservator and distributor was coordinated with that of Bernard M. Baruch's war industries board; and it would take several pages to explain its domestic and foreign ramifications.

After the Armistice of November, 1918, food supplies had to be distributed all over Europe; and as chairman of the food section of the Supreme Economic Council it was Herbert Hoover's business to see that this was done. Millions who were at death's door from starvation were rescued by means of relief efforts that Hoover organized and directed. When the Republican Convention of 1920 refused to unite upon either of the two leading candidates, General Wood and Governor Lowden, Mr. Hoover would have been the most popular and acceptable compromise. But the politicians were more narrowly partisan in their choice. President Harding, however, made amends by giving Mr. Hoover the opportunity, as Secretary of Commerce, to build up the most efficient public agency for the promotion of domestic and foreign trade that had ever functioned in any country.

Mr. Hoover remained at this post through the Harding and Coolidge administrations, with Mr. Hughes and Mr. Kellogg as colleagues successively at the Department of State. In 1928 Mr. Hoover was nominated for the Presidency in response to a popular demand that went beyond the limits of party or section. He had been intensely occupied for fifteen years with political and economic conditions that gave him a wider knowledge of affairs in Russia and Central Europe, in China and the Far East, and in Latin America as well as in all the English-speaking countries, than any other living man. This might have been true without being universally recognized; but in point of fact Mr. Hoover was known everywhere, and the world at large expected more from him and his administration than adverse winds of circumstance made possible in the years 1929-33.

However, Mr. Hoover had been in the White House less than six months when the time came to proclaim the ratification of the Pact of Paris, and it was expected in some European circles that he would make an extended address on American policy. Instead, his remarks were brief and avoided any commitments beyond the obvious ones that were expressed in the treaty itself. He called it "a proposal to the conscience and idealism of civilized nations." He followed that remark with several sentences further characterizing the treaty: "It suggested a new step in international law rich with meaning, pregnant with new ideas in the conduct of world relations. It represented a platform from which there is instant appeal to the public opinion of the world as to specific acts and deeds." He congratulated the signatory states and the entire world "upon the coming into force of this additional instrument of humane endeavor, to do away with war as an instrument of national policy and to obtain by pacific means alone the settlement of international disputes."

The new thought in Mr. Hoover's statement, and the one that is most pertinent to the position of the United States since 1939, is contained in the sentence that calls the Kellogg Pact "*a platform from which there is instant appeal to the public opinion of the world as to specific acts and deeds*." Mr. Henry L. Stimson was President Hoover's Secretary of State, and he had read the address from which this sentence is quoted on the day before it was delivered and had given it his complete approval. Mr. Stimson, who is now Secretary of War in President Franklin D. Roosevelt's Cabinet, is a man of logical mind and of convictions that might seem rigid at times, but never wavering and always courageous and definite.

There was no need in the summer of 1929 to dwell in an official utterance by the President or the head of the State Department upon the fact—scarcely realized by the American public—that the Pact of Paris marked a further turning-point in American policy. We were the exponent of new ideas in the conduct of world relations. We were in a position to judge specific acts and deeds when they violated the Pact of Paris. Mr. Simonds realized that we were moving toward the danger of a second embroilment in Europe's resort to war, and probably Mr. Stimson also knew that this departure from traditional aloofness—while intended to inoculate Europe and the world with our prophylactic safeguards—might have the opposite effect of drawing us into the vortex of European strife.

At least we were making it more necessary to discriminate, and to stigmatize the real aggressors. The Pact of Paris left little chance for the further assertion of the Doctrine of Neutrality as having any moral standing or legal value. Neutrality became merely a waiting or a temporizing attitude, reflecting the natural dread of war as a terrible expedient. Or, in case of small nations close to scenes of major war, neutrality was to signify little else than helplessness or the day-by-day anxiety to survive.

There was a genuine endeavor on the part of Mr. Hoover and Mr. Stimson to enrich our relationships with other countries by various measures of agreement and cooperation. At this middle period between two world wars, the hopes of lasting peace were so widely expressed that they might have seemed to give real promise of what Mr. Neville Chamberlain ten years later, refusing to look facts in the face, called "peace in our time." Ours was a satisfied nation, and we had not the slightest possible temptation to use force aggressively.

IV.

If Europe had weighed the cost of war as against the covetousness of particular countries, peace might somehow have been bought, and the present war averted or indefinitely postponed. Briand and Stresemann were friends, and if there had been a willingness on the part of the principal powers that had written the Versailles Treaty to support Briand in a program intended to make the German people also a satisfied nation, peace might have been secured. This is speculative, and not at this moment a profitable line of discussion. The failure to provide a complete and overwhelming program of appeasement affords not an iota of excuse for Germany's deliberate policy of aggrandizement by bold aggressions.

But in 1929 the German mind was not yet in full captivity to the military doctrinaires. Also, Japan's Foreign Minister at that time was not a militarist but a man of good will. Aggression policies begin at home, with the suppression of the apostles of justice and peace. Responding to Mr. Hoover's proclamation, as I noted at the time, Baron Shidehara, Japanese Foreign Minister, called war a "wasteful and bitter institution" and declared that the treaty "marks the starting point from which the problem of disarmament can be properly approached." Dr. Stresemann, speaking as German Minister of Foreign Affairs, declared that "the Pact, which gives expression to the inmost yearning of the nations, has created a new foundation for the peaceful development of relations between the States. I trust it will prove effective even under difficult circumstances." Senator Borah, who was then chairman of the Foreign Relations Committee, thought the time opportune for an immediate reduction of war expenditures and urged an early conference to deal with the problem of needlessly large navies.

Even now we begin to see—what will be clear enough in longer perspectives, perhaps fifty years hence—that the significant date at the conclusion of the First World War was not the forced signing of the Versailles Treaty by dummy representatives of Germany, but the voluntary signing of the Truce of November 1918. Germany was at the point of military defeat, and surrendered to avoid invasion and collapse. The military machine was disarmed; but those who propagated its doctrines thought that Germany had done well rather than badly, in view of so overwhelming an array of adversaries. They were by no means converted to American doctrines. On the contrary, they thought their tenets were vindicated, and began to map the corrected strategies of the future.

It had been obviously necessary for the Emperor William to abdicate, for the Allies made him a scapegoat. Germany adopted republican forms, and the Weimar Constitution seemed to promise an era of popular, representative government. It would be more cynical than reasonable to argue that the plain people of Germany were unlike those of all other countries, and that they were not sincere in hoping to avoid further calamities of war for themselves and their immediate posterity. Furthermore, it would be equally unconvincing to argue that Germans of liberal mind like Dr. Stresemann were less desirous of an era of European peace than Frenchmen like M. Briand. But regardless of new forms, German democracy was not yet on firm ground.

President Von Hindenburg on the day before Mr. Hoover proclaimed the Peace Pact sent him a radiogram in the following terms: " On the occasion of the going into effect of the Pact for the Renunciation of War in the creation of which the United States of America had so prominent a part, I express to you, Mr. President, the most heartfelt congratulations. I cherish the hope that the Pact will prove its strength in the shaping of the relations between the nations and contribute to securing the peace of the world on the foundations of right." This seemed to have the genuine ring; but no Prussian war-lord could ever see the world through the Quaker eyes of a Herbert Hoover.

There followed a brief period of conferences and treaties, which greatly extended the scope of internationalism as regards arrangements for arbitration, and the promotion of intercourse and commerce. We cooperated in measures for sharp control of such nefarious practices as the slave-trade in Africa and the iniquitous traffic in narcotic drugs. These efforts in the fields of world-wide amelioration were not only well intended, but they were of permanent value for two reasons. First, they were justified as specific deeds that reflected the awakening conscience of mankind. Second, every effort to bring nations together in united action adds its testimony to the cumulative evidence that an orderly world is possible.

In the Presidential election of 1932 Hindenburg was re-elected as against Adolph Hitler, who was the candidate of the National Socialist Party. But the defeat was only nominal, for Hitler became Chancellor of Germany in January, 1933, with President Hindenburg acquiescing. The venerable head of the state surrendered governing authority and became a mere symbol of his country's military glory of former periods. Meanwhile Hitler set about the business of restoring Germany's prestige and power.

Clouds were gathering in all quarters. The Bolshevik revolution in Russia had not begun to reach a point of equilibrium, and it alarmed Europe and America. The United States had not recognized the Union of Soviet Republics, which had also caused alarm and reaction in England. Japan had seized Manchuria, and Mr. Stimson was protesting. Mussolini was demanding Treaty revision, and preparing for his African adventure. The rise of Hitler was ominous.

Not to summarize at this point the well-known record of events and experiences in Germany between the two wars, let it suffice to say that Europe had not found the basis of a peaceful settlement, and that—well before the end of President Hoover's term and of Mr. Stimson's incumbency as Secretary of State—the prospects across the Atlantic as well as in the Far East had become discouraging. Even then, however, too many of us were disregardful of the stormy horizons, because we were preoccupied. In our well-nigh desperate efforts to recover from agricultural and business depression, we were too much absorbed with affairs at home to be concerned about rapidly changing conditions across the friendly oceans.

It seemed enough for us to struggle out of the morass of unemployment and financial disaster; and we were no longer, for the moment at least, finding uplift or cheer in our so-recently glowing faith in a happy world of equal opportunity. In an effort to save our home markets for ourselves, we had enacted the Hawley-Smoot Tariff, which—though not quite as offensive to neighboring nations and the world at large as its later critics have asserted—was an unwise product of log-rolling and lobbying protracted through a year and a half of uncertainty that ruined humble lace-makers in foreign lands, and producers of other wares for our market. Mr. Hoover had signed that tariff bill, though undoubtedly with inward qualms and any feeling but warmth of approval.

But while this tariff policy had given offense to Canada and some other good neighbors, and had been met by the new and discriminating tariff policies of the "British Commonwealth of Nations," the Hoover Administration had by no means intended to make America a hermit nation in the economic sense. For eight years, as Secretary of Commerce, Mr. Hoover had promoted American trade in all nooks and corners of the inhabited globe. His hopes and aspirations for a world of economic as well as political harmony and progress had not given place to distrust and discouragement, although domestic policies had been baffling, with Congress majorities under hostile leadership.

Thus among the larger negotiations that were pending when Mr. Hoover was defeated for a second term in the election of 1932 was the World Economic Conference, which was actually held in the summer of 1933 at London, with President Roosevelt's Secretary of State, the Honorable Cordell Hull, as chairman of the American delegation.

Mr. John T. Whitaker, a keen observer and for many years a prominent member of America's group of brilliant foreign correspondents, recounts and interprets many European situations in a volume entitled *We Cannot Escape History.* No writer has made it plainer that the second war is a sequel to the first, that the interval between was a truce rather than a period of genuine peace, and that the primary objective of the present war as of its predecessor was the crushing of Russia's military power while still inferior to that of Germany.

V.

Hitler appears, under Mr. Whitaker's scalpel, as the creature of the war party, who crushes the social revolution to keep his great aim free of domestic complications. He becomes a disciple of the later exponents of the theories of "Geopolitics." The English geographer Sir Halford Mackinder had founded this school of military speculation as early as 1919. England had been long inspired by the teachings of the American Admiral Mahan, and had determined to maintain unapproachable supremacy of sea-power at all hazards. But the Mackinder doctrine took account of new means and weapons, including aviation, and argued that the world could be conquered from a land base that should include a contiguous region within which lay Germany and neighboring European lands, and a large part of European and Asiatic Russia.

This was called the "Heartland Base" from which—thanks to modern methods of transportation—the country that controlled it could disregard the oceans and outbuild the naval powers of the world. Mackinder held that if Germany had neglected France and overwhelmed Russia in 1914, thus securing the so-called

"Heartland," she would have conquered the world. Mr. Whitaker makes the following observations:

> This application of geography to global strategy was studiously pondered by the German generals, but it was seized upon by Hitler as a sort of divine revelation. The tendency of the British, French, and Americans to confuse their prejudice against Communism with the facts of Russia's geographic position seemed fortuitous to Hitler. He said repeatedly to the German generals from the day of the purge onward—as Blomberg himself twice told the author—that the new German army would fight but one war, the war against Russia. In his contempt for the democracies Hitler believed until the British and French declarations of war that they would be duped by his crusade against Communism. He believed that they and the United States would be conquered without a struggle.

The author, from whose chapter "Whom Does the Army Obey?" I have quoted the preceding paragraph, concludes that chapter with an allusion to the deposed Kaiser that carries us across the interval between the two wars, and illustrates the simple fact that the one is a sequel of the other:

> The purge had made the militarists supreme once again and it led inevitably and inexorably to the dark night of August 31 and September 1, 1939—the night when the Nazis marched into Poland and precipitated world war. The most apposite and revealing comment on what had happened to Germany was given by Kaiser Wilhelm II, exactly two weeks before the attack on Poland. The Kaiser was saying farewell to John Wheeler-Bennett, the distinguished British historian, who had been the German's guest at Doorn.
>
> "This is farewell forever," said the Kaiser.
>
> "Why" asked my friend.
>
> "Because the war will separate us and I will die long before its end."
>
> "But is the war inevitable?" asked Wheeler-Bennett.
>
> "Yes," replied the Kaiser. "The generals have got Hitler just as they got me. He can never stop the German military machine."

A very brief glimpse that I had of Hitler's Germany in that summer of 1939 would not suffice to qualify me as a competent witness of this complete military dominance—which the Kaiser understood so well after twenty years of saddened reflection. But I could make quick comparisons, by reason of numerous previous opportunities to note conditions in Germany. Although I could hardly realize it, fifty years had passed since I had first studied

German municipal and administrative systems, with Prince Bismarck nearing the end of his long period as master of German policies. The young William II was in his second year on the imperial throne, and was already disputing Bismarck's policies.

Although the great Chancellor had formed a defensive alliance with Austria and had secured Italy as a third partner in 1882, he was by no means preparing for an "inevitable" war with Russia, but on the contrary was trying to provide against such a war. He had recently made a treaty of so-called "re-insurance" with Russia that provided for neutrality under probable conditions. It is true that the momentum of Bismarck's balance-of-power policies was to postpone major war for another quarter-century. But the transition in German aims and methods became apparent soon enough, as events threw light upon them. Germany had become an aspirant for world empire; and her ambitions were attended with such preparations, moral as well as physical, for the use of force to accomplish her objects as had not been known in modern history.

One possible corrective or restraint lay within the German nation itself, but this could have come about only by a social revolution. When Dr. Dernburg visited the United States a few weeks after the outbreak of war in 1914, he made allusions to the popular strength of the Social Democrats, and to the organized Catholic party, as if Germany like the United States or England were in fact a democratic country in which free speech and a free press prevailed, and where equal votes under manhood suffrage gave controlling power to the common people. Germany was indeed well organized, under the most efficient civil service system in the world. Many social reforms had been instituted from above, in order to avert the menace of a possible social revolution. But Germany had become a military state; and revolutionary tendencies would have been suppressed before they had gained any ground whatever.

Like any other occasional visitor and observer, I could have recited from memory numerous incidents to illustrate the ubiquity and insolence of the professional military caste, as it rose superior to all the rules and regulations that civilians were obliged to obey. The vast military machine was not to be rendered meekly subordinate to a civilian society led by Social Democrats like

Liebknecht. The army and navy—that is to say, the immense body of professional officers—had joined hands with the great captains of industry and of commerce to gain control of the German mind and to shape German policy.

The older publicists of Germany were forgotten. The universities and technical schools were now controlled by the exponents of the new doctrines of German destiny and supremacy. German nationalism had grown into German imperialism; and the idea of leadership in central Europe had expanded to the conception of leadership throughout the world. There was no counteracting sentiment in Germany of sufficient strength to bring about a rejection of these views and policies. Even those German leaders who disclaimed the doctrines of the militarists were constantly complaining of Germany's unfair treatment in a world which was yielding its benefits to the expansionist policies of other countries. Notably at the end of the nineteenth century the German mind was affected by seriously distorted views of American and British territorial extensions of authority.

In the course of the Boer War it was natural enough that the Dutchmen of Holland should sympathize with their Dutch kinsmen of the Transvaal and the Orange Free State. But the bitter feeling against England in Germany at that time was not because of sympathy for the underdog in an unequal fight. Rather it was a wave of extreme jealousy, because the British Empire was gaining what Germany desired for herself. The Kaiser and his imperialists had looked forward to future expansions of territory in South Africa from the unprofitable area that they already held; but this had now become impossible. The Kaiser was rash enough to have attempted intervention; but his military authorities knew that nothing at that time could be gained for Germany by a war impelled by spite and resentment.

VI.

Learning much from visits to the Continent as well as to England in those years of the Boer War, I could understand that so-called "jingo" imperialism was an affront to the best British sentiment and was not an expression of the nation's permanent aims. What the Germans refused to understand was the freedom of public opinion in Great Britain. The so-called "pro-Boers"—among them John Morley, James Bryce, David Lloyd George, my own partner W. T. Stead, and most of the other Liberal leaders, along with John Burns and the Labor elements—did not cease to denounce the South African war adventure, and free speech was not suppressed. The typical swing of the party pendulum in a general Parliamentary election supplied the necessary correctives. The Liberals did not repudiate any achieved results of the war in South Africa, but they turned them to constructive and salutary purposes. They gave all of South Africa back to its own responsible inhabitants, in a fashion that was accepted as permanent not only by all parties in Great Britain, but by Boers and British alike in the new Dominion.

Thus, as a sequel to the Boer War, there came the Union of South Africa, with a constitution of the most liberal kind under which the Boers were given every opportunity for self-determined progress that reasonable men could desire. No finer tributes, whether in action or in word, have ever been paid by defeated leaders to their conquerors than those that the Boer generals Botha and Smuts paid during the war period (1914-18), in which they rendered such conspicuous service to the British cause.[1]

[1] A general election in the Union of South Africa held in the summer of 1943 gives firm majority control in both chambers of the dominion parliament to the Prime Minister, General Smuts, and his policies in support of Great Britain's war position. The attitude of General Smuts in both World Wars is in consequence of the statesmanship of Sir Henry Campbell-Bannerman's ministry, that conferred self-government upon the Transvaal and Orange River colonies, and federated South Africa. Young Winston Spencer Churchill, who had taken part in the Boer War, and who had been elected in 1900 as a Conservative member of Parliament, afterwards joined the Liberals and was made Undersecretary for the Colonies by Sir Henry Campbell-Bannerman. He took the leading part in the House of Commons in promotion of the Union of South Africa; and this earned for him the cordial friendship of General Smuts that has continued for about forty years.

The New York Times on August 14, 1943, apropos of Mr. Churchill's visit to Niagara, quoted the Prime Minister as saying that he had first seen the Falls in the year 1900. *The Times* further comments upon the fact that Mr. Churchill lectured in New York, in December 1900, on the Boer War. Irish sympathizers in the audience cheered at the first mention of the Boers, which did not in the least disconcert the lecturer. On the contrary, he praised the would-be disturbers for cheering the Boers, and remarked: "They are a brave people, and they deserve all the cheers you can give them."

It happens that Major Pond (or Mark Twain who sponsored the American appearance of Mr. Churchill) had given me a seat on the platform near the lecturer, and thus the occasion remains fresh in my memory. Major Pond had

Germany could not, or would not, understand. Through a long term of years, Mr. Campbell-Bannermann as Premier, then Mr. Asquith, and at length Mr. Lloyd George himself, with Foreign Ministers like Sir Edward Grey, had represented an England that stood for democracy at home and abroad and that held out the olive branch to all nations—not the least to Germany—in the desire for a world of harmony along lines of justice, progress, and good understanding.

I might continue with further allusions to the growth in colonial empire of the French Republic, so bitterly resented by Germany and so much contributing to that crystallization of German policy that I have already characterized. I might also allude to the process of Russification that had been sweeping over vast areas in central Asia. It is enough to remark that Russia's power to acquire political control over Asiatic regions and to assimilate Asiatic peoples had aroused the attention of all intelligent observers. It had led Germany and Austria to look forward with no little anxiety to a time when Russia's ability to put twenty million men in the field might be attended by a corresponding ability to equip such vast armies with the necessary arms and munitions, and to maintain them on southern and western fighting fronts.

The example of the United States in expelling Spain from Cuba, Puerto Rico, and the Philippines, after acquiring the Hawaiian Islands, had been cited in Germany in a manner that wholly failed to recognize the motives, methods, and objects of the American people. Germany had regarded the United States as, like herself, one of the newer industrial nations, with an inevitable tendency toward economic and political expansion. Germany, on her own part, had desired to acquire the Philippines, and had looked forward to obtaining bases in the West Indies, and colonies, perchance, on the mainland of South America.

Democracy in America, like democracy in England, was fully able to check imperialism and to transform the doctrines of pos-

advertised the youthful Churchill as " the hero of five wars, the author of six books and the future Prime Minister of Great Britain." The visitor forbade the further use of this particular form of advertising, as he repeated his lecture in a number of American cities. But Mr. Churchill has since 1900 written a great many more books, has had a part in several additional wars, and now finds himself as Prime Minister directing Britain's greatest war effort of all time.

session and exploitation into those of guardianship and tutelage. American sentiment had become almost too eager to cut the Philippines adrift. The efforts of the United States to create a system of education in the Philippines, to modernize agriculture, to establish security and justice in the daily affairs of life, to train the people in local self-government, and to give them political institutions for permanent insular self-rule, had been remarkably successful.

But Germany could only see that the United States was attaining a position of larger influence and wider scope in the outer world, at a time when the southern and western parts of the American republic, together with Alaska, still afforded ample opportunity for the growth of population and the development of resources. Germany, with a greatly restricted home area, was second to the United States alone in the volume of her industry, and ahead of the United States in some forms of manufacture and commerce. Furthermore, Germany had seen the United States fortify as well as construct the Panama Canal, acquiring dominant influence in Central America and the Caribbean Sea, while England had been constantly strengthening her naval and political authority along the Suez route, in the Red Sea, in Egypt, and in Persia.

Such was the world in which Germany felt it necessary to make her way, first by an unexampled training of her people and development of her industry and commerce, and second by devising a wholly unparalleled convertibility of human and industrial resources into the instrumentalities of war. Democratic transformation from within was impossible under these conditions. Was it possible, on the other hand, before the First World War, for the democracies of England, America, and France to have taken Germany so freely and generously into a partnership for developing resources and trade—while restricting land and sea armaments and organizing the nations for peace—as to have won the great moral victory for civilization?

The essential factors of progress characterizing the nineteenth and twentieth centuries had been international, and therefore indivisible by political boundaries. Could the rivalries of the nations have been modified, and the dangers of nationalism gradually reduced and removed, if America, Great Britain, and France had set more consistent examples? I believe the records will show that each of these three great countries had actually endeavored to do full justice to Germany.

Questions asked in the two foregoing paragraphs refer to the years that preceded the convulsion of 1914. Let us admit that imperialism, even of the missionary type, is never wholly altruistic. It is more likely to be stigmatized as hypocritical than admired or praised by countries not engaged in parallel adventures. Cecil Rhodes made a religion of his belief in the further spread of the Empire that his business enterprises were promoting in the southern half of the Dark Continent. "If there is a God," said Mr. Rhodes, "the best service I can render him is to paint the map of Africa British Red, to the extent of my ability."

This was not a crass doctrine of material gain in the mind of that empire-builder, for he had adopted the view in early life that justice and integrity were basic British principles, and that such safeguards of liberty were needed above all else in the wilderness of Africa, under protection of the British flag. Yet there was another aspect in which rival nations looked upon the British Empire in its historic growth. These rivals could accuse England of rapacity and greed, without pausing to reflect that British principles at home were constantly applying correctives in the far-flung fragments of crown colony or protectorate. Quite apart from my own prejudices against the acquisition of territorial gains by means of war—and I include also the methods used in our gain of the Philippines—I have not been able to discover that any expansionist policies of England, France, America, or Russia afforded Germany the slightest pretext for the war of 1914.

In an era of awakened nationalism and race consciousness, the principal safeguard against devastating conflicts lay in the application to actual life everywhere of the doctrines of liberty and democracy. When freedom and equality had been established among the inhabitants of a given locality, and among the peoples using a common tongue and inhabiting a national area, it became increasingly probable that a democracy thus grounded in the doctrine of human rights would not maintain a governmental policy that looked toward the permanent subjection of other races or peoples. Unfortunately, governmental autocracy had survived up to the outbreak of the war of 1914, to a far greater degree in some countries and empires than in others. In this obvious historical fact lies the answer to many questions.

Germany and Japan were the only nations in the entire world that were prepared for the Second World War, unless we should also include Italy. That other countries were not ready to protect themselves gave the aggressors their awaited opportunity, but did not on that account afford them excuses, much less justification. The mistakes of the twenty-year period could hardly have been more numerous even if some perverse spirit of folly had guided the councils of the nations that imposed the treaties of 1919 upon the central powers.

Yet those errors did not constitute a chapter of vindictiveness or oppression, pointing toward another war as a justified means of escape from hardships imposed by unrelenting foes. Germany was not embarked in 1939 upon a gallant struggle for liberty, but rather upon a ruthless campaign of militarism, and domination by plunder and terror. If Germany had become a truly democratic state by revolution, instead of relapsing submissively to the status of a military autocracy, there would have been ample room in Europe and the world at large for her continued growth in cultural influence and material prosperity.

CHAPTER V

WOODROW WILSON'S REVERSAL IN 1917

For more than two years after the beginning of the World War in the summer of 1914, President Wilson had clung to the idea that the aims of the belligerent groups might be reconciled, through the mediation of neutral governments under the leadership of the United States. Neutrality in his mind had not meant isolation. He thought of himself as a peace-maker, and after his re-election he appealed to all the governments at war to state their objects, thinking that their answers might "bring a new light into the affairs of the world." He still clung to the view that peace without victory was possible. He found the Germans much more ready than the Entente Allies for a peace conference.

The belief that the United States could keep aloof from the war and could join both groups of belligerents in shaping a constructive and permanent peace was a delusion. Taking it for granted that Mr. Wilson would live up to the slogan of his 1916 campaign and continue to keep America out of the war regardless of provocations, the Germans made a bold decision. All further thought of peace by compromise was laid aside, and they adopted the view that they could win a quick and complete victory over England and France by resuming the submarine policy that they had abandoned more than half a year earlier as a concession to the United States.

Their delusion regarding Wilson's character was greater than his had been about the prospects of a negotiated peace. He had enough elasticity of mind to adopt a different view of the war, and now regarded it as a challenge to the rights and security of all mankind. In a contest involving so many nations, the doctrine of neutrality had lost influence and standing. Germany was seeking victory through defiance of the principles that had made modern civilization possible. We entered the war in such a way as to make it clear that we were not seeking advantages for ourselves, but were upholding fundamental principles and employing force as a legal process.

The facts as they presented themselves after we had been in the war for a few months were strikingly similar to those that emerged in the course of the Second World War. This is shown in an extended statement of December, 1917, reproduced in this chapter. Germany's purposes of conquest had been deferred, but not abandoned, when the Truce was signed in November, 1918. The Truce saved the Germans from another winter of war that would have brought invasion and disaster to their Fatherland. The armistice gave Germany opportunities for recuperation. These were delayed and perhaps inconvenienced, but were not crushed, by the exactions of the Versailles Treaty.

Mr. Wilson's broad principles of international harmony and world organization were in keeping with those of earlier American statesmen, and have never been so fully and eloquently expressed by any other public man. His conceptions will be vindicated, and it will be perceived that the further course of German militarism—as revived and renewed under Hitler's Nazi leadership—was not in consequence of any mistakes of judgment or policy on President Wilson's part. German militarism had gone underground for a time, but had not been conquered when the fighting ceased in 1918. The Second World War was not due to anything that Wilson had done or left undone.

AS I HAVE remarked in a previous chapter, there came a time in the course of what we call the First World War when we abandoned all pretense of impartiality. Through what experiences did we change our attitude?

President Wilson was re-elected in a campaign so closely contested that the Republican candidate, Charles Evans Hughes, had been at first regarded as successful and was so acknowledged at the White House. The unexpected result in California, however gave Wilson a majority in the electoral college. It was reasonable that he should have deferred the announcement of any radical change in his convictions and in his views of American policy until it was ascertained whether he or Mr. Hughes would have to carry the burden of responsibility for the ensuing term.

Mr. Wilson had done his best during nearly three years to make our doctrine of neutrality substantial in practical applications. He had urged upon the belligerents the propriety of observing the rules of the Declaration of London in their maritime proceedings. As early as February, 1915, he had warned Germany against its submarine policy. At the same time he had protested against the deceptive use of the American flag by British ships. In further notes of 1915 he had denounced the British and French methods of blockade as illegal, while not ceasing to protest against German disregard of established principles, both as concerned the conduct of the war on land and the rights of neutrals in their traffic on the high seas.

The most startling occurrence in the earlier employment of submarines by Germany was the sinking of the *Lusitania* en route to England from New York, causing the loss of more than a thousand lives. More than a hundred of these victims were Americans. I shall not recount in detail the arguments presented in the diplomatic correspondence that followed this *Lusitania* incident. Germany attempted to throw the burden of responsibility upon the British for their illegal blockade, but offered to grant immunity to American passenger ships if distinguished by special marks.

This concession was not acceptable, for reasons clearly stated in a note dated July 21, 1915, signed by Secretary Lansing, but evidently framed by the President. Following a number of atrocious incidents and diplomatic protests of increasing sternness, Germany promised to modify submarine warfare in order to remove American causes of offense. It proved impossible, however, for Germany to operate her increasing fleet of submarines in such a way as to do the maximum of injury to her enemies and a minimum of harm to America as representing the rights of neutrals. There were further mishaps, and our State Department continued to lay down the principles of international law, and to arraign German policy.

In April, 1916, more than eleven months after the sinking of the *Lusitania*, Mr. Wilson appeared before Congress to deliver a special message in which he reviewed the controversy in every pertinent aspect. Having summarized the recent course of events which included many sinkings of unarmed ships without warning, the President declared: "Again and again the Imperial German Government has given this Government its solemn assurances that at least passenger ships would not be thus dealt with, and yet it has again and again permitted its under-sea commanders to disregard these assurances with entire impunity." There followed a citation of more recent instances that were as inexcusable and as shocking as the destruction of the *Lusitania*.

As a conclusion, he declared that the use of submarines "because of the very character of the vessels employed, and the very methods of attack which their employment of course involves, is incompatible with the principles of humanity, the long-established and incontrovertible rights of neutrals, and the sacred immunities of non-combatants."

Even if Mr. Wilson might have seemed to clothe his thoughts in over-elaborate periods, it should be remembered that as a young man he had modelled his style upon that of Edmund Burke. His meaning was as clear as crystal, although his sentences were sonorous and oratorical. He was leading up to the statement that "unless the Imperial German Government should now immediately declare and effect an abandonment of its present methods of warfare against passenger and freight carrying vessels, this government can have no choice but to sever diplomatic relations with the Government of the German Empire altogether."

On May 4, 1916, just one year (lacking three days) after the *Lusitania* incident, Germany made a long reply. Its essence is contained in the statement that the Imperial Government "is prepared to do its utmost to confine the operations of the war for the rest of its duration to the fighting forces of the belligerents." This reply further stated that the German Government would impose upon all its commanders at sea the limitations of the recognized rules of international law upon which the government of the United States has insisted."

Having thus agreed to conform to the demands of the United States, it was natural enough that Germany—using diplomatic phrases—should avow its expectation that the United States would also insist that the British Government observe the rules of international law.

In a dispatch of May 8 our ambassador at Berlin (Mr. Gerard) was instructed to accept the Berlin government's declaration of its abandonment of the policy which had so seriously menaced the good relations between our two countries. Mr. Gerard was also instructed to say, in order to avoid any possible misunderstanding, that Germany's agreement to respect the rights of citizens of the United States should not in anyway be made contingent upon the conduct of any other government affecting the rights of neutrals and non-combatants.

Thus ended the diplomatic phases of the submarine controversy. It may be considered that the pledge not to sink merchant vessels without warning and without regard for human lives was observed from May 4, 1916 to January 31, 1917, a period of nearly eight months. The hope that peace might be restored, and that the United States might exert still further beneficent influences was undoubtedly stimulated throughout this country by the apparent success of Mr. Wilson's appeals to Germany.

The Presidential campaign, as waged by the national and local managers of the Democratic party, presented Wilson as the world's foremost apostle of peace, and made unlimited use of the slogan "He kept us out of war." However much or little justification there might have been for the inference that the election of Mr. Hughes would precipitate an American war policy, that question is not pertinent to my present discussion. It is enough to say that Germany misunderstood both the trends of American opinion, and also the Calvinistic tenacity of Mr. Wilson's mind.

II.

Realizing the strength of his position, with official authority extended for a further term of four years, Mr. Wilson was determined nevertheless to make one more appearance in the role of a peacemaker. He sent a note to each of the two groups of belligerents which was phrased for the most part in identical terms. On the one side at that time were Germany, Austria-Hungary, Turkey and Bulgaria, known as the "Central Powers." On the other side were at that time ten so-called "Entente Allies": Great Britain, France, Italy, Japan, Russia, Belgium, Montenegro, Portugal, Rumania, and Serbia. Mr. Wilson's note was sent to each of those fourteen powers. It was explained that he was not proposing peace, not even offering mediation. He was merely seeking to ascertain the war objects of these governments in order to find out "how near the haven of peace may be for which all mankind longs with an intense and increasing longing." He was hoping for answers that might "bring a new light into the affairs of the world."

Interpreting the statements of official authorities on both sides in the most magnanimous way for reasons of conciliatory approach, the President summarized them in the following terms:

> Each side desires to make the rights and privileges of weak peoples and small States as secure against aggression or denial in the future as the rights and privileges of the great and powerful States now at war. Each wishes itself to be made secure in the future, along with all other nations and peoples, against the recurrence of wars like this and against

aggression or selfish interference of any kind. Each would be jealous of the formation of any more rival leagues to preserve an uncertain balance of power amid multiplying suspicions, but each is ready to consider the formation of a league of nations to insure peace and justice throughout the world.

To state objects of policy is not to attain the desired ends; but it has a clarifying influence, and it serves the purpose of a sign-post. Here was a pronouncement that intelligent and right-minded men could not repudiate, if they had any faith at all in the principles underlying our modern institutions and our common civilization. Germany was already seeking to enter into peace negotiations. For two years the Teutonic allies had held their line in France and Belgium, and were in control of Poland, Serbia and other large areas of Eastern Europe. Germany's answer to the President promptly reiterated the proposal of a meeting of delegates at a neutral place.

The French government replied for the Entente Allies in terms that seemed less encouraging. That is to say, the Entente Allies did not believe that the time had arrived when a peace could be secured that would be of lasting benefit to Europe.

On January 22nd the President addressed the Senate. He regarded the reply of the Entente powers as reasonable in its forecast of the things essential to a satisfactory settlement. Thus Mr. Wilson declared to the Senate, "We are that much nearer the discussion of the international concert which must thereafter hold the world at peace." He had found that in every discussion of the peace that must follow the war it was taken for granted that there must be some organization that would make it "virtually impossible that any such catastrophe should overwhelm us again."

It would not be possible to follow the course of Mr. Wilson's thinking, as it led him on to the war declaration of April 6, 1917, without careful attention to this address of January 22, in which he foreshadowed the objectives and the character of the kind of world peace that alone could be regarded as acceptable.

He owed it to the Senate, he affirmed on this occasion, "to disclose without reserve the thought and purpose that have been taking form in my mind in regard to the duty of our Government in the days to come when it will be necessary to lay afresh and upon a new plan the foundations of peace among the nations." Whereupon he proceeded to set forth a doctrine wholly different in principle from the purely negative and defensive theory of neutral isolation. His thinking had led him to realize that we could not stand apart from the task of reconstructing peace among the nations. He stated it in this manner:

> It is inconceivable that the people of the United States should play no part in that great enterprise. To take part in such a service will be the opportunity for which they have sought to prepare themselves by the very principles and purposes of their polity and the approved practices of their Government ever since the days when they set up a new nation in the high and honourable hope that it might in all that it was and did show mankind the way to liberty.

Such was the kernel of his discourse. He developed his thought in rounded and stately periods. If we were to participate in guarantees of future peace, the war must be ended upon terms that would win the approval of mankind. Speaking prophetically, we were to seek preliminary conditions that would justify us in supporting the "guarantees of a universal covenant." He declared further:

> No covenant of cooperative peace that does not include the peoples of the New World can suffice to keep the future safe against war. . . . Mere agreements may not make peace secure. It will be absolutely necessary that a force be created, as a guarantor of the permanency of the settlement, so much greater than the force of any nation now engaged or any alliance hitherto formed or projected that no nation, no probable combination of nations, could face or withstand it. If the peace presently to be made is to endure, it must be a peace made secure by the organized major force of mankind.

Mr. Wilson did not shrink from certain logical implications. First of all he held: "It must be a peace without victory. . . . Victory would mean peace forced upon the loser, the victor's terms imposed upon the vanquished."

I think it worth while to quote Mr. Wilson to the end of the paragraph, although the entire address has historical significance that gives it deeper meaning, as one reads it after the lapse of twenty-six years, than was attached to it at the moment of its deliverance. He was referring to peace terms forced upon the loser:

It would be accepted in humiliation, under duress, at an intolerable sacrifice, and would leave a sting, a resentment, a bitter memory upon which terms of peace would rest, not permanently, but only as upon quicksand. Only a peace between equals can last—only a peace the very principle of which is equality and a common participation in a common benefit. The right state of mind, the right feeling between nations, is as necessary for a lasting peace as is the just settlement of vexed questions of territory or of racial and national allegiance.

This address of Mr. Wilson's might have been more terse in its phrasing, but it could not have been more lucid in its disclosure of convictions. No pronouncement by men in high office since the Second World War began could well be compared in the quality of its thinking, the definiteness and firmness of its logic, and the eloquence of its phrasing, with Woodrow Wilson's address to the Senate of January 22, 1917.[1]

Having laid down his doctrine of equality of rights, and having declared that " mankind is looking now for freedom of life not for equipoises of power," and having further asserted that " no right anywhere exists to hand peoples about from sovereignty to sovereignty as if they were property," he said that he had " no desire to exalt an abstract political principle," but wished " frankly to uncover realities."

Whereupon he declared:

Any peace which does not recognize and accept this principle will inevitably be upset. It will not rest upon the affections or the convictions of mankind. The ferment of spirit of whole populations will fight subtly and constantly against it, and all the world will sympathize. The world can be at peace only if its life is stable; and there can be no stability where the will is in rebellion, where there is not tranquillity of spirit and a sense of justice, of freedom, and of right.

In order to bring his discourse and his train of thought more familiarly to the comprehension of the Senate, Mr. Wilson concluded the address with allusions to the Monroe Doctrine, and with paraphrases of language used by Washington in his Farewell Address. I shall proceed to quote the four short paragraphs with which Mr. Wilson concluded this memorable state paper:

[1] Written in September, 1943.

I am proposing, as it were, that the nations should with one accord adopt the doctrine of President Monroe as the doctrine of the world: that no nation should seek to extend its polity over any other nation or people, but that every people should be left free to determine its own polity, its own way of development, unhindered, unthreatened, unafraid, the little along with the great and powerful.

I am proposing that all nations henceforth avoid entangling alliances which would draw them into competitions of power; catch them in a net of intrigue and selfish rivalry, and disturb their own affairs with influences intruded from without. There is no entangling alliance in a concert of power. When all unite to act in the same sense and with the same purpose all act in the common interest and are free to live their own lives under a common protection.

I am proposing government by the consent of the governed; that freedom of the seas which in international conference after conference representatives of the United States have urged with the eloquence of those who are the convinced disciples of liberty; and that moderation of armaments which makes of armies and navies a power for order merely, not an instrument of aggression or of selfish violence.

These are American principles, American policies. We could stand for no others. And they are also the principles and policies of forward-looking men and women everywhere, of every modern nation, of every enlightened community. They are the principles of mankind and must prevail.

There have been many enlightened persons in America and in other countries whose broad humanitarian views have been expressed on public platforms or in printed form in terms as generous and far-reaching as the foregoing utterances of Woodrow Wilson. The difference lies in the fact that these sentiments were expressed officially at a critical time by an American President, who was disclosing his views to the Senate as the body which shared with him his responsibility in foreign affairs.

III.

I am not recording events in detail, especially those of military character; and it will suffice to say that with much difference of opinion in Germany the views of Admiral von Tirpitz prevailed. At the end of January, 1917, the submarine war was renewed with complete disregard of the promises made in the first week of May, 1916. Germany had continued to build up her submarine fleet, and her attacks were resumed upon merchant shipping, even more ruthlessly than ever before.

Great Britain and her Allies had become increasingly dependent upon supplies purchased in the United States. The German Admiral was right in thinking that he had developed the weapon that might win the victory for the German powers, if Wilson should continue to moralize and to abstain from interference. The German government was simply mistaken, however, in supposing that Wilson's eloquence in assertion was a cloak for indecision, and for inability to act with boldness.

The President appeared before Congress in joint session on February 3rd. On the last day of January the German government had announced its purpose to renew its practice of using submarines to attack all shipping entering certain designated areas of the high seas. This new policy was to date from the following day, February 1. Mr. Wilson informed Congress that he had taken steps to sever diplomatic relations between the United States and the German Empire. In conciliatory terms he expressed his further hope that Germany might reconsider and again change its course.

Peace sentiment was still prevalent throughout a large part of the United States, and Mr. Wilson was proceeding with due care because it was necessary to have the support both of Congress and of public opinion. On February 26, after about four weeks of Germany's new policy, he informed Congress that the practical results were not yet fully disclosed, although serious congestion of our commerce had resulted. He asked authority to arm merchant ships and to "employ any other instrumentalities or methods that may be necessary." The bill embodying his proposals failed to pass, because the last session of the Sixty-fourth Congress was expiring on March 4. The Administration decided that it already possessed authority enough to arm ships for defense.

On March 5 President Wilson delivered his second inaugural address, devoting it for the most part to a restatement of his principles as applicable to world peace and political stability. He waited almost a month longer, and then on April 2, having called the Sixty-fifth Congress in special session, he appeared before a joint meeting of the two Houses, and proposed that Germany's course be declared to be war against the United States.

The opinion of the country at that time was confused. In New York and elsewhere in the East war sentiment undoubtedly prevailed. In the Middle West there was no consensus of opinion, and the demand for peace in the States beyond the Mississippi seemed to accord predominantly with the views of such leaders as Mr. Bryan and Senator LaFollette.

If President Wilson at that time, admitting serious grievances, had nevertheless recommended further patience, and had advised measures short of war, Congress would not have over-ruled his counsels. In the public mind the larger issue was perhaps obscured by consideration of narrow alternatives. Were our own losses and grievances weighty enough to overbalance the costs in human life and material resources of participation in the European struggle? It was held that we could keep our ships in our own ports, live comfortably at home, and sell goods to any foreign nation that would take the risk of transporting them.

Mr. Wilson's war declaration was not based principally upon our own particular grievances. I think it important in this year 1943 to quote certain sentences from what is known as "Wilson's War Address." He declared:

> I am not now thinking of the loss of property involved, immense and serious as that is, but only of the wanton and wholesale destruction of the lives of non-combatants, men, women, and children, engaged in pursuits which have always, even in the darkest periods of modern history, been deemed innocent and legitimate. Property can be paid for; the lives of peaceful and innocent people cannot be. The present German submarine warfare against commerce is a warfare against mankind.

His emphasis was upon the fact that it was a war against all nations, and that the challenge was to all mankind. Even the right of neutrals to use arms on their merchant ships within proscribed areas had been denied. Mr. Wilson explained that there had been no change in his motives or objects, but only in his view of methods necessary to attain the ends that had been set forth in his previous addresses.

My purpose in this chapter is to make it clear in the most definite way that Mr. Wilson had abandoned the doctrine of neutrality as a basis upon which to proceed. The opposing groups could no longer be regarded as duellists who were disturbing the common peace, and who could be brought to order through the influence or the authority of the neutral and noncombatant world. Said Mr. Wilson in this address:

> Neutrality is no longer feasible or desirable where the peace of the world is involved and the freedom of its peoples; and the menace to that peace and freedom lies in the existence of autocratic governments backed by organized force which is controlled wholly by their will, not by the will of their people. We have seen the last of neutrality in such circumstances.

The country was too much concerned with the practical implications of the impending war to pay much attention to Mr. Wilson's philosophy of internationalism. Yet the present-day reader may find in that address a better expression of the objects that right-thinking men now have in mind, as we endure the pains and hardships of a still greater World War, than any one since Woodrow Wilson—whether in official utterances or in the countless books and articles that are current—has been so gifted or so inspired as to formulate.

In an earlier section of this war message, Mr. Wilson made an observation upon the nature and growth of the law of nations that well defines the processes that I am attempting to elucidate in this volume. I quote it with approval for its truth and discernment:

> International law had its origin in the attempt to set up some law which would be respected and observed upon the seas, where no nation had right of dominion and where lay the free highways of the world. By painful stage after stage has that law been built up, with meagre enough results, indeed, after all was accomplished that could be accomplished, but always with a clear view, at least, of what the heart and conscience of mankind demanded.

When one keeps in mind the state of public opinion in the spring of 1917, the clarifying results of the President's war message must be regarded as evidence of his strong influence and high prestige in that critical juncture. The address was delivered in the evening of April 2. The Senate on April 4 adopted the war resolution by a vote of 82 to 6. The House after continuous debate through the afternoon and evening of April 5, took its final vote (without adjournment) in the early hours of the following morning, and supported the President's position by a vote of 373 to 50.

On that same day President Wilson attached his signature to the war declaration as adopted by Congress, and thus our entrance upon the first World War bears the date of April 6, 1917. The President's proclamation, issued immediately, deals with the legal aspects of the state of war, prescribes regulations, and exhibits the efficiency with which a democratic government can proceed when so profound a change occurs as the sudden transition from the status of peace to that of war.

It had taken time for neutral countries to understand that warfare was so changed in its character, methods, and objects that they could no longer maintain a position of impartiality. War could not be limited; and when its ravages had spread from land to sea and from continent to continent, it was necessary to support the allied nations that represented law and order. It was not intelligent to say that rights and wrongs were equally balanced on both sides. The war itself had to be ended, and it was the business of neutrals to discover which side stood more clearly for the general cause of justice and freedom, and which side had finally shown by its methods and its policies that it represented aggression and relied upon the appeal to force to achieve unwarranted ambitions.

Through the experience of three years we had been forced to the conclusion that the Entente Allies, led by England and France, had the better cause. They did not disclaim the principles for which President Wilson stood, and which had been set forth as American doctrine. The break-down of the public laws that had defined the rights of neutrals—expressed in many treaties and agreements—did not indicate or foreshadow an approach to world anarchy.

IV.

International law was undergoing changes, but was not to be thrown to the winds as obsolete. It was moving toward the outlawry of war by stigmatizing policies of aggression. It was shaping a new definition of war as *a legal process* when directed against aggression, and against the calculated employment of force for political conquest and material gain. If there had been any doubts regarding the nature of the First World War, the terms upon which the United States took up arms in support of Great Britain and the Entente Allies may be said to have clarified the situation.

Mr. Wilson's fifth annual message to Congress, the first after we had become involved in war, was delivered in the opening week of December, 1917, almost eight months after Congress had given its prompt adhesion to his declaration in the war message of April that a state of war actually existed by reason of Germany's acts. This message of December contained significant passages, as regards the nature of the war and the terms upon which the United States could join in a post-war settlement. But before quoting from that message I shall reprint at length certain comments written by me later in that month for publication on New Year's Day, 1918.

The picture of the scene as it appeared at the time is more vivid than the less definite outlines that one's unaided memory could hold in perspective. In many aspects the parallel between that first war and the one in which we are now engaged becomes strikingly apparent if comparison is made with an account written at a time when there could be no thought of attempts to make it appear that history was but repeating itself.

> The efforts of the United States to prepare for an important, if not a decisive part in the war are on a great scale and have behind them the moral purpose of the nation. If, from the practical standpoint, these efforts have not been as efficient and as coherent as they ought to have been, it remains true, when the worst is brought to light and admitted, that much has been accomplished. The power of America to contribute to the defeat of the German cause will be expressed in terms of increasing war efficiency. Already the support of America is of large material value to the Allies. This aid will expand rapidly throughout the year 1918. It will not be until next year, however, that—besides supporting the Allies with money, food, war materials, and ships—America can if necessary becomes a very large and perhaps a decisive factor in the direct military determination of the war. The world-wide elements that enter into the situation have become so numerous and so complex that many things may happen that cannot now be foreseen. But if major factors are to work their logical outcome, and if the war is to be concluded through military pressure, it would be our present opinion that the end might come with defeat of the Central Powers in the autumn of 1919, after the war had lasted a little more than a full five years.

Judging affairs from the purely military standpoint, the collapse of Russia would seem to have delayed victory for the Allies by about a year. If the Anglo-French fighting on the Western front has been disappointing in its results during 1917, the blame cannot justly be laid at the door of the armies or their leadership. The German withdrawal early in the year, to the "Hindenburg line" while an acknowledgment of the formidable character of the British preparation for a spring offensive, was a clever strategic movement on the part of the Germans that gained for them more than they conceded to their foes. By the time they were ready for the tremendous pounding that General Haig visited upon the German lines in Flanders, it had become possible for the Germans to withdraw large bodies of men from the forces that had been operating in Russia.

But for this misfortune of Russia's failure to hold the attention of a due proportion of the German and Austrian armies, the French and English armies would almost certainly have driven the Germans out of northern France, back to the line of the Meuse, well before the end of 1917. The English would have taken a long stretch of Flanders shore line and destroyed some of the most pestiferous bases of German submarine and airplane activity. And they would have been in a position to drive the Germans entirely out of Belgium and across the Rhine in the spring and summer of the present year 1918. Thus it must appear a terrible misfortune for Europe and the world that Russia could not have held her ground on the fighting front for a few months longer. It would have meant peace for all mankind.

But while it is possible to outline the nature of the catastrophe—and only too easy to point out the immensity of the cost in lives and material things of a year's further prolongation of this appalling war—it is not necessary to be pessimistic as to the nature of the outcome. Victories that do not bring peace any nearer, and that do not bring any stable gains, can be of no value to Germany, while on the contrary they are likely to prove in the end to be greater misfortunes for the Teutons than for their opponents. Thus, while Germany's relative military position seemed stronger last month than ever before, and while her fighting machine seemed more than ever invincible, the rulers were not able to show the people that durable peace lay in the direction of her victories and conquests. She was merely demonstrating the more clearly that she had been first and foremost in militarism, and that her performances had compelled a reluctant and peace-loving world, of far greater aggregate resources than hers, to become militarized in order to defeat her.

Thus every demonstration of German military prowess meant the more certain and rapid development of opposing military power, and the greater punishment of Germany in the end. In the early stages of the war the Emperor William sneered at England's "contemptible little army." Since that time Germany has lost several millions of her best young men, and meanwhile the contemptible little army of Great Britain has grown to a superbly trained and equipped fighting force of perhaps five million men that—in spite of great losses—holds its maximum strength and efficiency for the year 1918. In like manner when the United States felt it necessary to recognize the existence of war, last April, Germany declared us wholly negigible in the military sense; and the Teutonic peoples were promised that the war would be well over before America could participate.

The highest German authorities promised their people that the submarines should starve England into making peace, while the German armies were winning on all fronts. Yet already the American Navy, and our merchant ship-building, have begun to turn the scales against the submarine. Our little naval force has expanded to more than a quarter of a million officers and seamen. Our Army under training has considerably more than a million men, and before the end of 1918 our war industries can be expanded to equal, if not to exceed, those of Germany. Brazil and other South American countries that have turned against Germany are not as yet on a military footing, but if the war is prolonged they could make very substantial contributions to the cause of the Western Hemisphere that the United States has championed. Thus the prolongation of the war must henceforth constantly reduce Germany's man power through attrition, while it brings fresh military factors to the replenishment of the Allies. The fighting power of Japan is unimpaired, while China, with the joint aid of the United States and Japan, could gradually render assistance not to be despised.

While, then, the German victories that prolong the war are inflicting frightful damage upon the peoples of Europe and suffering upon the world at large, they are not leading to success or stability for the German cause. They are merely convincing the world of the necessity of a supreme effort to break down the German program of audacity and violence. Even worse than her losses of man power—an attrition that must be felt more, rather than less, from this time on—is her loss of standing in a world which sets more store by justice and right than ever before.

Germany's methods in warfare, intended to provoke exemplary fear, have aroused the world's intense reprobation. Her corrupt propaganda, the horrid trails of which are being traced and exposed in every country, have had the most detrimental effect upon the German repute. No great country has ever so rapidly fallen from a place of honor to one of low esteem. Every year, every month, that prolongs the struggle brings Germany lower in the opinion of mankind. This, of course, applies to the

German Government and its policies; to the military and naval leaders of Germany and their atrocious methods; and to the religious and educational leaders, with their false doctrines and their tribal egotism.

Far more than Germany has gained by her mischief-making propaganda in various countries, she is losing by the exposure of such propaganda. For instance, we are now aware that much of the mysterious antagonism of recent years toward the United States, in several of the Latin-American countries, was due to the official expenditure of German money in subsidizing and maintaining anti-American newspapers printed in the Spanish language and pretending to represent Latin-American interests. We are further aware that much of the mysterious hostility to the United States disclosed in Japan was fomented by German agents expending Government funds to inflame the readers of sensational Japanese newspapers.

While Germany's commerce has been cut off from the seas, while her colonies have all been lost, while her trade with small neutral neighbors has been reduced through the embargo policies of the United States and Great Britain, the one apparently sound and enduring structure erected by recent German political and military efforts has been the great "Mitteleuropa" union for power and for commerce, extending from the Belgian coast to the confines of Persia. But even this imposing confederation has no sound basis. If its members are to cohere loyally under Prussian hegemony, they will have to face the alternative of an entire external world united against them. This external world will control all the seas. Every country would be compelled to choose its associations. Neutrality would inevitably fade away. Holland, Sweden, Denmark, Norway, would in due time have to take their stand with the free countries, or look inland to an exclusive association with Germany, becoming—like Belgium—vassals of Prussia. Heretofore they have been strictly maritime countries.

Nothing could be more detrimental to the interests of these small countries than the success of the German dream of aggrandizement. If the present siege line across Belgium, northern France, and northern Italy can hold out against German and Austrian assaults for another year, the Mitteleuropa project will fall to pieces like a rope of sand. By that time, moreover, Spain, Switzerland, Holland, and the three Scandinavian countries may begin to see that the assault upon Belgium was in principle an attack upon each one of them, and that they also must be willing to make some sacrifices to end the war. They could hardly have entered the struggle singly in 1917. But they may later see their way to join the Allies, as did Portugal earlier (and doubtless with Greece helping, too, by that time) in order to end the war and have a part in the peace-making that will guarantee their future as small nations. These six neutral countries of western Europe could easily put two million men in the field in 1918; and the United States and South America could render great help toward their provisionment and munitioning. All their future welfare calls for German defeat. Their united espousal of the Allied cause would probably bring victory without a blow.

Within the confines of the Teutonic military control are many peoples who are growingly out of sympathy with Prussianism. The Poles and Bohemians, the Croatians with their kindred South Slav races, the Hungarian masses, the Bulgarians, and even the Turks, are under the political and military leadership of the Prussian autocracy through force of circumstances rather than through loyalty and good-will. They do not wish to be Germanized, much less to be Prussianized. Thus while the Potsdam power plans the great Central Empire, the seething races and peoples contained within the boundaries of the new Potsdam map are making future maps of their own, and dreaming dreams of democratic self-government and national independence and security that are wholly at variance with the plans of the Hohenzollerns, the Hapsburgs, and the feudal lords of whatever breed.

The German negotiations with the Lenin-Trotzky socialist government of Russia last month further illustrated this amazing paradox of inevitable German failure through the doorway of seeming success. Russia for the moment was a prostrate, helpless giant. German greed began at once to overreach itself in its eagerness to despoil the giant while he lay broken and bound. Vast territorial demands were made by Germany, and commercial advantages for a long time to come were to be solemnly guaranteed. The Russian Socialists had begun by claiming the doctrine of "no annexations, no indemnities." If Germany had now accepted this doctrine in pretending good faith, in accordance with the Reichstag resolution of last summer she would at once have withdrawn all her soldiers from Russian soil as a peace preliminary and would have proceeded to make generous proposals that might have captivated the simple Russian heart, impressed the peace advocates of all other countries, upset the political balance in Italy, and weakened the morale of France. But Germany could not avoid revealing her true nature and character in a moment when an opponent was at a disadvantage. Her proposals included vast Russian annexations that further exhibited to the world her unshaken adherence to the doctrine that there is no law but might. Her terms gave fresh proof that Germany does not hold it incumbent upon any nation to adjust its own ambitions to what is right and just for one's neighbors.

These German proposals to Russia of last month were the denial of all international morality. They served notice upon the world of what it must expect from German victory in other directions. And seemingly no large element of public opinion in Germany has fairly grasped the idea that it is precisely such attitudes that have led the world to the conclusion that Germany must be defeated. It must be a humiliated and repentant German people that can be allowed to begin over again, and to resume their places in a friendly world. The new international society that is to set about the upbuilding of a fine civilization must rest upon cornerstones of justice and liberty, as well as upon those of science and social order. Only a reformed Germany can be admitted.

I am reproducing these comments of mine (which until now I had not read since their appearance in January, 1918) because they bear testimony to American views that were not in dispute at that time, but also, and especially, because the last of the foregoing paragraphs might have been written at any time since Hitler's sweeping invasion of western and southern Russia in 1941. The facts and the inferences set down in my editorial survey were in accord with President Wilson's fifth annual message, and with the overwhelming sentiment of both Houses of Congress.

V.

We had not, before that time, declared war against Austria-Hungary, and this was recommended by the President. Congress agreed, and three days later a joint resolution to that effect was adopted unanimously by the Senate and also by the House (with the exception of one opposition vote by a Socialist). Mr. Wilson had said in his message:

Austria-Hungary is for the time being not her own mistress, but simply the vassal of the German Government. We must face the facts as they are and act upon them without sentiment in this stern business. The Government of Austria-Hungary is not acting upon its own initiative or in response to the wishes and feelings of its own peoples, but as the instrument of another nation. We must meet its force with our own and regard the Central Powers as but one. The war can be successfully conducted in no other way. The same logic would lead also to a declaration of war against Turkey and Bulgaria. They also are the tools of Germany. But they are mere tools, and do not yet stand in the direct path of our necessary action. We shall go wherever the necessities of this war carry us, but it seems to me that we should go only where immediate and practical considerations lead us and not heed any others.

The message was devoted almost wholly to the ultimate objects of the war. The President had not addressed Congress for eight months— not since Congress, on his advice, had declared war— and he believed that it was "necessary to say plainly what we here at the seat of action consider the war to be for, and what part we mean to play in the settlement of its searching issues." As the chief spokesman of the American people the President thought he expressed their views in the following passage:

I believe that I speak for them when I say two things: First, that this intolerable Thing of which the masters of Germany have shown us the ugly face, this menace of combined intrigue and force which we now see so clearly as the German power, a Thing without conscience or honor or capacity for covenanted peace, must be crushed, and if it be not utterly brought to an end, at least shut out from the friendly intercourse of the nations; and, second, that when this Thing and its power are indeed defeated and the time comes that we can discuss peace—when the German people have spokesmen whose word we can believe and when those spokesmen are ready in the name of their people to accept the common judgment of the nations as to what shall henceforth be the bases of law and of covenant for the life of the world—we shall be willing and glad to pay the full price for peace, and pay it ungrudgingly. We know what that price will be. It will be full, impartial justice—justice done at every point and to every nation that the final settlement must affect our enemies as well as our friends.

The address is quotable in any of its parts, but I am attempting simply to make clear Mr. Wilson's thinking, as we were about to send men in great numbers to the fighting front in France. The following sentences may be regarded as true disclosures of the President's principles and aims:

Let it be said again that autocracy must first be shown the utter futility of its claims to power or leadership in the modern world. It is impossible to apply any standard of justice so long as such forces are unchecked and undefeated as the present masters of Germany command. Not until that has been done can Right be set up as arbiter and peacemaker among the nations. But when that has been done—as, God willing, it assuredly will be—we shall at last be free to do an unprecedented thing, and this is the time to avow our purpose to do it. We shall be free to base peace on generosity and justice, to the exclusion of all selfish claims to advantage even on the part of the victors.

Let there be no misunderstanding. Our present and immediate task is to win the war, and nothing shall turn us aside from it until it is accomplished. Every power and resource we possess, whether of men, of money, or materials, is being devoted and will continue to be devoted to that purpose until it is achieved. Those who desire to bring peace about before that purpose is achieved I counsel to carry their advice elsewhere. We will not entertain it. We shall regard the war as won only when the German people say to us, through properly accredited representatives, that they are ready to agree to a settlement based upon justice and the reparation of the wrongs their rulers have done.

The Armistice that was signed in early November, 1918, ended the actual conflict eleven months and seven days after Mr. Wilson delivered the address from which I have made the foregoing quotations. Although the Armistice was based upon Mr. Wilson's own proposals, first set forth by him in the numbered paragraphs known as the "Fourteen Points," it is quite generally forgotten that this so-called "program of the world's peace" was formulated almost at once after the address to Congress of December 4, and was embodied in another address delivered on January 8, when Mr. Wilson appeared before the two Houses in joint session, to state the war aims and peace terms of the United States.

The representatives of revolutionary Russia had been negotiating peace terms at Brest-Litovsk with the German and Austrian representatives, and there were indications that the Central Powers would like to "extend these parleys into a general conference with regard to terms of peace and settlement." Mr. Wilson praised the Russians for insisting upon open rather than closed conferences. In passages preliminary to the announcement of his formulated Fourteen Points, he declared that the processes of peace when they are begun should be absolutely open, and should permit no secret understandings of any kind.

The Russian Bolsheviks, with the Czarist archives at hand, had been publishing to the world the secret agreements that the Allied powers had made, looking to the distribution of conquered territories at the end of the war. Undoubtedly Mr. Wilson was expressing his disapproval of those hidden arrangements when he said: "The day of conquest and aggrandizement is gone by; so is also the day of secret covenants entered into in the interest of particular governments, and likely at some unlooked-for moment to upset the peace of the world." Since those secret treaties were the subject of a long private conversation that I had with Mr. Wilson, I know how intensely he resented them. His repudiation of them was made the subject of the first of his Fourteen Points.

I have no purpose in the present chapter to discuss in detail either the Fourteen Points or the inconsistencies of the Versailles Treaty as negotiated in 1919. As one now reads the address of January 8, which embodies the Fourteen Points but also further elaborates Woodrow Wilson's views, the olive branch seems to have been extended in a manner far too conciliatory. Mr. Wilson seemed to forget that the military machine was still absolutely dominant in Germany, and that his deferential allusions to "German greatness," which was in no manner to be impaired by anything in his program, would be taken as a sign of American softness and sentimentality. There was nothing at fault with the President's generous feeling, as expressed in the following sentences, except what one must regard as their untimeliness:

> We grudge her [Germany] no achievement or distinction of learning or of pacific enterprise such as have made her record very bright and very enviable. We do not wish to injure her or to block in any way her legitimate influence or power. We do not wish to fight her either with arms or with hostile arrangements of trade if she is willing to associate herself with us and the other peace-loving nations of the world in covenants of justice and law and fair dealing.

There were additional sentences equally conciliatory, as, for instance, the one in which the President said that "we do not presume to suggest to her [Germany] any alteration or modification of her institutions." It should be explained, however, that Mr. Wilson was basing his generous phrases upon the supposition that a liberal majority in the Reichstag was at odds with "the military party and the men whose creed is imperial domination." I would be doing injustice to this address, which stands as one of the foremost documents in modern history, without quoting its concluding sentences. The President intended, in his courteous—however untimely—appeal to German right-mindedness, no sort of compromise with the fundamentals of permanent peace, as his final phrases amply prove:

An evident principle runs through the whole program I have outlined. It is the principle of justice to all peoples and nationalities, and their right to live on equal terms of liberty and safety with one another, whether they be strong or weak.

Unless this principle be made its foundation no part of the structure of international justice can stand. The people of the United States could act upon no other principle; and to the vindication of this principle they are ready to devote their lives, their honor, and everything that they possess. The moral climax of this the culminating and final war for human liberty has come, and they are ready to put their own strength, their own highest purpose, their own integrity and devotion to the test.

There is a tendency that does not do credit to our intelligence or our patriotism to disparage the records of men whom at one time or another we have entrusted with leadership through our own democratic processes of choice. I did not belong to President Wilson's political party, but I had known him well as a personal friend for thirty-six years when at the end of the war he went to Paris to uphold American principles in the planning of world peace. His views were in direct line with those of Washington and Jefferson of the early period; of Webster and Calhoun in their day; of Lincoln and his successors; of Theodore Roosevelt, Elihu Root and Mr. Taft, and also of the men who followed him—Hoover, Hughes and Stimson—and of Franklin D. Roosevelt, whose Atlantic Charter is on broad Wilsonian lines.

Historians of the future will not hold President Wilson responsible for the failure of America and the Allied countries to realize that the Armistice granted German militarism a Truce, which the Treaty of Versailles did not convert to a status of established peace. The power of aggressors had to be curbed; but also aggressor countries had in due time to become vital factors in some larger political structure. In the shaping of that larger association, all the advantages would needs be on the side of peace and good will, even as they are now, and have always been, in the United States since our Federal Constitution was adopted.

CHAPTER VI

INTERNATIONAL LAW AND EARLY GERMAN INFLUENCE

As a post-graduate student at the Johns Hopkins University, Woodrow Wilson during two academic years studied International Law, among other subjects in the field of history and political science. He heard lectures and joined in discussions in the room known as the "Bluntschli Library." Lectures were based upon the international-law code of a famous Heidelberg professor of jurisprudence, whose special collection of books had been brought to Baltimore by German-born citizens.

No one could have stated more clearly than Mr. Wilson himself, thirty-four years later, the change that had come about in German aims and aspirations. In an address at Buffalo just a year before the Armistice, President Wilson said: "The war was started by Germany. Her authorities deny that they started it, but I am willing to let the statement I have just made await the verdict of history. And the thing that needs to be explained is why Germany started the war. Remember what the position of Germany in the world was—as enviable a position as any nation has ever occupied. The whole world stood at admiration of her wonderful intellectual and material achievements. All the intellectual men of the world went to school to her. As a university man I have been surrounded by men trained in Germany, men who had resorted to Germany because nowhere else could they get such thorough and searching training."

Further elaborating the description of Germany's earlier prestige and prosperity, he emphasized the contrast, declaring that the German government was not satisfied, although "there was nothing in the world of peace that she did not already have, and have in abundance. . . . There was lying behind its thought and its dreams of the future the political control which would enable it in the long run to dominate the labor and the industry of the world. They were not content with success by superior achievement; they wanted success by authority."

This change of German purpose was also explained by Mr. Wilson in concrete terms of geography. Yet he never ceased to believe that "the spirit of freedom can get into the hearts of Germans and find as fine a welcome there as it can find in other hearts." The world would have nothing to fear from Germany if the spirit of freedom came into control of government policies. "Power cannot be used with concentrated force against free peoples," declared Mr. Wilson, "if it is used by free people."

TO UNDERSTAND the course of affairs and the state of the world at a given time, it is as necessary to study the history of thought as the history of action. The Declaration of Independence was a great charter of human freedom. It set forth the views of the thoughtful men who signed it. It was not a process of sudden conversion that led his associates to accept the political creed that Jefferson expressed in such sweeping terms. The occasion had arisen at an historic moment; but the doctrines were not new or in dispute among the members of the Continental Congress. The Declaration was to stand as a document testifying to the emancipated thought of political philosophers in the eighteenth century. It was to influence further thinking, and then to justify action, as democratic ideas made their way around the world during the century and a half that followed.

The seven-year war for independence was a rough experience; and all the strength and endurance that American leadership could rally were needed to meet its predicaments. Long years had passed before the country had gained stability enough to pause and celebrate anniversaries of the Declaration and to glorify its principles as illustrated in actual achievement. Nevertheless that document stood as a great signpost; and its doctrines were an essential part of the firm foundation upon which the country was building its broad and permanent structure of nationality.

In a previous chapter I have quoted from President Wilson's addresses, and especially from his declaration of American motives and objects when he advised Congress to authorize a state of war in 1917. He had not awakened belatedly from exciting dreams or visions to proclaim a new heaven and a new earth. His words were no apocalyptic foreshadowing of an orderly world of freedom and justice. He had not improvised those generous and disinterested expressions as an excuse for leading the country into war.

Although he acknowledged the failure of his prolonged efforts to limit and shorten the European conflict by diplomacy and compromise, he was not proposing to fight merely because Germany had flouted and defied him. It is true that our maritime rights were affected; and to some extent our future safety was menaced. But the larger aims that Mr. Wilson expressed were not new.

They were in keeping with views that he had long entertained. Also they were in accord with the enlightened thought and aspiration of the best minds of Europe and America.

National governments could not have acknowledged that their theoretical sovereignty was less than complete and final. They had surrendered no functions or authority to a super-state. Yet our modern civilization was not patterned on the political geography of a defiant and unrelated nationalism. The web and woof of civilization's fabric stretched across oceans and boundary lines, with uncounted and ever-multiplying strands.

The processes that had been creating this fabric were age-long, although interrupted and obscured from time to time. The growing sense of a common heritage made urgent demands. It compelled the nations to sign bilateral treaties or collective agreements that recognized mutuality of interest, and that took form as expressions of public law transcending the self-sufficiency of individual states. The higher order was in process of creation. It had only to be recognized and welcomed by enlightened public opinion.

Admittedly, there were reasons more immediate and practical than the ultimate aims so eloquently avowed by the President for our assumption of belligerency in 1917. In its earlier phases the Russian revolution had been hailed by Mr. Wilson as adding to our hope for the future peace of the world. " The great, generous Russian people," he declared, " have been added in all their naive majesty and might to the forces that are fighting for freedom in the world, for justice, and for peace. Here," he exclaimed, " is a fit partner for a League of Honour! "

But Russia's military resources were failing through lack of modern equipment. Predominant American opinion had accepted the cause of the Entente Allies as relatively deserving of our sympathy, and of our moral and material support. The cause of Germany and her Allies had acquired meanings ever more sinister, as the war had proceeded through the first three years. The military exhibition of national power had been accompanied by a German doctrine of might-makes-right that was proclaimed without shame or apology.

Russia's defection greatly imperilled what we had come to recognize as the better cause. With no hostile army on our soil or at our gates, we were in a favorable position to militarize our resources and utilize our man-power. Russia had fought well at the beginning of the war, but had been invaded and subdued. With the disappearance of the Eastern Front, we were to help England, France, and Italy in the West, and thus to end the war by the Armistice of November 1918.

An ancient proverb reminds us that the clash of arms supersedes the reign of law. (As Cicero expressed it, "*Silent enim leges inter arma.*") For the time being, war becomes an engrossing task sufficient unto itself; but in due time principles assert themselves and the normal rule of justice seeks to recover its rightful place. Mr. Wilson, however, could not even for temporary reasons dismiss from his mind the high purposes that had impelled him to enter the war.

He was not a military man, but he could on occasion act with promptness and decision. He found competent civilian and military leaders and gave them appropriate authority. He cooperated with Congress, and organized the military, industrial, and transportation services that the emergency required. As for his own sense of responsibility and leadership, the President was thinking not so much of the war itself as of the organization of peace that should follow the expected victory.

II.

There were many men who could well claim some measure of familiarity with Woodrow Wilson's views, not simply as expounded in his Presidential years, but as he had entertained them for at least three decades before he entered the White House in 1913. He had not made active politics his chosen career, but he had been a life-long student of politics in the deeper and broader meaning of that word. He had studied law at the University of Virginia after graduation at Princeton, and had entered upon law practice in Atlanta. If he had continued to practice law, he would soon have been drawn into official life because of his unusual qualifications. Oratory had always opened doors of political advancement in the South; and no young man of his period surpassed Wilson in felicity and resourcefulness as a platform speaker.

After a brief experience, however, of law practice, he decided to enter upon a career of study and teaching. This meant no change in his mental attitude. The sciences of law and government had been his major subjects of reading and thought, even while an undergraduate at Princeton. The four-year interval of study, and practice as a lawyer, had contributed to his training and mental equipment.

He went to the Johns Hopkins University to pursue graduate studies of wide range in the field of history and political science. He was occupied primarily in exploring the field of comparative constitutional history and government; and while he carried certain related studies along with other young men, he was also writing his first book, with originality of method and maturity of style.

It was my privilege to be intimately associated with him at the Johns Hopkins University. The fact that on election day we might vote differently did not in the smallest degree affect our cordial agreement upon fundamental principles. We had taken up the study of international law, in those days at Baltimore, with an interest that derived especial stimulus from certain facts of time and place. I shall recount them briefly for two reasons, first, because of their relation to contemporary world conditions, and second, because they explain the circumstances under which I prepared a paper that forms the succeeding chapter of this book.

The influence of academic centers upon our political thinking in the United States has been, in the past as also it is at the present time, an indispensable factor in the forming of opinion and the direction of our public policies. In our colleges and universities Americans have studied the history of civilization and have formed convictions of a disinterested kind about the rights and duties of men in organized communities, whether small or great. The story of America in the earlier period of our national development could not be told with understanding, if Harvard, Yale, Columbia, Princeton and other centers of culture—where older men taught by precept and example, and younger men learned to think—were ignored in the recital.

It was eminently true of Williamsburg, the provincial capital of Virginia and the seat of the College of William and Mary, that it was a focus of political thinking in the eighteenth century not surpassed anywhere for its enlightenment and its stimulating influence. George Washington, George Mason, Thomas Jefferson, Patrick Henry, John Marshall, James Monroe, and many other men who became leaders and institution-builders, had derived their inspiration from the liberated intellectual life of Virginia's Colonial Capital. Williamsburg in that period was the world's foremost center of political philosophy, both in doctrine and in personnel.

While the older universities of the North maintained, with increasing prestige, their respective positions as centers of political influence in the larger meaning of that phrase, younger institutions were coming into existence and acquiring similar rank. Cornell had assumed a high place under the guidance of Andrew D. White, historical scholar, diplomat, and international statesman. The University of Michigan had attracted the attention of the entire world of scholarship under the inspiring leadership of the elder President Angell, also a diplomatist and statesman.

The Johns Hopkins University at Baltimore from its opening year in 1876 had assumed a character of international influence by virtue of the plan upon which it was founded. Its department heads were drawn from different countries. Its thinking was in terms of the advancement of knowledge and it had no narrow prejudices. In numbers it was intentionally a small institution, its purpose being to train men who could in turn become trainers of more men who in turn would train still others. Thus even in its earliest years it was assuming a position of intellectual authority, and was doing its share to set high standards for American scholarship.

To attempt a survey of American life as we were entering the Second World War—let us say at the opening of the year 1942—without giving thought to the moral and intellectual influence of our high schools, colleges, and universities, would seem unthinkable. The schools together with the churches at once took full control of the war, in so far as its animus and guiding principles were concerned. The colleges became training schools for the special requirements of the Army, Navy and Air Force, as preliminary to actual service for offensive or defensive warfare.

But in opening their doors for such training, they were unanimous in their essential points of view. They regarded the war as a necessary legal interposition, in order to remove alarming obstacles that were interfering with normal human progress. They believed in the intellectual and moral validity of education, as they have interpreted that word. They believed that right-mindedness and intelligence in the local community could bring the advantages of an improved way of life to all families. They held further that instructed and right-minded communities could maintain freedom and justice in states and federated governments. Finally, they believed that an international society for common purposes is possible, when founded upon the principles that underlie civilization.

Woodrow Wilson, Theodore Roosevelt, William Howard Taft, and many other political leaders of their generation entered upon public life, whether earlier or later in their careers, with principles in no way unlike those I have attributed to men of the teaching profession. And these views guided them throughout their lives. The same thing could be said of Elihu Root and Charles Evans Hughes, distinguished Secretaries of State, who were devoted to the cause of international peace through the establishment of tribunals and the application of all possible remedies for the evils of war.

Woodrow Wilson's efforts to establish a League of Nations, that should by degrees so strengthen itself in confidence and in authority as to become virtually a super-government, were not the result of convictions formed during the First World War. He had entertained such ideas through the scholarly environment of his early youth. He had arrived at a more definite view of the possibilities of world organization when he became a student of international law at the Johns Hopkins University.

III.

There are two ways to study the relationships of law between different governments or between citizens of different allegiance. One way is that of the practitioner, who learns the technicalities of admiralty law for example, and who appears in law courts, or who represents clients in some other practical manner. The other way of studying international law is that which deals with this subject as belonging to the sciences of politics and government. It is considered in its relation to diplomatic history, to the development of particular nations, and to all that relates to war and peace.

In the early days of the Johns Hopkins University at Baltimore the historical department was small in numbers, but its atmosphere was that of scholarly research. Institutions whether local or general were studied from the standpoint of their continuity and their modification from time to time. International law was subjected to the same method of historical analysis, and we were taught to note its evolution as it advanced through successive periods.

At the head of our department was Professor Herbert B. Adams who had gone from Amherst College to Germany where he took a degree at Heidelberg. Dr. Adams had studied under Professor Johann Caspar Bluntschli, who was undoubtedly the most distinguished law teacher of his generation. Returning to this country, still a very young man at the beginning of a teaching career, Dr. Adams was chosen to organize a group of postgraduate students from various American colleges, to give them lectures himself, to find other lecturers, and to encourage each man in doing his own individual work. His method was to reinforce the department by bringing in men from the outside, who would give brief courses and sit familiarly with graduate students in evening seminars for round-table discussion.

One of the men who stimulated the historical department at Baltimore in the year 1882 was the English scholar and author Edward A. Freeman, whose great work in six or eight volumes on the history of the Norman Conquest of England was the major opus among his many authoritative works. Among other subjects that he dealt with during his sojourn at Baltimore were his talks upon what was known in those days as the " Eternal Eastern Question." Tracing the course of events from the Roman Empire, its division of the East from the West, and the extension by armed force of the Turkish Empire, Mr. Freeman dwelt with wide knowledge and much enthusiasm upon the deliverance of subject Christian peoples, and the beginnings of new states in Eastern Europe. His outlook was that of an advanced Liberal and an ardent internationalist.

Immediately following Mr. Freeman, James Bryce, then Professor of Civil Law in the University of Oxford and also a

Member of Parliament, gave a course of lectures on the principles of Roman Law and their influence upon modern law codes, especially in countries of Latinic origin. Both Freeman and Bryce were interpreting law and history in the larger terms of international progress. Bryce also met the historical students in familiar evening seminar meetings, telling us of his plans for his proposed volumes on *The American Commonwealth* and inviting some of us to undertake researches that might be of assistance to him in gathering material for chapters of his great work, that made its appearance six years later.

Another lecturer in that academic year was Dr. Austin Scott, who had been the associate of the venerable historian George Bancroft in writing two important volumes on the history of the American Constitution. In these lectures Dr. Scott elucidated—more clearly than anyone else I have ever heard—the doctrine of what he called the Federative Balance. At times the Federal Government seemed to be encroaching upon the spheres of authority that had been reserved to the States. At times the pendulum might seem to be swinging the other way, or, to keep to his own metaphor, the scales might tip somewhat in favor of States Rights.

The protection of the adjustment between the states and the central power lay in the simple fact that the two agencies were under control of the same citizen voters. Americans would use the state for the more intimate concerns of families and localities. They would employ central government as their agency for the expansion of national interests. Dr. Scott expounded Federalism in such a way as to bring to life again the large Jeffersonian formula. If you fixed appropriate limits for the functions committed to centralized authority, you could also carry on your state governments and bring into the federal union still more contiguous states for strengthening the secure areas of peace and freedom. This conception of the Federative Balance appealed to our imagination as we were studying international law under Dr. Adams. It seemed to have its bearing upon larger forms of union, as we thought of world situations.

Professor Bluntschli, after long years of law study, had written a volume in which he undertook to systematize in the form of a written code all those principles of international law that seemed to him to have been sufficiently recognized to justify their brief expression in a treatise of logical sequences. This volume had been translated into French, and Professor Adams was hoping at some time to give it an English version, but he never actually accomplished it. He used the German text as a basis for lectures and discussions, and we studied it as a starting point for much collateral reading.

IV.

I am about to describe an occasion that was in some respects typical of prevailing states of mind in the period to which I have been making allusion in this chapter. Professor Bluntschli had died at Heidelberg, and his family had offered for sale the library of this eminent scholar and philosopher. It was not a large library, but it was highly specialized, distinctive in character, and of exceptional value in some of its classifications. It was found, when catalogued, to contain about five thousand items.

We had already been using Bluntschli's textbook of international law, when this library was purchased and presented to the Johns Hopkins University for the benefit of our department of historical and political science. Its presentation was made impressive by local formalities. The donors were a group of German-born citizens of Baltimore, perhaps forty in number, whose spokesman on the occasion to which I refer (December 20, 1882) was Colonel Raine, editor of the *Deutsche Correspondent.* German newspapers, it should be said, were numerous and flourishing in the United States, especially throughout the last half of the nineteenth century. They marked a transitional period, as many thousands of German families had come to the United States to live permanently after the liberal uprisings of 1848. Having expressed the belief that "a strong mixture of German idealism with American realism must in the course of time aid much in giving a loftier impulse to the development of our [American] national character," Colonel Raine made further remarks from which I quote the following passages:

> Bluntschli was at the time of his death one of the great authorities of Heidelberg's law school. You can trace in his works the powerful influence of the teachings and philosophy of such renowned men as Savigny, Schleiermacher, Niebuhr, and others.

As successor to Prof. Robert von Mohl, he devoted with noble zeal all of his energies to the religious and civil emancipation of the German people, regardless of reactionary influences which too often, by the bestowal of political favors, seek to embarrass free and independent thought. Yes, Prof. Bluntschli became under Germany's monarchial system more liberal than he had been under the republican rule of his Swiss fatherland. . . .

In thus dedicating Bluntschli's library to the Johns Hopkins University, I express the hope that the volumes now placed upon your shelves may prove to the students of history and law an incentive to further research, a greeting from the "Vaterland" to the last home of the Teutons.

These donors of the library were present in an audience otherwise composed of the trustees and officers of the University, the students of historical and political science, judges of Maryland courts and leading members of the Baltimore bar, and—to crown the occasion—the Chief Justice of the United States, who was present by invitation to take a part in the exercises. The gift was received by the Hon. George W. Dobbin, who was then president of the Board of Trustees; and he addressed himself to the men of German birth who were joint donors of the Bluntschli library. I think it worth while (because it is characteristic of American sentiment sixty years ago) to quote a paragraph or two from the address of Mr. Dobbin:

Knowing you to be representative men of that great body of American citizens who, by immigration and descent, have added to our population an element second to none other, we appreciate your approval as of priceless value. Indeed, our relations to your fatherland in an educational aspect are of the closest kind; for what problem in science, what question in literature, what disputed point in history, can be considered as satisfactory examined before the results of German research have been availed of? Our own estimate of the excellence of German scholarship and University teaching is attested by the fact that we have profitably borrowed many of their methods, and by the further fact that no scholar presents himself to us for our instruction as better accredited than one who brings with him the diploma of a German University. . . .

To no nation more than to us, as a self-governing people, is the study of these subjects more necessary and more profitable. We are glad to believe that we have already in our teaching staff young, vigorous, and active minds, who received their lessons from the lips of Bluntschli himself, and who have already shown that they are the worthy scholars of a great master. To them, and to others who may from time to time in the growth of the University be added to them, will be committed the use of these volumes.

From these historical treasures they will teach truths of political philosophy in its broadest sense, and considering themselves but the trustees for your sons and your sons' sons, they will make them through the power and instrumentality of your gift, true political philosophers—the proper synonym of good citizens.

From Professor Herbert B. Adams's commemorative address on that occasion, the following quotation not only summarizes the career of Dr. Bluntschli, but it throws a glowing sidelight upon the scholarship and the habits of thought that Herbert B. Adams himself had brought to his fruitful labors as a director of historical studies at Baltimore:

Bluntschli's first lectures, delivered in Zurich, his native town, were upon Roman law; but he soon became more interested in the law of his own canton. His first, and some think his best work, was upon the institutions of Zurich. This was the local phase of Bluntschli's career. Called in 1848 to the University of Munich, a broader field of Political Science opened before him. Here was written his first systematic work upon the State, or the Science of Government. His early historical training bore further fruit in his History of Political Science, and in his great Dictionary of State in twelve volumes, edited wth the co-operation of the ablest historians, jurists, and economists of Germany.

Bluntschli's Heidelberg career, begun in 1861, was, in a scientific sense, international. Here his life broadened into cosmopolitan habits of thought and intercourse. Political activity, begun originally in the canton of Zurich, found freer scope in Baden and in avenues of influence widening thence towards the new German empire, international conferences, and the *Institut de Droit International*, of which latter Bluntschli became the first president. His associations with the jurists and publicists of Europe and America were intimate and fruitful. The instructions prepared by Francis Lieber for the Government of the Armies of the United States in the Field, promped Bluntschli to codify, first, the Laws of War, and afterwards the Law of Nations.

From the outbreak of the Civil War in America, until the international duel between France and Prussia, Laboulaye in Paris, Bluntschli in Heidelberg, and Lieber in New York formed what the latter used to call "a scientific clover leaf." Bluntschli wrote opinions upon various international questions, such as the Alabama claims, the legal position of the Pope, the question of privateering (the latter at the request of the Russian Government). Bluntschli was always deeply interested in questions of Church and State. He presided over four different convocations of German Protestants. He was for many years president of the synod of Baden, and died at the close of its last session, October 21, 1882, in the seventy-fifth year of his age, having just closed the assembly with these words: "*Ehre sei Gott in der Höhe, Friede auf Erden, und dem Menschen ein Wohlgefallen.*"

On the occasion at Baltimore which I am describing, Dr. Daniel Coit Gilman, who had organized the University and was its first President, spoke briefly concerning the influence of Germany upon American education, referring especially to the life and work of Francis Lieber. There followed the presentation of a portrait of Chief Justice Marshall and the introduction of the Hon. Morrison R. Waite, then Chief Justice of the Supreme Court, who spoke upon the influence of John Marshall on American jurisprudence.

To sum up the life-work of Dr. Lieber was a congenial task for the Johns Hopkins President. Dr. Gilman was himself a university man of international experience and broad sympathies. In earlier years he had been a professor of geography at Yale; and his range of study included what nowadays we call "geo-politics." He had spent a year or more in the close study of foreign universities, before his little-heralded launching in 1876 of the institution endowed by the Baltimore merchant and philanthropist, Johns Hopkins.

In his address on that particular occasion in 1882, Dr. Gilman could refer to conditions in Germany at the opening of the nineteenth century, Francis Lieber having been born in the year 1800, and having fought in the German army that supported the Wellington troops at the Battle of Waterloo. The youthful patriot had volunteered as a soldier at the age of fifteen. Among later adventures Lieber had served in the war of the Greeks for independence, with high-spirited young men of British and various nationalities.

At the age of twenty-seven, Lieber—already one of the most accomplished young men of his epoch—had come to the United States, where for some years he was occupied in literary and editorial labors. With an encyclopedic mind, he was editing the *Encyclopedia Americana.* In due time he became professor of history and political economy in what is now the University of South Carolina. His connection with that institution continued for twenty-one years (1835-1856), and during that period he wrote and published works of lasting importance in the field of law and politics. In 1857 Dr. Lieber entered upon his professorship at Columbia University. He was much consulted by the Government during the Civil War, and died in October 1872.

The story of this German-American scholar, whose influence was international, ought not to be forgotten or disregarded as if it had no surviving value. Lieber lent international distinction to a Southern institution, and his work in New York laid the foundations of Columbia University's department of political science, with its unbroken record of authoritative scholarship and public service.

Not a few successors of Dr. Lieber at Columbia were also to reinforce the State Department at Washington from time to time, serving in an advisory capacity. One of them, Harlan F. Stone, long-time Dean of the Columbia Law faculty, is now Chief Justice of the United States; and another, John Bassett Moore, now emeritus professor of international law and diplomacy, has been for more than half a century one of the foremost authorities in his field, serving for long years as member of the Permanent Court of Arbitration at The Hague, and afterwards as a judge of the Permanent Court of International Justice.

V.

Why should I tell the story sixty years afterwards of a local academic ceremony so modest and unpretentious that it made little stir in scholarly circles at home or abroad? It was barely noted in the news of the day, apart from those excellent Baltimore papers, *The Sun* and *The American.* I am referring to it because it illustrates a phase of internationalism that for several decades had its focus in centers of advanced scholarship. It was approaching its climax in the last quarter of the nineteenth century. British scientists and Scottish theologians were drawing inspiration from German universities. More impressively, however, hundreds of young American college graduates were to be found studying in Germany, where they were earning the degree of Doctor of Philosophy, and returning to assume places of leadership in Western as well as Eastern institutions.

Under German leadership, Americans studied classical archaeology in Italy and Greece, and sought records of the ancient world in Egypt, Palestine, and Mesopotamia. Research in chemistry, physics, biology, and bacteriology drew young men from many countries to the German universities, Americans perhaps more numerously than men of any other nationality.

At the Johns Hopkins we students were associated with young instructors who had recently returned from Germany. They had not lost enthusiasm for their own country or their faith in its institutions. But they had acquired broader points of view and better methods of study.

The American people as a nation were, in some relative sense, arriving at a stage of maturity. Private means had become available for the endowment of universities and the creation of libraries and laboratories. States west of the Alleghanies could provide by taxation for institutions equipped to train advanced scholars and professional leaders. It was becoming less needful for young scholars to study in Europe; but the debt of America to German scholarship was then gratefully acknowledged, all the way from Cambridge to Palo Alto.

I might have gone to Europe in 1881, but it was much more convenient to go to Baltimore. It is enough to say that I found there every opportunity that I could have desired for the study of history, politics, and international relations. We were not limited to the University's immediate resources. All the library facilities of Baltimore and Washington were at our command. The State Department and other branches of the government were hospitable to our inquiries. The Government itself, as it was actually functioning, could be observed and studied as if it were a laboratory for the student of political science. The same thing was true of the governments of the state of Maryland and the city of Baltimore.

Some of the methods we used had been adapted from foreign experience. American university life was becoming cosmopolitan, though not less patriotic. America itself was under inspection as an international complex. This was in part because of the further extension of the federal system by the admission of new states.

Mainly, however, it was because immigration was at high tide, and millions of people were arriving from all parts of Europe to remain permanently. They were to become naturalized, and wholly American in sympathy and loyalty to the governmental system that was giving them freedom and opportunity.

They were here in sufficient numbers to have more than a slight or transient influence upon American life. Germans, Italians, Scandinavians, Poles, Russians, Hungarians—all these and still other peoples were arriving in sufficient numbers to reduce the original British stock to a possible minority in actual numbers, though not in continuity of influence. The result of all this immigration was in no sense discordant. The new elements were rapidly assimilated. People spoke complacently of the "melting-pot." The English language and American ideals were adopted as the universal possession of the children, regardless of the home speech of their parents. The United States was moving rapidly toward the achievement of a homogeneous nationality. We were a people capable of united purpose and action in times of emergency.

It was in this atmosphere of a seething, somewhat tumultuous, yet ardent and hopeful American progress, that I went from a Western college town to study at Baltimore. We could not then imagine America as ever becoming embroiled in the "power politics" of Europe. The United States seemed to represent the better dreams of a world at peace. We could think of international law as in slow but stately processes of evolution. Orderly arrangements of a permanent kind, we were bold enough to think, would make the nations of Europe content to live side by side in mutual appreciation.

It was in that year 1882, while studying international law with Bluntschli's work as a textbook, that I wrote an essay entitled "The Growth of Internationalism." It was read before our department of history and political science and accepted with approval. Some time afterwards it was published as an article in *The International Review*, a periodical of which Henry Cabot Lodge had been an editor. There were others who could have written that conspectus with better legal knowledge and greater maturity of judgment than mine. There was nothing in my essay to provoke dissent; and I believe that its tone of mild and hopeful optimism was generally entertained at that time by our leaders of the bar, federal judges, and scholarly men of diplomatic experience. I am re-publishing it herewith as the chapter immediately following this one, because it may be regarded as a report upon the development, in the last quarter of the nineteenth century, of what Dr. Nicholas Murray Butler—a somewhat younger contemporary, still eminent as a world leader along the paths that Lieber and his successors blazed—has continued to exemplify as the "international mind."

In certain fields of research—chemistry, physics, biology, bacteriology among others—German scholarship continued to exert a direct influence, both upon the advancement of scientific study in the United States and also upon our industrial and administrative progress, for some time after we had ceased to look further to Germany for leadership in cultural studies, and in the fields of moral and political sciences. But in absorbing so much of the spirit and method of the great political and legal authorities, the historians, the economists, and the humanists of Germany, our universities a half-century ago derived such stimulus and momentum that they no longer had need to look abroad. They in turn have become more influential, both separately and in the aggregate, than like centers of education and culture anywhere else.

From its earliest years until the present day, the Johns Hopkins University has continued to foster and promulgate those views of international relationships that were so dominant sixty years ago. Each of its successive Presidents has been influential not merely as director of an institution for advanced studies, but as a man of wide experiences and sympathies, engaged personally in promoting international friendship. A great number of scholarly men who have been connected with this Baltimore center as professors and lecturers, or as students in one department or another during almost seventy years, have rendered conspicuous service in extending far beyond the boundaries of our own country that same spirit of helpfulness and cooperation.

When I make these allusions to a single institution it is not because I am unaware that as much, or even more, might be said of the influence emanating from certain other American universities. I refer to the Johns Hopkins because it supplied the initial point from which my own definite views of international justice and order took form, so that throughout life I have thought of civilization as not divisible on nationalistic lines, but as one fabric which was to be maintained on some collective plan.

In writing of the influence of Professor Bluntschi and of the ceremony of 1882 at Baltimore, I have not forgotten the apothegm of that British statesman who warned his fellow-members of Parliament that they could not indict a whole nation. Woodrow Wilson in that period, as I remember well, kept his volumes of Edmund Burke always within reach on his desk. He did not like certain German writers, and he detested von Holst; but he would not refuse homage to the best German thinkers, and neither could he ever find it possible to think that the nation itself was hopelessly reprobate.

Certainly since that happier period, in the case of Germany there has been a shocking repudiation of the ideals that were so justly praised half a century ago. Scholarship except as it promotes war ends and strictly material objects has lost standing, and there is no freedom of thought or teaching. Nor is any true university life allowed in any part of Europe that has fallen under control of Hitler's New Order.

Yet Americans descended from those Baltimoreans of German birth who brought the Bluntschli Library from Heidelberg to their new University have held true to the generous and humane sentiments of their parents or grandparents, because they have continued to live under free institutions. Life in Baltimore has not degenerated but has steadily improved under the influence of democratic ideals. These Americans of German ancestry, who keep the philosophical temper and the historical mind, would probably agree that a regenerated Germany can be counted upon to take its appropriate place in Europe when militarism is destroyed along with racial antagonisms. The experiment of political freedom has never had a fair opportunity to work its miracles in Germany. Reasonable minds, considering the intellectual attainments and moral leadership of many eminent Germans of the last century, believe that in some better time there may come from beyond the Rhine a new group of great-souled men fit to be named with Bluntschli and Lieber.

CHAPTER VII

GROWTH OF INTERNATIONALISM (A CONSPECTUS OF 1882)

The essay which constitutes the present chapter was written by me as a student of international law at the Johns Hopkins University, and read at a meeting (in May, 1882) of the Historical and Political Science Association. It was published in the *International Review* for April, 1883. This prefatory note is written just sixty years after its appearance in print.

I had been profoundly impressed by the methods of study under Professor H. B. Adams which emphasized the historical development of political institutions, whether of local types or of larger forms. I had already written upon the transplantation of township and county systems to the new states of the West from the early Massachusetts and Virginia forms, which in turn had British origins.

By the same method of historical approach we had studied the backgrounds of the British and American Constitutions. This subject of comparative national types of representative government was one, especially, that held the attention of Woodrow Wilson, who was writing the opening chapters of his book (*Congressional Government*). But Mr. Wilson, with whom I was intimately associated in those days, was also a fellow-student of international law; and he was in complete accord with my method of treating this subject of "the growth of internationalism."

I have no hesitation in bringing this forgotten essay to light again as a convenient summary of information relating to its topic as of the 1882 date-line. Chiefly, however, I reproduce it for its bearing upon current ideas of world organization to follow the Second World War. In the course of sixty years much has taken place along lines that were indicated or predicted in this essay. A summary of the further developments of international law would require more space—even for the briefest recital—than I gave to the tendencies that were in evidence sixty years ago.

Even at that time I could assert that war was changing its character, and becoming "a legal process" for the defense of the civilized world and the vindication of justice and order. It is the perception of that change, more evident now than ever before, that has made us one of the United Nations in their crusade against unprovoked aggression.

IN 1789, as a fruitage of his materialistic, utilitarian philosophy, Jeremy Bentham prepared his "Plan for an Universal and Perpetual Peace," the main features of which comprised the reduction of military establishments, the abandonment of the colonial system, and the organization of an international congress and a "common court of judicature." Just six years later, without any suggestion from Bentham's "Plan," which for many years remained unpublished,[1] the German transcendentalist, Immanuel Kant, from the diametrically opposite standpoint of his metaphysical ethics gave to the world his sublime essay "Touching Perpetual Peace,"[2] advocating the formation of free constitutional governments in every State and an international congress to legislate for a confederated world. Within our own century philosophers of every school, religious bodies of every creed, peace congresses, learned societies, philanthropists, jurists and statesmen have drafted unnumbered schemes for world-union, with a view to substituting law for force and making natural ethics the crowning source of practical international law.

The world at large has been disposed to regard these schemes as millennial visions or utopian dreams, rather than as the sage forecasting of institutions which will be the every-day realities of a near posterity. For, despite the optimistic belief of eighteenth century philosophers that mankind even in their day was about ripe for perpetual peace and brotherly accord, this present skeptical generation finds that nations still cherish unworthy hatreds and ambitions; still pursue sinuous and unfathomable policies, and still wage bloody wars on flimsy pretexts. Hence there arises the question: Is it true that the nations of Europe and America are making no tangible progress toward the goal of universal peace and international government? Is the world not appreciably nearer that goal than it was three hundred years ago, when good King Henry and his minister, Sully, announced to the world their "great design" for the federation of Christendom?[3] Laying aside theories and philosophies and taking up the humbler

[1] Bentham's "Plan," though written in 1789, was not published till 1839. It may be found in Vol. VIII of his *Complete Works*.

[2] "Zum Ewigen Frieden," Kant's *Works*, Vol. V, pp. 411 *et seq.*, Leipsic edition, 1838.

[3] Sully's Memoirs—Bohn Series.

but safer study of political and social history, can we discover no definite tendencies toward that consummation so devoutly wished for? To this end we will direct our present inquiry.

Of one thing let us be certain at the very outset. The nations will never fix upon a precise date when, like the tribes in the *Song of Hiawatha*, they will all lay aside

> --------the feuds of ages:
> The hereditary hatred;
> The ancestral thirst of vengeance,
> *　*　*　*　*
> Smoke the calumet together,
> And as brothers live henceforward.

Great movements are not so accomplished in the real world. "Sudden changes are made only in theaters," says a modern French writer, who also bids us beware of those "alchemists of thought who imagine that society can be made to undergo a transformation between the rising and setting of the sun."[4] That greatest contribution of our time to legal and political science, the historical and comparative method of study, in establishing the essential unity of all history, and in demonstrating the marvelous continuity of customs, laws and institutions, has shed a flood of light both on the nature of progress and on the true method of reform. It has shown us that the permanent institutions of society are things of slow and gradual growth—never artificial contrivances superimposed. For example, Sir William Blackstone was content to attribute "that masterpiece of judicial policy, the subdivision of England into tithings and hundreds, if not into counties,"[5] to the wise legislation of King Alfred; but a modern student, like Professor Stubbs or Sir Henry Maine, working under the new method, will readily trace those local divisions and governments back to the Saxon invasion, show their essential identity with Teutonic township life as Tacitus saw it in the woods of Germany, and conjecture their lineal descent from the prehistoric Aryan village communities of India. At most, King Alfred only improved what was already grounded in immemorial usage.

[4] Wolowski—*Essay on the Historical Method.*
[5] Blackstone's *Commentaries*, Book IV, Chap. 33.

To take another illustration, those writers show no adequate comprehension of American history who fix a date for the beginning of our national life and say that it came first into being with the adoption of the Constitution or with the Declaration of Independence. To the true historian those instruments are but the expression of a development whose " roots run deep into the soil of the past." Mr. Bancroft's ten volumes, preliminary to the constitutional era, will stand as a monument to the truth that national institutions do not spring full-grown from the brain of heroic revolutionists, nor from their combined sagacity in great conventions; but have their real origin in almost hidden springs—in unobserved and remote causes. The student of the English Constitution who has failed to catch this idea of historical development has missed the one grand unifying principle which gives unbroken continuity and logical sequence to English history, politics and law for fourteen hundred years.

Schemes of government, however complete in theory, fail most signally unless they are en rapport with national life and character. Witness for example the attempts of Central and South American States to make a constitution modeled after ours fit their different social structures and their different historic traditions; or call to mind that magnificent system prepared for the infant colony of Carolina by Locke, the philosopher, and Shaftsbury, the statesman.[6] We are told that their plan proved " so ill-suited to the condition and wants of the straggling colonists that no efforts of the lord proprietor could long uphold it." The colonists made their simple laws as they needed them, and there grew up naturally in Carolina a system adapted to actual conditions. It was precisely upon this principle of adaptation that Solon acted when he gave the Athenians, not the best laws he could devise, but the best they could bear.

II.

If, then the local and national institutions of society are things of slow growth and of only gradual change, we need not expect that international institutions will come into full being except it be by these same processes of development. Indeed, in the very

[6] The full text of Locke's "Fundamental Constitutions of Carolina" is given in *Charters and Constitutions of the United States*, Vol. 11, pp. 1,397 *et seq.*

nature of things we should reasonably predict for them a tardier and more imperceptible progress. There must be the day of small things. Long before the realization of any of those admirable and highly organized schemes for world federation which have been the dream of political philosophers in every country, analogy would teach us to expect to find undercurrents of tendency, isolated points of contact and assimilation, irregular fragments of organization, and a hundred half-hidden forces in every department of social life, co-working to promote an "international consciousness" and to assimilate mankind. We might expect, also, that such a social atmosphere would be productive of those philosophic visions of human brotherhood which, however impracticable under present conditions, are nevertheless suited to nourish that broader and more humane public sentiment which in turn can alone make possible the realization of such visions. For, as Bentham says, "what can be better suited to the preparing of men's minds for the reception of such a proposal than the proposal itself?"[7]

The landmarks of history are not abrupt peaks. Every one of them, on approach and inspection, proves to be merely the climax of a gradually ascending series of events; and, therefore, if international organization is to be an accomplished fact a few generations hence, that organization must be the simple and naturally progressive outcome of the present state of things, and its form must be largely shaped by tendencies now at work. Its history must now be actually forming around us, and its future historian will be under necessity of devoting long chapters of his work to the nineteenth century, and even to its predecessors.

The more complete of the schemes for international organization which have been outlined in recent times have generally concurred in providing for an international code of law, a judicial tribunal for the determination of controversies under the code, and a congress of nations with legislative functions. In our present inquiry we will make use of this division of the subject. It is true that in their germinant stages political institutions are never highly differentiated. One department overlaps or merges into another. Nevertheless, without too rigid adherence to the

[7] Bentham, "Plan for an Universal and Perpetual Peace."

method, it may be found convenient for purposes of discussion to consider, first, the tendencies and forces, if any, which are making toward the formation of an international code of law; second, toward an international legislative body.

In form, an international code is simply " an extended treaty." It will comprise a clear and precise statement and a systematic arrangement of that vast body of rules governing the intercourse and mutual relations of different States and of their citizens which has grown up through the centuries by express agreement between States, or by the tacit consent of long usage. All civilized nations profess to be bound by international law; but opinions diverge very widely as to what the law really is in many critical cases. Its sources are numerous and of varying authority. Treaties and conventions, especially those which have been signed by several States; principles of natural ethics; immemorial customs; the writings of eminent jurists; the legislation of individual States upon subjects of international concern, and the judicial decisions of such eminent tribunals as the Supreme Courts of the United States and England, are all to be included among the most important sources of international law. Out of this confused and indefinite condition of public law arises no inconsiderable proportion of the disputes and conflicts between nations, and no arguments can be necessary to prove that codification would materially enhance the authority and effectiveness of the law of nations, and thereby promote the progress of the world.

The adoption of such a code need in no wise affect our modern theory of the State as a sovereign and independent personality. Every nation today recognizes, as a part of its body of law, numerous treaties with foreign powers, which involve in one connection or another every important principle of international law. Our proposed code would but consolidate and unify such principles in the mass of existing treaties as are of general application and acceptance, and the perfected product would itself go into operation as a treaty, binding only those nations which should give their assent to it.

As the law of nations is the most voluntary of all law, depending solely for its sanction upon general recognition, we must not expect to find a body of public law developing simultaneously in all its parts. Thus we find some principles to be perfectly developed and recognized, others less perfectly, and still others only beginning to emerge from the nebulous background of the general consciousness. While this remark in some sense applies to all systems of constitutional or municipal law, it is peculiarly true of international law, because the latter acknowledges no authorized lawgiver. Evidently, then, before our systematic code can be constructed and adopted, its parts must have been evolved from time to time in fragmentary chapters.

There is nothing more gratifying to the student of international law than to observe how constantly principles have been passing over from the theoretical side—the law as it ought to be—to the practical and positive side—the law as it is. Every such operation furnishes a chapter or a page for our future code. It is in the treaties and declarations of European congresses and diplomatic conferences that this process is most apparent. Hugo Grotius, the founder of the modern science of international law, published his great work on *The Laws of War and of Peace* [8] during the progress of the Thirty Years' Religious War. Its influence was beyond estimation. It is said that Gustavus Adolphus, the Protestant champion, carried Grotius' cumbrous tome through all his campaigns, and nightly placed it under his pillow. And when in 1648 the treaty of Westphalia, "which laid the foundation of modern Europe," was signed, many of the advanced international principles which Grotius had first clearly enunciated passed over into the realm of positive law, made binding by solemn treaty.

From Westphalia in 1648 to Berlin in 1878, that process had been going on continually. Let us take a hasty illustration or two from our own century. A protocol of the Vienna Congress of 1815 furnished the chapter relative to ambassadors and diplomatic intercourse. The same congress denounced the slave trade, and made it an international crime. The Congress of Paris in 1856 provided a valuable chapter on naval warfare by their declaration abolishing privateering, exempting from capture an enemy's goods under a neutral flag and neutral goods under an enemy's flag (contraband of war of course excepted), and establishing the law of blockades.

[8] Grotius: *De Jure Belli ac Pacis.*

And to these four propositions must now be added the famous "three rules" of the treaty of Washington, 1871, which formulate the duty of neutral States in respect of maritime warfare. The rules of navigation—"the law of the road at sea"—prescribed by Parliament for English vessels by the Merchant Shipping Act of 1862, have been made applicable, by consent of their respective governments, to the ships of more than thirty countries; and these rules may certainly be called another chapter of our international code.

A convention at Geneva, in the summer of 1864, participated in by twenty-four States, adopted rules for the amelioration of the hospital service and the better care of wounded soldiers. Again, at St. Petersburg, in 1868, seventeen States agreed to renounce in war the murderous use of small explosive projectiles. Both these conventions have furnished material for our code.

III.

The first codification of international articles of war was the work of Dr. Francis Lieber of Columbia College, New York. It was prepared at the instance of President Lincoln, and formed the basis of the famous "General Order No. 100," issued by the War Department in 1863, as "Instructions for the Government of the United States Armies in the Field."[9] These same articles, with some modification, were adopted by the German Government in the Franco-Prussian war. In 1873 Russia issued a circular to the Cabinets of Europe, submitting a draft of a war-code, and asking a convention to discuss it.

Accordingly all the European powers met in conference at Brussels in 1874, and after much argumentation drew up a series of articles which are known as the "Brussels War-code."[10] To quote from a resolution adopted the following year by the Institut de Droit International, the Brussels code, while "having much resemblance to the American instructions of President Lincoln,

[9] The full text of these "American War Articles" may be found in the General Orders of the War Department for 1863, or among Lieber's *Miscellaneous Writings*, edited by D. C. Gilman. Bluntschli gives them in the 1st appendix to his Völkerrecht.

[10] Text of the Brussels Code may be found in an appendix to Bluntschli's Völkerrecht, and in various publications.

has the advantage over them of extending to international relations a regulation made for one State, and of containing new requirements at once practical, humane, and progressive."

It is with just pride that Americans may claim the war-code of Europe, which records a humanitarianism so far in advance of Grotius and the early writers, as the direct outgrowth of the labors of an American college professor. Dr. Lieber's "Old Hundred," as he jocosely termed his articles of war, will be an abiding monument to his memory; for it has given him a place among the framers of the world's great future code, which, when in process of time fully developed, will be a work "second to none in dignity or importance among the events which have illustrated the world's history."

Let us take still another illustration of the growth of a code. David Dudley Field, writing in 1876, says: "The late postal treaty is a code as far as it goes, or rather one chapter of a code. The fact that such a treaty has been made between sixteen different nations is proof that a general treaty can be made embracing one subject. Why may it not be made to embrace all, or, if not all, nearly all subjects of international concern?"

Communication by means of telegraphs and railroads on the continent of Europe is governed by a system of treaty stipulations which is fast attaining the uniformity of codification. The same may be said of European copyright laws. The use of oceanic cables and of interoceanic canals is sure to be fixed at an early date by specific international rules; and sooner or later we may reasonably expect to find such subjects as Sea-signals, Quarantine, Money, Weights and Measures, Longitude and Time, each the title-heading of a chapter in the code of nations.

These illustrations will suffice to indicate the processes by which the ethical speculations, the vague and verbose moralizings, of Pufendorf, Wolff and the early writers are gradually becoming reduced to a system of authoritative legal rules. To this end the writings of learned publicists have conduced greatly. Their efforts in our own times to bring the whole body of public law into the form of a complete code must, without doubt, facilitate the ultimate adoption of such a code.

The late Professor Bluntschli, of Heidelberg, was the pioneer in this field. It is interesting to notice Bluntschli's acknowledgment that it was the appearance of Lieber's American war articles which prompted him to undertake, for international law as a whole, what his American friend had done for a part of it.[11] Probably the most remarkable attempt to bring the whole body of law into a form suitable for adoption by the nations has been made by an American jurist, Mr. David Dudley Field. His *Outlines of an International Code*, revised 1876, is a volume which has received world-wide commendation.

The labors of two great international societies—the Institute of International Law and the Association for the Reform and Codification of the Law of Nations, the one founded at Ghent in September, 1873, and the other inaugurated at Brussels a month later—have both already proved highly effective, and have a growingly auspicious future.

With all their lingering prejudices, their jealousies, and their supposed conflict of interests, the nations are scarcely prepared as yet to adopt in toto so comprehensive a code as Mr. Field's. Nevertheless, there are many portions of it upon which agreement is already general; and for one who realizes the constantly accelerating tendency toward unification—which is the mark of our age—it is not hard to believe that differences will in so far vanish as to permit the adoption of a working code before the world is many decades older.

IV.

"Recourse is had to war only for want of a better expedient." Such were the words of the illustrious Sully, three centuries ago, when he announced to Europe his elaborate project for an international tribunal, which was to obviate "the necessity of passing through war to arrive at peace."[12] Ten generations have passed away and Sully's plan in its details still seems a visionary one. Nevertheless, the world is deeply conscious that it has grown toward unity; and an international court of judicature would by no means so irreconcilably violate the existing nature of things in our day as formerly. Institutions come by growth, and growth is always conditional upon a rightly constituted soil. Even, there-

[11] See Bluntschli's letter, Introduction to Lieber's *Miscellaneous Writings.*
[12] Sully's *Memoirs* Vol. II, p. 353; Bohn's series.

fore, if we could not claim that the institution of a tribunal of nations had yet so much as germinated, it would still be of genuine significance if we could show that the prerequisite soil was in process of formation.

We may readily find three important elements of that soil: First, the development of the science of jurisprudence. The scientific and comparative study of law is giving the constitutional and municipal systems of various nations a strong tendency toward uniformity; and this growing harmony in legal ideas and methods must evidently facilitate the establishment of an international court of law.

The second element is the growth of a law-abiding spirit—the recognition which has obtained throughout civilized society of the supremacy of law as opposed to force. As, under the constitutional regime of this century, law has everywhere become more stable and more just, and its administration in like manner has become more pure and disinterested, so respect for its authority and submission to its requirements have become well-nigh universal.

This spirit of self-restraint and submission to law is not alone manifested in the dealing of man with man or in the internal regulation of a State. It also appears when a Geneva or Halifax award is honorably paid, or when public sentiment holds a strong nation to the terms of a treaty stipulation contrary to its supposed advantage. Such a public sentiment is the good soil in which international organization can find firm rooting.

The third element is the radical change which has come about in the character of war. War was formerly regarded as the directly opposite condition of law. But today it is regarded as the instrument of law—a legal process for defending rights and redressing wrongs.

International law forbids wars for conquest, aggrandizement, plunder, hatred, revenge. It requires that war shall be resorted to only in the failure of peaceable means, and that no injury shall be done the enemy beyond what is needful to attain the lawful end in view. It prescribes rules to be observed in war, just as municipal law may provide rules which the sheriff, or constable, or policeman must observe in making a seizure or an arrest.

In the history of private law we find a stage of self-help, when men avenge their own injuries and maintain their own rights; but the subsequent development of courts of justice follows as a logical necessity. The analogy is morally sure to obtain in the progress of international law. The idea of war as a legal instrument once completely recognized, its replacement by the better instrument of a judicial tribunal becomes but a question of time.

That branch of jurisprudence known as private international law, or the Conflict of Laws, which has to do with the rights and relations of private individuals in foreign countries, does not require a system of international courts. In cases wherein its principles are involved, the ordinary courts assume a quasi-international character, and are guided by international law in their judgments. The appearance of this comparatively new department of law, and its practical recognition by the courts of all nations, are significant facts in the growth of internationalism.

Many consular courts in Oriental countries—and especially the mixed tribunals in Egypt—partake yet more decidedly of the international character. In these Egyptian courts, which were established in 1876, European and native judges sit together to try all mixed cases, without respect to nationality, using a code based on the Mohammedan law and the Code Napoleon.

Modeled somewhat after this Egyptian precedent, it has been proposed to erect an international court in Belgium, with jurisdiction over cases of private commercial law. Such a court, limited to the cognizance of cases arising under a single branch of private international law, could perhaps be organized with little difficulty; and while it would have no influence in the determination of great public questions, it might contain the potency and promise of a future tribunal with wider functions.

But it is for the settlement of disputes between sovereign nations rather than those affecting individual rights, that a tribunal is most urgently needed. "Even if," says Professor Sheldon Amos, "for a time very few questions were in fact submitted to it, its very existence would be a type and pledge of an institution which the community of States must inevitably hereafter develop, and must facilitate the way to its formation." [13]

There are jurists who see the imperfect beginnings of an inter-

[13] *Political and Legal Remedies for War*, p. 123.

national tribunal in the national courts which adjudge prize captures in naval warfare. In a restricted sense these may even now be regarded as international; for, although constituted by a belligerent to pronounce on the validity of captures from the enemy or from neutrals who are alleged to have violated neutrality, and therefore always liable to the imputation of unfairness and partiality, these maritime courts are nevertheless controlled in their decisions by international law, and their judgments are acknowledged as valid and final by all foreign governments.

In a series of papers in the *Revue du Droit International* a year or two ago, a French jurist, Bulmerincq, discusses the present organization and procedure of these prize courts of all countries, and explains a project for making them more broadly international. Upon the outbreak of a war he proposes that each belligerent shall name a judge, and that these two, together with a third who shall represent the interests of neutral States, shall constitute a court, holding its sessions on the neutral soil of Belgium, and pronouncing final sentence on all captures. Or, as an alternative, he suggests a court of twelve members, one each to be named by Great Britain, the United States, France, Germany, Russia, Austria, Italy, Spain and Portugal, Turkey and Greece, Holland and Belgium, the three Scandinavian Kingdoms, and the South American States. Such a court, sitting only in times of war, and deciding only upon sea-captures, might readily, in that writer's opinion, be the germ or the prototype of a permanent tribunal which would ultimately do away with wars and sea-captures.

V.

Other writers and jurists regard the court of arbitration as the prototype of the world's future tribunal. History records a great number of international disputes which have been settled by arbitration. Especially in loose confederacies like ancient Greece and medieval Germany such a system had a highly effective place. In no less than sixteen cases the United States has resorted to this mode of settling controversies. It must be admitted, however, that most of these were of very minor importance, the most serious difference ever adjusted in this manner being our *Alabama* claim against England.

There are obvious reasons why courts of arbitration, as usually constituted, are an imperfect and uncertain means of international pacification. On this point Mr. A. H. Stoiber, of New York, in a recent monograph says:

> From the single fact that a court of arbitration depends for its very existence and origin upon a formal treaty between nations, results the uncertainty whether a pending quarrel will not lead to an open rupture before the diplomatists have finished their labors in effecting a treaty.[14]

Says the same writer:

> The essential elements of the court of arbitration are that the arbitrators are quasi-judges; that their appointment results from a special treaty; that the arbitrators can exercise their functions only in the single case for the decision of which they were chosen, and that the rules of procedure are also determined only for the particular case in question. It is evident that we have here nearly all the essentials of a civil court of justice, with this exception, that in the case of the court of arbitration the party representing the plaintiff has no acknowledged right to summon the supposed offender to the bar of justice, but must rely on the latter's sense of honor to consent to the creation of a court for the purpose of obtaining a judicial decision.

Mr. Stoiber advocates the erection by treaty of a standing court of arbitration, the nations who are parties to the treaty agreeing to submit their controversies to the court and to abide by its decisions. The jurisdiction of the court would be limited to subjects mentioned in the treaty or to questions arising under a code which also would be adopted by treaty.

Mr. David Dudley Field favors a somewhat similar plan, and provisions for the establishment of such a tribunal form part of his proposed code. Mr. Field's plan,[15] in brief, is this: When one country has cause of complaint against another it must make out and submit to the offending party a formal statement of grievances. If satisfactory explanations or amends are not forthcoming each government appoints five members of a joint high commission. In case the commission should fail to adjust the controverted matter each of the other nations who are parties to the code selects and duly transmits four names, and from the list

[14] *On the Establishment of an International Tribunal*, New York, 1881.
[15] See his *Outlines of a Code*, New York, 1876.

thus impanneled the disputants alternately reject names till only seven remain. These seven constitute a high tribunal of arbitration, and their decision shall be final. Any nation violating the code or disregarding the judgments of the court incurs the risk of a war with the whole family of nations.

Now if these, and numerous other projects somewhat diverse in detail which we might describe for the erection of a great world tribunal, were merely the ingenious and philanthropic schemes of imaginative gentlemen, if statesmen and law-making bodies had given them no consideration, it might be unsafe to cite them as indicating definite tendencies of the times. But the facts are otherwise. International organization has held the eloquent and life-long advocacy of Americans like Sumner and Englishmen like Gladstone. It has become a custom, not only with the United States, but with many other countries, to insert in treaties provisions for resorting to arbitration in case of disputes arising under the treaty.

Moreover, governments have in so far recognized the possibility of improving the present imperfect system that in 1873 the British Parliament passed a bill favoring the establishment of a *permanent* system of arbitration, while in 1874 the Congress of the United States adopted a resolution authorizing the President to negotiate with all civilized powers for the formation of such a system. Russia, Italy, Sweden, Holland, have all expressed themselves as advocates of arbitration, and other European powers have more or less directly committed themselves. The significance of such expressions will not be denied.

For near a hundred years the Supreme Court of the United States, the unquestioned and incorruptible arbiter between the constituent members of the Union, has stood an object-lesson to the world. John Stuart Mill calls it "the first example of what is now one of the most urgent needs of the civilized world—a real International Tribunal." The recent confederation of the British Provinces of North America, and the erection of a Supreme Court for the Dominion of Canada, is another move in the same direction, well illustrating the power of a neighborly example.

And now as our Supreme Court may adjudicate between Maine and New Hampshire, and as the Supreme Court of Canada may decide between Nova Scotia and New Brunswick, and as both these tribunals were formed by the consent of the parties concerned, why also should not differences between Maine and New Brunswick, that is to say, between the American Union and the Canadian Dominion, be adjusted by an International Tribunal, also constituted by agreement between the parties concerned? It is hard to avoid the conclusion that some such tribunal is inevitable. It may not be the evolved product of consular or commercial courts; it may not result from the expansion of maritime prize courts; it may not find its prototype in the court of arbitration, and it may not be formed upon the model of the Supreme Court of the United States. But in a certain sense all of these are its forerunners, at once conditioning and heralding its consummation.

VI.

In accordance with our proposed outline, it remains to consider briefly the subject of an International Congress. Mr. Field's code, which we have already cited, provides for an annual conference of the representatives of nations, to meet successively at the various capitals for the purposes of discussing provisions of the code and their amendment, averting war, facilitating intercourse and preserving peace. A more ambitious scheme has been propounded by Professor Lorimer, the Edinburgh jurist. His project [16] includes an International Legislature, consisting of a Senate and a Chamber of Delegates, with its seat at Constantinople, which city is to be made an international possession, bearing the relation to the family of nations which the District of Columbia sustains to the States of the Union; a Supreme International Judiciary, with an international army to enforce its decisions; and the military and naval disarmament of Europe.

Such schemes are admirable, and are only wanting, as Sheldon Amos might sarcastically remark, in regard for the true political difficulties which at present have to be overcome. "An International Senate and an International Parliament," says Dr. Bluntschli,[17] "will long remain beautiful wishes. Nevertheless Europe is awaking to the need of an organization; and in my opinion, its

[16] Professor Lorimer in *Revue de Droit International*, 1877.
[17] Bluntschli, *Moderne Volkerrecht*, p. 109.

attainment will only be possible when the attempt at an organization *over* the States is abandoned, and an organization *through* the States is adopted."

Dr. Bluntschli's view is manifestly right. The sovereignty, independence and equality of States as organic personalities are ideas too firmly grounded at present to permit the formation of an international congress which is not simply a diplomatic body, or to admit the validity of any international legislation that does not take the treaty form and acquire its force as law through the formal ratification of individual sovereign States.

In the history of confederated governments there is a preliminary stage, a period of diplomatic alliance, leading up by more or less distinct transitions to federal union or consolidation. Thus, the American Union, before 1789, was in form an international league, the Articles of Confederation constituted a treaty between sovereign States; and the Congress was a diplomatic body composed of representatives not of the people but of the governments of the several States. And even this imperfect state of confederation had its earlier beginnings in the occasional cooperation of the Colonial Governments, as in Indian wars, for example.

Even under our present national Constitution, the equality of representation in the Senate is a survival of the period when we were not one but thirteen. The history of the Swiss Confederation, of the Argentine Confederation, and of the German Empire similarly illustrates the progressive stages in the growth of federal governments. It is only by such stages and from such tentative beginnings that the great world-congress of the future can come into being.

A European union has not yet been formally organized, but its idea can no longer be called a dream. For centuries there has been growing up a European constitution. Its development has been neither rapid nor symmetrical, and has been subject to many reactions, but it has been real and cognizable nevertheless. A leading principle of that constitution is the accountability of each individual State to the family of States in matters pertaining to external policy. While the principle of non-intervention in the private internal affairs of a State has become continually better established, it has become equally well established that every great question which affects the well-being of Europe shall be decided by the united voice of Europe.

The doctrine of the balance of power, the essence of which is "that the nations shall together judge of the infraction of the public law by any one of them and act in concert to prevent it," is one phase of this general principle. The diplomatic congress or conference, as the exponent of this general European sentiment, is another of the marked features of the growing constitution of Europe. Several of these great gatherings have already been referred to as of importance in the development of a code.

It was the Congress of Westphalia which secured the results of the German Reformation and laid the foundations of Prussia. The great congresses of Nimeguen, Ryswick and Utrecht restored the balance which had been overthrown by the ambitious Louis XIV. Of the congresses at Soissons, in 1727, and at Aix la Chapelle, in 1748, we are told that they renewed and confirmed the treaties of Westphalia, Nimeguen, Ryswick and Utrecht, "so that their labors formed a continuous series and identical body of international legislation," covering an entire century.

Within our own century there have been gatherings not less notable. The Congress of Vienna, 1815, which met to readjust Europe after Napoleon's downfall, made more changes in geography and politics than the Corsican had wrought. The Congress of Paris, 1856, at the close of the Crimean war, humiliated Russia, bolstered up the decrepid Turk, neutralized the Black Sea, and abolished privateering. The Congress of Berlin, 1878, says Mr. Field,

> was the most conspicuous and successful example of an international congress to avert impending war. There were settled questions not merely of European, but of Asiatic interest; questions affecting not only Russia and Turkey, but England, Austria and Greece as well; questions of supreme importance to the diverse populations of vast provinces, while millions of armed men stood looking on ready to spring into the arena if the counsels of peace had not prevailed.

The Conference at St. Petersburg, in 1825, led to the independence of Greece. The Conference at London, in 1831, secured the separation of Belgium and Holland, and made Belgium a perpetually neutral State. Another conference at London, in 1871, restored to Russia her ancient rights on the Black Sea, which the Congress of Paris had taken away fifteen years before. These familiar events are by no means here adduced as a list of European gatherings but merely as a citation of instances to illustrate the practice which will ultimately become invariable of solving the great questions which concern all Europe through the united counsels of the European States.

VII.

It is generally characteristic of legislative bodies in their earlier and forming stages that they deal with concrete and special questions even more than with abstract and general questions, thus performing many offices which at later periods are assigned to executive and judiciary departments. It may not be unreasonable to predict that this differentiating process, which is well illustrated by a comparison of the functions of our Continental Congress with those of our present Congress, will also be repeated in the slow upbuilding of a European organization.

Upon the formation of an international tribunal, or standing court of arbitration, many of the particular, concrete subjects heretofore dealt with by congresses and conferences will be assigned to the judiciary, and the congress will more and more tend to become a strictly lawmaking body, working out those principles and statements of public law which shall guide and control the judiciary in their adjustment of specific controversies.

It will mark a great progress when the European Congress—which we may regard as the prototype of that more broadly international organization which must also include America—shall begin to hold regular and periodic sessions. In this connection may be mentioned as significant that provision in the international postal treaty which calls for a convention of revision every three years. A periodic conclave of the nations of the world, though but for the single object of revising a postal treaty, is a prognostic the import of which can hardly be exaggerated.

After all, it is chiefly through such agencies as the postal system, the telegraph, the growth of commerce, the new facilities for travel, emigration and popular information, that old prejudices are vanishing, the nations are becoming acquainted with one another, and the world is ripening for an era of law and peace. A Monetary Conference, a meeting of the Evangelical

Alliance, a scientific gathering like the recent Congress of Electricians at Paris, the meetings of the great societies for the improvement of international law, great world fairs like those of Vienna, Philadelphia and Paris—all these are vastly more full of significance as showing the drift of our time toward internationalism than are even such splendid political pageants as the Berlin Congress.

That noble international affiliation of relief societies wearing the badge of the Red Cross of Geneva, an association whose magnificent service has been so conspicuous in the alleviation of suffering on every recent battlefield, recognized and protected by every civilized government, is a potent sign of the times. Even that once dreaded and denounced communistic order, the workingmen's "International," has had, indirectly, its useful mission in teaching lessons of organization, human brotherhood, the universality of social problems, and the identity of interest among the world's toiling masses, regardless of national distinction.

It has not been the purpose of this paper to promulgate any doctrine or to advocate any scheme. The attempt has been simply to note here and there a floating straw on the life-current of the age, that we may know assuredly in what direction that current is flowing. And if we conclude that the world is making strong and tangible progress toward union, law and perpetual peace, it is not alone upon sentiments of benevolent optimism, but also upon the facts of history and society, that we base our conclusion. Many years ago, in an address at Paris, Victor Hugo uttered the following prediction:

> A day will come when the only battle-field will be the market open to commerce and the mind open to new ideas. A day will come when bullets and bombshells will be replaced by votes, by the universal suffrage of nations, by the venerable arbitration of a great sovereign senate, which will be to Europe what the Parliament is to England, what the Diet is to Germany, what the Legislative Assembly is to France. A day will come when a cannon will be exhibited in public museums just as an instrument of torture is now, and people will be astonished how such a thing could have been. A day will come when those two immense groups—the United States of America and the United States of Europe—shall be seen placed in presence of each other, extending the hand of fellowship across the ocean.

CHAPTER VIII

THE MEDITERRANEAN: AGE-OLD CENTER OF WORLD INTEREST

The modern world has other centers, but the Mediterranean Sea continues to hold its place as the most influential one. The recovery of its control by the United Nations affects not only southern Europe, northern Africa, and the Near East, but because of its essential character as a trade route it concerns every country in the world.

The landing of a great American force in Morocco in the autumn of 1942, besides helping to accomplish the larger world-wide objects of the war, will undoubtedly have some bearing upon the future of this strategic area occupying the northwest corner of Africa. The Western Hemisphere is interested in the control of the Atlantic ports, as well as in the safety of the passage for world purposes between the Pillars of Hercules.

The control of Morocco formed a strategic place in the ambitious conceptions of Germany, as the Kaiser was casting about for imperial possessions, and taking one step after another that led inevitably to the First World War. This chapter recites the circumstances of the Algeciras conference on Morocco, to which President Theodore Roosevelt sent representatives. Five years later, Germany attempted to secure the port of Agadir on the Atlantic Coast, but accepted a compromise. Whether or not Morocco is to be restored to France for administrative purposes—which would seem to have advantages—it will form an outpost of world stability under some form of collective guardianship and security.

This chapter further raises the question of stability at the opposite entrance to the Mediterranean, where Great Britain has long controlled the Suez Canal under international regulations. Ground work laid by Gladstone sixty years ago for constitutional government in Egypt has survived all vicissitudes, because it had fundamental and permanent qualities. The same thing is asserted in my account of the restoration of the Upper Nile Valley, which is governed under a "condominium" plan, as the Anglo-Egyptian Sudan. Arrangements thus made from the days of Gladstone to those of Cromer, and maintained through the period of the Second World War, can be made to fit well into the pattern of things to come.

THE ARRIVAL of American forces in North Africa in 1942 opened another volume in the age-long and incomparable story of the Mediterranean Sea as a theater of international strife, mitigated by periods of peace based upon concessions and agreements—often multilateral. One hundred and thirty-eight years had elapsed since an American naval expedition under Decatur had entered the harbor of Tripoli, and put an end to the piratical exactions of North African tribal chiefs and their enslavement of Christian captives.

In the eventful course of the nineteenth century and the first four decades of the twentieth, there had been almost countless changes in external conditions affecting the freedom of the Mediterranean for legitimate traffic. But startling new challenges, not so different in principle from those of 1804, had again involved us in that area of ancient civilizations. Italy—not waiting to be supported by Germany—had in the twentieth century adopted the public morals of the old-time Barbary pirates.

When the second World War is ended, certain doctrines of world-wide application will have been agreed upon by the United Nations, and will be applied in practical ways. One of these will relate to the freedom and security of the seas for the commerce of all nations great or small. In keeping with the broad principle there will be regional agreements, more detailed in their bearings. A good-neighbor policy on our side of the Atlantic, applicable to the Caribbean Sea, will not be difficult to arrange, because it already exists in effect and is associated with the equal use of the Panama Canal.

More complicated, perhaps, but undoubtedly susceptible of harmonious agreement will be the pact providing for the equal use of the Mediterranean by a dozen or more nationalities bordering upon its shores, and by the ships of all maritime powers. It is safe to predict that this middle sea of the ancient world will not in the days to come be haunted by submarines or tormented from the air by explosives.

When fair adjustments are finally arranged, it will be discovered that many local solutions, accepted at intervals of the past when sanity and reason prevailed, will be brought to light as good examples. If for an unspecified term the British should retain authority at Gibraltar, at Malta, and at Suez, it would be in discharge of the duties of guardianship for the common good, rather than in assertive proprietorship.

Gibraltar: A Stronghold for World Security

It was at Gibraltar that the greatest convoy in all maritime history entered the Mediterranean in November, 1942. It assembled somewhere off the Eastern coast of the United States and crossed the Atlantic under the protection of an armada of battleships, cruisers, destroyers and submarines. This vast tonnage of shipping, counted by hundreds of units as the British half of the expedition joined the American, found anchorage under the protecting guns of a fortress that had now become a principal bastion of the United Nations in their determined struggle to redeem the world from the forces of banditry and piracy.

The reign of terror that the Axis powers had extended elsewhere was also encompassing the basin of the Mediterranean. It had been preceded by a Civil War in Spain so devastating that the Spanish people were left demoralized, impoverished, and near the point of starvation. France had succumbed to the German onslaught. Conditions in North Africa, extending from the Pillars of Hercules to the Suez Canal, were involved in political as well as military contradictions.

The British had been massing forces in Egypt to hold Suez, although for a time their position was so precarious that they were entering the Red Sea by way of the long voyage around the Cape of Good Hope. At Gibraltar, however, with supplies of munitions and food well stored to last if necessary for a period of years rather than of weeks, they were impregnable in the deep chambers of their famous Rock.

It is quite natural to accept plausible conclusions about things that do not concern us directly. For example, if only a few years ago Dr. Gallup's Institute of Public Opinion had asked Americans to express their views about the rightful occupancy of Gibraltar, a majority of them would have replied with assurance, though without any deep feeling, that Gibraltar ought to be transferred to Spain as a matter of obvious propriety. Such an expression would not necessarily have implied anti-British prejudices. It would merely have signified a memory of school-day lessons in geography. It seems so suitable that maps should determine political boundaries. Yet to assume that Spain should control Gibraltar would indicate little knowledge of history, and even less understanding of those modern relationships that affect world intercourse and commerce.

If a "public-opinion test" were to have been made in 1943, no intelligent American would declare that Gibraltar ought to be relinquished by the United Nations, and turned over to the government of General Franco as an integral part of the Spain over which he ruled as a military dictator. However much one likes the appearance of completeness and symmetry, geography cannot in all cases answer questions relating to political dominion. It is true that Spain has often looked with possessive desire towards the peninsular point that is crowned by the fortress of Gibraltar. But the entrance to the Mediterranean has concerned many other nations—perhaps more vitally than it has ever concerned the Spaniards.

If Gibraltar had been ceded to Spain as a gesture of British good will on some past occasion, when perchance royal families were inter-marrying, what would the consequences have been? Obviously, in this period of the second World War, the fortress would have been strongly held at first by General Franco with a Spanish garrison. But Germany and Italy together would have lost no time in convincing the Dictator at Madrid that the Axis must be allowed to hold the Strait of Gibraltar and the Pillars of Hercules. We might, indeed, have landed troops on the Atlantic Coast of Africa; but we would not have been able to enter the Mediterranean without military and naval preliminaries for which we were unprepared.

For a long time, perhaps seven hundred and fifty years, Gibraltar belonged to the Moors. The Spaniards acquired it in the fifteenth century, a few years before Columbus discovered America. It has been held by the English since 1704, a period of almost two and a half centuries, during which time nothing else has been so stable in the Iberian Peninsula. Portugal occupies a portion of that peninsula, and was separated in the eleventh century from one of the kingdoms into which Spain was then divided. Federalism is a political formula natural to the American mind, yet it would hardly occur to us to assume that Portugal must needs be united with Spain. Through a long period England exercised a certain undefined guardianship over Portugal, due to the predominance of the British navy, and to the further fact that Gibraltar was a Crown Colony.

Even if I had an opinion as to the future status of Gibraltar, I should not express it because the facts seem to carry their own argument. It may be said with confidence that since Gibraltar is today one of the strongholds of the United Nations that have agreed to uphold universal standards of justice and freedom, it will not fail henceforth to be controlled in the interest of our common civilization. Gibraltar stands as one of those foundation-stones, both in literal fact and also in symbolic terminology, upon which peace and good relationships can and must be established around the shores of the Mediterranean. Meanwhile, it stands also as one of the major guarantors of a safe thoroughfare for the traffic of Asia, Africa, and Australia with the continents of Europe and America.

Morocco: Henceforth also an American Concern

Across the Straits from Gibraltar lies Morocco, which occupies the northwest corner of the African continent. It extends about two hundred miles along the Mediterranean from Ceuta (the point exactly opposite Gibraltar) to Algeria. It stretches a much greater distance southward along the Atlantic coast. It supports the nominal rulership of an Arab Sultan, but most of the area of more than 200,000 square miles has been under predominant French influence since 1904, by virtue of a secret treaty with Spain and a more open understanding with England. For almost or quite a quarter of a century afterwards the French were carrying on wars of subjugation against fierce tribesmen living in the unexplored fastnesses of mountains and uplands.

A limited fraction of the northwest part of Morocco has been under Spanish control for many years, and the Spanish army has suffered humiliation at times in its wars with the tribesmen. The seaport of Tangier, once the haunt of pirates, was internationalized in 1912, and in recent years had been under the joint administration of Great Britain, France, Spain and Italy. The largest Moroccan seaport is Casablanca on the Atlantic Coast, within the zone of the French Protectorate.

The landing of American forces in the autumn of 1942 has naturally revived interest in the past history of that region, and even more in the problems of its future control and administration. About Algeria there is no question, because it has long been recognized as an integral part of France.

Tunisia, a comparatively small country of less than 50,000 square miles lying east of Algeria, has been administered as a French protectorate since 1881. The victory of the Allied Nations at the ports of Bizerte and Tunis in May, 1943, brought an end to the German-Italian military occupation. Since the United Nations will have no avowed object in considering the future of North Africa beyond the establishment of permanent peace and good order, and the welfare of the inhabitants, there can be no reason to suppose that there will be arbitrary reversals of administrative authority, especially as regards Tunisia. But the United Nations, including the United States, having liberated Tunisia at great cost of life and treasure, will insist upon some form of international oversight.

As regards Morocco, if the promises of international cooperation have any meaning at all, that country will pass from the status of a protectorate with military government (and frequent wars with the Riff Berber tribes) to an administration of international character, devised for the welfare of the population. The virtual French Protectorate (acknowledged in 1911) had its beginning with the conceded right of the French forces in Algeria to protect their western border. Gradually through a maze of diplomatic negotiations, veiled threats, naval expeditions, and horse-trade dickers among the powers engaged in dividing up Africa, the French were accorded predominant interest in Morocco. The difficulties of their protectorate have been so great, however, that it has been of questionable value to them in view of what it has cost, except as related to their general position in Africa. Their principal object in demanding predominance in Morocco, as if it were a valuable prize, was in former years to keep the German Kaiser from seizing control.

Directly or indirectly, all the leading European powers were involved in the Morocco dispute; and the story has current importance as a warning against the dangers of nationalism run amuck and extended to a mad quest of ambitious rivals for colonial empire. Almost contemporary with the Algeciras conference on the control and management of Morocco (to which I shall refer in later paragraphs), was an incident that led to the participation of the United States in that meeting of European diplomats. The incident had to do with the kidnaping of an American citizen, a brilliant writer with a Greek name, who had once obtained naturalization papers in the United States although he had long been a resident of Tangier.

President Theodore Roosevelt and the State Department under John Hay took such vigorous steps in the matter of this kidnaping that all American and European newspapers gave it as much prominence as if a war had broken out. Diplomatic circles also were much concerned. Turning to editorial pages of my periodical for July, 1904, I find the following statement:

It comes as an odd coincidence that a United States naval commander, with United States war vessels, should be carrying out in Morocco, in the first years of the twentieth century, what an American commander, with American ships of war, was doing in the opening years of the nineteenth. In 1804, Captain Decatur attacked and chastised the 'Barbary pirates' for attacks on American commerce. It is a far cry from his frigate the *Philadelphia*, to the splendid warship the *Brooklyn*, upon which Rear-Admiral Chadwick flies his flag today. With the internal troubles of Morocco we have no concern, and our government has acquiesced in the provisions of the Anglo-French agreement by which France's preponderance of influence in Morocco is recognized.

The presence of American and British warships in the harbor of Tangier for several weeks in May and June was due solely to the fact that an American citizen, Ion Perdicaris, and a British subject, Cromwell Varley, had been captured by a Moorish bandit, Muley Ahmed, or Raisuli, as he is called, a descendant of the most venerated of Moroccan chiefs, and held for the purpose of extorting money and other concessions from the unhappy Sultan. Raisuli seems to be a man of ability and power. He has several strongholds in inaccessible mountain districts, and the Sultan is practically in his power, as the American and British governments are demanding the safe return of their citizens and the Sultan's treasury is bankrupt. Raisuli originally demanded fifty thousand dollars and certain other conditions which would give him immunity from punishment and practical political authority over the districts he now controls. Later, he demanded more.

Recognizing France's peculiar position of authority in Morocco, our State Department requested the cooperation of the French Government in securing the release of Mr. Perdicaris (who, by the way, has been a resident of Tangier for many years, and is an American in nothing but his naturalization papers). If Raisuli, with all his piracy, can wring from the Sultan some concessions which will make for better government in Morocco, the world will forgive him for this particular kidnaping. It will certainly follow with the best of good wishes France's efforts to civilize the country.

The conclusion of the incident was reported by me in the following month. The matter derives its subsequent importance from the light it throws upon the course of affairs in the tangle of diplomacy relating to the European partition of Africa:

Within the month covered in our present record, the State Department has given several new illustrations of its successful methods. It has closed the Morocco incident by securing the release of Mr. Perdicaris, safe and sound, from the bandits who held him for ransom. Our European squadron was promptly assembled off the coast of Morocco to make a due impression upon the lax and decadent government of the Sultan Mulai-Abed-el-Aziz, but meanwhile the State Department was pulling just the right strings in its representations at Paris. A recent treaty between England and France had recognized the paramountcy of French influence in Morocco. Mr. Hay paid due deference to this treaty, and made the French Government see readily how usefully its African ambitions might be promoted if it should accept this American recognition and at the same time earn it by securing the release of Perdicaris. Mr. Hay had demanded "Perdicaris alive or Raisuli dead." No guarantees of any kind were given by our government, nor were any demands made on the Moorish Government for indemnity or punishment.

The whole reorganization of Moroccan government and finances will be the work of France, and the republic takes the credit for securing the release of the prisoners. The $70,000 was paid to Raisuli from the new French loan to Morocco of $12,500,000, and the net result to Europe is that France exerts to the full the control permitted her over Morocco by the recent Anglo-French treaty. M. Raindre, formerly French consul at Geneva, will take charge of the custom-houses at Moroccan ports, the receipts from which will secure the French loan. A French police force is also to be organized in Tangier. From beginning to end, the episode was creditable to American diplomacy.

The Morocco question was not of such vital character, if nothing else had been involved; but it became the key to other pending issues of larger consequence. Although it was settled with results that were regarded as favorable to European peace, it was in reality nothing less than one of the preliminaries that were leading to the First World War. Germany was staking out claims in various directions, regarding the time as opportune for colonial acquisition.

Major European events were closely coordinated. The Russo-Japanese war of 1904–5 had ended in a brilliant victory for the Japanese. President Roosevelt, though not acting as mediator in the strict sense of that word, had persuaded the governments of the Czar and the Mikado to accept terms of peace that seemed reasonable, and a treaty was signed at Portsmouth, New Hampshire, in the summer of 1905. While the Japanese were elated, and their militarists were planning further victories and conquests, the Russians were wildly indignant at what they regarded as corruption and mismanagement on the part of their own generals and admirals. In direct consequence, revolutionary activities prevailed throughout the vast domains of the Czar. There resulted many liberal improvements and reforms in Russian government; but for some time after her crushing defeat by sea and land, Russia's loss of prestige, and her serious problems of internal disorder, made her of no immediate value to France as an ally.

This situation had much to do with the German Emperor's sudden claim to an interest in the affairs of Morocco on behalf of the rights of German merchants and traders. Through the months of 1905 the Morocco question continued among the foremost subjects in the European and American press and in the chancelleries of Europe. The Kaiser had sailed in his yacht to Tangier, and on March 31, 1905, he had made a spectacular landing and a theatrical declaration. He had denounced the agreement of 1904 (which had come later to his knowledge) between England and France, in terms of which the British government recognized French predominance in Morocco, while the French acknowledged English claims to superior influence in Egypt. The Kaiser demanded absolute independence for Morocco, and much diplomatic controversy followed. France was calm but unyielding, and the support of England was unshaken.

Bargaining at Algeciras and Agadir

President Roosevelt was credited with having used influence behind the scenes to lessen the tension and to promote the holding of a diplomatic conference of all the powers interested. It was not a stiff or formal offer of mediation on the part of the United States, but a personal approach, growing out of a remarkable interest that the German Emperor had shown in the striking qualities and career of Theodore Roosevelt. Referring to the untimely loss of a promising young man in New York who had taken up a political career under Colonel Roosevelt's auspices, the President once remarked to me, "Now that poor G——— is dead, the German Emperor is my most prolific correspondent!"

This personal relation between two public men who exchanged letters with frequency and in a friendly spirit, involved no official commitments on either side. There was a Venezuelan situation at that time in the outcome of which our government was credited with having asserted the Monroe Doctrine against the attempts of several European governments, notably Germany, to use their navies to collect private debts. The President and the Department of State secured acquiescence in their proposal of arbitration. The blockade of Venezuelan ports was lifted, and the episode ended in surprising complacency, on all sides. The happy adjustment of this menacing Venezuelan case had made it relatively easy for Mr. Roosevelt to use tact—without any pretense of intervening in European affairs—in helping forward the agreements that resulted in the conference on Moroccan affairs.

The Kaiser, who was exceedingly fond of sailing and had been much interested in international yacht-racing, had ordered the construction of an American sailing boat. It was ready for launching early in 1902. He had asked the President if Miss Alice Roosevelt would attend the launching as sponsor, and he had sent his brother Prince Henry with a retinue of prominent men including Admiral von Tirpitz to make the occasion a notable one. There were circumstances in this visit of a Hohenzollern prince that elicited much comment, in a courteous vein; but it is enough for me to quote only two sentences from my editorial remarks of March, 1902:

It is a somewhat curious fact, and certainly well worth noting, that the visit of Prince Henry to this country has been taken with profound seriousness by the whole of Europe, and has been characterized as the most important international event since the consummation of the Franco-Russian alliance. In this country, on the other hand, it has been taken with easy good-nature, in the spirit of friendly hospitality, and without the slightest implication of political meaning—except, as we explained last month, that the exercise of international hospitality always has the useful result of diminishing prejudice and mitigating the rivalries that to some extent are inevitable between stirring and ambitious modern nations.

The belief in foreign circles that this visit had under-currents of profound significance merely points to the fact that European governments were uneasy and apprehensive. The people of Europe did not want war; and they felt more confidence in the friendliness and goodwill of the United States than they felt in their neighbors. Thus, when the Algeciras conference plans were taking shape, all of the interested governments were glad to have the United States represented. They did not expect America to be present as an arbiter, but rather as helping to relieve the tension and make the atmosphere more agreeable.

The conference began its sessions at Algeciras in Spain on January 16, 1906, and at that time I presented the following editorial paragraphs in explanation of the circumstances:

Algeciras is a little Spanish town of some six or seven thousand inhabitants, just across the bay from Gibraltar. In this quiet little place (not at Madrid), there assembled a conference of diplomats to deliberate over questions of international policy—a conference which bids fair to make the Algeciras treaty as significant as that negotiated at Portsmouth, N. H., last summer. The much-discussed and long-postponed Morocco conference, called ostensibly to formulate and provide for the execution of certain reforms in the Moorish empire in North Africa, is really a test of strength between France and Germany, with the rest of Europe ranged directly or indirectly on either side.

Briefly, the Moroccan problem is as follows: Algeria, which borders Morocco on the east, is a colony of France, and the republic has had considerable trouble during recent years in keeping order along the boundary because of the unsettled condition of Morocco and the lawless character of its wild tribes. For some time France has been attempting to extend her influence into Morocco, primarily to maintain order in Algeria, and secondarily, to obtain trade. It will be remembered that, by the Anglo-French agreement of 1904, France promised to recognize England's exceptional position in Egypt in return for a similar recognition of her own exceptional position in Morocco, in which country she was to have a free hand to influence the Sultan toward reforms. Later, this agreement was strengthened and complemented by arrangements with Spain and Italy. According to an official Yellow Book just published by the French Government, M. Delcassé, then Foreign Minister of the republic, duly communicated the scope of these agreements to Germany. The German ambassador in Paris had shown a friendly disposition, and, even as late as the spring of 1904, had assured M. Delcassé that he found French declarations with regard to Morocco "quite sound and reasonable."

Soon afterward, however,—remarkably soon after the serious defeats of Russia by Japan in the Far East—the Berlin government showed signs of dissatisfaction in regard to Morocco. Then came the German Kaiser's visit to Tangier, and his dramatic speech to the German residents and some of the Sultan's officials, in which he asserted his intention to protect German commercial rights and the political integrity of Morocco. Following this came some months of active diplomatic correspondence between France and Germany, and of growing anxiety lest the relations between Paris and Berlin be strained to the point of actual war. On June 6, last, Minister Delcassé was forced to resign, actually (though indirectly) because of German pressure, the Berlin government not having forgiven him for bringing about the Anglo-French agreement.

In October the details of the French Foreign Minister's resignation, with some additions largely imaginary, were published by a Parisian newspaper, the *Matin*, creating a sensation, mainly because of their assertions that, in case of German provocation, the British Government would extend military support to France. Delcassé was succeeded by Rouvier, the present Foreign Minister, and, despite sensational reports of the mobilization of armies and fleets, both the French and German governments have insisted upon their pacific intentions, and agreed to leave to this international conference at Algeciras (called at the initiative of the German Emperor) the final settlement of the question as to who shall hold Morocco in "its sphere of influence."

All the great powers, including the United States, are represented at this conference, the American delegates being Mr. Henry White, our Ambassador to Italy, and Mr. Gummere, our minister to Morocco. Count von Tattenbach-Askold, German minister to Morocco, heads the German delegation; M. Paul Révoil, ex-Governor of Algiers and formerly French minister to Morocco, leads the French delegation; the Marquis Visconti Venosta, former Minister of Foreign Affairs, is at the head of the Italian members; Sir Arthur Nicolson heads the British delegation; while Morocco is represented by a large delegation, at the head of which is the venerable Mohammed El Torres, the Moroccan Minister of Foreign Affairs, who is over eighty years of age. There is one Austrian delegate, who represents also the Vatican, and who will present, on behalf of the Pope, a proposition for freedom of worship in Morocco. The representative of King Alfonso, the Duke of Almodovar, Spanish Minister of Foreign Affairs, was elected president of the conference.

The first subject coming up for discussion was the question of contraband trade in arms across the Algerian-Moroccan border and over-sea from France, Germany, and Spain. It may be said in general that Germany concedes the special position of France, and that both agree to and contend for the "open door" in commerce. It is simply a question of who shall be permitted to police the country: France because of the nearness of her Algerian colony, which is the French contention, supported by England, Italy, and Spain; or an international gendarmerie, which is the German contention, supported by Austria and some of the smaller European nations. A reorganization of Moroccan finances is also a question which will come up for settlement. The conference opens with many protestations of peaceful intentions on the part of all participating.

Passing over our comments and reports of progress (or deadlock) in March and April, I find a hopeful summary of results at Algeciras in the issue for May, the conference having been in session for three months. It had reached conclusions, and had adopted agreements providing plans that were to be given a trial for a period of five years. It will be noted that it was my habit to discuss all matters of this kind from the standpoint of their bearing upon the American desire for the adjustment of differences by arbitration or by conference and agreement:

Undoubtedly there was behind the scenes deep apprehension throughout Europe lest the differences of opinion between Germany and France, as shown in the tedious delays of the Algeciras conference, might lead to a war the consequences of which would have been unspeakably calamitous. But, happily, wise counsels at length prevailed, and the outcome of the conference has left Germany and France on better terms than at any time within a generation. The French feel that they have not lost the opportunity to develop what they regard as their rightful policy in North Africa, and the Germans feel that they have made secure for themselves and for other nations certain commercial advantages which might have been forfeited in the ultimate absorption of Morocco by France.

It is the opinion throughout Europe that the presence of the delegates of the United States in the conference was helpful, and that the conduct of these delegates was at all points wise and judicious. However slight may have been the real danger of a war growing out of the Morocco dispute, it is an unquestionable fact that there was anxiety and dread in the hearts of millions of people who longed for peace beyond almost anything else whatsoever.

Thus, the amicable and sensible conclusions reached at Algeciras are to be set down as a boon to mankind and a notable historical achievement. Each like result helps the cause of permanent peace and makes easier the solving of future difficulties by similar methods. While our American participation at Algeciras was of slight consequence when compared with the part we took in the bringing about of peace between Russia and Japan, it is considered in Europe that we are to be congratulated upon having rendered material assistance in making good feeling and bringing harmony out of threatened discord.

The five-year period that followed the Algeciras conference was not one of political tranquillity, whether in the domestic affairs of countries and regions or in the field of diplomacy and international relations. Russia was making every effort to restore order, and was entering upon a program of rearmament, hoping to regain prestige and self-confidence after the disasters of her war with Japan. Both France and Germany were strengthening their military machinery. The tone of the Wilhelmstrasse Foreign Office grew more assertive. There were troubles in the Balkans, and further signs that the old order in the Ottoman Empire was disintegrating.

As regards the ambitious projects that were taking form in the minds of leaders who surrounded the Kaiser, Morocco continued to be a key point. It might be used to challenge the British stronghold at Gibraltar. Its harbors might shelter naval expeditions to Brazil. France and England had been extending their colonies or protectorates at great speed across immense areas of Africa, and this was looked upon with ill-concealed covetousness at Berlin. At the end of the five-year Morocco experiment Germany was ready with another surprise. I shall quote a part of my report upon that incident from my comments for August, 1911. Germany did not wait for the completion of the fifth year. Without serving notice of her unwillingness to renew the agreement for another term, she chose to act first and explain afterwards:

The agreement reached by the great powers of Europe at the conference of Algeciras in 1906 for the settlement of all disputed matters in Morocco was to continue for five years. That period expires on the last day of 1911. It was the protest of Germany against the Anglo-French Convention of 1904 regarding Morocco, which brought about the Algeciras conference. Again it is Germany, which, by a bold move, proclaims to the world her dissatisfaction with the workings of the present agreement, and indicates her intention of having a better share in any understanding that may be reached to supplement the Algeciras convention.

On the first day of last month, the German Foreign Office made an announcement that startled the world. On account of the fear of German merchants in southern Morocco, said the statement, that the present disorders among the tribesmen would spread, the German warship *Panther* had been ordered to Agadir, a port on the Atlantic coast of Morocco. The principal powers which agreed at Algeciras (France, Great Britain, Spain and Russia), as well as Morocco, were informed that the appearance of the warship had no unfriendly significance. Its presence at Agadir, moreover, was to be only temporary.

As was to be expected, this move on the part of Germany aroused French sensibilities to a high pitch, and caused a good deal of popular discussion in Great Britain as well. The continental stock markets became excited and war was freely discussed. President Fallières, at the time the announcement was made, was on an official visit to the Netherlands. Premier Caillaux, who had only a few days before succeeded M. Monis, at once opened diplomatic correspondence with Herr von Schoen, the German Ambassador at Paris, and M. de Selves, the new French Minister of Foreign Affairs, instructed M. Cambon, the French Ambassador at Berlin, to declare to the German Government that France could not conceal her surprise and regret at the action of Germany.

Without exaggerating the gravity of affairs, the Foreign Minister instructed Ambassador Cambon to point out that the manner chosen by the imperial German Government to manifest its anxiety for German interests in Morocco was likely to seem very strange to French opinion. Particularly, in view of the fact that a new ministry was then taking office in France, and the President had departed on a foreign tour, this action by Germany, "while certainly not of a nature to create a grave situation, is, nevertheless, hardly in conformity with the intention of the two powers (France and Germany) as enunciated in the agreement of 1909, to treat each other with mutual cordiality."

The French press remained calm, but, without exception, urged the government to hold the situation with a firm hand. Intense public interest was manifested in England. Replying to a question by Mr. Balfour, in the House of Commons, in regard to Morocco and the attitude the British Government intended to take in view of the Anglo-French understanding, Premier Asquith said, on July 6:

"I can say little at this stage, but wish it to be clearly understood that the government considers that a new situation has arisen in Morocco in which it is possible that future developments may affect British interests more directly than has hitherto been the case. We are confident that the diplomatic discussion will find a solution, and in the part which we will take in it we shall have due regard for the protection of those interests and the fulfilment of our treaty obligations to France."

The smooth phrases of diplomacy were maintained, but in practical effect France was asking, "What do you want?" and Germany was answering, "What have you to offer?" The small German gunboat *Panther* was replaced by a first-class cruiser at

Agadir. Then a French warship was ordered to that port, while both France and Germany were giving pleasant assurances to the world. They declared that they would soon begin a series of "conversations," with a view to "settling definitely the status of the Arab empire, which, standing at the gateway of Europe, has been constantly regarded as a possible cause of international difficulties." No conference was held, but Spain, England, and Russia were invited to listen in, while the conversations were taking place.

Undoubtedly Germany had some intention of remaining permanently at Agadir. That port lies many hundreds of miles south of Gibraltar and the Straits; and if Germany could have acquired control of it by some bullying, with face-covering compensations, it would have been developed into a powerful naval station. The firmness of France and England, supported at that time by Spain and also by Russia, found Germany unable to gain her point by diplomacy; and she lacked sufficient excuse to precipitate a war. Thus it happened that the French Protectorate was extended and confirmed, assuming virtually the same character as that of Tunisia.

Germany as the price of her acquiescence accepted from France a fraction of the desert territory known as the French Congo or Equatorial Africa. She had demanded much more than she received, but accepted what she could get and annexed it to her West African protectorate known as the Cameroons. Thus the Germans were eliminated from the Moroccan situation, although doubtless they had begun to think of acquiring colonies by war rather than by diplomacy, and expected sooner or later to dominate North Africa and the Mediterranean.

The French were superior administrators, although they had no reserve of colonizing population. They were soon made uncomfortable by the Spanish claims in northern Morocco, and in later years they were to observe the emergence of General Franco's army, that was to make war upon the liberal government of Spain.

Thus a series of wars has again stirred up a hornet's nest of African problems. These can be dealt with only through some form of international organization, strong enough to supervise the economic and social development of African territories and peoples, and possessing authority enough to exclude imperial rivalries and adventures.

Egypt and Suez in Retrospect

In the year following my preparation of the paper on "Internationalism" that is reproduced in the preceding chapter, I was on duty as an editorial writer in the West; and I find in a scrapbook two articles that I wrote in July, 1883, soon after the British intervention in Egypt.

The use of force, on the part of a powerful government with almost unlimited naval strength at its command, to restore order in some smaller country where chaotic conditions prevail, can be justified only by disclosure of good motives and by results of unquestionable value. Of that character was the intervention on the part of the United States to liberate the people of Cuba in the year 1898. The editorial that I am about to quote was written fifteen years earlier than our Cuban adventure, and was concerned with the policy of the British Government under the Liberal administration of Mr. Gladstone in 1882, when intolerable conditions in Egypt seemed to justify European action. For reasons that were well understood at the time, the French government was indisposed to act with the British in a joint effort on behalf of the persecuted Egyptian people.

Six years after I wrote the editorial praising Mr. Gladstone for dealing by summary action with a state of affairs that could not be remedied by speech-making or diplomacy, I was travelling in Egypt and making note of the improved conditions that had resulted from a system of honest taxation and local security, in the villages of the Nile Valley. I was also enabled to observe the satisfactory administration of the Suez Canal, with its impartial treatment of merchant ships under all national flags. The first editorial, which follows herewith, was entitled "Universal Suffrage in Egypt."

Perhaps, however, to make my object clear beyond any possible confusion, I should explain that the information thus summarized by me sixty years ago in the *Minneapolis Tribune* was not of transient importance. There have been changes in the higher government of Egypt in accord with the popular demand for national independence. But the fundamental character of Egypt's political system was established in that Constitution of 1883, which provided for representation by village units.

The British Government was well advised when after the first

World War, Egypt having been utilized as the British base of operations in the Middle East, it abandoned the proposal to administer that country as a part of the British Empire. The independence of Egypt, with a liberal constitution under a parliamentary system, was confirmed, with British good-will. The system of local freedom and justice throughout the Nile Valley remains, however, as it was established under the benevolent auspices of Mr. Gladstone. It is from the groundwork of simple and familiar but permanent reforms of this kind in times past that future stability is to derive much of its assurance. There are other regions where the Egyptian pattern can be applied, with ready adaptation to local or tribal customs.

My editorial, entitled "Universal Suffrage in Egypt," appeared in July, 1883, and I reproduce it herewith:

The latest nation receiving the blessings of a constitutional government is the ancient land of the pyramids. For centuries the down-trodden Egyptian peasantry—the Fellaheen—have been practically the slaves of an arbitrary and despotic oriental government. Taxation has been robbery, and the people, those who toil and produce, have had no rights, no education, barely a subsistence. The storming of Alexandria [1882] raised a loud cry against the aggressive policy of England, and the conscientious Mr. Bright was obliged to leave the cabinet of a government that interfered and meddled everywhere; but already Mr. Gladstone's government has been enabled to make the Egyptian nation a present of one of the most enlightened, discreet, and liberal constitutions of modern times.

From the cruel and rapacious government of a Mohammedan prince to government by constitutional forms and elective machinery is a long distance. No people can make the change by a single stride. First, there must be restraints placed on the arbitrary sovereign; second, there must be the gradual development of self-governing power in the people. For some years the first of these forces had been in operation. England and France had placed many restraints upon the Khedive, and had, as it were, stood between the people and their insatiate rulers. Now the second force is in operation. The new constitution will be the instrument by which the people will be taught to use political power.

The constitution is grafted ingeniously and wisely on existing institutions. The Khedive remains, and nominally retains most of his authority. But the existence of a legislative council and a general assembly practically limits the Khedive and his ministers in the management of national affairs; and the erection of provincial assemblies will restrain the oppressive rule of the Khedive's officers in the various localities of the realm.

The agency of the people is indirect. Until they have become more accustomed to the exercise of power, and better enabled by education and improved material conditions to take large part in government, their influence must remain comparatively limited. For the present they are represented in the following way:

Egypt has some 6000 villages. Every Egyptian is connected with a village. Every male Egyptian above the age of 20 votes for an "elector delegate" from his village. The peasantry will invariably vote for some prominent and competent person in whom they have confidence. They are said to be shrewd judges of character, and therefore perfectly qualified to choose this delegate. Egypt has fourteen provinces, each containing several hundred villages. The "electors-delegate," one representing each village, choose the members of the provincial assembly. Each provincial assembly chooses one member of the national legislative council, which is a small body. The village electors-delegate also choose from each province two or three members of the national general assembly. The Khedive, his ministers, and the legislative council, are all included in the make-up of the general assembly. The legislative council must meet as often as once in two months, and the general assembly must be called by the Khedive at least each alternate year. This latter body has special authority to act in respect to proposed changes in tax laws, national loans, railroad and canal grants, and questions which affect the public purse. The constitution is sufficiently elastic to admit of constantly enlarged grants of power to the people so fast as they become ready for its exercise.

England had a grand opportunity, and she has improved it. Instead of using her power over prostrate Egypt for annexation or selfish purposes of gain alone, she has used her irresistible influence to oblige the Khedive to give his people a free government. Egypt will have a slow and toilful road to enlightenment and strength, but there is hope for her. In the patient and industrious Fellaheen there is the material from which to build up a solid, vigorous people.

The reader of the second editorial of July, 1883, to which I have alluded, will discover that in my ardent youth I was strongly Gladstonian and Liberal in my political sympathies, as I followed the course of British affairs. But this was true of Americans of all parties at that time. We regarded Mr. Gladstone as the foremost statesman of the nineteenth century, because he set an example of good conscience and high moral purpose in public policies. The Suez Canal, which had been built by a French company under an Egyptian charter, had become so vital to British commerce that certain imperial elements were urging its seizure.

In times of great emergency, as in both world wars, there has been no question about the unhampered and vigilant guardianship of the British at Suez. But the principles that Mr. Gladstone established have never since been disregarded. The international character of the Canal has been maintained, and ships under all flags have received fair and equal treatment. The editorial that follows herewith was entitled "International Sunday-School Politics," this having reference to the sneers of Mr. Gladstone's opponents, who found his moral scruples opposed to their views of imperial expansion. The doctrines of the great Liberal leader seem to have foreshadowed those of the so-called "Atlantic Charter." When Mr. Gladstone in the early Eighties gave the Egyptians their representative system of government, and confirmed the international character of the Suez Canal, he was making permanent history. Such achievements will stand the shock of world wars because they are at once magnanimous in spirit and practical in their detailed applications. Herewith follows my article of July, 1883, on the Gladstonian treatment of the Suez question:

If an old-line British statesman or diplomat could have come back to life and appeared in Downing Street, he would have been surprised and shocked at what was going on the other day. The decay of a "bold" foreign policy, the decline in the science and art of diplomacy, the prevalence of a "tame," open, honest habit of dealing with foreign countries, the desire to respect obligations, the admission that other powers—even weak ones—have rights, the disposition to international morality and equity; all these things would have troubled the ancient politician's soul, and would have seemed the marks of his country's decadence and humiliation. The change which he would find has come about very gradually, but it is real. Relatively speaking, this is an era of Sunday-School politics in international affairs.

The other day the British ministry invited a Frenchman, Ferdinand De Lesseps, to cross the channel and talk over Suez Canal business with them. De Lesseps is the brilliant engineer who projected the canal, made the surveys, organized a company of capitalists, got a concession from the Egyptian government, raised the money, took the risk, gave the world the Suez Canal, and is president of the company. Just about the time, after years of risk and labor, that the canal was completed, England found out there was something in it. Trade with India and China began to discover the new and short road. England became the great user of the canal. She sent more than ten times as many ships through it as any other nation.

In fact she has been using it three times as much as all the rest of the world put together. It became greatly to her interest to control it, as the key to her Indian empire. Gibraltar, Malta, Cyprus secured the freedom of the Mediterranean, and the control of the canal would have added the most important link of all to her imperial chain. But the canal belonged to a French company to whom Egypt had guaranteed exclusive rights.

England's opportunity came. Arabi's revolt and the Khedive's helplessness gave her the right, and under the circumstances made it her duty, to invade Egypt and reorganize the government. Her complete success made it possible for her to have annexed Egypt to the empire, deposed the Khedive and assumed absolute control of the canal. Her paramount commercial interests seemed to many to justify her in such a policy. But she voluntarily relinquished it. She gave the Egyptian people a wise constitution, and while remaining the sponsor, ally and friend of Egypt, refused to be guilty of any usurpation. This was Sunday-School politics of a sort to prove that the world grows better.

International commercial interests are at present demanding an increase of facilities which can best be met by the cutting of a parallel canal. It was with reference to this that De Lesseps visited Gladstone; and here we have another startling exhibition of Sunday-School politics. The Suez Canal is a monopoly. Tolls are rather high, business is immense, and dividends have been exceedingly cheerful for the stockholders. When there is a really good paying thing, John Bull wants it; and English commercial men have been wanting to dig the new canal themselves, regulate their own tolls and pocket the profits. This is natural enough, for these Englishmen furnish most of the canal traffic and they hate to pay toll to a Frenchman. Moreover, relations between England and France are in a strained condition, owing to French aggression in Madagascar.

Under the circumstances it would have been very easy for Mr. Gladstone's government to find pretexts justifying England in digging a new canal of her own or getting practical control of the present one. But right here Mr. Gladstone's moral principles came in the way. As he and his ministry understand it, Egypt had given the Lesseps company exclusive canal rights; and England's present position as ally of Egypt made it morally obligatory upon the former to help maintain the latter's contracts rather than to violate them. This looks plain and honest, but it arouses great indignation among the surviving friends of the late Lord Beaconsfield, who liked to have the British lion roar and shake his mane. It also greatly irritates the commercial interests.

The newly-made bargain with De Lesseps is simply a business matter, with no politics in it at all. The English government agrees to loan the canal company a large sum of money at 3½ per cent, with which to construct the canal. The company on its part will reduce tolls and further accommodate British vessels by increase of facilities. The bargain looks fair and advantageous to both parties. In 1875 England bought the Khedive's stock in the canal, and therefore, as a very large stockholder, England will share in whatever prosperity the company may have. It is true the company has a good thing; but Gladstone is right in holding that England has no business to gobble it up so long as it is managed impartially.

The canal company is entirely outside of politics, and should be kept so. The time is not far distant when inter-oceanic canals will be neutral, international highways, their use regulated by an international code of rules. Everything points to this conclusion. The Suez Canal is practically assuming this status. As a financial enterprise, it may appropriately remain in the hands of the private corporation which built it; but Europe will soon decide that no power shall use it for purposes of military or political advantage.

This is the growing sentiment of Europe, and Mr. Gladstone has recognized it in his amicable bargain with De Lesseps. There is great danger lest a parliamentary coalition of Tories, Irish obstructionists, and Liberals representing commercial constituencies, may defeat the bargain and overthrow the ministry on the strength of it; but it is certainly to be hoped that such a calamity may be averted. England can afford, in the interest of international equity, courtesy and progress, to forego the opportunity of getting a fat thing by a dishonorable policy.

I am not attempting to set down even in bare outline the full story of Anglo-Egyptian relations since the historic adjustments of the first Gladstonian intervention. The further course of British cooperation in the Nile Valley led inevitably to a second intervention, and one on a much larger scale.

THE ANGLO-EGYPTIAN SUDAN—A HALF-CENTURY TEST

The word Sudan applies to a vast African area stretching across the continent south of the Sahara, and including French West Africa which is one of the largest colonial areas in the world. My present remarks, however, relate to the region south of Egypt, formerly known as the Egyptian Sudan. Arabized tribes under the Mahdi Mohammed had broken away from Egypt in the early Eighties, and the region had sunk into chaotic social conditions.

The control of the Upper Nile Valley seemed essential to the welfare and safety of Egypt. Efforts to reconquer this important area had failed until General Kitchener completed the task in

1898. Since that time, the region has been known as the Anglo-Egyptian Sudan, and it has been under the joint sovereignty of the two countries. The administration of the Sudan, centering in a Governor-General at Khartoum, so distributes the functions of government as to graft European principles of justice upon local and tribal customs.

The reconquest accomplished in 1898, after two years of a carefully planned campaign, was resisted by fanatical hordes of tribesmen led by the so-called "Mad Mullah," and resulted in great loss of life at the battle of Omdurman. But there followed that battle a reign of peace; and good order has prevailed, with improved health conditions, village schools for the children, and economic prosperity continuing and expanding, now for almost half a century.

The pages that follow herewith are quoted from comments of mine published in October, 1898, and January, 1899. Since I was endeavoring to write of current events in the spirit of historical interpretation, I am now republishing my contemporary comments because they dealt with a settlement that has long since been justified by its results. An armed intervention that a doubting world at first regarded with outspoken disapproval, was soon recognized as making for stability, for freedom and for human welfare, in an important area of the African continent.

The great attempt of the Anglo-Egyptian troops, under command of Sir Herbert Kitchener, to move an army from Cairo up the Nile to the capital of the revolted Soudan provinces has been crowned with complete success. The battle of Atbara on April 8, [1898]—a battle in which many thousands of the Khalifa's men were slain—marked the beginning of the last stage of an expedition that had been on the move for about two years. The remaining march to Khartoum had simply to wait for the proper condition of the Nile from the point of view of the gunboats accompanying the expedition.

Omdurman, it should be understood, is the new capital of the Soudan, built by the Mahdi after his seizure and destruction of Khartoum in 1885, at which time General Gordon was killed. Omdurman had grown to be a much larger town than Khartoum ever was, but its buildings were far less substantial. As General Kitchener's expedition of 25,000 men, mostly native Egyptian troops, approached its final objective at Omdurman, the Khalifa's army rashly but bravely came forth to meet the enemy. Machine guns played a large part in the fearful massacre of the brave Dervish fighters. The British losses were, comparatively, only a little handful of men. The first reports were to the effect that 5,000 of the Khalifa's men were left dead on the field, while subsequent reports made the number very much greater, some estimates going up almost to 20,000.

The fanatical movement of the early '80's, led by the Mahdi, had resulted in the absolute closing up of one of the most promising and prosperous regions of the whole African continent, a region occupied at that time by not less than 12,000,000 people. Mahdism had desolated the Soudan; agriculture and trade had been destroyed; the population had been reduced about one-half—and the fire of fanaticism had at length burned itself out. If the result of the victory of the United States over Spain shall have resulted in the material improvement of the condition of 8,000,000 people in the Philippines and 2,000,000 or more in the West Indies, it is to be remembered that this splendidly managed expedition of General Kitchener will have brought even greater succor and blessing to the millions of human beings in the eastern Soudan.

To declare, in the language of the German Emperor's dispatch, that the victory at Omdurman "at last avenges poor Gordon" is to take altogether the wrong tone. Englishmen can afford to be superior to the spirit of revenge in dealing with African problems. We prefer to regard General Kitchener's expedition not as a war of revenge, but as a practical manifestation of the spirit of peace and good-will toward men—a constructive task in the interests of humanity and civilization.

It will not do us any harm in the United States to understand how systematic was every feature of this expedition. The care of the troops and the working out of difficult problems of supply constituted the real triumph of General Kitchener's management. In justice to ourselves, on the other hand, it must be remembered that former British expeditions have been fraught with disaster, and that the perfect organization of this latest one grew out of much sad and bitter experience. General Kitchener had a free hand in organizing the expedition; and although we are told that a great deal of social and political pressure was exerted by various people who wanted commissions or some other sort of honorable or profitable connection with the affair, all such pressure was sternly resisted and every man chosen on his strict personal merits.

It is wonderful how a bit of well-earned success sometimes clears the atmosphere, and how fair-weather friends at once come crowding about with their congratulations. It had been seriously feared in the earlier stages of General Kitchener's expedition that the French were proposing to cut across from their holdings in the western Soudan to a point on the Nile above Khartoum, at or about Fashoda, for the sake of preventing the English from going any further. The seriousness of such a proposition can only be understood when one remembers the peculiar nature of the

Nile. If the French were in full possession even at so remote a point as Fashoda, they could at any time they chose so divert the water as to ruin the whole of Egypt, which owes its life to the periodical overflow and to irrigation.

The French, however, have now quite disclaimed any intention to regard the Fashoda expedition as anything else except a private exploring party, and there is no disposition in any quarter to oppose the still further advance of the English. With Khartoum as a headquarters, General Kitchener will readily make his authority felt in every outlying direction. The French press has spoken in high terms of the expedition, the Germans have assumed a wholly congratulatory tone, and, in short, Kitchener's success gives the touch of prestige that was needed to assure once and for all the entire British programme in the African continent.

It is true that Mr. Cecil Rhodes, though elected himself, has failed to secure a progressive majority in the Cape Colony Parliament. Nevertheless, the Cape Colony elections have been so heavily counterbalanced by the brilliant achievement of Sir Herbert Kitchener, and by the Anglo-German agreement about the control of Delagoa Bay, that nothing can now prevent the very rapid carrying out of Mr. Cecil Rhodes' great project of a through railroad from Cape Town to Cairo.

Three months later, in an editorial survey at the beginning of the year 1899, I referred again to the conquest of the Egyptian Soudan in its broader bearings, as follows:

Everybody in England expects that General Kitchener, by virtue of the attainments and qualities he has exhibited in his successful reconquest of the Soudan, will be allowed an almost unrestricted hand in the great work of reorganizing the country, creating for it systems of police, finance, and justice, and a full scheme of civil and governmental institutions. What General Kitchener will do with this magnificent opportunity will be one of the things worth living to observe, through this auspicious new year 1899. The people of Great Britain will be highly interested in General Kitchener's work in the Soudan, but it will scarcely occur to any of them that he is not competent to do it unless he has the assistance of Parliament at every point.

The status of England in Egypt and the Soudan is one that cannot be explained under the forms or terms of international law. Egypt is a quasi-independent state, owing nominal allegiance to the Turkish Sultan, through whose government at Constantinople its international affairs are, in theory at least, conducted. Those parts of the great Soudan that have now been recovered by General Kitchener, were formerly known as the Equatorial Provinces of Egypt.

General Kitchener's expedition has been prosecuted in his capacity as Sirdar—that is to say, commander-in-chief—of the forces of Egypt. He holds no official position under the British Government, whether civil or military. He was formerly an engineer in the British Army, but has for some years served the Khedive of Egypt in a capacity which makes him the chief military official of the Egyptian Government, subject to the Khedive and the Khedive's minister of war.

The funds for the expedition have been provided chiefly out of the Egyptian treasury. Where, then, does England come in, and why are the British pluming themselves so highly upon their great victory at Omdurman? In order to get rid of the anomaly, a great many people in England would be glad if legal fictions were abandoned, the transparent mask thrown off, and the whole of the country tributary to the Nile boldly declared to be a part of the British Empire. But at present the English Government thinks it better to make sure of the substance and pay little attention to the shadow. British withdrawal would be cruelty to the people of Egypt and advantageous to no legitimate interests. On the other hand, to annex Egypt as France has annexed Madagascar would stir up a great pool of bitterness and wrath. And so England holds to the *status quo* and does not bother about definitions.

It is not to be expected that the people of the United States could put up with so anomalous a condition. Our eagerness to push things to logical conclusions is not so great temperamentally as is that of the French, but we have so long lived under paper constitutions that it distresses us to be unable to classify relationships and to show that all things are in conformity with prescribed plans.

The foregoing passages were written by me forty-five years ago, and I then declared that foundations were well laid for political stability in the regions drained by the Nile. In almost half a century so many changes have occurred that it is reasonable to inquire whether those interventions of the British, during the two last decades of the nineteenth century, have left any permanent results. I am sure that any honest and intelligent answer would be in an affirmative tone.

When Sir Evelyn Baring (the First Earl Cromer) resigned in 1907, after a long period of residence in Egypt as plenipoteniary representative of Great Britain, he was called the "Maker of modern Egypt," and he published volumes that justified the appellation. The British had done a good job, to use current language. Cromer did not live to see the end of the First World War, but died in 1917.

Meanwhile, Egypt had served as British headquarters for campaigns throughout the Middle East, in consequence of which changes of great moment have occurred in the Arabic world. Lord Cromer would probably have advised against the attempt of Great Britain to annex Egypt after the lapse of the Turkish suzerainty. Since, however, the Egyptians objected so strenuously, declaring that they had been promised their complete independence, their feelings were respected and their independent sovereignty was recognized by Great Britain in 1922.

The new Egyptian regime was ambitious, and naturally it claimed too much at the outset. It had to prove its efficiency and its capacity for administration before taking over complete control of the Sudan. The English would not give up their interest in the region that Kitchener had redeemed from savagery and transformed by means of good government and modern agricultural methods. The British had made large investments in the Sudan, and had built dams and irrigation works. Their cotton-fields were made productive by the flow of water in the Blue Nile, which in turn is made secure by the control of Lake Tsana. This considerable body of water is in Ethiopia, but it is essential to the prosperity of the Anglo-Egyptian Sudan because it is the source from which the Blue Nile emerges and makes its way northward across the border.

While the League of Nations was putting pressure upon Italy, and employing "economic sanctions" in condemnation of Mussolini's expeditionary war to conquer Ethiopia, the British were accused of carrying on secret negotiations with the Italian government. They were in fear lest the waters of Lake Tsana should be diverted to irrigation projects within Ethiopian territory. It was an embarrassing situation, illustrating the importance of the first of Woodrow Wilson's Fourteen Points, that which calls for open diplomacy. But the underlying difficulty was not one of diplomacy but of shameless aggression.

Italy has now lost its ill-gained African empire, and Haile Selassie, King of Kings, is restored to his throne of fabled antiquity. If the League of Nations had been formed on a plan that gave it direct authority, Italy would not have marched up the barren hills of Ethiopia only to march down again in humiliation and complete loss. Nor would an English statesman have been compromised in his endeavor to protect lawful economic interests in the Sudan.

Finally, the ruler over a venerable African kingdom whose independence had been duly acknowledged by European powers, and whose government had been admitted to membership in the League of Nations in 1923, would have been upheld, and aided in many ways to improve the internal conditions of his domain of 350,000 square miles. The League of Nations knew what ought to be done, and made some salutary gestures. The story of the rise and fall of Mussolini's African empire affords an excellent illustration of the need of a powerful world organization, having authority—among other things—to supervise the development of the Dark Continent for the protection of just interests and, above all, for the defense of native populations against slave-drivers, internal disorders, epidemics, and European exploitation.

Chapter IX

WE CONSIDER GREECE, SYRIA, PALESTINE, AND THE NEAR-EAST PATTERN

The position of the Greek race, after its achievement of independence more than a hundred years ago, illustrates the need of a firm and strong society of nations. Greece has been a victim not only of local wars but also of the strategic operations of two world wars. In this chapter there is an account of the war of 1897, when the Greeks attempted to rescue their compatriots in Crete from Turkish oppression. They were defeated, and the great powers of Europe intervened in a half-negligent fashion to protect Greece from impossible war indemnities.

The expulsion of Greeks from their homes in Asia Minor in 1923, where they had been domiciled long before the Turks had established themselves in Anatolia, added a large new element of population to Athens, Salonika and the farmlands of Macedonia. This evacuation of Asia Minor was a hardship, but it brought a desirable element of new population to the ancient Greek homeland. The migration was assisted by the United States Navy and by the American organization known as Near East Relief. A few years later, Turkey and Bulgaria cooperated in an exchange of populations with Greece, supervised by an American, the Hon. Henry Morgenthau, former Ambassador at Constantinople.

Greece was adjusting itself to these new conditions with remarkable energy and good-will. There was peace with the neighbors, and notable educational and agricultural progress. There was new consciousness of the ancient glory of Greece, and determination to fit worthily into the life of the modern world.

Then came the dastardly attack of Italy following the lawless seizure of Albania. Greek resistance was heroic and it won the admiration of the world.

Germany came to the support of Italy with superiority of air force, and British efforts to relieve the Greeks both on mainland and in Crete were gallant and memorable, though unavailing.

German occupation resulted in frightful deprivations and almost unbelievable loss of life through starvation. Turkish initiative opened the way for civilian food relief; and the neighborliness shown by the authorities of the Turkish Republic gives promise of a wholly new condition in the Near East, when the United Nations clear the enemy from the lands around the Mediterranean.

This chapter endeavors to show that "good deeds will never die." It recites the story of Corfu and the Ionian Islands, and their return to Greece in 1864. It upholds the view that the Bosphorus and Dardanelles will become fully internationalized, with Constantinople a hospitable center of United-Nations activity. It ends with a discussion of the Syrian mandate held by France, and the Palestine mandate under authorized British administration. It attempts to show how these entities will fit into the intelligible pattern of a world that has hitherto looked like a jig-saw puzzle. A United Nations oversight, evolving into a form of collective world control, will give security to all these Mediterranean and Near East situations.

IF THE United Nations carry the second World War through to the fulfillment of the purposes they have avowed, the people of Greece—in their European Peninsula and in their neighboring islands—will have such security and such assurance of stable conditions as they have never known in ten or perhaps twenty centuries. They experienced a renaissance in the war (1820–32) that gave them Independence, after five hundred years of Turkish over-rule and oppression. But the Turks, continuing to rule their empire from Constantinople, were dangerous neighbors on the Eastern border of Greece, and were clinging tenaciously to important Greek islands, especially Crete.

Toward the end of the century there were Greek uprisings in Crete and massacres in reprisal. A war to relieve and rescue the Cretan people resulted disastrously for the Greek kingdom. As for the attitude of Europe, it is sufficient to remark that the great powers, having keen rivalries of their own, were treating Greece as an inconvenient and upstart stepchild. They were showing a kind of deference to the Sultan that was not creditable to the policies of collective Christendom. Nevertheless, the Powers had the grace to intervene and save Greece from the extreme exactions that the victorious Turks had imposed.

The more recent history of Greece is familiar, and leading facts will be readily recalled. After the Balkan struggles that preceded the first World War, Crete was at last transferred to Greece, Turkey (in 1913) having relinquished her sovereignty by the Treaty of London after a Mohammedan occupation of more than a thousand years.

The quality of Greek patriotism could never be doubted after the gallant defense that drove back the invading Italians in 1940. British aid was not sufficient to stem the ensuing German invasion; and the sufferings of the Greek people under Nazi occupation might have exterminated a less resilient and courageous people.

In the larger view, however, the Greek position is clarified as never before in the eyes of all people who love justice throughout the world. If other nations gain freedom, and the right to order their own lives without aggressive and cruel interference, the Greeks will assuredly share those benefits of victory. Greece will not henceforth be the victim of mysterious moves on the checker-board of European politics. The small states are no longer to be mere pawns in a game of balance.

In that war of 1897 for the liberation of Crete, the Greeks might have won but for the vacillation of the royal family, connected as it was by close relationships with the reigning dynasties of Germany, Russia, and Denmark, not to mention others. I will reproduce some paragraphs from a contemporary summary of mine, that had at least the merit of a narrative written with the facts fresh in memory. It appeared in the summer of 1897, and I begin my quotation (without describing earlier battles) at the point where the Greeks were defeated, beyond further power of resistance, and knew they must accept results and obtain the best terms that they could. The passage is quoted from the *Review of Reviews* for the month of June, 1897:

M. Ralli's government appealed to the powers to intervene and asked for an armistice. The powers agreed to use their influence with Turkey to bring the war to an end, on condition that the Greeks would withdraw from Crete and accept such terms as the powers might be able and willing to arrange. To these conditions the Greek government gave its prompt assent. The brave Colonel Vassos gathered his troops together thereupon, and withdrew from Crete. This ought to have been the end of bloodshed.

But the Turkish government—somewhat intoxicated by its victories, and urged on by the fanatical "Old Turk" party, which for the time being had the ear of the Sultan—kept Edhem hammering away, and evidently proposed to march straight to Athens. Turkey allowed it to be known that she would grant peace to the Greeks on condition that the great northern province of Thessaly should be ceded to Turkey, that a war indemnity amounting to forty or fifty millions of dollars should be paid, that the Greek fleet should be turned over to Turkey to hold while the indemnity remained owing, and that among other concessions the Greeks should no longer have in the Turkish Empire the status under the so-called "capitulations" which the citizens of all other nations enjoy—such privileges, for instance, as those that entitle Europeans to the benefit of their own consular courts. These demands were obviously preposterous. Nevertheless, the European powers went about their task of arguing with Turkey in the most leisurely fashion, while the Turks kept up the fighting with great loss of life and destruction of resources on both sides.

At length on the 17th of May a great and destructive battle was fought at Domokos, in which about fifty thousand Turks, at the cost of great slaughter, stormed and took the well-fortified positions of an army of perhaps thirty thousand Greeks, driving the Hellenic forces back toward Lamia and the pass of Thermopylae. Whereupon Russia concluded that the war had gone far enough, and called upon the Turks to halt. The Sultan was informed that, under the influence and advice of Russia, the Bulgarian army would be immediately mobilized against Turkey. Then it was that the government of the Sultan saw a new light and telegraphed to Edhem Pasha to cease hostilities; and thus the war seems to have come to an end.

The Turkish government had presumed too much upon the seeming friendliness and encouragement of the great powers. Their apparent hostility to the Greeks was due, in no sense, to a preference for the Turks. It was merely to give emphasis to their disapproval of the campaign, and their determination to prevent any shifting of relative advantages among the Balkan states. It was not the purpose of the great powers that Turkey should gain any Grecian territory, nor was it the will of Europe that the Turks should exact an impossible indemnity.

Nevertheless, this war will have had the effect of putting a new spirit of hope and fervor into the whole Mohammedan world, and will probably retard considerably the process of disintegration in the Turkish Empire that must some day in any case work out its logical results.

On the other hand, the war has made a military people out of the Greeks. As a nation they have conducted themselves with heroism, and they are entitled to high credit. Their modern career, far from being ended, is only beginning. The New York *Tribune* of the 20th of May [1897] accurately stated the facts concerning the Greek population in the following sentences:

"There are five million or six million Greeks in the Ottoman Empire. They form nearly one-third of the population of Constantinople itself. They form a majority of the population of Chalcis, of the Aegean coast of Thrace, of the European coast of the Sea of Marmora, of the Black Sea coast from the Bosphorus to Varna, and of Smyrna and the whole western coast of Asia Minor, while they form nearly all the population of the islands from Samothrace to Rhodes."

The Greeks are anything but a declining race. They are the rich and prosperous men of Alexandria, Smyrna and many another great town of the Orient. They send their sons to the University of Athens to be educated, and their power and position as an ethnic factor in the life of the Levant make constant gains. This little war is embarrassing for the treasury of the Greek kingdom, and it has cost the Greeks the lives of some thousands of brave young men; but as for the Greek race, as a whole, the effect of the war will not have been disheartening. The present seems to be with the Turks; but the future is inevitably against them. The Greek race will find its expression some time in a government really representing the wealth, power, intellectual force and rapidly developing population of the Greek nationality. That government ought by all means to be a republic.

After the first World War an upheaval in Asia Minor was to result in the wholesale expulsion of Christian elements of the population, including especially the Armenians and the Greeks. These Greeks were domiciled in Asia centuries before the disbanding of the armies of Alexander the Great. They were evacuated from the harbor of Smyrna, with American assistance. They were welcomed at the ports of Greece, and many of them were settled north of Salonika (Thessaloniki), on the farmlands of Macedonia.

II.

Perhaps no country has ever received so large an accession of refugee immigrants at a given moment, in proportion to its total population, as this sudden transfer of Greeks from Asia Minor to the ancient home of their race. At the end of the second World War, if the forces of law and order shall have prevailed, the people of the United States will not be content to send food to Greece, or to contribute through their churches and Sunday Schools to well-conducted private agencies like the Near East Relief. These things they will do; but also they will understand that the forces that have been successful in defeating and punishing aggressors must not be disbanded.

The collective security that is the declared aim of the United Nations will not exempt the United States from obligations to continue indefinitely. Greece will not henceforth be dependent, as it was after its defeat in the War of 1897, upon diplomatic relations with neighboring states, or upon power politics and reluctant favors from the chancelleries of four or five dominating governments.

Among the happier portents of this second war period, when the Greeks, downtrodden under Axis domination, were dying in the streets from lack of food, was a timely intervention on the part of Turkey that will take its place in history as one of those beneficent acts that encourage the lovers of peace and concord. The Germans and Italians in their own interest were seizing the normal food supplies of the Greeks. The British with superior maritime force were blockading all the shores of enemy-occupied Europe. American agencies, led by Mr. Hoover, the Near East Foundation, the Friends, and the Red Cross, were seeking to send food supplies to the starving women and children of Greece, but were stopped by the British refusal to open the blockade.

This British attitude was not due to lack of sympathy with the suffering Greeks, but to the belief that the army of occupation would not allow relief materials to be properly distributed. How the blockade was broken in the summer of 1941 has been told in a statement made jointly by Mr. Herbert Hoover and Mr. Hugh Gibson.[1] British policy had been determined by a statement made in the House of Commons by Mr. Churchill in August, 1940. It was not until August 3, 1942, that Mr. Sumner Welles, Under-Secretary of State, wrote to the President of the Greek War Relief Association expressing the satisfaction of the American government with what he described as "feasible attempts, with adequate safeguards, to save a heroic people from annihilation."

What had happened in the meantime? The facts were revealed to Messrs. Hoover and Gibson by the Turkish Ambassador at Washington. He admitted that he himself was responsible for having broken the dead-lock. He prefaced his explanation by the illuminating statement that "although the Turks and Greeks had been age-old enemies, they had settled their quarrels and were both determined to go on being friends." I will quote at this point from the statement made by Mr. Hoover and his associate:

When disaster overtook Greece, and wholesale starvation spread throughout the country, the Turkish government considered it had a moral obligation to its neighbor; the ambassador was instructed to approach the British government and urge that relief operations be allowed for the Greeks. In due course, he received the customary reply, enumerating the usual arguments against any help for populations under Nazi occupation.

This unfavorable reply was forwarded to Ankara, and, a short time later, came a telegram instructing the ambassador to inform the Foreign

[1] *Collier's*, February 20, 1943.

Office that on such and such a date, such and such ships loaded with food would sail from such and such ports in Turkey for such and such ports in Greece. This did the trick.

Most countries could not have carried it off in this way. But Turkey is a highly important neutral that could not be antagonized. Not only were the ships allowed to go through to their destination, but when experience proved that the operation involved no danger to the Allied armies, that it in no way benefited the Nazis, the volume of relief was increased, and financial facilities were provided by Britain and America. The whole operation was regularized by agreements set up by the Swedish and Swiss authorities and placed under the guardianship of the International Red Cross.

Admittedly there were serious obstacles to be overcome; and yet it is a matter of profound regret that Greece could not have been relieved sooner, and that similar methods could not then have been employed for the relief of Norwegians, Belgians, Netherlanders, and Poles. Mr. Hoover had believed it possible, and for almost two years he had been urging the American and British governments to give aid and support to relief attempts.

The object of my allusions in this chapter, however, is not to open the question of war-time relief for civilian populations. I am calling attention, rather, to the change of attitude on the part of the Turkish authorities. The new Turkey, hoping to avoid war and seeking no territory beyond its present boundaries, has no desire to take advantage of the misfortunes of neighboring states. The old Turkish Empire in 1897 sought to annex Greek provinces, and in other ways to despoil a gallant enemy defeated in a war that did the Greeks no discredit. The new Turkey opens the way for American relief ships, and is prepared to take a leading part at the end of the war in re-establishing peace and order among the Balkan states, and throughout the Near and Middle East.

The Balkan states one after another—as in the nineteenth century they gained their freedom from Moslem rule—were intoxicated with the sense of a great destiny for their respective nationalities. They revived the study of their ancient racial histories and, one and all, they fell under delusions of grandeur. They were involved in boundary altercations, and they quarreled and fought for bits of disputed territory.

The discipline of suffering will now have relieved them of

these false ambitions; and the friendliness of Turks for Greeks will help to extend the principles of good neighborhood to Bulgarians, Serbians, and Rumanians. During this process of restoring the Balkan states to political sanity and economic cooperation, the advice of the United States will perhaps prove to be a determining factor in the adjustment of various details.

During a long period, the influence of American educators at Constantinople has been felt throughout the Near East; and this is not less true of the American University at Beirut on the Syrian Coast than of Robert College on the Bosphorus. American diplomacy, cooperating with educational leadership and with our relief agencies, enhanced the reputation of the United States throughout the Near East for disinterested good-will. Such Ambassadors as Oscar Straus and Henry Morgenthau, not to mention other American officials, did their full share to create an influence that will assert itself in the period of post-war adjustment.

It was in 1930 that a treaty with Turkey resulted in the systematic and careful completion of an exchange of populations. The evacuation of Greeks from the port of Smyrna in 1923 had followed the defeat of Greece by Turkey in a war that resulted in part from unwise government control at Athens. Bulgaria joined in the supervised exchange of racial elements, and it was carried out under the auspices of the League of Nations.

The Hon. Henry Morgenthau, who had been American ambassador at Constantinople, accepted the invitation to return as high commissioner in charge of a movement that resulted in the withdrawal of about 800,000 Turks and a like number of Bulgarians from Greek territory. Greeks in similar or greater numbers were added to the population of the little kingdom whose language they spoke and whose ideals they cherished.

III.

Digressing briefly from my survey of certain situations of major importance in the theatre of the Eastern Mediterranean, I think it worth while to revert to an instance of adjustment made some eighty years ago. It illustrates those tendencies in the world—as the sway of reasonableness makes its slow but hopeful way—that seek permanent solution of vexatious problems. I refer to the political history of Corfu and the associated islands that constitute the Ionian group, once known as the Heptanesus.

Not to consider their place in the annals of ancient Greece, the later history of Corfu and its sister islands had covered a thousand years of political drift and change, with some transitions that were abrupt and tragic, until the year 1864. Transfers of authority were at a bewildering pace in the last years of the eighteenth century, with Venice, Austria, France, Russia, and Turkey tossing the Heptanesian title about, regardless of the unhappy inhabitants.

During the Napoleonic Wars the British began to acquire the Ionian Islands, one after another, completing the process by occupying the principal island, Corfu, after the abdication of Napoleon. The Treaty of Paris (1815), signed by Great Britain, Russia, Austria, and Prussia, placed under exclusive British control what was then called the "United States of the Ionian Islands." The British made harbor and highway improvements, and gave thought to the welfare of the inhabitants; but they were tenacious and arbitrary in their interpretation of the Treaty of 1815. Also, when the inhabitants wished to aid in the cause of Greek Independence in 1821, British authorities obstructed their laudable efforts.

More than twenty years later, during the wave of liberalism in Europe that had its climax in 1848, there came changes of policy. The Ionian islanders, who were clamoring for union with Greece, could no longer be kept down by the British garrison. Their local parliament adopted a resolution favoring immediate union with free and independent Greece. Then came the appointment of William E. Gladstone as a high commissioner to the Islands, with discretionary power to deal with the situation on the spot. Gladstone had been a friend of Greek independence, but he did not find that the mass of the Ionian islanders were ready to have the British Protectorate abolished.

There followed long years of delay, during which various reforms and improvements were made, until in 1864 the five great European powers signed a treaty by virtue of which the British consented to withdraw, and the islands were at last annexed to Greece. A part of the delay had been due to the extensive fortifications of Corfu, and the desire of the powers that these islands should be neutralized and have a future of immunity and peace.

Since that agreement became a part of the public law of Europe, it has been periodically violated in times of war; yet it holds its historic place with no further question, and it represents an intelligent effort to provide for a future of orderly life on the islands and among the border peoples of the Mediterranean.

In writing of Gibraltar as a focus of permanent international concern, and of Suez as another such focus, I do not forget the Bosphorus and Dardanelles as a source of historic controversy and of never-ceasing rivalry. The geographical position of Turkey gives that country natural jurisdiction over the Straits connecting the Black Sea with the Mediterranean. This was acknowledged in 1936 by the eight powers signatory to the Treaty of Lausanne when they gave consent to Turkey's request for a revision of the agreement, so that she might remilitarize the shores of the Dardanelles and the Bosphorus. But Turkey will not question the international character of a passage so essential to Russia. Whether or not the passage is assigned in future to the joint guardianship of Turkey and Russia, this water route will undoubtedly be neutralized by the United Nations and treated as a third approach to the Mediterranean which must be held inviolate for common use of commercial ships under all flags.

While Ankara will doubtless remain the capital and administrative center of the Republic of Turkey, it is not improbable that Constantinople may become once more a great cosmopolitan center, a meeting-place for peoples of all races and religions.

Since there can be no further question of Russia's rights in the Black Sea and in the waterways that connect the ports of the Ukraine, the Crimea, and the Caucasus with the sea-lanes of global traffic, I believe that we are justified in regarding that situation as no longer subject to serious controversy. Peace and harmony at this third focal point of the Mediterranean water system would seem to hold bright promises alike for Eastern Europe and Western Asia.

IV.

I shall proceed to make some observations upon two situations that are more complicated and less obvious than the future of the Black-Sea outlet. One of these concerns Syria, and the other relates to Palestine. Neither situation can be understood without considering special arrangements that were made at the conclusion of the first World War.

Syria is a large area south of Turkey and fronting upon the Mediterranean Sea. It was formerly a part of the Turkish Empire, but has had no political connection with Turkey since the first World War. In times past the French government had asserted a continuing though rather indefinite responsibility for the welfare of Christian minorities in Syria. Although the French had never undertaken to set up a political protectorate over the country itself, as against the Sultan's overlordship, they had intervened with military and naval force at certain junctures, when Christian elements were under persecution of an extreme sort at the hands of neighbors.

The most notable of these expeditionary ventures on the part of France occurred under direction of the Emperor Louis Napoleon in 1860, when Christendom was startled by an outbreak of violence in the Lebanon region. The Druses, a strange racial offshoot of the Moslem tradition, were massacring inhabitants of Maronite villages, the Maronites being a branch of the Eastern Christian church with Roman Catholic rather than Greek-Orthodox affiliations.

Europe approved of the French intervention, and certain administrative improvements were the result. Although the whole of Syria remained nominally a part of the Turkish Empire, a large district known as the Lebanon, because it included the rugged upland region of the Lebanon Mountains, was accorded an autonomous administration of its own, beginning in 1864.

Some twenty-five years after the formation of the privileged Lebanon province, I spent several weeks with a guide, riding horse-back on sure-footed Syrian steeds among the hundreds of flat-roofed villages, traversing the stony trails where they overlooked the Mediterranean, and where they led down the precipitous descent to the valley of the famed Orontes. I was studying what I termed (in a memorandum that I wrote at the time), "The Autonomy of the Lebanons."

The entire district was closely dotted with the compact stone-built villages, each one having its own religious character and each keeping suspiciously aloof from other villages, however near. But profound peace reigned throughout the area, because of a system of representative government based upon village units, with a central council made up of twelve members. Four of these were Maronites; three were Druses; there was one Turk, then came two Orthodox Greeks, one Greek Uniate, and one so-called Metawalli. As ruling head of the province there was a military governor, who must be a Christian of Latinic rather than Greek affiliation, while acting as a sort of pro-consul in the loyal service of the Sultan. His appointment from term to term had to be approved nominally by the European powers (actually by France). This might seem cumbersome as I try to describe it; but it had the merit of working well.

Order was maintained by an efficient native police force, and the central council, as I witnessed it, seemed to me a highly dignified group of native citizens, capable and fair-minded. I was merely a casual visitor in the region, with a medical brother-in-law teaching in the American college at Beirut. My observations had no importance for anyone but myself, and I never sought to publish the account that I wrote.

The value to me lay chiefly in the fact that I had obtained a close-up glimpse of a kind of representative system in local government resembling in principle and method the system that had (much more recently) been established for the villages of the Nile Valley in 1882, and that was applicable elsewhere in the Turkish Empire. The population elements in the Lebanon were by far more mixed and inharmonious than in Egypt. In the Nile Valley there were Coptic Christians, and Arabs belonging to one branch or another of Mohammedanism, while in the Lebanon there were distinct villages of perhaps a dozen mutually antagonistic religious persuasions.

It was my impression at the time that the French capacity for understanding non-European peoples, and for creating administrative systems skilfully grafted upon local and tribal customs, was most exceptional. This French genius for government was to be credited with the prevalence of order and peace in a region where discord was perhaps more natural than anywhere else in the world. Let it be noted that this system of Lebanon government, under the "Organic Statute" accepted by the Sultan in 1864, lasted for fifty years and was ended only by the outbreak of World War in 1914—moreover, it had never ceased to work successfully.

French influence had waned in the course of later changes in the Turkish Empire. But when Turkey as a result of the first World War had lost suzerainty over outlying provinces and peoples, the mandate system was invented and applied in the distribution of forfeited domains among the allied victors.

Among the understandings at an early stage of the first World War was an acknowledgment by the other Allies of the claim of France to succeed Turkey in control not only of the Lebanon district but of the whole of Syria. When the peace treaties took final form, the Turkish Empire had lost more than 400,000 square miles of territory, and was left with less than 300,000. But what it retained, and what now constitutes the Turkish Republic, was a compact and well-defined area south of the Black Sea, which includes four-fifths of the population that was formerly under Turkish rule.

Turkey is wholly reconciled to the loss of suzerainty over Arabia, Syria, Palestine, Armenia, and the greater part of Mesopotamia. The regions that we formerly knew as Arabia and Mesopotamia have, within defined boundaries, become the independent kingdom of Iraq. It was formed under the guardianship of Great Britain by consent of the Allies, with Bagdad as its capital. Iraq is a constitutional monarchy with an elective legislature. In 1930 by virtue of a treaty signed at Bagdad the British mandatory rights were renounced, and the full independence of Iraq was acknowledged. The final section of the Bagdad Railway was completed in 1940, and Turkey has now the advantage of rapid communication and profitable business relations with the valley of Mesopotamia.

The mandate that awarded Syria to France was not acceptable to the population as a whole. The tribes of the interior belong to that Arab world which was persuaded during the first World War to rise in revolt against the Turks. They were promised by British military leaders—and above all by their trusted friend "Lawrence of Arabia"—that they were not only to have deliverance from the Turkish yoke but that they might look forward to an independent national existence.

The French government sent distinguished military leaders to enforce order throughout Syria, and nationalist uprisings were sternly suppressed in the early '20's. But during most of the time between the two world wars, Syria was ruled under martial law. The plan was adopted by the French authorities of separating the Lebanon district, and the coastal area including Damascus and the ports of Beirut and Tripoli, from the less populated areas of the central and eastern parts of the country. To make the division seem more impressive and final, this western district was called "The Republic of the Lebanons" with Beirut as its capital. It was evidently intended to prevent the nationalist movement from developing in a unified way.

We may assume that after the end of the second World War the mandate system of twenty years ago will be renounced. There had been an unjustifiable tendency to regard regions acquired by mandate as permanent possessions, rather than as temporary trusteeships. In the case of Syria it is reasonable to suppose that a national constitution will be adopted, with French encouragement and supervision. The long experience of representative institutions in the Lebanon district under French auspices has provided a pattern that may well be applied to the other parts of Syria, with due allowance for wide differences in the density of population, and in the customs and economic status of the interior tribesmen.

V.

Immediately south of Syria lies one of the smallest countries in the world, but by no means one of the least famous. Palestine is similar in area to our state of Vermont. It has been conquered many times since the Israelites led by Joshua crossed the Jordan and laid siege to the city of Jericho. The Jews since their banishment and dispersal early in the Christian era, have always yearned for Palestine as their "homeland." Christians of different communions have called it the Holy Land, and have at times engaged in deadly quarrels among themselves over its sacred places.

The Turks had ruled it for four centuries before General Allenby drove them out when he entered Jerusalem in triumph in December, 1917. The British were accorded a Mandate over

Palestine in the peace treaties, and they set up a civil government in 1923, following three years of military rule. For the past twenty years a succession of British High Commissioners at Jerusalem has ruled the country, usually with impartial concern for the welfare of the inhabitants.

What seemed at the time a passing remark rather than an official pronouncement on the part of Lord Balfour to the effect that Great Britain would convert Palestine once more into a homeland for the Jews, was taken literally and with great seriousness. The "Balfour Declaration" became the political basis of the Zionist Movement. It was estimated in 1920 that there were about 80,000 Jews in Palestine, four-fifths of them living in the cities and towns. Almost twenty years later, a careful estimate of the Palestine population found about 850,000 Moslems, about 425,000 Jews, and about 115,000 Christians of all creeds.

The Moslems (usually designated as Arabs) greatly resented the influx of several hundred thousand Jews, most of them from Europe and some of them from America. Immigration was halted, however, several years ago, partly because of racial friction, but chiefly because no more agricultural land was available for settlement, and other opportunities for employment were lacking.

Meanwhile, there has been remarkable improvement in living conditions alike in town and country. The best authorities are convinced that the population elements of diverse races and creeds can learn to tolerate each other, and can live at peace when they are assured of justice and political security. It has become evident that the Moslem majority, long in occupation, will not allow themeslves to be dispossessed by the zeal and insistence of the Zionist leaders. When the persecution of Jews is ended in Europe, their refugee flight will cease, and migration will be reduced to normal ratios. There is little reason to suppose that Jews will ever outnumber the Moslem population in Palestine, unless by slow processes of natural increase.

The interest of many nations in the future of Palestine is so great that the British Government will not assume to exercise permanent or exclusive control by virtue of a mandate of the League of Nations that was granted after the first World War. A revised plan of government can be adopted that will give fair and equal representation to Arabs, Jews, and Christians, with a national police service under central authority.

Half a century ago Russian pilgrims by the thousands were accustomed to make their way on foot from Jaffa to Jerusalem and thence down the Jericho Road, to bathe in the sacred waters of the River Jordan. If Greek Orthodoxy should again prevail in Russia, we may be assured that the Palestine Republic of the future will not be less hospitable to pilgrims than were the Turks in the days when it was said of them that they were "on guard to keep Christians from cutting one another's throats."

A well-ordered and reconciled Palestine is so obviously a part of the forthcoming adjustment of peoples, governments, and conditions in the Mediterranean theatre, that only the skeptical and pessimistic could doubt the prospect. The British will have no further temptation to subdivide tiny Palestine in order to separate the Jews from the Arabs, while keeping for themselves a convenient port and naval station, and an outlet for the pipe-line that brings oil for their ships from the wells of Iraq. The collective security that guarantees Palestine will also protect such British economic and maritime interests as have validity.

Quite apart from the pretentious legalities of the mandate system stands the simple fact that the British government in assuming political control of Palestine also obtained authority from the other allies, in their distribution of Turkish assets, to govern the area known as the Trans-Jordan or Transjordania. Much of this region formed a part of the land of Canaan that was divided among the twelve tribes of Israel.

The British gave the area a distinct political set-up, but placed it under the responsible supervision of the High Commissioner for Palestine. They created a friendly environment for the Trans-Jordan by selecting as "Emir" to administer the country a brother of King Feisal of Iraq. Since this district extends somewhat indefinitely to the eastward, its boundaries have not been precisely delimited, but it probably contains about 35,000 square miles, its population of perhaps 300,000 consisting almost entirely of tribal Arabs.

It may be regarded as probable that the Trans-Jordan will in future be administered as a hinterland territory of Palestine. It already has a typical representative government suited to the nature and needs of the population. The Emir has a council of advisors, and in 1929 there was established an elective legislative assembly of twenty-two members. A railroad from Jerusalem and regular air service bring what was once the wild and remote Trans-Jordan country into ready communication with the world of modern activities.

With the dawn of a new era that will insure social justice and political stability, it is quite possible that long-deferred engineering projects may open new areas of intensive agriculture in Northern Palestine, irrigated from the Jordan. Chemical research also gives promise of important industries that will resolve the composite salts of the Dead Sea into valuable commercial products. But above all else Palestine will remain the land of places sacred to Jews, Christians, and Moslems, where ethical experiments in tolerance can be worked out as in a laboratory of human relationships.

CHAPTER X

THE MONROE DOCTRINE AND PAN-AMERICAN ACCORD

At the end of the Second World War the establishment of peace under world cooperation may not prove as difficult as it seems when we study the proposals of those who would begin at the central point of a systematic project. Accord will grow out of concrete situations that already exist.

This chapter relates to the Western Hemisphere, to its method of settling international disputes, to the so-called good-neighbor policy, and to the Pan-American Union. It endeavors to explain the Monroe Doctrine in its origins and applications, and in its larger significance.

The Monroe Doctrine is treated as an extension of the Declaration of Independence. It proposed to uphold the application of the Jeffersonian doctrine of democracy and federation to the political evolution of Central and South America. Early American statesmen were internationalists, believing in a system of self-government for specific entities like our States, and in federation of such entities for the larger objects of security and general welfare.

One of the first applications of the Monroe Doctrine had to do with rival claims affecting the Oregon country. Agreements with Russia on the north, and with Mexican-Spanish claimants on the south, fixed the line of northern California at the 42nd parallel. Then came disagreement between Great Britain and the United States over the so-called Oregon country lying between the California line and the southern line of Russia's Alaska claim, which was the 54°–40 parallel.

The long dispute was settled appropriately in 1846, by an agreement which gave what now constitutes the states of Oregon and Washington to the United States, and the Province of British Columbia to Great Britain.

Having cited at length my own interpretation of the Monroe Doctrine as possessing a distinctly international character, this chapter proceeds at length to discuss the assertion of that doctrine in our claim to the Oregon country for actual settlement, as against British demands at a time of unrestrained imperial adventure.

The purpose of the chapter is to indicate the persistent quality and character of the Monroe Doctrine through the experience of one hundred and twenty years. Its acceptance by Europe has come about with repeated tests of the good faith of the United States.

The Doctrine could be asserted again on occasion, but it has for the most part been merged in the more comprehensive aspects of Pan-Americanism. The United States government does not seek predominance, but prefers a joint sponsorship by the American republics in conference, when any case arises that affects their relations with each other or with a trans-Atlantic government.

ACCORD IN the Western Hemisphere is the foundation upon which the international policy of the United States is based. The accomplishment of that accord—which stands today as the most substantial achievement ever realized in the larger field of national inter-relationships—has not been a simple or uneventful experience.

It was in 1823 that our government made a statement of its views which has since been known as the Monroe Doctrine. Many diplomatic incidents (and some of a military character) have given practical demonstrations of the firmness with which the American government through more than a century has adhered to the policy enunciated by President Monroe.

It was not a merely personal attitude that the fifth President of the United States assumed, to meet what might have proved to be only a temporary menace to the new republics of South America. The country was experiencing what was known as the "Era of Good Feeling" that followed the conclusion of the second war with Great Britain. John Quincy Adams of Massachusetts was Secretary of State, and there was no living statesman in Europe or elsewhere more thoroughly trained than this son of our second President in the diplomacy of the revolutionary and Napoleonic periods. Jefferson was eighty years old and living in retirement at Monticello; but he was keenly aware of every political move, and was always consulted. John Adams, who was several years older than Jefferson, was still the political mentor of New England, and was enjoying a delightful correspondence with Virginia's philosopher and democratic idealist.

President Monroe had recently made a good-will tour of New England. Thomas Jefferson and John Adams had been fellow-members of the committee of the Continental Congress that drafted the Declaration of Independence, and Jefferson had referred to Adams as the "chief pillar" on the floor of Congress in support of that Declaration. The Monroe pronouncement was actually a second Jefferson-Adams Declaration. It was not intended to set forth any narrow doctrine of Americanism. It was not a partisan, sectional, or individual statement. On the contrary, it represented the collective views of surviving leaders of the Revolutionary epoch and of their sons and successors, including John Quincy Adams, Henry Clay, Andrew Jackson, and many others.

The liberties that the revolting American colonies had demanded for themselves were those, as they believed, that in the course of human events all other men would eventually seek to gain. The Monroe Doctrine almost half a century later was in effect a re-affirmation of the principles of 1776. We were about to recognize the new governments of South America. Europe after the downfall of Napoleon was under the spell of imperial reaction, and the "Holy Alliance" of dynastic autocrats was encouraging Spain to renewed efforts for recovery of her colonial empire in the Western Hemisphere. While America was in sympathy with Latin-American independence, and hailed it with genuine popular enthusiasm, the Monroe Doctrine was not wholly altruistic. The re-establishment of European colonialism might have interfered disastrously with American ambitions. Jefferson and many others believed that our federal system would at no distant time extend all the way to the Pacific.

Underlying the Monroe Doctrine, therefore, were large conceptions of democracy and of federation. The visions of a world where mankind everywhere would assert its unalienable rights to life, liberty, and the pursuit of happiness, were entertained by our forefathers without apology and as a matter of course. They believed that governments "deriving their just powers from the consent of the governed" would lay their foundations on such principles "as to them shall seem most likely to effect their safety and happiness." They were not seeking military conquests on behalf of the United States, and believed that our expansion would come by peaceful processes of settlement, local self-government, and federal union.

They had no desire for another war, but they believed that the peaceful evolution of self-government in the Western Hemisphere was a cause worth fighting for. They realized that this Declaration of 1823 might not only give serious offense to European governments but might actually involve us in an unwelcome conflict on land and sea. There was shrewd diplomacy, however, behind the statement of December 1823, and Secretary Adams was aware of the support of the British Foreign Minister George Canning. Our announcement of the Monroe Doctrine was followed almost immediately by the British recognition of the independence of the Spanish-American colonies.

In an address on the future bearings of the Monroe Doctrine made at a Conference in the summer of 1917, about two months after we had entered the first World War, George G. Wilson, Professor of International Law at Harvard University, remarked that "the purely national and American character of the Monroe Doctrine may be said to have been waived." He proceeded to make the following observations:

> The next step—the recognition by the world of the general principles underlying the doctrine as likewise sound for world policy—would not now be a long step for the United States. When the Monroe Doctrine was originally published in Europe it met with approval from liberal statesmen, who hailed it as shedding "joy, exultation, and gratitude over all free men in Europe." The reactionary Metternich maintained that it was a natural calamity following the establishment of free states. Later, Bismarck regarded it as a piece of "international impertinence." At home the propositions of Monroe were received with a degree of proud self-satisfaction. By many it was regarded as giving to the Declaration of Independence a wider scope. Many other interpretations followed, and these were frequently adapted to temporary policies, but the doctrine was always regarded as a choice American contribution toward the well-being of the western continent. . . .
>
> In a sense the Monroe Doctrine aimed in 1823 to make the western hemisphere "safe for democracy." The President's war message of April 2, 1917, said, "The world must be made safe for democracy." In this broad conception the United States may thus be said to be fighting for a Monroe Doctrine for the world.

The Conference at which Professor Wilson made the address to which I have referred, was held under the auspices of the Academy of Political Science in the City of New York, in cooperation with the American Society of International Law. Its programs extended through five days (May 28 to June 1 inclusive, 1917) and they were devoted wholly to the "Foreign Relations of the United States." Members of the Conference were brought from all parts of the country, and included many distinguished lawyers, publicists, and editors of leading newspapers.

II.

There was remarkable agreement in the Conference upon ideals and principles, with full concurrence in the belief that the United States must take a generous part at the end of the war in plans for the better establishment of international law and for the maintenance of peace. Charles Evans Hughes, afterwards Secretary of State and Chief Justice of the United States, concluded a notable opening address with the following sentences:

> Shall we not at least be hospitable to the thought that America has its obligations to the world? We cannot live unto ourselves. What promise does the future hold if treaties and conventions are made only to be broken? If we can see at all into the future we know that it offers no chance for isolation to the United States. We have vast resources and extraordinary privileges and we cannot shirk our duty to mankind. Self-interest as well as a proper sense of obligation demand that we should aid in rearing the structure of international justice, and certainly that we should not make its establishment impossible by holding aloof.

The subject assigned to me for presentation at that Conference was "The Monroe Doctrine and the Evolution of Democracy." I am reproducing in the following pages of this chapter the full text of my address on that occasion, chiefly because it interpreted the Monroe Doctrine as an extension of the principles set forth in the Declaration of Independence, and as a statement having permanent bearings of an international character. Another reason for giving it a place in my present discussion of the backgrounds and foundations of future peace lies in the fact that it found acceptance in certain responsible quarters, in contrast with views of the Monroe Doctrine that were regarded as nationalistic and controversial. My address was made on May 30, 1917, and is reproduced herewith:

> The power and persistence of ideas lie at the base of all historical movements. Policies have a tendency to form themselves around doctrines and theories, and in due time precedents begin to support policies and to reflect credit upon doctrines. The Monroe Doctrine has run some such course, until now the tendency has been to glorify it as well as to accept it. In order that hope may not die within us and that pessimism may not paralyze our power to press forward, we are compelled to believe that the millennium is about to dawn, that the great war of nations will end in the near future, and that in the happiness of a world peace we shall

somehow find solutions for all the problems hitherto unsettled. I like to indulge in these rosy, optimistic dreams, although I have observed too much and studied too widely to suppose that in plain reality a great war will have enlightened all understandings, chastened all spirits, and made everybody at once right-minded and true-visioned.

We shall continue to live in a world that is highly unequal in its stages of development. Some parts of the world will be much more unfinished than other parts. The future will have very difficult questions to deal with that are not involved in the present war. Nevertheless, if many great things that we deem righteous and just can be established at the end of this war, the future course of progress and civilization will be rendered accordingly less difficult. We shall have our western-hemisphere problems, but we shall also, I hope, have found improved ways of dealing with them.

I should like to say a few words upon the relation of the Monroe Doctrine to a far larger doctrine that had been earlier proclaimed and that persisted in the convictions of some of the men concerned with the Monroe Doctrine's formulations. The political teachers of the eighteenth century, who were the mentors and prophets of the revolutionary period, not only proclaimed their doctrines of the rights of man and of political and social democracy, but they also held firmly to the doctrine of world organization. Europe lost the great vision and entered upon a period of unrestrained nationalism after the collapse of the Holy Alliance. But the American leaders, notably Jefferson, kept alive both parts of the great conception of the revolutionary reformers. That is to say, the authors and defenders of the Declaration of Independence not only stood for democracy, but also believed in the confederation of democratic sovereignties and in the abolition of international conflict.

Thus our American union of states was consciously built upon both parts of the great conception of a reformed political life for the world. The first part was the democratic rule of communities, and the second part was the confederation of sovereign states. In both parts we have made a marvelous success of the practical demonstration. This success was based not merely upon the doctrines themselves, but also very greatly upon wisdom and generosity at moments of crisis.

Two great steps stand out among others. Hamilton's leadership in securing the assumption of the revolutionary debts of the states by the confederation as a whole was most admirable in its effects. Still more important was Jefferson's leadership in persuading Virginia to cede her western lands, with the result that the Northwest Ordinance gave us a series of magnificent states while pointing the way toward creating another group of states south of the Ohio and east of the Mississippi. The conceptions embodied in the Northwest Ordinance have been projected across the continent. They have given us forty-eight sovereign states, not by any means of equal size and importance, but sufficiently alike in their averages of population and resources to constitute a true and permanent sisterhood of commonwealths.

It was because of the persistence of this great conception of democratic self-government in the particular states, with the common interests of them all merged in the higher structure of the confederation, and with a higher machinery of justice to deal with possible misunderstandings between them, that Jefferson could see no necessary limit to the extension of a system thus firmly based upon human equality and universal education. He expressed the opinion repeatedly that a confederation thus formed might expect in due time to comprise the whole of North America and ultimately to include Central and South America.

Canada has, indeed, had a different history thus far from that which both British and American statesmen had anticipated until a very recent period. Yet the course of things in the Dominion of Canada has not, upon the whole, been widely divergent from that which Jefferson and others had predicted. The great northwestern areas have been divided into states, in each of which—as in Manitoba and the rest—there is now to be found a thoroughly modern and strictly democratic government, with all the attributes of autonomy. The Canadian states, from the maritime communities of the east to British Columbia in the west, are united in a confederacy that is quite in harmony with the Jeffersonian conception.

So closely akin are the essential principles that control the individual states and the Canadian confederation with the principles that control our individual states and our union, that there is visible an increasing harmony between the two halves of the North American continent. There is practically little more danger that Michigan will quarrel with Ontario, or that Minnesota will quarrel with Manitoba, than that either Michigan or Minnesota will quarrel with Wisconsin. I hope and believe, however, that in case of a quarrel, as over a boundary line, there may in due time be an authoritative tribunal as between Alberta and Montana, so that the diplomatic methods of the past that dealt with the Maine boundary and the Alaska boundary may be superseded by an institution more analogous to our Supreme Court. Suffice it to say that North America has upon the whole worked out fairly well the eighteenth-century conception of the democratic autonomy of states and the confederation of neighboring commonwealths extending over continental areas.

Jefferson and the men of his time undoubtedly realized that democratic institutions could not be so easily developed where people were lacking in homogeneity or were made up of races lacking in education and unequal in economic development and position. Yet those statesmen of the revolutionary period had supreme faith in democracy, and they were not so contemptuous of the so-called inferior or backward races.

The Monroe Doctrine was inspired by two things: first, a large vision; and second, an exigency of statesmanship. I shall not, I am sure, be thought to touch upon matters of historical controversy when I ascribe the Monroe Doctrine to Jefferson in so far as the larger vision is concerned. His correspondence with Monroe affords all the evidence that one needs. For the statesmanship of John Quincy Adams I have the most unqualified regard, as also I have for the Pan-Americanism of Henry Clay and those of his school. The independence of Latin America was favored by our political leaders and thinkers in the United States as the great preliminary step.

There were also those in Latin America who cherished the earlier ideals of the French Revolution, and who believed both in democracy and in the federation of states for the preservation of peace. It was plain enough that even with admirable paper constitutions prescribing democracy, it would be a painful task to build up the intelligent and capable body of democratic citizens without which mere paper institutions cannot give freedom or security. But Jefferson, Adams, Monroe and their contemporaries believed that Latin America would have a better future if it were free to go on in its own way, creating through arduous experience the reality of a series of democratic republics, than if it were brought back under the yoke of European colonialism by the united military and naval efforts of the emperors of the Holy Alliance and the Spanish crown.

It is true that the nature and the motives of the Monroe Doctrine have been construed in different ways at different times by statesmen in Europe, in South America, and in North America. These different constructions have been due chiefly to practical problems involving the possible application of the doctrine. It can never be rightly or fully understood, however, unless one keeps in mind not only the historical circumstances but the political doctrines and the large visions under which it had its origin.

I repeat, then, that the conception of the American union of self-governing states was in no small measure the outgrowth of that still larger conception of world federation and perpetual peace that German and British thinkers, as well as French and American, were entertaining in the latter part of the eighteenth century. The Monroe Doctrine was intended to save the whole of the western hemisphere for the processes of democracy and interstate organization, for the abolition of war and the promotion of the concerns of the common civilization.

I have never had much respect for that view of the Monroe Doctrine which has made foreigners think of it as a sort of Yankee jingoism. Doubtless at certain times and in certain aspects our own national interests have been involved in the assertion that Europe must not meddle in western-hemisphere affairs. We have desired to keep the western world from becoming militaristic, and in this sense we have helped to make the Monroe Doctrine a success.

From the Straits of Magellan to Baffin's Bay and the Northwest Passage, there has been no state or community that has founded itself upon the doctrine of military power as against its neighbors. For a region so relatively undeveloped in natural resources, and so far from maturity in the creation of its bodies politic, South America in recent decades has been singularly free from the din of arms. Brazil, Argentina, and Chile have learned to be good neighbors; and there is little evidence anywhere in Latin America of the existence in any country of a party or a leadership that has in mind the securing of a dominant position as among neighbors by the militarizing of national resources on the European model.

It was precisely to prevent the growth of such military policies, and to encourage friendly and helpful interrelationships among the American democracies, that the men of Monroe's time took their stand against the extension to the western hemisphere of the European system of exploited colonies. The survival of that system in Cuba remained as an awful example and a standing justification of the principles that Monroe and Adams enunciated and that Mr. Canning seems to have supported.

It is necessary, I think, to have this larger vision in mind in order to judge at times of the value of practical applications. It happens that the confederation of our forty-eight sovereign states becomes relatively less a confederacy of sovereigns, and relatively more a national union of subordinate parts, simply because of the great homogeneity of the older American stock and the wide distribution of our newer immigrant elements. But for these facts the states would be relatively more individual and the union would not absorb power quite so easily.

I am making this remark because of its relation to the future of entities that have distinct populations. Thus, Puerto Rico can derive security and much economic and social progress from her place in our confederation while exercising democratic self-government according to the genius of her own people and with the enjoyment of her own language and customs. Cuba, in turn, can, for purposes of international policy, derive benefit from a limited connection with our confederacy while working out her own destiny as a self-governing people. I am of opinion that the two principles of democracy and confederation may also secure for all of the Central American states, and even for Mexico, some advantages from special or limited partnerships in our confederation, with full freedom of domestic evolution.

As respects the larger nations of South America, the Monroe Doctrine has become for them and us merely a family concern. As against European imperialistic assertions, we may indeed at times have been justified in declaring that ours was the place of leadership in the western hemisphere, and that we would make it our business to see that no small American state should be treated by any European empire as Serbia was treated in 1914 by the government at Vienna.

But, as among ourselves in the western hemisphere, it was not the purpose of the Monroe Doctrine to create or set up a position of overlordship. Much less was it any part of our doctrine that Europe must find her spheres of interest and exploitation in Asia and Africa in order that we might have the western hemisphere as our sphere of commercial or political exploitation. So far as Brazil and the other larger and more stable republics are concerned, the Monroe Doctrine is to be interpreted as one of mutual help and good understanding. We seek increasing friendship with our South American neighbors, and rejoice in their progress and welfare.

It is entirely in accord with the spirit of the Monroe Doctrine that the Pan-American Union has been established, and that various Pan-American conferences have been held from time to time. Our interests in the European struggle were identical with those which we asserted in the period of the Monroe Doctrine. We stand now, as then, for democracy, liberty, non-militarism, and friendly adjustment of all international differences. We have joined in the war against Germany, not to help one set of European powers obtain the advantage over another group of powers for selfish reasons of their own, but because the interests of all the American republics, as of democracies everywhere, were imperiled by the methods which Germany had adopted and by the doctrines and policies that Germany and her allies were supporting with an organized application such as the world had never seen, of science and skill to military ends.

The Monroe Doctrine was a part of that larger message of peace, democracy, and universal friendship that the best thinkers of modern times had delivered to Europe and America in the latter part of the eighteenth century. With many blunders, but faithful in the main, North America and South America have gone forward trying to realize in practice those great dreams of democracy and international peace. Over against these high doctrines, announced in the eighteenth century by utilitarian philosophers and Christian moralists alike, we are now combating the destructive and hideous doctrine of the right to dominate in the affairs of the world by unrestrained force.

The object of the Monroe Doctrine was the peaceful evolution of democracy in the western hemisphere. Our participation in the war against Germany is in strict fulfilment of the aims of the Monroe Doctrine. We are fighting for the rights of democracy and the claims of international peace. Fundamentally, the whole of the western hemisphere, South America no less than North America, had become imperiled by the doctrines and methods of Germany and her allies. The cause of the United States in this war, therefore, is also the cause of Brazil and the other South American republics. We are entitled to the moral support, if not to the physical aid, of all the members of the Pan-American Union. If in this crisis the western hemisphere shall see alike, it will be fortunate indeed for the future relations of the United States with the sister republics of South America—with the communities of the mainland and of the islands around the Caribbean.

III.

When on a previous page I referred to Western Hemisphere accord as a substantial achievement, I had no thought of it as standing four-square and unshakable. It is by no means complete and finished, much less is it static and monumental. There is constant movement and relative change within all national areas, and especially within the imperfectly developed countries of our Western world. Agreements, even among friendly neighbors, have to be reconsidered and revamped from time to time. The worst disasters of our modern era have been due to the fact that nations and their leaders could not—or would not—understand that keeping the peace is a business that requires unceasing watchfulness and "trouble-shooting" effort, and one that justifies large expenditure of various kinds.

One per cent of the money that the United States government has been spending to meet the costs of the second World War would probably have sufficed to maintain peace for another twenty years—if it had been devoted at the right time to the right objectives. Money alone might not have bought "peace in our time," but pecuniary investments in peace-keeping bargains would naturally imply an intelligent understanding of other people's points of view, and the open-mindedness that is prepared to make concessions and compromises, except where principles of justice and fair play are at stake.

Such moral reflections, I am sure, would not find contradiction anywhere as long as they are kept in the safe sphere of glittering generalities. It is in the application of theories to particular circumstances that troubles begin and persist. Since there is no prospect whatever that we shall speedily obliterate national boundaries and race distinctions, and merge all peoples in a single global democracy, it will be well to remember that peace is primarily a local affair.

It begins with the willingness of the individual to accept responsibly the rules that make for justice and order in his own community. From this firm standpoint of political and social self-rule where one has his domicile, we can extend our principles of democracy and representative government throughout a great confederacy like the United States. It so happens that favorable circumstances have given to our nation a much larger aggregate of population, wealth and power than to any other in North or South America. Does it not follow that we ought to know whether or not we could ever be tempted to use superior force for advantage or aggrandizement at the expense of some less powerful neighbor?

It may now be said that a survey of public opinion would find the people of the United States virtually unanimous in holding that we consider our country pledged never henceforth to use military power to take advantage of any neighbor, great or small. It is one thing, however, to believe that we have attained that consciousness of good intentions even under stress and strain, and a different thing to persuade the neighbors to believe that we can be trusted not to rely upon superior force, in case some dispute should arise.

If then it is true that a substantial accord has been reached throughout the Western Hemisphere, it must mean that we have renounced in good faith all reliance upon force as an instrument of public policy (except to withstand aggression); and also that we have brought the neighbors to the point of believing that we are sincere, and would not yield to the first temptation to violate our avowed principles.

But two other things, also, are implied, if a general Western Hemisphere accord has indeed been attained, with a reasonable prospect of permanence. One of these is the purpose of the other American republics to deal with one another in the same spirit of justice and mutual goodwill. The other necessary implication is the willingness of each of these American republics, our own included, to renounce the idea that it can be a law unto itself, in the case of an issue of dispute with a neighbor. There must be sacrifices of absolute sovereignty at the point where disputes—otherwise stubborn and dangerous—could be settled by a tribunal of arbitration or by reference to a high court of international justice.

If the Monroe Doctrine has had any large and generous purpose, it finds its fulfillment in two results. First comes the acceptance throughout the states of the Western Hemisphere of the principles of democratic self-government, along with the settlement of inter-state disagreements by peaceable methods. The second result is the approving acquiescence of Europe and the world at large. If these results have been attained in large measure, as we have reason to think that they have, what remains to be done about it? Well-informed men would reply that such a field of human endeavor must never be neglected, but must be fertilized and cultivated if it is to be fruitful and beneficent.

It is not enough to see that boundary disputes are settled by friendly negotiation or by submission to arbitrators. There are always questions of trade and commerce, with liberal sentiment inclining toward increased freedom of exchange. There are matters affecting public health, education, cultural relations, improvement of communication facilities, and various other things that have been considered in numerous Pan-American conferences.

In Europe, Asia, and Africa war rather than peace is the prevailing condition at the present time. Within the Americas from Canada to Patagonia there are relationships of peace. Our welfare is not disturbed by lack of harmony within the Western Hemisphere. The Monroe Doctrine one hundred and twenty years ago meant simply that the Americas were on guard against aggression from beyond seas. At the present time that Doctrine stands for the same thing in a larger way. The Americas are again on guard against aggression from abroad that would disturb us in the enjoyment of all that we have gained through the trials and discipline of more than a century.

If these regional experiences on our side of the encompassing oceans had involved only a few difficulties, they would have fewer lessons for Europe and the world at large. But the obstacles and predicaments have been real; and the experiences through which we have advanced to our present condition—that of well-behaved neighbors throughout the Americas—have been instructive enough to justify a re-statement of some of the more significant episodes. I shall venture, in the following chapters, to recount several of those attempts to adjust differences. Familiar as they are to students of American history and diplomacy, they are not familiar in detail to our citizens, especially those of the younger generation.

It was remarked in a previous sentence that our applications of policy in concrete cases might at times have justified the prevailing European cynicism. It was said of us that we were more intent upon winning stakes in our own game of expansion than upon a benevolent guardianship of the revolted areas of Latin-America. After the second war with Great Britain (1812–14) our statesmen were beginning to think of the United States in continental terms.

It happened that their interest was directed to the Oregon country of the Far Northwest much earlier than to California. John Quincy Adams thought Russia was making claims that extended too far southward on the Pacific Coast. A well-informed authority summarizes the dual motive of the policy enunciated by President Monroe in his Message to Congress of December 2, 1823, in the following explanation of the origin of the Monroe Doctrine:

> The doctrine grew out of two diplomatic problems. The first was the minor clash with Russia concerning the northwest coast of North America. In this quarrel, Secretary of State John Quincy Adams in a note to Monroe expressed the principle that the American continents were not to be considered any longer as a field for colonization by European powers. This was incorporated verbatim in the presidential message. The other, and more important, part of the doctrine grew out of the fear that the group of reactionary European governments commonly (though incorrectly) called the Holy Alliance would seek to conquer and reduce again to colonial status the Latin-American states that had recently revolted from Spain. The United States had just recognized the independence of those states, and Great Britain did not care to lose the markets of Latin America.

The fact that the Monroe Doctrine as set forth in the Presidential Message had reference to our claims in the Far Northwest has been quite generally forgotten. John Quincy Adams carried his point with Russia, and a treaty between the United States and the government of the Czar was actually signed in 1824. Under the terms of the treaty, Russian claims were withdrawn from territory south of latitude 54° 40′ N.

This parallel line was then fixed in the minds of ambitious Americans as a permanent landmark on the shore of the North Pacific. It was considered by our pioneers, explorers, fur-traders, and prophets of "Manifest Destiny" that our northernmost boundary line, extending inland for a great distance, perhaps two thousand miles, had been settled for all time, beyond any further doubt or question.

We had also been concerned about the southern line of this so-called Oregon country. As a part of Spain's great province of Mexico, administered by a Viceroy whose seat of government was Mexico City, there was no question about the Spanish title to California. The Spanish claims, however, extended indefinitely northward to meet those of Russia, without any understanding as to the exact line of demarcation. During Madison's presidency our government had succeeded in purchasing West Florida from Spain by the treaty of 1819, five years earlier than our boundary agreement with Russia.

Although the Oregon country was far removed from West Florida in terms of geography, this was a situation in which diplomacy could clear up several points at the same time. In the treaty of February, 1819, a northern boundary for California was agreed upon. Spain relinquished to the United States all Spanish territorial claims north of the parallel of 42°, running from the Pacific Ocean to the Rocky Mountains. Taken in conjunction with the Russian agreement made five years later, the United States had apparently acquired a fairly good title to an extensive territory on the Pacific north of California, extending to the new "54–40" line. So our expansionists thought a hundred years ago; and they did not believe that they were claiming anything that belonged in good conscience to any other jurisdiction.

A fourth claimant, however, had appeared upon the scene—a claimant far more tenacious and insistent than either Russia or Spain had ever been. Before the War of 1812 an American fur trader John Jacob Astor had established a colony at the mouth of the Columbia River. The British navy had seized the coast, and Mr. Astor's operations were suspended "for the duration." Afterwards he resumed his project under assurance that his rights would be protected in accordance with a clause in the treaty of December, 1814, which guaranteed the restoration of all American territories seized or occupied by the British during the war.

We had not then enunciated the Monroe Doctrine; but our government held the view that we were destined to settle and develop this so-called Oregon country. The British had adopted the device of extending their imperial holdings through private trading companies, operating under royal charters. British India had been expanding in this way; and in the far northwest of our continent the Hudson's Bay Company had not only established trading-posts, but was exercising jurisdiction over vast unsettled regions comprising most of what was called British America. The Company's sway was so extensive that it governed perhaps four-fifths of what is now the undisputed domain of the provinces that are parts of the Dominion of Canada.

The definite competition between American and British-Canadian fur-traders had extended southward to the regions drained by the Missouri River and the Upper Mississippi. President Jefferson had taken a keen interest in these rival claims, and as early as 1803 he had sent Meriwether Lewis and William Clarke on their famous expedition to the Upper Missouri and the Northwest Coast. Dr. James M. Callahan, who is an unquestioned authority upon American policy in Canadian relations, remarks of Jefferson that in 1810 (two years after his retirement from the Presidency) "he considered that an early American settlement on the Western Coast would be a 'great public acquisition,' and he looked forward to the time 'when its descendants should spread themselves throughout the whole length of the Coast' covering it with free Americans independent and self-governing."

IV.

In a subsequent chapter I shall deal with relations between the United States and Canada, and at this point I am referring to the Oregon dispute only because it took its place as one of the earlier controversies in which we were asserting the Monroe Doctrine on our own behalf. It was the American belief that we were destined to settle the Pacific Coast and develop it with our own people, just as we had begun at that time to settle Ohio and the states created under the Northwest Ordinance. Meanwhile the British conceded our right to re-establish the Astoria settlement under the American flag.

I shall not try to convey to the reader of these summary allusions any adequate conception of the intricacy of our further negotiations with Great Britain, and the persistence with which the two governments asserted their rival claims for almost forty years. In 1818 our negotiators offered to accept as a boundary the line of 49° with the proviso that there should be free navigation of the rivers and free use of ports and harbors by inhabitants of each country. The British would make no such diminution of their claim, and after much dickering a treaty was signed that provided for joint occupation of all the territory in dispute until some time in the future when a final decision could be reached. This agreement was ratified at Washington on January 30, 1819, less than a month before the signing of the treaty with Spain in which the United States acquired whatever territorial rights Spain had previously claimed north of the parallel of 42°.

Far from being limited to the Pacific Coast, there were boundary disputes affecting the state of Maine, the Great Lakes, and various other Anglo-American differences that might have led to war if either of the two countries had thought it worth while to indulge in a third armed contest. It was not until the negotiation and adoption of the Webster-Ashburton Treaty in 1842 that eastern boundary disputes affecting the line between Maine and New Brunswick were finally adjusted.

Meanwhile migration to the Oregon country had set in, and pioneer farmers were following the toilsome Oregon Trail in steadily growing numbers. Agitation was aroused throughout the country, but especially in the Mississippi Valley, for the establishment of American sovereignty in Oregon, and for grants of land based upon United States jurisdiction.

Negotiations were re-opened in 1844 between Secretary Calhoun of our State Department and the British Minister to Washington, Mr. Pakenham. The British offered to agree upon a division at the 49th parallel, as formerly proposed by the United States, but Mr. Calhoun declined the proposal. Mr. Pakenham then offered (January 1845) to arbitrate, but President Tyler and Secretary Calhoun preferred direct negotiation.

Meanwhile the presidential election had been held in the autumn of 1844, in which James K. Polk defeated Henry Clay. The Democratic Convention that nominated Mr. Polk had declared that the United States was rightfully entitled to all of Oregon, and a party campaign slogan, "*Fifty-four-Forty or Fight*" familiarized the country with the idea that our rights were in danger on the North Pacific. In his inaugural address (March 4, 1845) President Polk declared not only that the United States had a clear and unquestionable title to Oregon from the California line to the parallel of 54–40, but that American jurisdiction should be extended over the entire region. This exhibition of assertiveness, as Dr. Callahan reminds us, was met by the British ministry in a similarly defiant tone. Sir Robert Peel, however, "referred to it with an expression of regret for the indiscretion, and with a calm assurance of British readiness to maintain British rights if invaded."

Fortunately the British authorities began to prepare the public mind for some compromise and retreat from earlier claims. On the American side, two men of wide experience were in position to conduct fresh negotiations. One of these was James Buchanan, the new Secretary of State, and the other was Louis McLane, our minister to England. I shall not attempt even briefly to summarize the arguments and proposals presented, first on one side and then on the other, in the course of this critical negotiation.

The British had naturally inferred a hostile disposition on the part of the Americans, and had begun to prepare for defensive military measures. President Polk did not relieve the strain when he decided in the autumn to re-affirm the Monroe Doctrine, and to make it directly applicable to the Oregon question. He referred the matter to his Cabinet, which approved of his treatment of the subject in his forthcoming annual Message to Congress. He proposed that notice should be given for termination of joint occupation. This would carry with it plans for extending American government and jurisdiction, and for defense of our new position.

The situation became increasingly ominous. Resolutions were presented in both houses of Congress to the effect that the American government had no power to transfer any portion of its soil, and "that the title to the territory between 42° and 54° 40′ was not open to compromise." Several offers to arbitrate were made by the British and declined one after another. Secretary Buchanan, now committed to President Polk's policy, not only refused to arbitrate, but declared: "If the British Government intends to make a proposition to this Government, they have not an hour to lose if they desire a peaceful termination of this controversy." In concluding, he declared: "The President will accept nothing less than the whole territory, unless the Senate should otherwise determine."

A careful study of all the facts and circumstances proves beyond doubt that war was by this time expected by Great Britain. The Canadian authorities were instructed to make specified military preparations. Mr. McLane, who was a tactful diplomat and had once been Secretary of State himself, sent word to Secretary

Buchanan that Pakenham's refusal to consider a division on the 49th parallel was now disapproved by both parties in England; and he evidently favored an attempt to compromise on a basis that our own government had offered in the preceding July.

Buchanan gave several weighty reasons to Pakenham against arbitration and in favor of direct settlement between the two countries. McLane (writing from London) reported that negotiations were made embarrassing by free expressions of public opinion in American newspapers and periodicals, some of which were encouraging the persistence of the British in extravagant claims and in war preparations.

Then came the outbreak of our war with Mexico, which called for complete and undivided military effort. Obviously, we could not fight two wars at once, in opposite directions. Our government had already served notice of the abrogation of the Treaty of 1819, which had provided for joint occupation of Oregon. Meanwhile, there had come about a change of party government in England, due to issues of domestic policy. It was a favorable time for an effort on the part of the British to take the initiative in re-opening the Oregon question, and they offered once more to agree upon the boundary at the 49th parallel.

President Polk now shifted responsibility, and referred the question to the Senate, admitting that rejection of the British proposals might result in war. After a debate of only two days (in June 1846) the Senate by a vote of 37 to 12 favored the acceptance of the British proposal. There were details with which we are not concerned in this summary. The subsequent proceedings were not delayed. Three days after the Senate vote, Secretary Buchanan signed a treaty with the British minister, Mr. Pakenham. The Senate ratified it at once by a vote of 41 to 14.

V.

Dr. Callahan, whose account is perhaps the most complete and accurate that is available for general readers, makes the following comments: "Thus, a serious boundary controversy, which threatened to precipitate war, was peacefully adjusted by a reasonable compromise which established a logical line of division—probably the most logical that geographers and statesmen and politicians could plan."

In the foregoing resumé of the Oregon dispute, I have touched only upon high points and principal decisions. A patient scholar like Dr. Callahan, who is a veteran in the field of diplomatic history, goes to direct sources and gives all the lights and shades that belong to the complete picture. The citizens of our state of Washington and of the adjoining Canadian province of British Columbia are justified in studying the details of their past history. They cannot well avoid having in mind several questions: First, had either side a reasonable claim to the entire Oregon territory, as compared with the other? Second, would British Columbia have been better off if the United States had secured all that it demanded? Third, as a matter of historical speculation, was the prompt acceptance at Washington of the final British proposal due to fear of British attack while we had the Mexican War on our hands? I would answer all three questions with a qualified, cautious negative.

Viewed in retrospect, the claim of the United States might be regarded as superior, because the facts of history have justified Jefferson's anticipations of 1803. A network of contiguous free commonwealths has spread from ocean to ocean. The United States was simply seeking to secure the unoccupied territory it would need in the near future for the natural expansion of its homogeneous population.

The British, on the other hand, were at that time engaged in imperial adventures having a commercial basis, and they were supporting their trade in the Pacific by superior naval strength. While the Oregon dispute was approaching its climax, Britain's empire-builder, Lord Palmerston (the very same Palmerston who served a seven-day ultimatum on Abraham Lincoln in 1861) had brought to a successful conclusion his Opium War against China. An impartial encyclopedic record sums it up in a sentence or two as follows: "China, attempting to end the opium trade at Canton, came into conflict with Great Britain who insisted on maintaining the trade. The British won the war and by the Treaty of Nanking treaty ports were inaugurated, and indemnity was paid. Hongkong was ceded to the British, and China gave up some of her share in the fixing of tariff duties."

We may be frank enough to remark that the British navy in the Forties of the last century was prowling widely and handsomely in the broad Pacific. It was actually seeking what it might devour. It was trying to find an excuse for seizing the Hawaiian Islands, which were then independent under a native dynasty. But Britain's armed ships were also in the Atlantic, patrolling the African Coast against the kidnappers (largely American) who were engaged in the illicit slave-trade.

I have never been inclined to disparage the broad Jeffersonian Americanism of President Polk; yet I agree with Dr. Callahan in believing that the compromise by direct negotiation was an honorable and wise solution of the Oregon dispute. It was not until twenty years later that the political ambition of Canada reached out with full consciousness from the Province of Ontario and the great Hudson Bay to Vancouver Island and the meandering coast of the North Pacific.

Looking at these strategic movements with more generous and disinterested retrospects, I am inclined to believe that the political evolution of the Dominion of Canada has been the best single piece of good fortune for the United States that has fallen to us in our external relations since the Civil War. If we care at all about peace and harmony—in a world that has been made small by the airplane with a rapidity almost too dangerous—we will cultivate further good relations with Canada as the first specific article in our international program.

As these lines are written it has been a hundred-and-one years since Great Britain seized Hongkong and forced the opium of India upon the Chinese. England was in advance of other countries in her industries at home, and in her trade that carried the Union Jack to all seaports. Our New England seamen at the same time were quick to avail themselves of the open ports that England secured from China. These hardy seamen of Gloucester and Salem were also engaged in the African slave trade, and were bringing the rum of Jamaica and the West Indies to comfort and support the theologians of rugged New England. I am not aware that American moralists at that time objected to Lord Palmerston's imposition of opium upon the Chinese. At a great cost, not yet fully repaid we have atoned for the wickedness of our slave trade. We would be cheaply sentimental if we were assuming now to reproach our British friends for their seizure of Hongkong one-hundred-and-one years ago.

Smuggling opium into China was wrong, and kidnapping negroes on the African Coast in order to smuggle them into the

United States was even worse. We may feel that our international manners and morals have improved; and many of us have come to believe that the Golden Rule could be adopted with safety even across the boundary lines of sovereign states. If we learn to think of our neighbors in a proper spirit, we will not covet their possessions and we will relax our support of isolationism in the sphere of economics. I conclude with the thought that the Monroe Doctrine served us well in its narrower application to the Oregon question, and that we may now think of it with less concern for ourselves and with more regard for the welfare of other nations.

In the following chapter I am treating the case of the Venezuela boundary line, in relation to the alleged encroachments of British Guiana. This was a typical case of the application of the Monroe Doctrine under circumstances in which we were making claims not upon our own behalf but upon that of a sister American republic. As in the Oregon case, the results were all that could have been desired.

VI.

As regards Venezuela, there occurred another intervention on the part of the United States government during the administration of President Theodore Roosevelt that, as it turned out, was creditable to our own administration, and to several European governments that were involved. President Castro had governed Venezuela most disastrously, acquiring great wealth which he transferred for safely to European banks. The disordered finances of Venezuela, with a bankrupt treasury, created a situation that European naval expeditions undertook to terminate by occupation of seaports and forcible collection of claims.

Venezuela was at fault, but the European method of collecting private debts owed by citizens of a weakened, ill-governed country was not regarded at Washington as properly applicable to Latin-American conditions. Skillful diplomacy on the part of our government led to international adjustments well worth recalling briefly, because they illustrate the better way of dealing with such disputes. It was in 1902 that Venezuela's financial collapse had so greatly disturbed European creditors that their governments undertook a joint debt-collecting intervention on behalf of their aggrieved citizens.

Great Britain, Germany, and Italy sent a joint naval expedition into Venezuelan waters. Our own relations with Venezuela were also in bad case, because of Castro's outrageous conduct as a dictator. Germany, seeming to take the more aggressive part in the expedition, seized Venezuela's gunboats and blockaded her seaports. Early in 1903 our government completed diplomatic intervention on the basis of the Monroe Doctrine. By virtue of President Roosevelt's good offices the blockading powers withdrew, on agreement that their respective claims should be adjudicated by mixed commissions. This process of straightening out claims and counter-claims was carried on at Caracas in 1903.

There was a minor question which attracted the attention of international law authorities. Should the blockading powers have their claims treated preferentially, as against the claims of other powers that did not undertake to collect by force? This detail was referred to the Hague Tribunal, and decided in favor of the blockading powers. The South American republics, meanwhile, had been much agitated over the violation of Venezuelan sovereignty by powerful European countries, and their views were expressed by a distinguished Argentine statesman and international law authority Luis Maria Drago. He was minister of foreign affairs at Buenos Aires, and he enunciated what was known as the Drago Doctrine. This was regarded as supplemental to the Monroe Doctrine.

Senor Drago's formulation was, however, an international law principle, rather than a policy applicable solely to our hemisphere. It condemned the use of force by governments for the collection of debts owed to their nationals by foreign governments or their citizens. In a modified form it was afterwards accepted at the Hague Conference of 1907, and thus obtained some standing in a general code of public law.

I shall not attempt to specify other interventions on the part of the United States to protect American republics such as Haiti, San Domingo, or Nicaragua from European debt-collecting adventures, or from anarchy through incessant revolutionary strife. In no case has the United States intervened to assert domination on the part of this country. Its object has been to help small American countries, at some critical stage in their affairs, to make recovery and go forward upon the principles of orderly self-government. They have all accepted such principles, and embodied them in constitutions and laws. But some of them have found it hard to master the arts of orderly political life.

In 1943 it would be possible to adduce many evidences of accord in the Western Hemisphere. We may regard present conditions as the fruitage of fairly consistent policies that have been tested by more than a century of experience. What has been accomplished can be maintained and vastly improved, but only on the condition of unceasing effort to make the good-neighbor policy productive of ever better political and social conditions.

It would not be appropriate, however, to conclude this chapter without acknowledgement of the critical study that our historians have given in recent years to every phase of our relationship with the Latin American countries. Such studies have been productive of at least a dozen volumes based upon lecture courses given at Baltimore in the annual series known as the Albert Shaw Lectures on Diplomatic History. Two of these courses were given by Dr. Dexter Perkins, Professor of History in the University of Rochester. As the author of four volumes on the Monroe Doctrine, Dr. Perkins' comprehensive researches have made him our foremost authority in this particular field. He lectured at the Johns Hopkins in 1932 on the Monroe Doctrine in the period from 1826-1867. In the year 1937 his lectures dealt with the Monroe Doctrine as tested in the period between 1867 and 1907.

Quite apart from the value of these contributions to American history as models of thoroughness and accuracy, they have much to teach us regarding (1) the methods of diplomacy; (2) the intricacy of situations involving a number of governments approaching a subject from different standpoints, each with its own motives; and (3) the importance that is justly attached to the peaceful adjustment of a dangerous situation in which diplomacy triumphs over threats of violence and war.

Dr. Perkins devotes seventy-five pages to his chapter on "The Venezuelan blockade of 1902-03." Much discussion has turned upon the nature and extent of Theodore Roosevelt's activities in securing the discontinuance of German and British naval aggresion in Venezuelan ports, with an agreement of multi-lateral character to settle all claims against Venezuela by arbitration. As I have remarked in a foregoing page, a certain matter of detail was referred for arbitration to the new Hague Court that had been established in accord with agreements reached at the Hague Conference of 1899. The European claimants, including the German, British and Italian governments, had joined with Venezuela in asking President Roosevelt himself to act as arbitrator.

At the very moment when he was completing his negotiations with these European powers he wrote a letter to me that throws so much light upon his spirit and method in diplomacy, and his unshaken adherence to the Monroe Doctrine, that I think it worth while to extract it from my files and give it publicity for the first time. The letter follows herewith, and students of that complicated episode will note the fact that its date of December 26, 1902, has especial significance:

Personal

WHITE HOUSE

Washington

December 26, 1902.

My dear Dr. Shaw:

First let me say that, as I expected, you have done exactly what I wished in setting forth my attitude on the trust matters, and I thank you most sincerely for it.

Now as to Venezuelan arbitration. You have also doubtless noted that we have carried our point and after no little difficulty have persuaded all the contending governments to accept the principle of arbitration by the Hague court. I regard this as a great triumph. At the same time if one or other of the governments had stayed out I should certainly have accepted the position of arbitrator myself rather than to have seen the failure of all efforts to get arbitration.

We are not out of the woods by any means, for we shall find difficulty in getting acceptance of all the terms of agreement for the arbitration, as the contending parties will doubtless strive to insert provisos which their opponents will severally regard as unacceptable; but it certainly looks as if we could now obtain agreement. There was one reason, and only one, which made it in my judgment better that I should arbitrate myself. This was the fact that in such case there would be no possibility of the court rendering a decision which might conflict with the Monroe Doctrine.

Of course I take it for granted that you would support me in refusing to acknowledge the power of the Hague court or of any other tribunal or of any other power to overrule us as regards our attitude on what I consider the cardinal feature of American foreign diplomacy. But the terms in which England and Germany have put their request relieve me of apprehension on this score, for they especially stipulate that arrangements shall be made for the satisfaction of the award, and this will enable me to explain that said satisfaction must not consist in the acquisition of territory (which indeed I have done in my note of today to the Powers). I am very well satisfied with the results of our attitude so far.

As with the trusts, my position has been consistent for a long time on the Monroe Doctrine. I supported President Cleveland in 1896 on this point, and in an article I then wrote which was republished in my "American Ideals" I took the ground which I elaborated later in both of my special messages to Congress, which I set forth very plainly, although very courteously, in the letter to Germany of last spring.

The principles we there set forth were explicitly accepted by both Germany and England, and of course nothing that they have done or threatened to do so far has in any way or shape conflicted with our contention as to what the Monroe Doctrine means. But the chances of complication from a long and irritating little war between the European powers and Venezuela were sufficiently great to make me feel most earnestly that the situation should be brought to a peaceful end if possible.

I would be much obliged if you would tell Holls the substance of this letter.

Faithfully yours,

(signed) THEODORE ROOSEVELT.

Dr. Albert Shaw,
13 Astor Place,
New York, N. Y.

The allusion in the last sentence of President Roosevelt's letter not only deserves, but actually requires, some explanation. The Hon. Frederick W. Holls was a New York lawyer who served as the executive officer and most active member of our delegation at the First Hague Conference. He was one of my most intimate friends, and was a close adviser of Mr. Roosevelt, especially in his period as Governor of New York. In the year 1900 Mr. Holls published an elaborate volume entitled *The Peace Conference at the Hague and Its Bearings on International Law and Policy.* Our delegation had gone to the Hague prepared to promote a general arbitration treaty; but, as Mr. Roosevelt was aware, I had made a suggestion regarding the Monroe Doctrine that the State Department accepted and noted in its instructions to the delegation. Mr. Holls had taken the initiative at the Hague in this particular matter, where he was strongly supported by Dr. Andrew D. White and Admiral Mahan. The so-called "American Declaration" was accepted and affixed to the signatures of the American delegates, in the following language:

Nothing contained in this Convention shall be so construed as to require the United States of America to depart from its traditional policy of not entering upon, interfering with, or entangling itself in the political questions or internal administration of any foreign state, nor shall anything contained in the said Convention be so construed as to require the relinquishment, by the United States of America, of its traditional attitude toward purely American questions.

In commenting upon the importance of this proceeding, Mr. Holls declared that "never before that day (July 25, 1899) when this declaration was read by the Secretary of the Conference, had the Monroe Doctrine been officially communicated to the representatives of all the great Powers, and never before was it received with all the consent implied by a cordial acquiescence, and the immediate and unanimous adoption of the Treaty upon that condition."

President Roosevelt's allusion had these facts in mind. All the important phases of the Venezuela controversy had been settled in strict accord with the essentials of the Monroe Doctrine. The reference of a detail to the Hague Tribunal was a graceful and suitable recognition of the work of a Conference to which the American delegates had contributed so much of encouragement and hopeful effort. Mr. Holls was well satisfied with the settlement of the Venezuela case; and this meant something, in view of his exceptional contacts at that time with the German authorities.

CHAPTER XI

BOUNDARY SETTLEMENTS BY AGREEMENT: OREGON, BRAZIL, VENEZUELA

In the chapter to which these lines are prefatory, the effort is made to show that when international adjustments take place through diplomatic conference or arbitration, the findings are likely to be permanent, and to provide points of stability that will remain unquestioned in times to come. For instance, reference is made to final boundary settlements in Puget Sound, twenty-six years after the general agreement of 1846.

The most typical settlement of a boundary dispute, however, was that of the embittered controversy between Venezuela and Great Britain relating to alleged encroachments of British Guiana, with successive changes of the boundary line, each change including more territory. More than one Prime Minister refused to arbitrate, and along with his refusal he pushed the Guiana boundary further inland. President Cleveland and his Secretary of State, Richard Olney, decided to champion Venezuela's position. An American commission of distinguished authorities was appointed to study the case and report upon its merits.

The British newspapers had never previously been represented in the United States, and now for the first time they began to take note of American news. Colonial matters had been handled in its own fashion by the inner circle of empire-builders, and the British public had never even heard of the Venezuelan question, although the dispute had raged for forty years, and had kept Latin-American opinion dangerously exasperated. President Cleveland's proposal aroused great excitement in England, where it was regarded as a threat of war.

Fortunately Lord Salisbury yielded to the pressure of opinion, and discovered that the Venezuelan question was one eminently fitted for adjustment by arbitration. The important question was not one of the extent or value of the territory in dispute, although that meant much to Venezuela. The real issue was that of a strong power disregarding a reasonable principle of settlement in the case of claims made by a weak power. The righteous adjustment of that case forms a substantial portion of the historic background that renders Anglo-American cooperation possible under present conditions, with hopeful promise for the future.

Under American influence at that time, France proceeded amicably to settle a long-standing dispute involving a still larger extent of territory between Brazil and French Guiana. In various directions the cause of arbitration or other peaceful methods for settling disputes was advanced by the firmness of President Cleveland, and by the timely change of attitude in Downing Street.

IN THE bewilderments of a global war, with many boundaries overrun, and with deadly conflict of theories and purposes regarding older and newer orders in Europe and Asia, we are compelled in the very nature of our mental processes to discover points of stability from which to make our reckonings. Whatever may happen after the war, the line between California and Oregon will not be in dispute; and not less firmly established will be the line that was settled by reasonable agreement between what are now the political entities known as the State of Washington and the Province of British Columbia.

Readers who have given their attention to my chapters thus far will understand that I am reviewing events of an international character not to re-state familiar facts found in textbooks of history, but rather to give fresh meaning to some of them as seen in retrospect, and to interpret them as fitting into the pattern of things to come. After almost a century of experience, we can feel assured that these specific lines (and many others) on the political map of North America are to survive for generations yet to come.

In the compromise agreement of 1846, Vancouver Island—not then regarded as valuable by the Americans—was conceded as a whole to the British, although a considerable fraction of it lies south of the Forty-ninth parallel. There are, however, numerous smaller islands between this larger one and the mainland of the state of Washington, and a troublesome controversy soon arose regarding the line of demarcation as it meandered through the water-passages.

Conflict of claims appeared especially regarding the ownership of San Juan Island, where Americans had settled; and local authorities disputed about the right to collect taxes. Our General Harney—an impetuous person with the prestige of his record in the Mexican War—happened to be stationed in the far Northwest, and he took it upon himself to encamp soldiery on San Juan Island. President Buchanan, always judicious and slow to wrath, sent the head of our army, General Winfield Scott, to calm the troubled waters of Puget Sound. This paragon of all the antique virtues removed the American troops at once, and arranged for a joint control of San Juan Island until a final adjustment of the boundary line could be made through the Strait of Georgia.

Again our Government was confronted with the irritating

Palmerston-Russell manner. (Lord Palmerston and Lord John Russell were at this time respectively Prime Minister and Secretary of State for Foreign Affairs. They were frequently caricatured by John Tenniell in *Punch* as "Queen Victoria's bad bays," and they dominated British imperial policy through a large part of the nineteenth century. They played the game always with British Empire assertiveness, in the initial stages of any negotiation. Lord John Russell declared that "the British Government would accept no settlement which did not provide for reservation of San Juan to the British." This of course was a supercilious attitude, which could not be maintained as against the quiet insistence at Washington upon the determination of a disputed title by amicable methods.

Few things have done so much to provoke controversy about border-lines and jurisdiction as the discovery of gold in waste places. This is precisely what happened in the Puget Sound islands, and on the mainland of New Caledonia (later called British Columbia). Thousands of American mining prospectors flocked to those regions in the Fifties. It was not until 1863 that the British Government was willing to settle the various disputes that had become acute since 1846 in that far northwestern area. Finally, a joint commission, working with an impartial umpire or arbitrator, rendered decisions that were accepted as conclusive. Besides settling various financial claims, the jurisdiction over disputed islands was permanently fixed, and the maps now show San Juan well within American limits. The German Emperor acted as arbitrator, and he awarded that island to the United States in October, 1872.

The significant thing from the historical standpoint was not the decision itself, as regards title to an island lying off the coast of the state of Washington, but rather the methods by which the decision was reached. A boundary dispute, whether between two farmers or two nations, is likely to make trouble unless adjusted by conciliatory means. We abandoned long ago the shotgun method of dealing with private quarrels of this nature. As regards public disputes of title, international law has provided legal remedies which no nation great or small may henceforth reject with impunity.

II.

The most typical case of a disputed title that has ever led to the assertion of the Monroe Doctrine on the part of the American government was that of a controversy between Venezuela and Great Britain. It concerned the exact limits of the crown colony on the northern coast of South America known as British Guiana. This territory was first occupied by the Dutch West India Company in the very year (1620) remembered as the date of the Plymouth Rock landing.

Having signed the treaty of 1783, thus recognizing their loss of the thirteen united American colonies, the English were seeking imperial compensations elsewhere, in accordance with the spirit of the age. They made war upon the Dutch and seized the Cape of Good Hope in 1795, expelling the Dutch East India Company which had been established there for almost a century and a half. In 1796 they took possession of that portion of the Dutch holdings on the coast of South America which they still retain.

Lying east of British Guiana is the present Dutch possession of Surinam, or Netherlands Guiana. Americans might care to remember that Surinam was confirmed to Holland by the English in 1667, in exchange for the Dutch colony of New Netherlands, afterwards called New York.

The British took Surinam from the Dutch in 1799, but returned it as one detail of a general treaty between the two governments signed at London in 1814, and confirmed it in the larger settlements after Waterloo in the following year. Dates have importance in the adjustment of boundary disputes; and those concerning the Guianas were not to be ignored as geographers and historical scholars were brought to the aid of governments, when Venezuela's complaints at length secured attention. Two further dates had some significance: The establishment of the independence of Colombia in 1819, after the successful revolution against Spain, and the organization of the Republic of Venezuela in 1830, following amicable division of the earlier Colombian area.

Americans have been strongly inclined to the view that surviving European colonies in the Western Hemisphere are either usurpations or anomalies. Such a view, however, requires careful study of both sides before it can be justly applied to a particular situation. Spain was not pretending to have authority over English, Dutch, and French Guiana when the South Americans gained their independence; and the Guianas were not involved. This trio of colonies on the South American Coast had been held for two hundred years by European governments other than Spain, when Colombia (and other parts of Spanish South America) gained independence.

Soon after the organization of the Republic of Venezuela its governing authorities at the city of Caracas began to complain that the British were encroaching upon Venezuelan territory by following the rivers ever further into the wilderness interior, searching for gold and other valuable things. These protests became more insistent as the years went by, because the British authorities were changing their maps from time to time, marking new lines and including new zones of hinterland. Whenever they deigned to give momentary attention to the complaints (as it seemed to the exasperated Venezuelans) the British made a new map, claiming more territory each time.

Meanwhile, the British public was completely unaware of the existence of a controversy that was disturbing South America. Neither had it gained serious attention in the United States until after Grover Cleveland had entered upon his second administration (which began in March, 1893). Mr. Cleveland was a careful but firm man, who possessed a logical mind, had the courage of his convictions, and lacked little but a background of information and experience. He appointed a federal judge, Walter Q. Gresham of Indiana, as Secretary of State. Mr. Gresham had been a Republican and a Cabinet member in two previous administrations. He was a man of character and intelligence, but was without the knowledge of foreign affairs that some, at least, of our Secretaries of State had possessed in earlier periods.

The United States had become absorbed in domestic problems. Twenty-eight years had elapsed between the inauguration of James Buchanan and that of Grover Cleveland in 1885. The Democratic party, in power again after such a long interval, was occupied in dispossessing Republican office-holders and in revising internal policies, and these processes were resumed when, after the four years of President Harrison, the Democrats were again in office.

At that time our Department of State (our Foreign Office, as

Europeans would call it) had only a member or two besides the Secretary himself, except for routine clerks. England had a government highly aware of foreign affairs, and a public knowing little or nothing about them. In the United States, on the contrary, we had many private individuals who were informed in special ways about external conditions, with a government that had surprisingly little knowledge.

It can do no harm to give point to this last remark by mentioning an incident that has never heretofore been made public. This relates to the first year of Mr. Cleveland's second administration. There were revolutionary disturbances in the Dominican Republic, which occupies the eastern half of the island of Santo Domingo. An American company, having business interests that were in jeopardy, sent one of its managers with a New York lawyer to Washington to explain the situation, and to suggest that if a naval vessel should happen to make a timely call at the port of Santo Domingo, it might exert a quieting influence.

Mr. Cleveland gave his approval, and sent his callers to Secretary Gresham. As they left the White House, the President remarked: "Santo Domingo, as I remember, is where we have a coaling and naval station." The visitors were too polite, and too well pleased with Mr. Cleveland's ready compliance with their wishes, to correct his last statement. They went to the State Department, found Mr. Gresham equally cordial, and again were reminded that our Navy was in possession of a station on the coast of Santo Domingo.

It was in 1870, during the second year of his first administration, that President Grant had negotiated a treaty providing for the purchase by the United States of Samana Bay, a deep and spacious natural harbor having maritime and strategic advantages of exceptional value. Senator Sumner was chairman of the Foreign Relations Committee, and his opposition resulted in the refusal of the Senate to ratify the treaty. Singularly enough, both President Cleveland and his Secretary of State, while remembering about the treaty, were entirely oblivious of the fact that it had never been ratified and thus had been rendered void. The New York lawyer, himself a man of wide knowledge of foreign affairs, returned to New York to tell me what seemed to us both a surprising lapse of memory on the part of our highest officials, charged with the conduct of foreign relations.

Yet Cleveland and Gresham were both lawyers of more than ordinary ability, and they were capable of statesmanlike policies and decisions. Their mistake about Samana Bay was not culpable. They could learn things when a case was in hand. They had not as yet been giving thought to the Caribbean Sea and its environing coastal shores and harbors, whether insular or on the mainland. However, they were soon to have their attention called to that important region, although not until after they had made themselves responsible for certain steps in the successive transactions that finally resulted in our annexation of the Hawaiian Islands.

Their first experience in the adjustment of a Latin-American dispute was an affair of minor significance, yet it was typical of a number of efforts that were to follow, during the next thirty years, as we helped to clear up undesirable situations. Also, the Nicaragua affair, which I am about to recall, gave Mr. Cleveland a certain zest for taking up forlorn causes, and it was a prelude to his diplomatic intervention in behalf of Venezuela.

Having made editorial allusion to President Cleveland's recognition of the Hawaiian Republic (in October, 1894) I proceeded with the following paragraphs of comment upon an episode of American diplomacy relating to Central America:

Another of the small States practically under the friendly patronage of the United States is Nicaragua. For many months past this little republic of Central America has been the scene of a controversy that has attracted almost as much international attention as the Hawaiian revolution, and it is fortunate that the Nicaraguan affair has also been settled upon lines of apparent justice and permanence. The controversy has been over the relations to Nicaragua of a portion of its eastern or Gulf-of-Mexico slope, known as the "Mosquito Coast" or the "Mosquito Reservation." The government of this district has borne some such anomalous relationship to that of Nicaragua as the Indian Territory's has borne to that of the United States.

The Mosquito Indians have had a chief of their own and have been independent of Nicaragua in local affairs. Their port is the town of Bluefields, and under the long established regime of the Mosquito Reservation this port has not been subject to the customs regulations of the republic of Nicaragua. Accordingly many American and other foreign traders and merchants dealing in the fruits and various semi-tropical products of the region have settled there, have obtained great influence over the conduct of local affairs, and have profited greatly by the immunities which freedom from Nicaraguan laws and regulations has permitted them.

It needs no argument to make it clear that this quasi independence of the Mosquito Reservation has been most disadvantageous to Nicaragua, and constantly humiliating as a limitation upon the nation's sovereignty over its own territory. So indefensible an arrangement could not have lasted all these years but for the real or pretended existence of a certain vague and shadowy British protectorate over the Mosquito Indians, which has enabled the merchants of the coast to bring dire and sundry threats against Nicaragua when the little republic has been inclined to assert itself. Of late, however, the Nicaraguans have grown bolder, and have simply advanced into the Mosquito Reservation, claimed possession, and reduced the district to the status of an unprivileged, ordinary portion of the republic of Nicaragua. In the proceeding, despite the loud complaints of American residents at Bluefields, whose special immunities are cut off, our government at Washington has promptly and heartily acquiesced. The phantom British protectorate has vanished into thin air, and Nicaragua is wondering at her own former timidity and congratulating herself upon the ease with which she has cut the Gordian knot.

For foreigners resident at Bluefields who are discommoded by the assertion of full Nicaraguan jurisdiction over Nicaraguan territory, we beg to express our sympathy; but we will not for a moment admit that their interests are superior to those of Nicaragua or that the power of the United States should have been employed to maintain a humiliating curtailment of Nicaragua's authority and sovereignty within her own boundaries.

It is reported that many of these irate Americans trampled upon the Stars and Stripes and renounced allegiance to this country in favor of Great Britain, because Mr. Cleveland and Secretary Gresham were not willing to help drive the Nicaraguans out of a vital part of Nicaraguan territory. In point of fact our government has done its duty in supporting the just claims of an American republic over its own soil and its own fiscal arrangements, as against private and foreign interests.

III.

Immediately following the foregoing comment upon the so-called "Mosquito Coast" of Nicaragua, there appeared an editorial paragraph in which I presented the current American view of the Venezuelan dispute. I am reprinting it regardless of its value as a disinterested statement, because it serves as preface to a narrative account of a first-class diplomatic controversy. I gave it close attention from first to last, as from obscure beginnings it gained the attention of statesmen and diplomats on both sides of the Atlantic and of journalists throughout the world.

It should be noted that Secretary Gresham, whose health had been failing for some time, died late in May, 1895, and was succeeded as Secretary of State by Richard Olney of Massachusetts. Mr. Olney was a successful corporation lawyer in Boston when President Cleveland appointed him to the office of Attorney General. On the death of Secretary Gresham, he was transferred to the Department of State. He had some of the qualities of Charles Francis Adams, whose Americanism was unbending and whose manner was cold and austere. The chief personages in the Venezuelan discussion were Secretary Olney on behalf of his complaining client Venezuela, and Lord Salisbury who had become master of the British Empire's foreign policy. The paragraph in question is given herewith:

There is another American republic whose rights within her own proper territory require the most considerate attention by our Department of State. We refer to the republic of Venezuela, great and valuable portions of whose territory seem to have been encroached upon by Great Britain. Beginning with a trading post or two on the coast, the English have extended their claims until they now assert authority over a great region which was formerly regarded by everybody as an integral portion of Venezuela. Far from increasing their territorial claims on the north coast of South America, the British ought by all means to prepare definitely to withdraw altogether. It is wholly contrary to the ethics of modern international relations that a European power like Great Britain should hold by force of arms a region that belongs naturally to the home territory of a friendly nation.

In the issue of my magazine for the month of December, 1894, I made a more extended statement which was *ex-parte* on behalf of Venezuela, using information that had not then been definitely contradicted. After a lapse of almost half a century my tone might well seem not only indignant but unduly provocative. All that I desired however, was to have enough attention focused upon the matter to have the boundary line settled, once and for all, by some judicial process. My highly argumentative presentation was in the following terms:

It is to be remembered that President Cleveland already has on hand a delicate piece of work as arbitrator in a South American boundary dispute. The position which this country holds in respect to the arbitration of differences between nations has come to be a commanding one. The list of disputes on our own account that have been peaceably solved by tribunals of arbitration is surprisingly long, and in addition to this our government has had a part in the arbitration of a considerable number of disputes between other nations. It would be a marked triumph for the principle of arbitration, and a striking illustration, moreover, of the growing influence of the United States if our government should at last secure a righteous settlement of the grave boundary dispute now pending between the republic of Venezuela and Great Britain, and should be able to bring it to the judgment of a disinterested umpire or a regularly constituted council of arbitration.

But a state of affairs exists in that portion of the American hemisphere that it is high time every American citizen should understand. The encroachments of Great Britain upon Venezuelan territory have been progressing steadily for more than fifty years. Furthermore, the Republic of Venezuela has asked Great Britain probably not fewer than a hundred times since 1840 to submit the boundary differences to arbitration. As if conscious of the flimsiness and weakness of her claims, Great Britain has constantly refused to arbitrate. Again and again the United States government, with delicacy and tact, has offered to adjudge the relative merits of the rival claims. Venezuela has been willing; Great Britain has refused.

Most of the Spanish-speaking republics, from Mexico to the Argentine Confederation, have at one time or another made their representations to Great Britain in favor of a reasonable and peaceful settlement of this standing scandal and international disgrace; and Great Britain has refused them all. If there were any consistency whatsoever in England's claim, the grounds for moral indignation against her might not be so great. But England has now occupied and fortified a vast region which only a few years ago, during the pendency of this very dispute, she freely admitted to be Venezuelan territory beyond any question. The simple fact is, so far as we can understand, that England has not the shadow of a lawful claim to any territory west of the Essequibo river. She has gradually stolen the coast line as far as the Orinoco, and has set up a claim to vast and rich interior regions, which ten years ago she admitted to belong to Venezuela.

A renewed attempt on the part of Venezuela to secure some agreement on a boundary line in 1886, resulted in claims on the part of Lord Rosebery, then Minister of Foreign Affairs, which went so far beyond the utmost limits England had ever claimed before, that Venezuela was compelled to break off diplomatic relations. In 1890, however, another approach was made, and Lord Salisbury informed Venezuela that he would be willing to compromise on a boundary line which, in its turn, encroached very much further upon Venezuelan territory than Lord Rosebery's audacity had carried him in 1886. Finally, Venezuela's confidential agent in London made a last attempt in 1893 to reach some basis of settlement with Lord Rosebery, again restored to office; and this enterprising statesman, after that discipline of delay to which England usually subjects the representatives of minor powers before answering their requests, magnanimously proposed a settlement on the basis of a boundary line which not only kept intact Lord Rosebery's own encroachments of 1886, and those added ones of Lord Salisbury's in 1890, but made still further large increases of England's claim!

Thus Lord Rosebery has put himself in the position of asserting that what he admitted in 1886 that Venezuela might justly claim as her own, has, by virtue of the British policy of refusing to come to terms, been lost to Venezuela and gained by England in the lapse of seven or eight years. At the present rate, Great Britain will within a decade or two be demanding the whole Orinoco valley.

The latest edition of the *Statesman's Year Book*, which is virtually official so far as English claims are concerned, declares that British Guiana extends from 8 degrees and 40 minutes north latitude to 6 degrees 45 minutes, and from 56 degrees 15 minutes west longitude to 61 degrees 40 minutes. Lord Rosebery's latest proposal, as we understand it, is a compromise on the basis of England's taking a still further slice of Venezuelan territory not heretofore claimed as British. Comparing the present official bounds of British Guiana with those claimed only a few years ago, it is interesting to note the fact that the English Cyclopedia of Geography, which is a standard work and which does not scruple to sustain all English claims, was content only a few years ago to inform the world that British Guiana contained 50,000 square miles. Nobody has ceded England any further territory in that region; yet 109,000 square miles is the existing area, according to all the latest British statistical works.

Unfortunately, Venezuela is weak and defenseless. But England's aggressions in South America, and her refusal even to consider arbitration of boundary claims, constitute both an insult and a menace to every autonomous government in the Western Hemisphere. The least permissible penalty should be the full restoration to Venezuela of every foot of territory west of the Essequibo River. Not one of the dozen different boundary lines proposed by Great Britain since 1840 should any longer be considered for an instant.

Moreover, the United States, Mexico and the South American republics, having declared themselves upon this question at different times, and having met England's disdainful refusal to arbitrate a question that belongs to the Western Hemisphere, should appoint a joint commission on their own account to investigate Venezuela's claims, should agree upon a just settlement of the true historical boundary line, and should thereupon give notice to Great Britain that they would jointly sustain Venezuela's claim to the territory on her side of a boundary thus determined.

Any hesitation on the part of Great Britain to accept such a verdict, in view of her countless refusals to arbitrate, should be followed by the further agreement among the autonomous states of North and South America that England's conduct had justified total forfeiture of all her claims whatsoever on the South American coast, and that they would jointly sustain Venezuela in the occupancy of what is now properly known as British Guiana.

The Monroe Doctrine is recognized by all Americans as a part of the public law that they are in honor and in patriotism bound to sustain. That doctrine holds that the United States cannot tolerate European encroachments upon the soil of American republics which have thrown off their old-world allegiance. When this doctrine was declared in set terms seventy years ago it was with the heartiest concurrence and approval of Great Britain. At that time there existed an Alliance of continental monarchs, who were proposing to assist Spain in the recovery of her revolted South American colonies, with a view to apportioning them and forever holding them in bondage to Europe. It happened that England's interests were at that time adverse to those of the Alliance; and America's announcement of the Monroe Doctrine, sustained by England, saved the South American republics and formed a brilliant episode in our national history.

When this country was distracted with civil war, France and Austria thought to set at naught the Monroe Doctrine by subjecting Mexico to the rule of an Austrian prince. Having settled our own differences, we proceeded to reassert old principles in a manner which made its due impression and which saved Mexico as a self-governing republic. There is only one government, at present, which is showing any disposition to play fast and loose with the principles of the Monroe Doctrine; and that is the very government which seconded President Monroe and John Quincy Adams in their famous assertion of the claims of the new world.

We are assured that England has no desire to quarrel with the United States; and nothing in the world is farther from our intentions and wishes than a quarrel with our excellent kinsmen. But our tolerance and good nature ought not to make us forget justice and duty. If these scandalous British encroachments had affected our own territory, our resentment would have been quick and conclusive. But we are also under obligations to exert ourselves in behalf of a sister American republic, when in her feebleness she suffers from insolent and unscrupulous European aggression. Fortunately Venezuela has now secured an eloquent and able advocate in William L. Scruggs, a Southern diplomat and jurist, who was recently minister of the United States to Colombia and Venezuela, and who has made an exhaustive study of every legal and historical phase of the boundary question.

If there was ever a sound reason for the convening of a pan-American congress, there exists a reason today in the circumstances of this dispute between an American republic and a great European power which is coolly annexing American territory and fortifying each new strip of stolen ground. It is time for the American republics to inform England that America is neither Turkestan nor India; and that the methods by which Russia and England are gradually appropriating the whole of Asia will not be tolerated on this side of the Atlantic. Nor is America in the stage of original discovery and colonization. England, France and Germany may carve up Africa to suit themselves, and the United States will give itself small concern. But England's habit of conquest and of disregard for the rights and claims of feeble folk who cannot protect themselves must eliminate the Western Hemisphere from its future field of operations.

I should do myself some injustice if I seemed over-anxious to apologize, long years afterwards, for the asperity of those comments written in earlier years. I had spent much time in London, and was almost as familiar with English politics and the journalism of the British metropolis as with affairs in Washington and New York. In those days English newspapers had no correspondents in the United States, and the British public at large hardly knew the name of the American President. I was not passing judgment upon ascertained facts, but was calling attention to a dispute that had been too long neglected.

Four long years were to elapse before the Venezuela question was settled, and it required some agitation in the United States to carry the echoes of our stormy talk across the Atlantic. Frank discussion did no harm; on the contrary it was helpful, as results abundantly proved. I shall restrict further quotations; yet it seems worth while to follow the subject through to the end.

Only a month later than the appearance of the preceding paragraphs, I made the following comment:

We are glad to observe that President Cleveland has taken occasion in his message to Congress to call attention to the dispute between Venezuela and Great Britain, regarding the boundary lines of British Guiana, and to express his wish that Great Britain should consent to an arbitration of this question. In view of the history of the case, as outlined in these pages last month, Mr. Cleveland might well have expressed himself with greater emphasis. The subject is one which ought to be dealt with by Congress. Boundary disputes are in constant process of adjustment by joint commissions or outside arbitration, and there is no conceivable reason why the metes and bounds of British Guiana should not long ago have been determined. It is reported that Mexico and Guatemala have just now yielded to good counsels by agreeing to submit for adjustment by a joint commission what had begun to be a very acute boundary quarrel.

Four months later appeared the following allusions to current affairs in the Western Hemisphere, Lord Salisbury still refusing to arbitrate the Venezuela case:

There has been sincere gratification throughout the United States over the peaceful adjustment by Mexico and Guatemala of their vexatious boundary dispute. Hostile feeling had run high in both countries, and war seeemd almost inevitable. The details of the friendly compromise are far less important than the fact that war was averted. There is a renewal in Central America of the many times interrupted movement in favor of a union of the group of quarrelsome little republics. Every good reason is on the side of their forming a close confederation. The thing which has stood most in the way in the past has been the personal ambitions of petty generals and statesmen.

There has been much discussion of England's peremptory demand that Nicaragua should pay $75,000 as an indemnity for the expulsion from Bluefields of Mr. Hatch, the alleged English Consul. The reason why England sets her own price, and demands prompt payment without any discussion of the justice of the claim, lies simply in the fact that England is strong and Nicaragua weak. Much the cheapest and best thing for Nicaragua to do is to pay the sum demanded; while there would seem to be nothing for the United States to do except to give close attention and make a careful memorandum of the incident.

As for England's refusal to submit the Venezuelan boundary claim to arbitration, it is not so certain that this country should remain passive. In view of the recent attitude of Great Britain and other great European powers regarding affairs in this hemisphere, there are many arguments that might be urged in favor of the assemblage of a Pan-American Conference. A committee representing the American republics could investigate the Venezuelan claim, and could help to bring about a final solution.

Such a Pan-American Conference might be of use in helping to adjust Central American difficulties, and might, furthermore, have some influence in the settlement of the Cuban question. Cuba is part and parcel of America, and the Spanish yoke under which Cuba has so long been held down against her will is also an annoyance, a scandal and a positive injury to the whole western hemisphere. It is to be wished that some concerted action might be taken by the United States, Mexico, Brazil, Argentine, Chili and other American republics regarding such questions as the Venezuelan boundary, the independence of Cuba, and the European annoyances to which Central America is subjected.

IV.

The foregoing observations were wholesome and timely, and can be quoted in after years without regret. Our representative in London at that time was the courtly Mr. Bayard, who had been making well-phrased speeches here and there in England, in the course of which he had fallen into an injudicious habit of referring to the crudities and limited intelligence of the American people. When, therefore, the Venezuelan question came to the front in Washington, it went against the grain for our Ambassador to mention it to Lord Salisbury without minimizing the issue.[1]

At Paris by way of contrast the Hon. James B. Eustis, United States Minister to France, was perhaps too emphatic in asserting American views. He had evidently inherited a strong bias in favor of the Ostend Manifesto, and thought the United States ought to annex Cuba. As for the attitude of Great Britain towards trans-Atlantic affairs, Mr. Eustis exercised no diplomatic restraints. Although less polished and urbane than Mr. Bayard, Mr. Eustis was a man of force and adaptability; and his views were freely imparted to the head of the French Foreign Office, who was at that time perhaps the ablest statesman in Europe. Certainly M. Hanotaux was the most capable director of the foreign policy of France who had held that office for a long time. In my comments for the month of August, 1895, occur the following references to a speech that had been made by this French statesman:

> Unless we are greatly mistaken in reading what seems as simple as the alphabet, the French republic has wisely concluded that the best possible course for the French to pursue in their dealing with Western Hemisphere questions is to consult frankly and cordially with the United States and to make their policy so far as possible conform with the policy and wishes of the country. In his speech M. Hanotaux said of the United States that this nation is "employing admirable practical sense and legitimate authority among the nations to restrain warfare and develop the benefits of peace."
>
> Two highly significant steps have followed. One has been the announcement that France and Brazil will settle by friendly arbitration the dispute

[1] The Hon. Thomas F. Bayard of Delaware had been a Senator from his State for sixteen years when in 1885 he entered Mr. Cleveland's first Cabinet as Secretary of State. In 1893 he was appointed Ambassador to Great Britain.

which has lasted for several generations concerning the boundary line between French Guiana and the great South American republic. Meanwhile the administration of the disputed strip of territory is to be in the hands of a Dual Commission in which France and Brazil are to have equal representation.

The piece of territory which France and Brazil both claim is large enough to have very considerable importance, but the principle at stake is much more important than the strip of territory. The United States, France and Brazil are the world's three greatest republics. It is through the influence of the United States that France and Brazil have been willing to settle this boundary dispute by arbitration. It is now expected that the President of the Swiss republic will be arbitrator.

Following this step, as if by way of acknowledging the influence of the United States in bringing about so fortunate a termination of so disagreeable a dispute, the French Chamber of Deputies and the French Senate have concurred in adopting a resolution asking M. Hanotaux and his ministerial colleagues to endeavor to negotiate a permanent treaty for the arbitration of all disputes that may ever arise between France and the United States. We must beg to assure our readers that we consider the policy of M. Hanotaux toward North and South America, and his great desire to cultivate intimate and cordial relations with the United States, as one of the greatest steps in the progress of the world that the past month has revealed.

In that period the correspondents of the *London Times* at Paris, Berlin, and Vienna were men of such knowledge and influence that it was often said of them that they held positions equal if not superior to those of the British Ambassadors, except for ceremonial rank and dignity. The head of the *London Times* bureau at Vienna, Mr. Brinsley Richards, whom I knew well and to whom I was much indebted, was a foremost authority not only upon the Austro-Hungarian Empire but upon everything relating to the rivalries of Austria and Russia, as they affected the Balkan States and the changing fortunes of the lands held in suzerainty by the Turks.

The other newspapers of London, and also the *Manchester Guardian* and several provincial and Scottish newspapers, gave close attention to European news. But there was not a newspaper in the British Isles that thought it worth while to have a correspondent in the United States. A few copies of American periodicals found their way to England. My views, as it happened, became somewhat widely known through Mr. W. T. Stead's

English *Review of Reviews* by reason of a cooperative arrangement, and free exchange of articles.

Henry Cabot Lodge, United States Senator from Massachusetts, contributed an article to the *North American Review* on "England, Venezuela, and the Monroe Doctrine" which was incomparably more challenging and provocative than anything I should have dreamed of writing. Mr. Lodge declared that Great Britain had almost reached the limit of what could be secured in Asia, Africa, and the islands of the Pacific, and was now turning her attention to South America. Since Lodge was regarded more highly as historical scholar than as politician, and had been thought more friendly to the British than were Southern and Western politicians, his article made an exceptional impression. I think it suitable, therefore, to quote the sentences that follow from the concluding paragraph of this article by a Harvard scholar and United States Senator:

If the United States are prepared to see South America pass gradually into the hands of Great Britain and other European powers and to be hemmed in by British naval posts and European dependencies, there is, of course, nothing more to be said. But the American people are not ready to abandon the Monroe doctrine, or give up their rightful supremacy in the Western hemisphere. On the contrary, they are as ready now to fight to maintain both as they were when they forced the French out of Mexico. They are not now, and never will be, willing to have South America and the islands adjacent to the United States seized by European powers. They are resolved that the Nicaraguan canal [2] shall be built and absolutely controlled by the United States. It is high time, therefore, that steps should be taken to maintain the policy of Washington and Adams, to which American statesmen of all parties have adhered down to the present time. It is not too late to peacefully but firmly put an end to these territorial aggressions of Great Britain and to enforce the Monroe doctrine so that no other power will be disposed to infringe upon it. But immediate action is necessary.

Theodore Roosevelt (not then so well known as Mr. Lodge, but destined to be President of the United States only six years later) published an article asserting the Monroe Doctrine in equally firm tones, and demanding its application to the Vene-

[2] At that time it was expected that the United States would finally adopt the Nicaraguan route for the isthmian canal.

zuela case. A popular correspondent, Richard Harding Davis, went to Venezuela, aired the wrongs of that republic, and invoked the Monroe Doctrine somewhat flamboyantly. The newspapers of the United States, with an exception of two in New York and Boston, were publishing editorials in the tone of Senator Lodge. Both houses of Congress had already expressed their belief in the justice of Venezuela's demand for arbitration, and public men throughout the country were making speeches more violent than well-informed.

At this juncture a great organ of the Liberal party in London (the *Daily Chronicle*) which had been intelligent enough all along to understand that the United States asked nothing but investigation and arbitration, sent a special correspondent to the United States whose comprehensive articles reached a large section of the British public. Also the *London Times*, as an almost startling innovation, decided to place in the United States a regular correspondent of the same high ambassadorial rank as its representatives in European capitals.

The *Times* engaged the services of Mr. George W. Smalley, a brilliant American journalist who had organized the *New York Tribune's* London bureau in 1867 and had remained there for twenty-seven years. No one could have been more familiar with English politics and British Empire affairs than Mr. Smalley, and he knew how to interpret American views in such a way as to reassure an awakened and disturbed British public, which had been told that the United States was threatening war. Inasmuch as English statesmen of more recent periods have declared that "public opinion" must rule world affairs and decide the issues of war and peace, it is well to understand that the newspaper press is the chief agency through which the public is guided in forming conclusions.

V.

In the history of the growth of improved understanding between America and Great Britain, the year 1895 is a significant date, because it denotes the discovery by English newspapers that news from the United States is of importance to their readers. I shall proceed with further comments upon the Olney-Salisbury correspondence, and the manner in which the Venezuela case was brought to a creditable conclusion. But I may anticipate the remaining part of the narrative by a few added words of reflection upon public opinion as a force in the conduct of affairs. In an early chapter of the present volume I have referred to the rapid growth throughout Europe of elementary education and newspaper reading as a source of international difficulty during the nineteenth century. This was not because the development of popular sentiment was undesirable in itself, but because it was so sharply restricted and localized by political, racial, and language limits.

As against conflicting sentiments in Bulgaria and Serbia, for example, there was no sweeping public opinion throughout the Balkan States to uphold the advantages of harmony and cooperation. For the best interests not only of the English-speaking nations but of the world at large, nothing could have been more necessary than the discovery and nurture of common sentiments. If it could be found that there were basic ideas of justice, freedom, goodwill and fair play that were entertained in England as well as in America, it might then be possible to utilize the force of Anglo-American public opinion in times of great emergency regardless of differences of manner and custom.

I express these thoughts—as I continue to discuss certain events of the five years that ended the nineteenth century—because it was in this period that relations between Great Britain and the United States were tested in several serious emergencies, endured the strain, and ended the century with well-justified hopes for the future. I am willing to defend the thesis that Anglo-American public opinion, as we entered the twentieth century, had become a substantial thing—one of the sign posts on the way to a better world.

Mr. Cleveland's message to Congress at the opening of the session (December 3, 1895) was a carefully elaborated document, and it indicated a diligent study of our foreign relations. He had been President for almost three years of his second term, and had given studious attention to the duties of his responsible office. He informed Congress that a dispatch had been sent to the British government through our Ambassador at London in July, in which the facts relating to the Venezuela case were set forth as he and Mr. Olney understood them. Also, in that communication it had been argued that the territorial dispute could be settled only by friendly and impartial arbitration. The British government had previously intimated that it might be willing to draw a line to include the minimum of its claims, and then submit to arbitration the portion lying outside of that limit. Our government insisted upon submission of the territorial controversy in its entirety to an arbitral tribunal.

To show his lack of excitement, Mr. Cleveland went off on a hunting trip to be gone for a week or two, although he knew that the British reply was on its way in the ocean mails. Congress and the press were unduly impatient, and the President was sharply and generally criticized for absenting himself. I remarked at the time: "It is altogether possible that the President went to North Carolina expressly to avoid the necessity of sending the Venezuelan correspondence to Congress until the public feeling on that subject might grow somewhat more calm." This proved to be the case. He had to consider carefully the bearings of what he was proposing to do.

It was on the 17th that Mr. Cleveland transmitted to Congress a special message on the Venezuelan question, together with a full summary of the correspondence that had passed between Secretary Olney and the British government. Mr. Olney's exposition of the meaning of the Monroe Doctrine and of the attitude of the United States with reference to questions on this side of the Atlantic was regarded by Congress and the country as constituting a state paper of historic rank. In its essential purport Lord Salisbury's answer could be summed up in the statement that whatever Great Britain might choose to do with Venezuela or any other Latin-American state was absolutely none of the business of the United States. To quote his exact words: "It is a controversy with which the United States have no apparent practical concern. It is difficult indeed to see how it can materially affect any state or community outside those primarily interested, except, perhaps, other parts of Her Majesty's dominions, such as Trinidad. The disputed frontier of Venezuela has nothing to do with any of the questions dealt with by President Monroe."

President Cleveland's special message controverted Lord Salisbury's position, and invited Congress to support a plan that he proceeded to outline. He declared that "the dispute has reached such a stage as to make it now incumbent upon the United States to take measures to determine, with sufficient certainty for its justification, what is the true divisional line between the republic of Venezuela and British Guiana." His recommendation was accompanied by the remark that "it is a grievous thing to contemplate the two great English-speaking peoples of the world as being otherwise than friendly competitors in the onward march to civilization, and strenuous and worthy rivals in all the arts of peace." Yet he held that "there is no calamity which a great nation can invite which equals that which follows a supine submission to wrong and injustice, and the consequent loss of national self-respect and honor, beneath which is shielded and defended a people's safety and greatness."

There followed in both countries a period of discussion that was for the most part ill-informed regarding all phases of the particular issue, but the general effect was advantageous. It is essential to note the fact that Congress without delay and by a *unanimous vote of both Houses* endorsed the President's recommendation for the appointment of a special commission to determine "the true divisional line" between British Guiana and Venezuela, and $100,000 was appropriated for its necessary expenses.

When the President named the members of his commission of inquiry, the correspondents of English newspapers who had made their way to this country could find no occasion to be critical or to alarm the British public. If the selections had been made by the British Ambassador himself, he could not have improved upon Mr. Cleveland's appointments for assurance of impartiality, learning, and mature judgment. Besides two judges and an international lawyer of repute, there were two scholars who had founded universities and were as well known in England as in America, namely Andrew D. White of Cornell and Daniel C. Gilman of the Johns Hopkins. The choice of such men lifted the discussion out of the muck of ignorant controversy, and placed it at once on a high plane of historical and legal investigation. I shall allow myself to quote the comments I made upon the announcement of the selection of these gentlemen:

The Venezuelan Commission is very strongly composed. The Supreme Court of the United States is confessedly the most eminent tribunal in the world, and Justice Brewer is regarded as one of the ablest and most deeply learned members of the Supreme Bench. The Appellate Court of the District of Columbia also occupies a very high place, and Judge Alvey has long been held in peculiar esteem by jurists and lawyers. Mr. Coudert of

New York has a great international reputation as a lawyer, and his experience has made him unusually familiar with the history, laws and languages of the Latinic countries, whether European or American. The wit, eloquence, and good temper which he displayed, along with much learning, as one of the American counsel before the Bering Sea Arbitration Board, was fittingly acknowledged at the time.[3]

The Hon. Andrew D. White, formerly President of Cornell University, and Dr. Daniel C. Gilman, President of the Johns Hopkins University, belong to a group of influential American citizens who hold positions not exactly duplicated in any other country. The president of an American university is at once a scholar and a man of affairs. He represents citizenship in its best form, and stands for the highest national aspirations. President White has filled the great diplomatic positions of Minister to Germany and Ambassador to Russia. He is an eminent historical scholar, having in his younger days occupied the chair of History in the University of Michigan. It would be impossible to name a man in the entire country better fitted than President White, by virtue of the whole training and experience of a lifetime, to serve upon precisely such a commission.

President Gilman also has very exceptional qualifications. Like President White he has been a great traveler. One of his most cherished lines of study has always been geography, both physical and political. He has filled many important public trusts with great acceptability. He is the biographer of President Monroe. Like President White he has a wide acquaintance among the best and most influential Englishmen, who repose confidence in his attainments and know his disinterestedness. These five gentlemen will regard the rights of England as scrupulously as if they had been selected from the ranks of such Englishmen as Mr. Morley, Mr. Bryce, Sir John Lubbock, Mr. Balfour, the "law lords" of the House of Peers, or the Justices of the Queen's Bench.

Only careful students of that period can comprehend the vast range of problems with which Lord Salisbury was confronted, as he found it convenient within a few weeks to change his attitude completely toward the United States. Conditions in South Africa had led to a sharp difference between London and Berlin. The British government had improvised a Monroe Doctrine of its own, in accordance with which it was making such claims regarding a great portion of the African Continent as Mr. Olney was making

[3] Hon. Frederic R. Coudert was for many years chief legal advisor in the United States of the French, Italian and Spanish governments. He was a gradaute of Columbia University and an outstanding citizen of New York. In 1888 he had been a member of the International Conference at Berne for the codification of the law of nations.

in reference to our interest in the political development of the Americas. There were matters for England to adjust with France and Russia, and these were in process of settlement.

When Parliament opened Lord Salisbury was ready to explain in the House of Lords—and to have Mr. Balfour, as government leader in the House of Commons, explain, in the same conciliatory spirit—that nothing could be more plain or reasonable than the right of the government of the United States to give itself the most constant concern regarding the freedom of the smaller American republics from European oppression. The Monroe Doctrine was in effect conceded as a general principle of American policy, by his lordship and by his nephew, the Right Honorable Mr. Balfour; nor was there any serious attempt made to maintain the arguable thesis that the principle of the Monroe Doctrine was not involved in the Venezuelan dispute. The American Venezuelan Commission, far from being treated by Lord Salisbury and Mr. Balfour as offensive to the British government, and therefore to be protested against or else ignored, was referred to in terms of high respect and approval.

It was officially explained that the British government had consented to facilitate the inquiries of this commission at Washington by laying before it with the utmost possible expedition all the information bearing upon the matters in dispute that the government could find and arrange. This seeming reversal of attitude on Lord Salisbury's part met with the warm praise of the leaders of the Liberal opposition. It became evident at once that President Cleveland's firm position had really won the respect of Great Britain, and that, far from weakening the essential bonds of good will which bind together the people of England and the United States, the American policy in the Venezuelan matter was clearly destined to strengthen those bonds.

The appointment of our Commission had been regarded by President Cleveland not as a final step but as a preliminary one. It was hoped that a report of these legal and historical authorities would lead either to a settlement between England and Venezuela by negotiation, or to the appointment of an arbitration board. The Commission actually went more deeply into the historical aspects of the case than had either of the two governments concerned, although both presented voluminous materials to support their respective claims.

The Venezuelans had begun to feel such confidence in the Commission that they were awaiting its report with intense interest and hopeful anticipations. Meanwhile, however, the English Liberals—who had been badly defeated in the last General Election—were finding that the Venezuelan question offered them a timely opportunity to upbraid and criticize the Tory ministry. The Liberals were saying that never since time began had there ever been a clearer case for arbitration. Whereupon Lord Salisbury, discovering how consistent was the American belief in such methods for the settlement of international differences, began to discuss with Mr. Olney (in a series of amicable diplomatic exchanges) the precise terms of a treaty between England and the United States for a permanent tribunal to deal with all future differences that might arise.

Meanwhile, the British government was now ready to arbitrate the Venezuelan case without waiting for a report of the American Commission. This was gratifying, although there was a justifiable desire—in South America particularly—to know what such high authorities as Dr. Gilman, Dr. White, and Justice Brewer might have recommended. It should be remembered that in all boundary disputes affecting European settlements in new countries there is likely to be a conflict between the legalistic and traditional titles and the realistic or presumptive claims of the people who are creating a nationality upon the territory in dispute.

This conflict of ideas had involved us in the war with Mexico. Old Spanish or Mexican titles to land-grants as asserted by private owners were generally respected from Texas to California. But the American pioneers, soon constituting a majority of the population, refused to recognize Mexican sovereignty based upon the broad Spanish claim which in turn had owed its validity to a Papal Bull. The Venezuelans thought that their realistic title was better than the legalistic title of the previous Dutch proprietors, and far better than the British title based upon what the British lawyers themselves called "the right of conquest."

It is true enough that early international law writers treated the so-called "right of conquest" with great respect. I am repeating the phrase because to the twentieth century mind it seems little better than an invitation for the strong to prey upon the weak. Germany and Japan have now held up the mirror before the gaze of empire-builders whose gains by "right of conquest" had indeed been earlier in time, and certainly less abhorrent in practice, but not so different in principle.

As I have remarked, our Commission at Washington employing experts had examined the archives of Holland at The Hague, of Spain at Madrid, and of the Vatican at Rome, and had entertained with due respect the information and arguments presented by Venezuela and Great Britain. It was about to report, and President Cleveland expected to present the results to Congress in his Annual Message of December, 1896. But all this was superseded by Lord Salisbury's eagerness to proceed at once to arbitrate the dispute. I remarked at the time that "the scholarly, thorough and impartial methods of the Commission have become recognized by the whole world, and it is clear that if its decision were once given it would be practically impossible for either claimant to make good any other boundary than the one pronounced just and right by these American Commissioners."

Under the arrangement agreed upon, England was to name two arbitrators, the United States two, and the four were to select a fifth. It was prescribed in the agreement that where British subjects had been in actual occupancy for at least fifty years, their claim was to have consideration. Venezuela accepted the proposals with good grace. As finally arranged, the names of the arbitrators were inserted in the treaty, and it was signed at Washington by Sir Julian Pauncefote for England and Minister Andrade for Venezuela on February 2, 1897.

Venezuela named our Chief Justice Fuller, and President Cleveland designated Justice Brewer. Lord Salisbury's government selected Lord Herschell and Justice Collins, both of whom were eminent jurists. It was arranged that the umpire or fifth member should be named by King Oscar of Sweden. The case having reached this point, there were delays to explain which would only encumber a narrative already too protracted.

Early in 1899 this special board of arbitration was in session at Paris, with Professor Martens of Russia—perhaps the foremost European authority on international law of that period—as its presiding officer. Further dignity was added to the proceedings by the appearance of our former President Benjamin Harrison, and a former Cabinet Member Benjamin F. Tracy, as principal counsel for Venezuela, while Sir Richard Webster and other eminent lawyers were in charge of the British case. The arbitration court remained with the membership I have mentioned excepting that Lord Chief Justice Russell had later replaced Lord Herschell.

The tribunal was fortunate enough to reach a unanimous decision. I shall not attempt to discuss the verdict itself. Both theoretical and practical claims were considered, and no one had occasion to question the justice of the conclusions reached. The announcement was made on October 3, 1899.

The case had become important chiefly through the principles that were brought into question. It was well worth while that the Chief Justice of the United States and the Lord Chief Justice of Great Britain sat together as members of the tribunal. It was remarked at the time that a permanent high court for treatment of international disputes might have settled this particular issue much more quickly. I expressed that opinion at the time, and this view was accepted in the United States, Great Britain, and South America.

But during the pendency of this dispute both the United States and Great Britain had become involved in wars of great historic significance; and the settlement of the Venezuela case at a European capital by such a spectacular array of Anglo-American authorities was a fortunate occurrence. It presented an object lesson to a disturbed world. Public opinion in England and America had discovered essential points of agreement, and had learned that when questions of justice and of right conduct were brought to the test, the basic views of our two countries could be brought into harmony. This was to hold good in times of far greater trial during the first half of the twentieth century.

Chapter XII

CUBAN INDEPENDENCE AND THE PANAMA CANAL

The Spanish-American War of 1898, in its causes, methods, and results, deserves re-study as it throws more light than any other episode upon the development of American foreign policy. It was an intervention to end a three-year struggle that had become deadlocked and increasingly disastrous.

The political and economic reconstruction of Cuba under American auspices throws some light upon methods that will have to be pursued by the United Nations, jointly or separately, in social relief and rehabilitation, and in temporary political control of one country or colonial area after another.

Besides placing chief emphasis upon the sanitary reforms that have changed all the conditions of life in the West Indies and the countries around the Caribbean Sea, I have considered the war of 1898 in its broader bearing as related to the Monroe Doctrine and Latin-American interests.

This chapter further summarizes the history of the Panama Canal, chiefly from the diplomatic standpoint and from that of the withdrawal of the Isthmus of Panama from connection with the Republic of Colombia. It recites the later transactions that created perfect accord between our government and that of Colombia, and that gave the small Isthmian Republic of Panama a status above reproach in the Pan-American family.

During the Taft administration Congress granted exemption from Canal tolls to American vessels engaged in coastwise traffic. A question arose regarding the consistency of this exemption with provisions in the Hay-Pauncefote treaty, under which Great Britain had renounced all claims to an interest in the construction or control of an Isthmian waterway. At President Wilson's instance, Congress revoked this exemption of tolls, in order that no question might be raised in any quarter as to the equality of treatment by the United States of vessels under all flags making use of the facilities of the Canal.

The chapter ends with the assertion that "our accomplishments at Panama have foreshadowed a world of peaceful commerce, of collective safeguards against epidemics, and of increasing harmony as intercourse tends to elevate the standards of living and to serve the common ends of civilized society."

IN the present chapter it is my purpose to consider the Spanish-American war, chiefly with reference to its avowed motives and purposes and to its results as they bear upon the pattern of international relations in the era following the present world conflict. The war of 1898 was of brief duration; but its consequences have had a profound effect upon our policies during the past forty-five years, and have made themselves a part of European and Asiatic history as well as that of North and South America, the Central American states, and the island domains not only of the West Indies, but also of the Pacific ocean.

We undertook the war as a relief mission. We were setting out in good faith to rescue the Cubans from a situation that had become intolerable. Our own grievances were slight and incidental, and we were embarking upon an adventure that was essentially altruistic. The revolt of the Cuban patriots had lasted for three years, and had reached a stalemate. We had looked on at the devastating scene, as the arrival of recruits from time to time had expanded the Spanish force in Cuba until it aggregated about 200,000 officers and men. The Insurrectos, under command of General José Gómez and other guerrilla chieftains—leaders of amazing audacity and persistence—controlled the hilly interior of the extensive island, while the Spanish troops held the seaports and the coastal areas.

The retention of Cuba as a surviving remnant of Spain's vast colonial empire in the New World was not merely a point of pride with the royal house and the political authorities at Madrid. It was demanded also by the Spanish people, with passionate sentiment. Any minister of the Crown who might have proposed to sell Cuba to the United States would have been dismissed from office before he could start negotiations. Yet Cuba had become by far too costly a jewel in the Spanish crown.

Almost a quarter of a million young soldiers and seamen were far from happy in their indefinite absence from the farms, villages, and seaport towns of the Iberian Peninsula. The patriotic rebels were supplied with guns and ammunition from the United States by a smuggling system that could not be suppressed. This was not carried on with the connivance of the government at Washington; but there was such general sympathy with the cause of Cuban independence that agents of the Insurrectionist leaders had little trouble in obtaining needed supplies from the United States.

European governments were not well disposed toward the idea of American intervention in Cuba, and did not hesitate to make joint expressions of their disapproval. Through inter-marriage the reigning house of Spain was widely connected; and European views were reflected in the hostile attitude of diplomats at Washington representing royalist governments. At first Lord Pauncefote, the British minister, seemed to take the lead in bringing this adverse pressure to bear; but his attitude was rather suddenly altered. The authoritative biography of Joseph Chamberlain published several years ago reveals the fact that this energetic Unionist statesman was entitled to full credit for the change of front in favor of the United States. Mr. Chamberlain had married an American wife and had learned to give close attention to American opinion. He was Secretary for the Colonies in Lord Salisbury's Cabinet, and was able to convince his chief that Britain would make a serious mistake if the Foreign Office should take the Spanish side, and frown upon a sincere effort by the United States to liberate Cuba. This British swing to the American side was to earn rewards that no one could well have anticipated.

Before explaining the steps taken by our government to make its disinterested motives convincing, not only to our citizens at home but also to foreign observers, it may be well to revert to an occurrence of the year 1854, also relating to Cuba. Forty-four years had elapsed, and the so-called "Ostend Manifesto" bore no relation whatever to American policy in 1898, yet it was not forgotten in Spain. President Franklin Pierce's Secretary of State was Mr. Marcy of New York. At his instance, three American diplomats met at Ostend in Belgium to take counsel together regarding the interest of the United States in the island of Cuba. These were James Buchanan, then our Minister at London (who was to succeed Mr. Pierce as President); John Y. Mason, who was United States Minister to France; and Pierre Soulé, our Minister to Spain.

These well-known leaders of the Democratic party drew up a report that was afterwards widely promulgated—at least by their Republican opponents. It held that Cuba by situation and destiny was already within the territorial and political orbit of the United States, and that its control by a foreign power was detrimental to our interests. The Manifesto proposed that an offer should be made to Spain to purchase the island, and in case of

Spain's refusal, it was declared that "by every law human and divine we shall be justified in wresting it from Spain, if we possess the power."

This was perhaps the most frank and undisguised statement of a belief in the heaven-ordained "right of conquest" that was ever issued as if by authority of an American administration. Its adverse effect upon opinion everywhere was such that it was repudiated at Washington even by those who had been responsible for it. The Republican party was then in process of formation, and its first Presidential Convention was held in 1856. One of the planks in its platform was phrased as follows:

"*Resolved*, That the highwayman's plea, that 'might makes right,' embodied in the Ostend circular, was in every respect unworthy of American diplomacy, and would bring shame and dishonor upon any government or people that gave it their sanction."[1]

It was just forty years after the contest of 1856 that William McKinley was elected to the Presidency in a successful Republican campaign. The insurrection in Cuba had begun in the previous year; and there was no question about the general sympathy of Americans for the cause of Cuban independence. But Republican leaders were not to forget their party's historic denunciation of the Ostend Manifesto and they were not willing to have it thought in any quarter that the United States proposed to acquire the island.

II.

In entering upon the war against Spain the two houses of Congress in the early hours of April 19, 1898, adopted a preamble followed by four resolutions. Since the preamble presents certain facts, while the resolutions form a statement of American policy, it will, I think, be more desirable to quote them than to epitomize or paraphrase them:

WHEREAS, The abhorrent conditions which have existed for more than three years in the island of Cuba, so near our own borders, have shocked the moral sense of the people of the United States, have been a disgrace

[1] Dr. Dexter Perkins, our most exacting authority upon subjects relating to the Monroe Doctrine, reminds me that the "Ostend Manifesto" was not an official document, and cannot be justly attributed to Mr. Pierce's administration as a promulgation of American policy.

to Christian civilization, culminating, as they have, in the destruction of a United States battleship, with two hundred and sixty of its officers and crew, while on a friendly visit in the harbor of Havana, and cannot longer be endured, as has been set forth by the President of the United States in his message to Congress of April 11, 1898, upon which the action of Congress was invited; and therefore be it resolved:

First—That the people of the island of Cuba are, and of right ought to be, free and independent.

Second—That it is the duty of the United States to demand, and the Government of the United States does hereby demand, that the Government of Spain at once relinquish its authority and government in the island of Cuba and withdraw its land and naval forces from Cuba and Cuban waters.

Third—That the President of the United States be, and he hereby is, directed and empowered to use the entire land and naval forces of the United States, to call into the actual service of the United States the militia of the several States to such an extent as may be necessary to carry these resolutions into effect.

Fourth—That the United States hereby disclaims any disposition or intention to exercise sovereignty, jurisdiction, or control over said island, except for the pacification thereof, and asserts its determination when that is accomplished to leave the government and control of the island to its people.

On the following day, April 20, an ultimatum was sent to the Spanish government, and Spain was given three days within which to meet American demands and avoid a war. There was no reason to believe that Spain would yield to the ultimatum without at least some show of fight. Nor could any country that draws its sword against another ever foretell how soon it may turn again to its plowshares. Nevertheless, it was true for Cuba—although Spanish authorities could not believe it—that the long desired boon of independence was assured when President McKinley signed the joint resolution declaring that the people of the island are, and of right ought to be, free and independent.

The events of the 19th and 20th of April came as the culmination of a period of heated discussion that had lasted many days. Yet apart from differences of opinion about matters of detail there was remarkable unanimity upon the essential fact that Spain had inevitably forfeited Cuba. There had been delay in Congress because of strong divergences of view regarding the wisdom of an immediate recognition of the provisional Cuban republic. But this proposal, which was offered as an amendment by Senator Foraker of Ohio, was strongly supported on the Democratic side of the Senate, and was adopted by a conclusive majority.

In response to the American ultimatum, Spain declared war against the United States on April 24, and our Congress voted that war had actually existed since the 21st. On that date the foreign powers had been notified of our intention to blockade Havana (this being an act of war) and Admiral Sampson received sailing orders. On the same date a blockade of Manila harbor in the Philippine Islands by the Asiatic squadron under Commodore Dewey was decided upon and ordered.

As regards the war itself, a few facts and dates will suffice for the present purpose. The principal Spanish fleet under Admiral Cervera sailed from the Cape Verde islands on April 29, and took refuge in the harbor of Santiago on the south coast of Cuba. On July 3 this Spanish admiral led his fleet out of the harbor in an attempt to run through the American blockade, but in the naval battle that ensued his ships were destroyed within four hours.

Commodore Dewey had sailed into Manila Bay a little more than two months earlier; and on May 1 he had annihilated the Spanish fleet that was guarding the Philippine archipelago. American land forces in Cuba were speedily victorious after several actions in July, especially at Santiago and San Juan Hill, where Colonel Theodore Roosevelt's Rough Riders took part in the fighting.

An armistice was signed on August 12, and the war was ended to the great relief of all concerned. It had lasted for a week less than four months. The Spanish government had been told by European naval experts of repute that the United States was inferior to Spain as a maritime power. But the American officers and men were incomparably superior in training, morale, and efficiency. It was an intervention to end a war that was ruining Cuba and bankrupting Spain. Each side had reason to be grateful, although the blow to Spanish pride was grievous.

No other American leader, as it happened, was so conspicuously affected in his public career by the war with Spain and its results as Theodore Roosevelt. For more than a year he had been Assistant Secretary of the Navy in the McKinley administration, and he had foreseen the probability of a test of strength between our naval forces and those of Spain. He had been given a free hand in directing the training of our seamen in gunnery, and had personally selected Admiral Dewey for command in the Pacific. Upon the approach of war, having done what he could to prepare the navy, he recruited his regiment of Rough Riders which was commended for its part in the battle of San Juan. Returning with his men to Long Island where they were disbanded, he soon found himself drafted by the Republicans as their candidate for Governor of New York, and was elected to that office in November.

Entering upon his duties at Albany at the beginning of the year, he delivered an extended message to the Legislature (January 2, 1899) which was devoted principally to state affairs, but which opened with a noteworthy statement referring to the war in which he had taken part. I am not aware that people of the present day have ever had their attention called to that expression of Roosevelt's views about the meaning of the Spanish-American War. I am quoting it especially because it throws light upon the convictions of a man who was within less than three years afterwards to assume the responsibilities of the Presidency, and to direct certain policies that have had lasting consequences. It follows herewith:

> The people of New York, like the people of every other State in the Union, are to be congratulated, because during the past year the nation has carried to a brilliant triumph one of the most righteous wars of modern times. When last spring it became evident that the interests of humanity and of national honor alike demanded that we should drive Spain from the Western Hemisphere and free from her tyranny the subject peoples of the islands of the sea, New York responded with eager zeal to the call for volunteers, and in the Cabinet, in Congress, and in camp, her representatives did all they could to ensure the success of the American policy. We are not merely New Yorkers. We are Americans; and the interests of all Americans, whether from the North, the South, the East or the great West, are equally dear to the men of the Empire State.
>
> As we grow into a mighty nation, which, whether it will or not, must inevitably play a great part for good or for evil in the affairs of the world at large, the people of New York wish it understood that they look at all questions of American foreign policy from the most thoroughly national standpoint. The tropic islands we have taken must neither be allowed to lapse into anarchy nor to return under the sway of tyranny.
>
> War is a grim thing at best, but the war through which we have passed has left us not merely memories of glory won on land and sea, but an even more blessed heritage, the knowledge that it was waged from the highest

motives, for the good of others as well as for our own national honor. Above all, we are thankful that it brought home to all of us the fact that the country was indeed one, when serious danger confronted it. The men from the East and the West, from the North and the South, the sons of those who wore the blue and of those who wore the gray, the men of means and the men who all their lives long had possessed only what day by day they toiled to earn, stood shoulder to shoulder in the fight, met the same dangers, shared the same hardships and won the same ultimate triumph.

The foregoing statement, with which Colonel Roosevelt opened his first official communication in his new capacity as Governor of New York, was published as one paragraph; but I have broken it into three for more convenient reading, and because there are sentences in it that justify emphasis. Two generations have grown to manhood and womanhood since these avowals were made, just four weeks after a treaty of peace had been signed at Paris between Spain and the United States. The Governor's theory of the war was entertained by President McKinley, both House of Congress, and quite generally by right-minded people throughout the country.

I had known Theodore Roosevelt with intimacy for some years, and was consulted by him in the preparation of this message to the Legislature. I am competent, therefore, to testify to the sincerity with which he asserted that the recent war was waged from the highest motives, and that the United States must inevitably play a great part in the affairs of the world at large, as we grew into a mighty nation. In his mind, we were acting as an agent for the forces of civilization.

III.

Behind this action was the unified opinion of our forty-eight states; the endorsement and approval of the government and people of Canada; the moral support of most Latin-American countries, and the timely understanding and good will of the British people of both parties, expressed through the Conservative government of Lord Salisbury. Furthermore, the disapproval of continental Europe as expressed in narrow governmental circles was limited and superficial rather than popular.

It could not have been sufficient, however, merely to avow high motives when we undertook an intervention by force in affairs not strictly our own. Our conduct had to be justified not only in the eyes of onlookers at that time, but also in results that could be evaluated half a century later. There were certain immediate consequences, however, that many survivors in Cuba (then children in *reconcentrado* camps) hold in memory today. Spain had exploited Cuba with so little regard for the welfare of the inhabitants that there had long been a ferment of discontent, with earlier wars for independence that had failed.

The three-year struggle beginning in 1895 had been accompanied by terrible privations for women and children. The situation grew worse progressively. In his determination to end the war, the Spanish commander, General Weyler, had adopted the plan of herding women and children (together with such men as he could capture) into concentration camps to keep them from rendering aid to their compatriots who were fighting in *commando* raids from their strongholds in the hills. During the three years more than 200,000 lives were said to have been sacrificed, including those killed in fighting on both sides, and the greater number who died of starvation and disease. This was perhaps one-eighth of the entire population, which in 1895 had amounted to approximately 1,600,000.

One of the most highly respected members of our Senate, the Hon. Orville H. Platt of Connecticut, had visited Cuba in order to ascertain for President McKinley and Congress the nature and extent of those bad conditions, regarding which we had received startling accounts. Senator Platt was a man of philanthropic character, while also an accurate and trustworthy observer. His report had much influence upon the subsequent decision of Congress to intervene.

To restore normal conditions of safety and order, to provide food for the hungry, and to reconstruct the economic life of the island were obvious tasks of emergency that the United States proceeded to perform. No mature person will suppose that our invasion of Cuba and our attempt to set up an independent republic could have been carried off like a well-conducted holiday cruise. Such undertakings on the part of a peaceable nation like ours are rough-and-tumble affairs, replete with incidents that show unpreparedness and unskillful management. Our small regular army had been in scattered detachments at Western posts, and no American general at that time had ever commanded as many troops together as would constitute a small brigade.

But in the perspectives of history we may see the forest without considering the underbrush. Theodore Roosevelt was keenly aware of ineptitudes and of mistakes to be corrected. His great merit lay in the fact that he could see clearly what were the impelling motives of the country, and could anticipate—with reasonable forecasts and without inflamed imagination—the greatly broadened position that the United States in the twentieth century would have to assume in world affairs.

The treaty with Spain having been signed at Paris on December 10, 1898, Governor Roosevelt had been aware of its principal terms for three weeks before his completion of the message from which I have quoted. He knew that we were to be occupied with the reconstruction of social and political life in Cuba, and that we were taking over the administration of Puerto Rico as a dependency of the United States in the West Indies. He knew also that we were to extend Admiral Dewey's occupation at Manila indefinitely, and were to assume control of the great Philippine archipelago in the interest of its inhabitants as well as for reasons of large international import. This decision regarding the Philippines is one that I shall discuss in a chapter concerning our interests in the Pacific; and I shall return to the Cuban situation for some further remarks.

As a naval power Spain had been virtually obliterated; but having lost the valuable remnants of her empire alike in the West Indies and the East Indies, she had little cause to regret the loss of needless armored vessels. Her navy had been maintained in traditional regard for memories of the great days when it protected the treasure ships of her merchant marine.

The pressing task was not to rebuild the useless navy, but to bring back more than two hundred thousand homesick soldiers—most of them mere boys—lingering amidst the scenes of hunger and epidemic disease on the shores of Cuba. Upon that topic I shall reproduce in several following paragraphs the gist of what I wrote in August, 1898, a few days after the armistice, or so-called "peace protocol," that was signed on August 12. The comments relate particularly to the arrangements for evacuating the Cuban troops.

The completeness of the settlement of the West Indian situation, which was set forth in the summary of the protocol, afforded a justification of the policy pursued by the United States, while it also entitled President McKinley, with his Secretary of State and his other principal advisers, to the gratitude and esteem of all friends of progress and humanity. The surrender at Santiago, followed by the remarkable arrangements for the deportation of the army of Generals Linares and Toral back to their native shores, furnished the outlines of a plan upon which the complete evacuation of Cuba and Puerto Rico would be carried out in the course of the next few weeks or months.

In the case of the troops surrendered at the eastern end of Cuba in July, the United States had agreed to provide transportation at its own expense back to Spain. Bids having been called for, it turned out that the principal transatlantic steamship company of Spain had made a more advantageous offer than any other of a considerable number of competing transportation agencies. The United States Government had, accordingly, accepted the Spanish proposition.

And thus it happened that in the very midst of a vigorously prosecuted war the victor at a given point was amicably paying the expenses of sending a conquered army across an ocean, employing for that purpose the merchant marine of the enemy, and carefully bargaining with the hostile contractors that they should furnish safe and suitable accommodations and provide ample and proper food for the men of their own army, whom they were being well paid to carry home. Nothing like this had ever happened before in all the history of warfare. The incident threw light upon the spirit in which the United States had prosecuted the war from the very beginning.

If the United States had merely recognized first the belligerency and then the independence of the Cuban republic without active armed intervention, the Spaniards would have been ultimately forced out; but they would not have withdrawn without first destroying Havana and leaving the whole island in a state of chaos and ruin. We were now to witness a quiet and orderly removal of the Spanish armies, aggregating scores of thousands of men, from Cuba and Puerto Rico back to their homes in Spain. Their coming and their going constituted a military episode without parallel, for it must be remembered that never before in the history of the world had there been any movement of troops across an ocean on a scale even half as great.

Those who had formed the habit of speaking of Spain as a

decadent and inefficient nation, while having much truth on their side, ought at least to have remembered that the assemblage of two hundred thousand Spanish soldiers in Cuba, and their maintenance there for two or three years, gave evidence of a very considerable degree of energy and vitality. It was enough to say that Spain had forfeited all claim to the further management of distant colonial possessions. Her civil administration of those possessions had been hopelessly corrupt and oppressive, while the scandalous rottenness of her military administration afforded the chief explanation of her failure to subdue the Cuban insurgents. The Spaniards at home in their own peninsula were more likely to exhibit a renaissance than a national decline as a result of this war with America. Our soldiers who faced the Spaniards regarded them as brave and vigorous opponents. Good leadership and honest government was their great need.

When the last contingents of Spanish soldiery were evacuated from Cuba and Puerto Rico, there came to an end a military occupation that had been unbroken for several centuries. Also there came the end of a system of colonial administration that had provided places for hordes of Spanish civilians, whose chief purpose was to acquire wealth enough to return to Spain and live in comfort. Nothing had been done to train the Cubans as a whole for the political, economic and social tasks of a well-ordered republic. They were not without men of education and professional training, and there were numerous " politicos " and military leaders. But even a reformed colonial administration, such as Spain had promised to institute, would have been better than an immediate assumption of political independence without external support.

Had Congress been unwise in declaring, just before its ultimatum to Spain, that the " United States disclaims any disposition or intention to exercise sovereignty, jurisdiction, or control over said island, except for the pacification thereof, and asserts its determination when that is accomplished to leave the government in control of the island to its people? " When that declaration was made on the eve of war, it was not debated. Its object was to give a broad general assurance to the Cubans themselves, to the Latin-American republics, and to the cynical statesmen of Europe, that the United States had no purpose to annex Cuba " by right of conquest."

After the armistice the Spaniards had been less eager to withdraw, and they had kept part of their army at the western end of the island while waiting for the final peace settlement. The Spanish court at Madrid entertained lingering hopes that European powers might engage in some form of belated interference to curb Yankee aggression. Such ideas of course were vain and futile; but there were many influential Spaniards who had private interests in Cuba, and these had to be protected in so far as they were legitimate. Continued military occupation by the United States was essential. To have withdrawn immediately would have left Cuba in chaos, and would have heaped reproach rather than honor upon the adventure that Theodore Roosevelt justified so sincerely at the end of 1898.

IV.

Further remarks that I shall make upon the reconstruction of Cuba and its launching as a hopeful member of the family of nations are intended to have some bearing upon problems that will be faced at the end of the second world war. No two situations will be exactly alike; but certain principles were observed, and certain methods applied in the case of Cuba more than forty years ago, that have been justified in results, and that have gained the approval of qualified historians. American policies were guided with a tactful hand by President McKinley; but two men whom he appointed to critical positions after the conclusion of the peace treaty with Spain are entitled to more prominence than any others in the assignment of credit for the achievements of a three-year period.

By rapid promotions from May to December, 1898, Colonel Leonard Wood, who had been an Army surgeon until May (when at Roosevelt's request he was made Colonel of the regiment of Rough Riders) found himself a Major-General. He was left in charge of affairs at the eastern end of the island with his headquarters at Santiago. When he left Cuba some months later for a brief visit to the United States (as Ray Stannard Baker wrote at the time): "All Santiago came down to see him off and cheered him lustily. They presented him with a diploma of regard, a beautiful hand-work scroll written in Spanish—'the people of the city of Santiago de Cuba to Gen. Leonard Wood. The greatest of your successes is to have won the confidence and esteem of a people in trouble.' "

This tribute was a foreshadowing of the larger success that was to attend the services of Leonard Wood in Cuba. Soon after the middle of the year 1899 the McKinley administration was to be strengthened by the appointment of Mr. Elihu Root of New York as Secretary of War. Mr. Root was well known as one of the country's ablest lawyers, who had shown in his own state a talent for constitutional and administrative reforms. Toward the end of that year Mr. Root sent General Wood from Santiago to Havana, and made him Military Governor of the entire island. He retained that office from December 12, 1899 until the government of Cuba was transferred to the new Cuban Republic on May 20, 1902.

Four years had elapsed since our decision to expel Spain from the West Indies and make Cuba a self-governing entity. In view of the difficulties to be overcome, this was not too long a period. Writing after two years had elapsed since the ratification of the treaty with Spain, I predicted that history would accord us praise for the record we had already made in the island, and continued my comment as follows:

> Although our temporary government has been exercised through the War Department, its spirit has been civilian and statesmanlike rather than military. We have not filled the civil offices of Cuba with 'carpet-bagging' Americans, but to the very utmost have endeavored to fill them with Cubans. We have not hesitated, however, to furnish administrative, educational, financial, and sanitary experts, in order to set a high standard for the new regime in the long-suffering island. General Wood as Governor has at once held the deserved confidence of the people of Cuba, the respect and esteem of the people of the United States, and the firm support of his immediate superiors, Secretary Root and President McKinley. He has taken such good care of public affairs in Cuba that Cuban agriculture and commerce have had some opportunity to recover themselves. It would have been very fortunate for Cuba if General Wood could have continued, for at least four or five years to come, to manage the public affairs of the island on the present system. But democracies are impatient, and opposition parties have no nice scruples. It was perfectly certain that if Mr. McKinley and the Republican party had proposed to defer for several years the withdrawal of the United States, there would have been no end of nagging accusation brought against them.

Meanwhile, Cuban delegates had met in constitutional convention to provide a plan for the domestic government of the island, and to open negotiations with the United States to settle the future relations between Washington and Havana. They had yet (1) to give the final touches to their domestic constitution; (2) their agreement with the United States had to be worked out; (3) Cuba's first general election would have to be held; and (4) the transfer of government from the United States to the new authorities and the withdrawal of the American troops would be the final step.

Cuba was to be self-governing and was to take a place of dignity among the Latin-American republics. Yet the circumstances were such that there had to be arrangements of exceptional intimacy between the United States and the tentative republic. It was desirable, in view of Cuba's safety as well as our own best interests, to acquire an American naval station on the Cuban coast (without involving Cuba in any expense) and Mr. Root was able to arrange this without difficulty. Our situation (then arranged for) at Guantanamo on the southeastern coast near Santiago has been available for ships of the Pan-American countries, and at the service of the United Nations in the present war.

A more difficult question was that of trade agreements. I was one of those who thought that the relations between Cuba and the United States ought to be so intimate at all points as to justify entire freedom of trade, with no tariff barriers whatever between the two countries. This could have been accomplished, but for the sugar question. The beet-sugar interests of several of our Western states were more powerful at Washington than in the commodity markets. They were willing to admit a large quantity of Cuban sugar on preferential terms, but not the entire crop. It is obvious enough that Cuba has already been too greatly dependent upon the fluctuating demand for sugar in world markets. Economic adjustments in Europe at the end of the present war, it is hoped, will assist Cubans in securing stable markets and improved financial conditions.

As one looks back upon the results of the Spanish-American War as regards its influence upon conditions in the Western Hemisphere, I should give first place to the sanitary reforms that were achieved almost immediately, and that have paid increasing dividends throughout the decades that have followed. Upon this topic I made comments and predictions while the question of Cuban-American relations was still under discussion:

> It is not fortresses or naval stations or commercial relations that are chiefly important to us as regards Cuba, but something wholly different. Through our entire lifetime as a nation we have been sorely plagued and incalculably harmed by epidemic diseases that have visited us from the West Indian ports, and particularly from Havana. In times past we have thus imported smallpox, typhus, cholera, and, worst and most frequently, yellow fever. Since the American occupation of Cuba we have been doing all we could to improve sanitary conditions there for the good of the Cubans and also for our own benefit. We are making some wonderful demonstrations as to the way in which yellow fever is propagated, with the prospect that we may in a few years stamp it out altogether. It would be worse than frivolous folly — it would be criminal — for a handful of Cuban politicians on the one side, and a handful of nagging partisans and self-righteous American newspapers on the other, to force a precipitate independence upon Cuba that would simply mean the yearly dread of yellow fever, and the occasional dread of cholera, to our entire Southern seaboard. The people of the South should see this matter clearly and in its true light, and should insist that their representatives at Washington put important considerations first.

It had been a matter of common consent that the United States could not install a Cuban government and withdraw, without having first approved of Cuba's constitutional arrangements for the internal government of the island. Furthermore, the acceptance of some plan that would provide for American oversight and possible control in emergencies had to be worked out and agreed upon. In the international sense, Cuba had fallen under the jurisdiction and sovereignty of the United States since 1898; and after the lapse of three years the outside world had ceased to care about the form of future Cuban-American relations. It was assumed in Europe that the island would remain under the tutelage or sponsorship of the United States government. From our own standpoint, however, and from that of Cuba also, the arrangement had to be made explicit.

It took form in what was known as "The Platt Amendment," so-called because it was added to a bill authorizing the President to withdraw from the military occupation of Cuba. The Connecticut Senator who had introduced it had for some years shown a deep interest in the welfare of the Cuban people. It was in several clauses, the first of which was intended to protect and guarantee the independence of Cuba, and the second was meant to insure the island's financial solvency. The third clause embodied Cuba's consent to the exercise of intervention by the United States if necessary to preserve independence and the maintenance of responsible government. Another clause related to the execution of plans mutually agreed upon " for the sanitation of the cities of the island to the end that recurrence of epidemic and infectious diseases may be prevented thereby assuring protection to the people and commerce of Cuba, as well as to the commerce of the Southern ports of the United States and the people residing therein."

Not to specify the nature of one or two other appropriate clauses, it is enough to say that the eighth and last one required the embodiment of the entire series in a permanent treaty between Cuba and the United States. The author of the arrangements included in the Platt Amendment was Secretary Root, whose object was to give the more intelligent citizens of Cuba such support as they would need in establishing a government under the difficult conditions of popular suffrage.

During subsequent crises the United States intervened more than once in accordance with the agreement, always however to maintain peace and order for the best interest of the Cuban people themselves. In 1934 the treaty was abrogated by common consent, perhaps as a so-called " good neighbor " gesture. If serious disorder should occur, it is probable that the countries of the Pan-American Union would act together in an endeavor as conciliators, to protect Cuban interests from the recklessness of rival military leaders seeking to rule the island and set themselves up as dictators.

Diplomatic history and international relationships may be said to bear some resemblance to pictures of the impressionistic school. They must be viewed with proper perspective in order to have any meaning. Only those concerned with such affairs—diplomats and students of history—could have even a faint idea of the commitments and entanglements that are involved in the history of a small Caribbean state, Nicaragua or Santo Domingo for example. One might wonder how such a small state as Nicaragua, frequently distracted by revolutions and always engaged in diplomatic transactions with other governments, can find safe storage for the official materials that accumulate year by year in its archives.[2]

If the records were examined in close detail, with no attempt to deduce conclusions from results over (let us say) half-century periods, one might turn away in bewilderment, doubting the reality of human progress. When, however, one accepts the view that nations great or small have hitherto made their way through trouble, toil, and pain, we may take for granted the rough road and terrible detours, and find some encouragement in broad comparisons. All progress is at the cost of grim struggle, though its results may read like a fairy tale.

The greatest boon that has ever been conferred upon the peoples of Central America (as well as the West Indies, and the continental areas of North and South America bordering upon the Caribbean Sea and Gulf of Mexico) may be summed up in the terms "tropical medicine" or "public-health administration." A new life-saving dispensation may be said to have begun with the Spanish-American War, and with the decision by the United States Government to construct an Isthmian canal as a national enterprise.

V.

The details as related to the history of the canal are tedious and complicated. They may be read in a shelf full of books in several languages dealing with this great engineering project from technical and scientific standpoints. They may be studied also in the diplomatic history of France, England, the United States, and several Latin-American countries. From still another angle they may be studied in the great medical library founded by Dr. William H. Welch in association with the School of Public Health at the Johns Hopkins University, and in other libraries that devote attention to the subjects of tropical medicine, bacteriology, the control of infectious diseases, and the prevention of epidemics.

Portuguese and Spanish explorers and colonizers were relating their dreams of a canal across Panama almost a hundred years before the English settlements of Virginia and Massachusetts.

[2] Research historians tell me that West Indian and Central American archives are "in terrible shape." But so were ours at Washington until our scholars and scientists persuaded Congress to provide an Archives building, and to see that official papers were properly filed and preserved.

From our North American standpoint, the subject of transit across the Isthmus became a practical one after the Mexican War, when gold was found in California and the migratory rush set in for the Pacific Coast. Early in the century the naturalist and geographer Humboldt had mapped alternative routes for a canal, and Spain had proposed to begin construction at the very time when all her aims and objects in the Western Hemisphere were ended by the revolutions that made Spanish America independent. A railroad had been built by American capital at Panama in 1855, which facilitated transfer of passengers and freight from the shipping of one ocean to that of the other during the continued migratory movement after the acquisition of California. From that time forward, however, there was unceasing discussion of the canal question; and a private company which had obtained a local charter was proceeding with surveys and subscription of capital.

This led to an agreement between the United States and Great Britain in the year 1850 known as the Clayton-Bulwer Treaty, the object of which was to provide that neither country should obtain advantages over the other in the control or use of such a canal, in case of its actual construction. Since the project, in contemplation of which the treaty was drafted, failed of realization, the agreement was generally regarded as in abeyance, but its continuing validity was asserted half a century later.

It was in 1878 that the Republic of Colombia, which then controlled the Isthmus of Panama, granted a concession which became the property of the Panama Canal Company. This was a French organization, under the leadership of Ferdinand de Lesseps who had previously built the Suez canal. M. de Lesseps began his preliminary work in 1881 and for some time he carried on excavations with notable energy. But after eight years had elapsed, the company was unable to meet its ever-increasing expenditures. Work was suspended and bankruptcy and liquidation followed. The chief obstacle this French company encountered had been the frightful ravages of epidemic disease of one kind or another, which had caused the death of many thousands of imported laborers and had disabled other thousands through recurrent illness.

Meanwhile, the war with Spain was to provide an object lesson for Americans which created an irresistible demand that an Isthmian Canal should be constructed as a measure of national defense. Certain fighting ships of our small navy had been ordered to join the fleet in the Atlantic, in order to give Admiral Sampson the force regarded as necessary at Santiago. The battleship *Oregon* was in the North Pacific, and its long passage around Cape Horn was observed throughout the country with anxiety. Our new responsibilities, after the decision that kept the American flag at Manila, gave an added reason for a water passage between the oceans.

A commission of American engineers was authorized in 1899 to study all possible routes and to make a report to the President and Congress. It was an exceptionally able group that President McKinley appointed, and its surveys and studies were more thorough than any that had been previously made. After three years this engineering board reported in 1902, and recommended a route across Nicaragua. The United States had already secured necessary concessions, and Congress proceeded to make financial provision in accordance with the engineers' report.

Many thousands of thrifty French peasants and small investors, having great faith in Ferdinand de Lesseps, had invested savings in the Panama Canal Company. Their plight had become a disturbing political topic in France. A new French company was formed, to take control of such assets as might be salvaged. These included the unexpired concession from the Colombian government at Bogotá; some miles of excavation actually accomplished; a vast quantity of abandoned machinery and rusting implements.

The people of the United States were determined to construct an Isthmian canal. The Nicaragua route was much nearer to this country, and it had been chosen by competent engineers and accepted by Congress and public opinion. Our board of engineers, having been instructed to take account of political and diplomatic obstacles as well as those of a physical nature, had rejected Panama in part because the French were holding their exclusive concession at a price that no possible buyer would consider. Incidentally, our engineers had estimated the practical value of the work already done at about $40,000,000, if the United States were to proceed upon the French plans. But if the United States should begin work on the Nicaragua route, as seemed imminent, no other company or government would pay anything whatever to the French company, and the Bogotá concession would lapse.

Forty million dollars was not a large sum in view of the extravagant outlays that the original French company had made, but it was much better than nothing at all. An accomplished French engineer, M. Bunau-Varilla, who was also a plausible diplomat, crossed the Atlantic and visited New York. He took with him an able lawyer, William Nelson Cromwell, to introduce him to the " key men " at Washington. The Canal bill (appropriating $180,000,000 for the Nicaragua Canal) had reached the Senate; and Mark Hanna of Ohio was chairman of the committee in charge of it.

Senator Hanna was deeply moved by the onset of the French engineer. The sudden discovery that frequent earthquakes would make it virtually impossible to maintain a Nicaragua canal, took the Senate and the Administration fairly off their feet. After a brief but open debate, and without any appearance of improper methods of persuasion, Congress was induced to accept the Panama route. The board of engineers had been asked to reconsider, and had now given its preference to the Panama route.

By that time Theodore Roosevelt was President (Mr. McKinley having died at the hand of an assassin in September, 1901). Philander Knox as Attorney-General found the French title valid, and was assured that the French government was authorizing and supporting the sale and transfer of the Panama company's assets to the United States. The State Department, meanwhile, had negotiated a treaty with the Republic of Colombia that gave the United States control of a strip of territory a few miles wide on each side of the proposed canal, with a cash payment of $10,000,000 to Colombia and a yearly payment thereafter of $250,000. This treaty, negotiated by John Hay as Secretary of State with Senor Herrán (Colombian envoy at Washington) was favorable in all respects to the South American republic, as I then believed, with no reason to doubt the justice of that view.

Unfortunately, that turbulent country was under the unstable rule of a President who was not strong enough to support Mr. Herrán. The Colombian Congress had not been in session for a period of about five years. When the Senate was called to meet at Bogotá to ratify the treaty—in accordance with the insistence of the United States upon at least a nominal regularity of action before investing American money in so large and hazardous an enterprise—the results were disappointing.

The opinion prevailed at Bogotá that if the treaty with the United States were rejected, or indefinitely deferred, the concession to the French company would expire through lapse of time, or could be invalidated. Then the assets of the canal company would be forfeited to Colombia, and the authorities at Bogotá, instead of receiving only the ten million dollars provided in the Hay-Herrán treaty, would be in position to claim the forty millions that the United States was about to pay for the reimbursement of French investors.

This was not a creditable proceeding, and it was as short-sighted as it was inappropriate. It was not intended as a hold-up of the United States, for our government had proceeded in a candid and straightforward manner throughout every phase of the canal situation. The intention was to intervene at a moment when the amount payable to the French for distribution to the small stockholders might be diverted for the benefit of a ruling clique at Bogotá. There seemed nothing for the United States to do but to turn again to the Nicaragua route, where there were no political or diplomatic obstacles and where physical difficulties might prove to be no more serious than at Panama.

The intrepid M. Bunau-Varilla, however, was not to be discouraged. It was reported that he had proceeded to Panama without a moment's delay. Perhaps he remained in New York. The point is not essential. I remember declining to see him when he came to my office, because I might be regarded as open to influence. Certainly Bunau-Varilla was no stranger in Panama, for he had been employed as an engineer on the canal in 1884, and had risen to the position of chief engineer, remaining there until 1889. He understood the project in every aspect, whether physical or political, better than any other living man. He had organized the new French canal company, and had hoped to secure enough money to complete the undertaking. This having proved impossible, the only practicable alternative was to sell the assets to the United States. I am quite certain that this last recourse, although it surprised the world, had been well considered in advance.

The political status of Panama was perfectly understood by this French engineer. The Isthmus was a distinct entity, small in area but of almost unequalled geographical significance. This fact had given it also a notable place in the history of early exploration and settlement. The city of Panama was founded by Balboa in the year 1519, and it remained an administrative center of large colonial areas for more than two hundred years. It was not until

1740 that the *Audiencia* of Panama was made subordinate to the vice-royalty of New Granada. After the revolution, the South American liberator Simón Bolívar created Greater Colombia, including Venezuela and Ecuador as well as New Granada. These three republics soon went their separate ways, however, and in 1832 the Republic of New Granada was established which—with four subsequent changes of name—became known in 1886 as the Republic of Colombia. Panama was included as a section of that republic.

It was said that Bunau-Varilla, landing at Colon, proceeded by the short rail line to Panama City, which lies on the Pacific Coast, and made the situation clear to the influential citizens of the Isthmus, whereupon an impromptu revolt, with an immediate declaration of independence, occurred on November 3. But I am not concerned here with these matters of detail. The argument for separation from Colombia was unanswerable to all whose interests were identified with Panama. The Isthmus had long been exploited by the government of Bogotá as a revenue-producing asset, but Panama had derived no benefit in return.

Bunau-Varilla had lived among them for years and enjoyed the confidence of the people of Panama. They accepted the assurances that were given. Their independence would be recognized at once by the government of the United States, and they would be protected from an attempt by Colombian troops to reclaim the district by force. By a coincidence that some men regarded as prearrangement, American war vessels arrived at Colon, and the naval officers —acting (it was alleged) in accord with a provision in the treaty of 1846 relating to the Panama Railroad—prevented Colombian troops from using the rail line to reach the scene at Panama City.

VI.

History was then made with a rapidity that engaged attention everywhere. The Republic of Panama was recognized by the United States on November 6th, and exactly a week afterward Bunau-Varilla appeared at Washington as accredited Minister from Panama, and was received in that capacity by President Roosevelt. Four days later (November 17) the Hay-Bunau-Varilla Treaty was signed, granting to the United States in perpetuity the use and control of a Zone from the Atlantic to the Pacific approximately ten miles in width. Panama received the ten millions that Bogotá had refused, and the annuity provided in the Hay-Herrán Treaty was accepted by the French engineer on behalf of the Republic that he had helped so expeditiously to found. France had recognized the independence of Panama on November 10, and Germany, England and Russia were not slow to follow.

Panama was restored again to its proper place of geographical and commercial significance as a focus of cross-world traffic that it had enjoyed in the old days of the Spanish galleons that came to Panama City from the Philippines and the Indies. Chagrin at Bogotá was deep, and resentment was bitter. President Roosevelt was charged with having fomented a conspiracy to steal its best treasure from a relatively helpless South American republic. As it happened, I was exceptionally well acquainted throughout that period with affairs in the State Department and also at the White House; and after the lapse of forty years I can testify to the good conscience and good faith with which every step in the proceedings was taken by all branches of the government at Washington.

The claim of sovereignty over Panama by an unstable government at Bogotá was no better than the claim of Spain had been to a perpetual domination of Cuba. Panama rebelled as the only recognizable means by which it could insure its future prosperity. If Colombian troops had quelled the uprising at Panama City, the United States would without delay have proceeded to build the canal across Nicaragua. European interests would not have combined to renew work on the abandoned Panama project, and the Isthmus of Darien, as it was once called, would have sunk to ruin and utter desolation.

Under a constitution drawn up in January and adopted in February, 1904, the provisional arrangements of November were superseded by the regular government of the Republic that has now been in existence for forty years. It was not until August 15, 1914, that the canal was completed and its opening celebrated. Three years had been occupied with preliminaries, and the world's greatest engineering project then required seven years for execution. The preliminaries included the necessary re-study of plans, the preparation for housing many thousands of workmen, the assembling of machinery, and careful provision for constant flow of supplies.

But all these things, together with ample funds, could never have completed the canal. It was the inability of the management to protect the workers from the ravages of infectious disease that had wrecked the French undertaking. Our medical authorities supplied the most essential preliminary.

The conquest of yellow fever by American surgeons and bacteriologists, and the safeguards provided by sanitary experts against malarial fevers and other forms of tropical and epidemic disease, achieved results hardly less than miraculous. From its record as the most unhealthy place in the torrid belt of the entire globe, Panama was so transformed as to be the most immune district in the inhabited tropics. It was this triumph over disease and death that made the construction of the canal possible, and that has made Panama a place where people could live during the past generation without fear of yellow fever or Asiatic cholera. These benefits were not confined to Panama, but were extended promptly to the coastal regions of Colombia and elsewhere throughout tropical or sub-tropical American areas.

Since Colombia occupies a large area with about five hundred miles of coastline on the Atlantic and a similar frontage on the Pacific, the proximity of the canal (and its use on the most favored terms) gave promise of great advantage when that republic, in times to come, was to develop its natural resources and comprehend its commercial advantages. It could better have afforded to grant concessions freely, and offer rather than demand subsidies, than to have the Panama route abandoned. The politicos at Bogotá could not reconcile themselves, however, to the consequences of their own mistakes, and it was not until the completion of the canal that a new regime in Colombia could face the facts with realistic appreciation.

In 1914 with the canal completed, the United States was ready to consider Colombia's sense of grievance over a lost opportunity. Under a new treaty signed in 1914 (although not ratified by either country until 1921) Colombia was paid $25,000,000 from the United States Treasury as evidence of good will on the part of the United States. It was not blackmail on the one hand, or abasement on the other. It was a small price to pay for reconciliation. The real purpose was to bring tardy but complete acquiescence in the liberation of Panama. Good relationships were established between Colombia and the smaller republic when in 1921 the treaty was consummated.

Other diplomatic questions were involved in the construction of the Isthmian Canal by the United States as a governmental undertaking. Secretary Hay, seeking to clear away certain issues that might present themselves, had signed what was known as the Hay-Pauncefote treaty with the British envoy at Washington. Its professed object was to secure the abrogation of the Clayton-Bulwer agreement that had been framed more than half a century earlier, and that had long been regarded as null and void.

John Hay had been Ambassador at London before President McKinley made him Secretary of State; and his desire to cooperate with England, while wholly commendable, resulted at times in mistaken activities. Of his own accord—not content with agreeing to annul the inactive and forgotten Clayton-Bulwer treaty—Mr. Hay had written into the new agreement a proviso for such international control as the European powers had demanded of Egypt and Turkey, when the private French company obtained its charter to construct the Suez Canal. It had been provided that the Suez passage should not be exclusively managed, but should be available on equal terms for all.

The United States was willing to guarantee the use of the Panama Canal to the commerce of all the world on equal terms, but Mr. Hay was putting the United States in a position that seemed to give the European powers authority identical with that which they asserted at Suez. It might in some future crisis have destroyed the power of the United States to protect its own greatest public work—a costly project intended to afford our navy more speedy access from one ocean to the other. I shall not dwell upon an episode in which there was not the slightest evidence of bad faith on either side. The second Hay-Pauncefote treaty was speedily prepared, in accordance with which the United States retained the authority to fortify the canal and to control it for its own safety, as well as for the welfare of all maritime interests. There had been no objection whatever, on the part of the British government, to the American view of its own rights and responsibilities.

There arose a question, however, as the canal was approaching completion, regarding the terms upon which it could be used by American ships engaged in coastwise traffic. No country permits merchant vessels under foreign flags to trade from port to port along its coasts. Congress had chosen to construe the canal as a part of the American coast line, for purposes of trade that began and ended in American ports. In 1912, during the administration of President Taft, Congress had passed a bill exempting vessels engaged in coastwise trade from the payment of Panama Canal tolls.

There had arisen a sharp debate in this country regarding the propriety of such an exemption. The trans-continental railroads naturally opposed it, as an unfair form of subsidy to a competing transportation system. But also there were many others who regarded such exemption as violating the spirit if not the letter of the Hay-Pauncefote treaty with Great Britain that had been concluded in November, 1901, several weeks after Theodore Roosevelt had become President.

Woodrow Wilson had been President for a year when he appeared before Congress (March 5, 1914) and urged the repeal of the provision of 1912 that exempted our coastwise vessels from the payment of tolls. His argument had solely to do with interpretations of the treaty. The President declared that however we might understand the Hay-Pauncefote agreement, there was only one opinion in England and in other maritime countries. He did not mention the fact that President Taft, than whom there could have been no higher legal authority, had signed the bill in 1912, believing that the exemption was consistent with the treaty. Mr. Wilson made his plea for what he called "a voluntary withdrawal from a position everywhere questioned and misunderstood."

He continued as follows: "We ought to reverse our action without raising the question whether we were right or wrong, and so once more deserve our reputation for generosity and for the redemption of every obligation without quibble or hesitation. I ask this of you in support of the foreign policy of the administration. I shall not know how to deal with other matters of even greater delicacy and nearer consequence if you do not grant it to me in ungrudging measure." These were the concluding sentences of a message in the course of which Mr. Wilson treated the subject as one of "grave and far-reaching implications." It is enough to add that Congress responded favorably and repealed the clause.

I have given a scanty, but perhaps sufficient, outline of international questions that arose in the course of our effort to construct and operate a water passage between the oceans. President Wilson's plea in 1914, a few months before the beginning of the

First World War, gave to the maritime nations a final and unquestioned assurance that the canal would be maintained and defended for the benefit on equal terms of all vessels, under whatever flag, using the seas for legitimate purposes.

The Suez Canal under a treaty signed at Constantinople in 1888 by Great Britain, Austria-Hungary, France, Germany, Italy, the Netherlands, Russia, Spain and Turkey, was declared open to all nations and free from blockade. But such agreements cannot hold against the exigencies of a war that involves more than two nations. If England should fail to hold the Suez Canal for the United Nations, Germany would capture it for the Axis powers. When the war is ended and new adjustments are made, the Suez and Panama Canals alike must and will have a full and free international character. If Great Britain should keep its controlling ownership of the Suez passage, and the United States should retain its authority in the Canal Zone of Panama, it would in either case be with the approval of the people most concerned.

Forgetting details of the tedious documents and papers that clutter the archives of foreign offices as regards the Panama affair, the American people can have the satisfaction of knowing that in transactions involving several countries—among them France, Colombia, and England—our government sought to act with justice and consideration. Our accomplishments at Panama have foreshadowed a world of peaceful commerce, of collective safeguards against epidemic, and of increasing harmony as intercourse tends to elevate the standards of living and to serve the common ends of civilized society.

Chapter XIII

WE CULTIVATE RELATIONS WITH CANADA AND MEXICO

The best guarantee of a peaceful world lies in good understanding between immediate neighbors. I have mentioned in a previous chapter the happy removal of all causes of discord between Turkey and Greece. The United States has had a long history of dealings with Mexico. Misunderstandings that were serious during the period of the First World War have now fortunately been cleared away. The contrast between the Diaz regime in Mexico and the existing situation under President Comacho represents a new era of progress south of the Rio Grande which it becomes our duty and privilege to encourage.

The Pan-American Union has become an agency which serves what we may now call the higher government of the Western Hemisphere. The Pan-American program has developed to such an extent that it may be said without undue optimism that our Hemisphere has outgrown the reliance upon force in relationships of American countries with one another.

More important both to Canada and the United States than their relationship to any other country are their associations with each other as neighbors. The present chapter deals with the history of reciprocity and trade relations, including an account of Goldwin Smith's commercial-union proposals, the British trade preferences, and our existing bi-lateral agreements.

Several negotiations of major importance that have affected our relations with Canada are described in this chapter, one of them being the settlement of the Bering Sea controversy relating to the fur-bearing seals of the Pribilof Islands. Still more important was the settlement of the Alaska Boundary, which was brought into question after the discovery of gold in the Yukon region.

A so-called "International Joint Commission," consisting of three American and three Canadian members was established in 1910, and it has dealt with one question after another, proving itself an agency of a highly useful type, that might well be imitated in parts of Europe and Asia.

Finally, in November, 1942, Secretary Hull formulated a general proposal relating to post-war economic policies between the two governments that was immediately accepted by the government of Canada. It called for the broadest kind of economic cooperation, to take such a form that it could be a starting point from which it might be extended; and it was agreed that it should be "open to participation by all other countries of like mind."

Thus a program of complete Canadian-American war-time cooperation will be followed by sincere efforts to assimilate the economic policies of North America, as a great step toward the removal of trade restrictions throughout the world.

RELEASED from captivity and enslavement, the Lord's chosen people returned to Jerusalem to restore their ruined capital, with fresh hope in the prospect of surcease from war and the enjoyment of liberty under the disciplines of Mosaic law. But they did not trust to divine favor as their sole protection against future assaults. They proceeded to rebuild the walls of the city for defensive purposes, and we are told that " every man built over against his own house." We will assume that this meant planned and organized cooperation, rather than haphazard work in a spirit of stubborn individualism. The moral is obvious, and anyone can write his own sermon from those ancient texts.

In a limited sense it is true that the world can be no better at any given time than the people who inhabit it. If this were wholly true, however, the course of affairs might be left to chance and fate, as if we could expect nothing more than "the struggle for existence " and " the survival of the fittest." Such doctrines ignore the vast progress that humanity has already made, with its demonstrated power of readjustment, its increasing deference to principles of right and wrong, and its capacity in certain national areas to attain higher levels under intelligent and far-seeing leadership.

We can hardly hope to provide full-fledged institutions of government for a harmonized world until we have established fairly stable conditions among races and tribes that have a tendency to jostle each other. This remark applies to neighboring states that regard themselves as civilized, and that profess to recognize the duties as well as the privileges of sovereignty. Through circumstances that have perhaps become too familiar to be properly estimated, the American government has gained a position of leadership that has been illustrated in several preceding chapters. The Monroe Doctrine has to a great extent been merged in a broader policy of cooperation among the American republics, with a reasonable measure of success in dealing with practical cases.

I mean by this statement to imply that the republics of Latin-America have been learning to settle boundary disagreements by arbitration, and to live on amicable terms with their immediate neighbors. The collective influence of official and unofficial Pan-Americanism is evolving a regional unity of purpose and aspiration. It is so far from perfection, however, that constant effort and close attention must be given to it if we would hold what has been gained and make farther advance.

"Pan-Americanism" is a term not too definite to exclude any effort public or private to promote good will, and work out some beginnings—however shadowy—of what we may call the higher government of the Western Hemisphere. This means (1) multilateral agreements that begin to constitute a code of public law; (2) the adoption of legal remedies for the settlement of disputes, and the relinquishment of force; (3) some executive agency to guard the peaceful progress of the western world, based upon the Monroe Doctrine as interpreted in the Pan-American Union.

Official Pan-Americanism proceeds upon the idea that peace and progress require systematic and vigilant oversight. This is best secured through definite arrangements. Since all of the twenty-one American republics are represented here, it was agreed that Washington would be the most convenient place for a permanent center. The name "Pan-American Union" was adopted in 1910, with the completion of the building devoted to its purposes, for the erection of which Andrew Carnegie had made a large gift at the instance of the Secretary of State, Elihu Root. A summary explanation of its functions may be quoted from a convenient source: "The Union is maintained by the Republics to disseminate information and promote understanding and peace among the nations. Its governing board is made up of the United States Secretary of State and the diplomatic representatives of the other American states. The management is in the hands of a director-general. The Union has the largest extant library of Pan-American materials. It issues bulletins giving commercial, economic, social, political and cultural information on the Republics."

In short, the beautiful building with its library and appurtenances stands as a visible symbol of purposes that recognize the past and look to the future. The vital element is the weekly meeting of the diplomats, with the American Secretary of State presiding. The periodic Pan-American Congresses or Conferences were first proposed by James G. Blaine as Secretary of State more than sixty years ago. As they met from time to time, their usefulness was demonstrated; and their standing "Bureau of Republics" took later form in the present Pan-American Union. After the first meeting at Washington, these Congresses have met at Mexico City, Rio de Janeiro, Buenos Aires, Santiago, Havana, and Montevideo, with the most recent one at Lima. They have assembled at five-year intervals as the more usual plan, though this is not a fixed rule. Since the Lima meeting there have been special conferences at Panama, Havana and Rio de Janeiro. These gatherings have had a marked influence upon the development of an inter-state public opinion in Latin-America.

II.

The long presidency of Porfirio Diaz seemed to Americans, while it lasted, to have brought a golden era of peace and prosperity to the people of Mexico, after more than half a century of violent political upheavals. Diaz as a youth of sixteen had taken part in the war with the United States; and twenty years later had been active in the patriotic movement that expelled the French troops and sealed the fate of Maxmilian. He attained the Presidency in 1877, and except for a brief interval in deference to a law prohibiting a second term, he served continuously from that date until 1911, a period of thirty-four years. He was an administrator of such skill and alertness that he knew how to meet opposition before it had gained strength.

He eliminated banditry, and secured civil order by organizing ragamuffins into smartly uniformed and well paid squads of a national military constabulary. He cultivated good relations with the United States; encouraged American capitalists to build Mexico's railroad system; promoted mining companies, and welcomed other foreign entrepreneurs. He looked forward to a long and happy period of capitalistic exploitation, in the profits of which he and favored members of his government were glad to have their share.

President Diaz was readily accessible to Americans with proper credentials, and on the occasion of a visit to Mexico City I found him as personable and courteous as American Presidents of the type of McKinley or Harding. The prosperity of Mexico was real, but was not well distributed. Individual holdings of land were on a vast scale. The péons of Indian origin who formed most of the population resembled the fellaheen of the Nile Valley under Turkish rule, and were even poorer. Governors of Mexican states re-elected themselves from term to term, with no one else seemingly aware that an election date had been passed.

I do not suppose that the Diaz regime needs abject apologies from any source. Mexican reforms were belated, but they had to wait for the emergence of leadership. Many of the more fortunate young Mexicans in the forty-year period before we entered the First World War had studied in the universities of their own country or in the United States, and had become lawyers, engineers, scientists, and capable men of affairs. Most of these men were patriots, and some were idealists. Among such men it was inevitable that leaders would appear, and that revolutions would deal unsparingly with the great landlords, the oil companies, the mining companies, the transportation companies, and with all those of the kind that one American President stigmatized as "malefactors of great wealth," and another called "economic royalists." The land situation was almost as anti-social as that which Arthur Young found in France just before the outbreak of the French revolution. It was probably worse than that which existed in Russia and other parts of eastern Europe before the First World War.

When such reactions occur, they are explosive and go to extremes. The processes of reconstruction have been less violent in Mexico than in most other countries where revolutionary leaders have proclaimed the era of the common people, in the language of Jean Jacques Rousseau or Karl Marx. The proximity of the United States, and the familiarity of many Mexican leaders with democracy and wealth-distribution north of the Rio Grande, have had a moderating influence upon the drastic policies of expropriation that were launched some years ago, under a new socialistic constitution. There have been mistakes of policy on both sides, as our government has sought to protect American interests in Mexico. But how ready the Mexicans were to show confidence in Americans of friendly spirit and understanding mind was exhibited in the success of Dwight Morrow, who was sent by President Coolidge as Ambassador to Mexico City. Mr. Morrow did not condone the confiscation of American property, but he had no sympathy with the threat of force to protect the profits of speculative investment.

The principal object of Mexican statesmen of the better type is to stamp out illiteracy, to abolish the extremes of poverty, and meanwhile to maintain solvency and pay the costs of social progress. It is a rough road that Mexico must continue to travel; but the idealists are no longer so few in number and they have an ardent belief in the future of their country. Also, it is possible that the United States may become a much better neighbor to Mexico in the future than at any time since—almost a hundred years ago—we fought to secure the independence of Texas, and ended a brief war by taking possession of California.

Under revolutionary conditions in 1915, Mexico's new policy of land distribution, and of opposition to the vested authority of a dominant church, broke upon the scene so abruptly and harshly as to arouse American and British protests on behalf of property interests. The new constitution promulgated early in 1917 embodied the principles of a revolution that was intended by its authors to rid the country of sixteenth-century land-based feudalism, old-time Spanish ecclesiasticism, and unregulated, monopolistic capitalism.

A few weeks after the new constitution took effect, the United States declared war upon Germany. The Zimmerman note, proposing to enlist Mexico in Germany's war against us, was intercepted by British agents and had some influence upon President Wilson's war policy.

A comparison of relationships between Washington and Mexico a quarter-century later brings evidence of gratifying contrasts in understanding and cooperation. Land reforms continue, under steadily improving methods; and in many ways Mexico shows educational and social progress. On June 1, 1942, Mexico declared war against the Axis powers, and has coordinated her programs with those of the United States under the guidance of a joint military commission.

Fifty years ago the American Minister to Great Britain was elevated to the rank of Ambassador. It did not change his functions, but it recognized the importance to both countries of Anglo-American relations, and enhanced his dignity as a member of the diplomatic corps at London. Of the fifteen countries with which we now exchange ambassadors, six are Latin-American Republics, with Mexico perhaps more important to us in the long run than any of the others, because of proximity and also because of the great future of development and influence that lies before the Mexican people.[1]

III.

Although comparisons are often invidious, it might be plausibly argued that relations between the United States and Canada more vitally concern both Americans and Canadians than the relations of either with any other country. Previous to the First World War Canada was represented at Washington by the British Ambassador. It was not until after the present status of Canada was made clear at the end of the First World War (recognized ten years later by the British Government in the Statute of Westminister) that Canada established her own legation at Washington, while the United States sent its diplomatic representative to Ottawa. I am not concerned with the nature of relationships between Canada and Great Britain. No two intelligent persons would be likely to explain them in just the same way. Canada in obvious fact has been a confederated democracy of continental extent, fully self-governing, for a period half as long as the recognized existence of the United States, that is to say, for almost eighty years—since the American Civil War, or to be exact since 1867.

Only well-informed students of diplomatic history could have even a vague conception of the incessant difficulties that were for a long time encountered in the process of adjusting relationships between these two neighboring countries. While the British government in the '40's of the last century was making certain of its half of the Oregon country, the small eastern provinces of Nova Scotia and New Brunswick, and the larger colonies on the St.

[1] After an academic career as head of the department of political science at the Universiy of Pennsylvania, Professor Leo S. Rowe after the Spanish-American War revised the laws of Puerto Rico, and soon became a recognized expert in Latin-American affairs. In 1915 he was appointed Director-General of the Pan-American Union at Washington, and has held that important position since that time.

In response to an inquiry by me regarding a newspaper report in March, 1943, Dr. Rowe confirmed the statement that the Ministers of the five Central American countries, and also those of the Dominican Republic and Haiti, have all been advanced to the rank of Ambassador. Their names had been sent to the Senate and had been confirmed. Thus all the representatives from Latin-American republics who gather at stated intervals around the board table of the Pan-American Union have the Ambassadorial rank, regardless of the size or importance of the country they represent. It would seem appropriate that the minister from Canada to Washington should also be an Ambassador, and that he should take his seat as a member of the Pan-American Union.

Lawrence were engaged (1) in agitations of bewildering complexity regarding the rights of American fishermen in waters under British jurisdiction; (2) in disputing about questions of navigation and transit; and most of all (3) in making demands for access to American markets. They were ready for free trade with the United States, for annexation to the United States, for war with the United States, or for any combination of these alternatives.

The British government was inclined to the opinion that either American refusal or American acceptance of a liberal policy of reciprocal trade, navigation, and fishing rights would result in annexation. But on sober second thought Mother Britain always does what she can to keep her wayward or restless children loyal to the family relationship. Lord Elgin came to Washington on a special mission, seeking to end ten years of menacing discord. This British diplomat and statesman was Viceroy and Governor-General of Canada from 1847 to 1854; and the crowning success of a creditable and eminent career was the achievement of his object on that occasion. After several weeks of genial intercourse with our public men he had overcome all effective opposition. He brought wisdom and broad vision to support his errand, and he made friends by his resistless charm and bonhomie. On June 5, 1854, after having ascertained for himself that the Senate would ratify, Lord Elgin persuaded Secretary Marcy to sign the treaty of reciprocity.

There will come a time when Lord Elgin's career will be studied afresh, and he will be accorded a place not merely among British empire-builders or Canadian viceroys, but as a man who had far-reaching views of economic unity and harmony throughout North America. The reciprocity of 1854 could not survive the upheavals of our Civil War period, which included the Morrill tariff adopted in Lincoln's administration. There were reasons on both sides of the line why the treaty lapsed in 1865. But it has held its place in tariff history, and it formed a precedent that was to strengthen future arguments. Sooner or later there would be further efforts to reduce trade barriers by reciprocal agreement.

Such an attempt came in 1911, when Mr. Taft was President and Sir Wilfrid Laurier was Prime Minister of Canada. Congress did not welcome the reciprocity idea with much warmth, but President Taft was so earnest about it, and argued for it with such strength of conviction, and such faith in the larger principles involved, regardless of mere schedule details, that the measure was negotiated and duly adopted at Washington by legislative enactment. Its fate was otherwise, however, in Canada.

Sir Wilfrid Laurier, who was the first French-Canadian to become Prime Minister of the Dominion, was one of the most brilliant and large-minded statesmen of his period. He had held the premiership longer than any predecessor in the history of Canada. A general election was pending, and it turned upon Canadian-American relations in general and the reciprocity treaty in particular. The Conservatives, opposing reciprocity, gained an outstanding victory over Sir Wilfrid Laurier's Liberal Party.

When the new Prime Minister, the Hon. Robert L. Borden, took office, I was able to secure from him a statement that constituted his first official message to the people of the United States. We were soon to commemorate in both countries the completion of a hundred years of peace that had followed the War of 1812. Mr. Borden referred to it, and expressed his faith that each of the two countries would "accomplish its destiny under the splendid inspiration of enduring and increasing friendship and good will." He opened his message with the following allusions to Canada's new ambition as an industrial country:

> In 1879 Canada placed upon her statute book a standing offer of reciprocity, which remained open to the United States for eighteen years, or until 1897, when it was repealed by the government of Sir Wilfrid Laurier. The United States always declined to entertain this standing offer and we never questioned their perfect and absolute right to take that course. In the meantime Canada had entered upon a policy which involved the development of her natural resources, the growth of her industries, and the preservation of her home market. Eight years ago I declared in the House of Commons that a factory in Canada was worth as much to our empire as a factory in Yorkshire. Our fiscal autonomy involving the complete control of our tariff had been finally completed and secured in 1879, and it will never be relinquished.

During the period when Elihu Root was Secretary of State and James Bryce was British Ambassador, many unsettled questions of detail involving public and private interests were adjusted by agreements that paved the way for the relatively harmonious relationships between Canada and the United States that have now existed during a third of a century. These two statesmen were so fair-minded that their positions might have been reversed—by which I mean that Canadian interests might have been placed in charge of Mr. Root, with American claims and viewpoints represented by Mr. Bryce.

As the climax of that period of fruitful diplomatic endeavor, a treaty negotiated in 1909 provided for reference of various questions still pending to a new kind of tribunal. This was the permanent "International Joint Commission," consisting of three American and three Canadian members. One might suppose that such a standing tribunal would within a short time finish its docket of cases and find itself unoccupied. This would be a wholly mistaken view, as Dr. Callahan proves in pages that describe the numerous activities of the Commission during a period of twenty years or more after it entered upon its duties in 1912.

As regards future trade relations, it will be more practical to consider barriers near home than to descant ecstatically upon the benefits that might flow from the removal of all tariffs, all quota systems, and all other trade regulations throughout an emancipated and unified world. Living conditions in Canada and the United States are not widely dissimilar. Moreover, there has been much commingling of population across the line. French-Canadians by the million have become domiciled in New England, while American farm folk in great numbers from Iowa, Nebraska, and other western states have helped to develop the fertile provinces of Manitoba, Saskatchewan, and Alberta.

There was a time when it could be said that by far the greater part of the population of Canada could be found in a strip along the boundary more than three thousand miles long but barely a hundred miles in average width. This is no longer true, however, and a vast expansion lies in the early future, when the present population of fifteen millions will be doubled. This Canadian development will call for joint efforts and greater freedom of movement for people and goods.

At Ottawa, the attractive Canadian capital, an "Imperial Economic Conference" was held in 1932 for the purpose of adopting a system of preferential tariffs in favor of imports from Great Britain, in exchange for quotas of wheat and other primary materials. The United States had long proceeded upon the plan of general tariffs, with import duties alike on goods from all countries. The Hawley-Smoot Tariff Bill had been enacted in June, 1930, with higher average rates than in any previous measure. For example, the import duties upon agricultural products were advanced from an average rate of about 38 per cent to approximately 49 per cent. Although Congress might have sought to protect our markets against the competition of Argentina, the new tariff in effect was most disadvantageous to Canada.

Two years later, in 1932, England gave Canada large quota allowances for wheat and other products, in exchange for a 25 per cent preference on manufactured goods that competed with like products of the United States. In 1934 Congress authorized the executive branch of our government to negotiate "bi-lateral trade agreements" with particular countries, thus modifying the general tarff rates of 1930. This new method of tariff revision has been continued by further extensions of the Act, at three-year intervals. Several successive agreements have been reached by special negotiation with Canada. Experience, it may be hoped, will lead to the appointment of a Joint Commission on Trade Relations to function continuously. Freedom of trade throughout North America should be the ultimate goal.

The most distinguished publicist who ever came from England to live on our side of the Atlantic was Professor Goldwin Smith. After twenty years as a Professor of Modern History at Oxford, he came to the United States in 1866, by persuasion of President Andrew D. White, and added lustre to the early days of Cornell University. From 1871 until his death in 1910, a period of almost forty years, Goldwin Smith resided at Toronto. He had opposed imperialist tendencies while in Great Britain, and he continued to write brilliantly for almost half a century for English, Canadian, and American readers. He was not an advocate of the annexation of Canada by the United States, but he urged the removal of trade barriers, and the adoption of a plan of Commercial Union between the two countries.

Goldwin Smith had strongly favored the Northern cause in the American Civil War, and was a life-long friend of Bryce, Morley, and many English Liberals. I knew him well in my early editorial years, and thought his arguments for commercial union were too sound to be refuted. The difficulty of realizing their objective lay in the fact that economics and politics are commonly so hard to reconcile. Mr. Borden defeated the reciprocity measure of Sir Wilfrid Laurier partly by championing Canadian home industry, but chiefly by sounding an alarm against tendencies toward Canadian-American cooperation. Trade reciprocity, he declared, might endanger the cause of British imperialism. He thought it a cunning device—like the Trojan horse—to conceal the enemy lurking at the very gates of Canada's proud isolation. In short, the defeat of reciprocity in 1911 was not upon the merits of the proposal.

The Ottawa agreements of 1932, in contrast, were in the nature of a practical bargain, with an economic *quid pro quo*. The recent trade agreements with the United States also proceed upon common-sense lines, with no political tincture whatsoever. Obviously Canada's legation at Washington should become an embassy, and Canada should join the Pan-American Union. Beyond that, Canada's political, military, and commercial alliances with Great Britain or with any other over-seas government are matters of her own discretion and choice, and do not, henceforth, concern the United States.

IV.

American interest in the Pacific Coast began with the Lewis and Clark Expedition ordered by Thomas Jefferson. It swelled to the point of enthusiasm with the pioneers of the Oregon Trail. The bold conception of a country facing on two oceans was realized completely when California was acquired. In our school geographies, within the memory of elderly people, a great squarish block of territory occupying the northwest corner of the mainland of North America was called "Russian America." It was acquired by the United States in 1867, by virtue of a policy for which the Secretary of State, William H. Seward, was responsible. Navigators of several countries had sailed along its rugged coasts, but Russia had made the first settlement, and had established claims that were undisputed.

This area, however, was not a source of any profit or advantage to Russia, and no persuasion was necessary on Mr. Seward's part to secure the title for the United States. He was a man of imagination, and declared that "Russian America" had resources that would make it a valuable acquisition. It was believed at the time that when the United States paid Russia $7,200,000 for this transfer of title it was a disguised payment for proffered naval support of the United States by Russia at a critical juncture in our Civil War. The name "Alaska" was an American invention, adopted by Congress.

Thirty or forty years earlier it is fairly probable that the British government would have objected to a transaction that forever limited the Pacific coastline of British North America to the frontage gained in the Oregon treaty of 1846. But the United States at the conclusion of the Civil War had new prestige and strength, was building trans-continental railroads, and was envisaging a great future on the Pacific. There were public men in England who did not resent the frequent prediction that Canada, including the fur-trading empire of the West, would soon be annexed by the United States. Whether or not it was ever proposed officially, the idea was afloat that American claims against Great Britain might be settled by the transfer of the western half of what is now Canada to the United States.

It is possible that a bargain of this kind might have been effected if those who succeeded Mr. Seward in influence at Washington had not preferred a lawsuit of the most imposing character. They actually won the arbitration case at Geneva, and Great Britain paid to the United States the sum of $15,500,000 in satisfaction of the claims of American ship-owners on account of depredations by Confederate cruisers built and fitted out in England. The negotiations that preceded this settlement were instituted by Hamilton Fish, who was Secretary of State from 1869 to 1877. The "inside" story of our foreign relations in that post-war decade is re-told with care and authority by Mr. Allan Nevins in a masterly biography (1936) of Mr. Fish.

Preliminary to the arbitration at Geneva—and much more important than this mere detail of a money award—was the Treaty of Washington signed on May 8, 1871. A Joint High Commission composed of half a dozen highly competent Americans and a similar number of eminent British statesmen and law authorities took counsel together at Washington for about ten weeks, and signed a treaty that John Bassett Moore (in his introduction to the Nevins volume) describes as a comprehensive scheme which adjusted for all future time a number of controversial issues. Says Mr. Moore in characterizing the Treaty of Washington: "Not only because of the fact that it provided for four distinct arbitrations, but also because of the magnitude of the questions submitted, it was the greatest treaty of actual and immediate arbitration the world had ever seen; and it still holds that preeminence. Moreover, the high water mark of international arbitration was reached in the proceedings and the award of the Geneva tribunal."

Students of Canadian relations in the period following our Civil War will be likely to discover the fact that while British authorities might not have objected to Canadian independence, or even to the annexation of Canada by the United States, Canadian sentiment was clearly opposed to either alternative. British Columbia desired annexation to Canada. As for Canada as a whole, while it was ready for the experiment of self-government through confederation of the Provinces, it did not wish to terminate the British connection. This was true of the French-speaking elements for reasons of their own, and of the English-speaking citizens of the Maritime Provinces and Ontario for reasons as definite though quite different.

Almost three-quarters of a century has elapsed since the Treaty of Washington adjusted certain acute difficulties on behalf of the hardy fishermen of the northeastern coasts, made navigation of the St. Lawrence and other rivers free, and arranged for arbitrations. In various other respects it showed to our own citizens, and to the world at large, how two neighboring countries could remain distinct in their institutions and their ways of life while finding reasonable methods by which to deal with new differences, whenever changing circumstances created unexpected situations.

A recent volume published in the French language at Montreal (1941) and written by several scholarly French Canadians (also sponsored by the Carnegie Foundation for International Peace) reviews with thoroughness and candor the relationships of the French Canadians with their American neighbors during more than three centuries. These writers fully confirm my impression that the interesting and excellent inhabitants of French North America remain as distinctive a social and political entity in this period of the Second World War as they were in 1871, when the separateness of Canada was in fact ordained, although the great Treaty of Washington made no allusion to it.

V.

The acquisition of additional territory will usually bring unexpected problems and complications that give employment to diplomats if not to navies. This soon proved to be the case with Alaska as a possession of the United States. Far to the westward there stretched the long, crescent-like chain of islands reaching from the American mainland most of the way to the Siberian peninsula of Kamchatka. This crescent forms the southern boundary of what is known as the Bering Sea. Well north of the Aleutian chain is an isolated group of small islands known as the Pribilofs.

A long controversy was incident to the American proprietorship of those remote islands of the Bering Sea, and it did not reach final settlement until the year 1911. The principal breeding place of the fur-bearing seals of the North Pacific was (and still is) on the Pribilof Islands. The United States government claimed a monopoly proprietorship in these animals and soon found it highly profitable. But the herd of two million seals after a decade or two had been reduced by more than nine-tenths.

This was due to the unregulated enterprise of Canadian, Japanese, and other marine fur-takers who prosecuted what was known as pelagic or open-sea capture of the seals, as with homing instinct those animals made their way to the breeding islands. The United States government, seeking to preserve the herd, made regulations and seized certain vessels that defied them. A violent dispute followed, with submission of certain questions to an arbitral board (1893). The United States paid damages for seizing a Canadian vessel or two, but ultimately secured the main point at issue, namely, the prohibition of the taking of seals in the open seas, as they moved to or from their breeding places.

The final agreement was reached by representatives of the United States, Great Britain, Russia, and Japan. A partnership arrangement was made, a patrol established, and the United States assumed general responsibility for the protection and further maintenance of the fur-bearing seals of the Pacific that were henceforth to have an international character. The settlement made in 1911 under the leadership of President Taft and Secretary Knox was of such a nature that it may be said to form a specific item in the elaborate code of maritime international law that will be agreed upon at the end of the present war. There will be other subjects, relating to the oceans and their animal wealth, more or less analogous in character to that of the Pribilof seals, that must be dealt with by a special tribunal or permanent commission.

The year 1911 was one of exceptional diplomatic activity on the part of the government at Washington. Although the treaty providing for tariff reciprocity between Canada and the United States was defeated in the Dominion Parliament at Ottawa, a general treaty of arbitration was negotiated between England and the United States that was more inclusive than any previous one. The negotiator on the American side was Philander Knox, President Taft's Secretary of State, while Great Britain was represented by Ambassador Bryce. In its tentative form the proposal was handed to Ambassador Jusserand representing France, and we were informed that the German Foreign Office would soon take up the matter of unlimited arbitration with this country, upon the basis of the Knox-Bryce treaty.

England and Japan were in alliance at that time under an agreement which was to expire in 1912. The terms of this alliance were revised in a new ten-year agreement signed at London in July, 1911. I explained it at the time in the following paragraphs, which derive new interest from occurrences that led to the present war in the Pacific. The opening sentences, as the reader will observe, relate to the ten-year extension (1912-1922) of the alliance between Great Britain and Japan:

> The principal change in the new agreement is that which states that if either party concludes a treaty of general arbitration with a third power, the alliance shall not entail an obligation to go to war with that power. It is understood that Japan readily agreed to this proposition, which, in the opinion of the Japanese, as well as the British press, precludes forever the possibility of war between Japan and the United States.
>
> Under the old agreement Britain was bound to lend aid to Japan in case of war with any other nation. Under the new one, taken together with the general arbitration treaty about to be concluded with the United States, Great Britain virtually announced that she would never support Japan in a conflict with the United States. The new treaty is to run for ten years. Some of the London journals characterize the situation as amounting almost to a triple alliance between Great Britain, Japan, and the United States, and compliment President Taft on his efforts in bringing it about.
>
> Japan's enlightened attitude in this matter should go far toward strengthening her position as a member of the family of modern nations. Meanwhile, on the seventeenth of last month, the new treaty of commerce and navigation between the United States and Japan went into operation. The important point of difference between the present and the former treaty lies in the omission from the new convention of that paragraph which, in the old, set forth the immigration restrictions objectionable to the Japanese. In the diplomatic note prefacing the treaty, Japan agreed to carry out the spirit of existing conditions with regard to Japanese coolies coming to America. A very gratifying opportunity to show our cordiality of feeling toward the Japanese people is afforded by the visit of Admiral Togo, who this month is to be the guest of the nation.

I am aware that the five foregoing paragraphs, relating to Anglo-American arbitration and to Anglo-Japanese accord, seem to violate chronological order, and to interrupt the thread of my discourse upon Alaskan diplomacy. But they have a bearing upon the spirit of confidence in which we were proceeding for many years to deal with Pacific problems.

VI.

As held by Russia and ceded to the United States, Alaska has a long shore-line, sometimes called the Pan-Handle, that extends southward to meet the original boundary of the so-called Oregon country (54° 40′ of N Lat). This pan-handle strip, perhaps five hundred miles in length, extends inland for a certain number of miles following a coast so irregular, and with so many deep indentations, that there had been no attempt to mark the boundary line in a mountainous and almost inaccessible terrain. East of this Alaskan coastal belt lies the vast northern area of British Columbia which now—like Alberta, Saskatchewan and Manitoba—extends to the 60th parallel of North Latitude.

No one was particularly concerned about this Alaskan boundary line until gold was discovered in the Yukon Territory of Canada, which lies directly east of the main block of Alaska. There was a rush of mining prospectors and camp followers to the goldfields, and the Canadians began to study old maps with a definite purpose. They adopted the theory that certain deep, navigable inlets actually penetrated the fringe of American territory, and that Canada was entitled to seaports far north of the 54-40 line.

The Canadian theory would have given the United States a broken coastline rather than a continuous one; and this would have failed to accord with the undisputed interpretations that had been placed upon the Russian claim for several generations. The agitation became almost as assertive in the Dominion's political circles and in the Canadian press as the American clamor for the Fifty-four-Forty line half a century earlier. On its face it seemed to the Canadians a reasonable view. Why should their great and valuable hinterland be denied access to the sea?

Direct negotiation with the United States might have resulted in a practical compromise, regardless of the historic Russian title. But the American government was not disposed to yield sovereignty over any part of its coastline, and Canada was too intent upon proving a belated theory. Free access might readily have been granted to designated ports. The whole subject of the Yukon-Alaska goldfields should have been settled easily and courteously by a give-and-take partnership arrangement. Unfortunately for Canadian aspirations, the British authorities were luke-warm, because their thoughts were centered upon other questions then pending.

Theodore Roosevelt was President at this time, and John Hay was Secretary of State (holding over, with other members of the Cabinet of the late President McKinley). Mr. Hay was anxious to arbitrate the question on some plan, and President Roosevelt was willing to refer it to a joint board of six members, with no outside umpire.

The Russian government had made a treaty with Great Britain in 1825 to describe the character of the boundary between Russia's coastal possessions and what were regarded by the Russians as westward encroachments of the Hudson's Bay Company, which asserted governing authority over the great continental interior under British charter. Dr. Callahan explains that while Canning, the head of the British Foreign Office at that time, was willing to grant a line a hundred miles back from the ocean, the Russians were not aware of this. So they agreed to accept a continuous strip some thirty miles wide, except where mountain barriers formed a natural dividing line.

At recurring intervals after Seward's purchase the desirability of a survey was urged, first by one government and then by the other. A reasonable compromise had come near acceptance in 1899, but was at length rejected. Then the Canadians proposed an adjustment by arbitration with an umpire. The American government insisted that the Alaskan controversy bore no resemblance to the dispute involved in the arbitration of the Venezuela boundary. The further story of the negotiations is not merely tedious but appallingly disagreeable as we look back upon it. The best minds in the governments of the United States, Canada, and Great Britain were insisting, suspecting, contradicting, and, in general, repudiating one another's claims and arguments as "evasive," "false," "outrageous."

Possessions too easily obtained often lead to unanticipated troubles, and become a burden. The eastern provinces of Canada and the early colonies of New England alike had earned their territorial claims, by virtue of actual settlement and the endurance of successive generations of toilers and civilizers. But the title of the United States to the Alaskan wilderness, like that of Canada to the vast Northwest, had cost next to nothing and lacked the solid basis of occupancy and development. Historic titles had little intrinsic value on either side of the line, yet the best legal and political minds in the world were engaged in angry controversy over free access for miners' supplies to one or another water-passage on the way to the Klondike goldfields.

To save appearances, agreement was reached at Washington to refer the dispute to a board of six men, and President Roosevelt appointed Elihu Root (who was the Secretary of War, but soon to enter the Senate), Senator Lodge of Massachusetts, and Senator George Turner of the State of Washington. King Edward appointed Lord Alverstone, Lord Chief Justice of England, Louis Jetté, Lieutenant-Governor of Quebec, and Mr. Aylesworth of the Ontario Bar. These gentlemen met at London in the summer of 1903. Attempts were made on the British side to defer proceedings but the Americans, who were accompanied by able legal counsel, insisted upon a forthright decision. On the main points at issue, Lord Alverstone sided with the three Americans and a verdict was reached.

Since the Americans were not open to conviction, a deadlock would have resulted if the Lord Chief Justice had sided with the two Canadians. In the last analysis this was not an arbitration, but a method of disguising the fact that the British government was accepting the American view, which undoubtedly was sound from historical and legal standpoints.

I have dwelt at some length upon this dispute only because of certain lessons that may be derived from it, and I have spared my readers by omitting at least a hundred tiresome and sordid details. In the first place, boundary agreements should be definite when made. Socalled natural barriers, whether mountains, rivers or inlets, do not always constitute desirable lines of demarcation. For east and west lines, parallels of latitude are often best. North and south lines through unoccupied regions may well be made to follow some degree of longitude. This, however, assumes good-will and peace as a prevailing condition. Instead of a meandering coastline for its pan-handle annex, Russia would have been wiser to insist upon a north and south boundary for Alaska much farther eastward, to be continued without deviation until it reached the ocean. This would have given the lower part of the pan-handle to the British, which they needed for access to the sea. British America was shut off from the Pacific entirely until it gained the upper half of the Oregon country by agreement with the United States in 1846.

VII.

Boundary lines and title claims have no real consequence, however, except as they affect the welfare of those who inhabit the adjoining countries. A few years after this Alaska dispute, when Mr. Root became Secretary of State and Mr. Bryce was British Ambassador, it was found quite possible to adjust one unsettled question after another that had accumulated in the course of years. If the Alaska dispute had been referred to those two men, they could have found a practical answer not based upon old maps or new maps, but upon actual conditions. It is extremely difficult to persuade people in the mass that the Golden Rule can be applied to international controversies with perfect safety to all interests.

The boundary dispute that was adjusted in 1903 would have no attention in these pages except for the fact that while it does not adorn a tale, it does point a moral. The United States and Canada, speaking relatively, have been good neighbors for a long time. But they have made far too much obstinate and dilatory diplomatic history out of details that were susceptible of prompt settlement upon some inclusive formula of sincere and friendly cooperation.

With new responsibilities before America, as we face a period of aggression and disorder in the whole theater of the Pacific, it has become imperative that there should be ungrudging cooperation between the two halves of the North American mainland. It will not be enough to fight the war to a successful conclusion. The problems of peace, freedom, justice, and good order will require statesmanship that rises above all the minor questions of detail affecting nationalistic claims and titles.

It promises well for post-war relationships that agreement upon broad principles has already been reached between Washington and Ottawa. Conversations among officials of the two governments had been in progress from time to time for a year or more when on November 30, 1942, our Secretary of State, Mr. Cordell

Hull, addressed an official note to the Canadian government through its representative at Washington, Mr. Leighton McCarthy, whose reply bore the same date. These notes are regarded as having as much validity as if their substance had been embodied in a formal agreement.

The two governments had previously agreed to provide mutual aid, both in defense and in economic matters, through what were known as the Ogdensburg and Hyde Park Agreements, and certain subsequent arrangements. Having referred to those agreements, Mr. Hull declared that "post-war settlements must be such as to promote mutually advantageous economic arrangements between them [the United States and Canada] and the betterment of world-wide economic relations." His note then proceeded with the following paragraph indicative of the purpose of the two governments to provide a broad formula for improved economic relations with each other and with other countries:

> To that end the Governments of the United States of America and of Canada are prepared to cooperate in formulating a program of agreed action, open to participation by all other countries of like mind, directed to the expansion, by appropriate international and domestic measures, of production, employment, and the exchange and consumption of goods, which are the material foundations of the liberty and welfare of all peoples; to the elimination of all forms of discriminatory treatment in international commerce, and to the reduction of tariffs and other trade barriers; and, in general, to the attainment of all the economic objectives set forth in the Joint Declaration made on August 14, 1941, by the President of the United States of America and the Prime Minister of the United Kingdom.

Mr. McCarthy's reply quotes verbatim the essential paragraphs of Mr. Hull's note, and then confirms Canada's agreement in the following sentence: "I am instructed to inform you that the Government of Canada concur in the foregoing statement of conclusions and agree to your suggestion that your note of November 30th, 1942, and this reply should be regarded as placing on record the understanding of our two Governments in this matter." This exchange of notes was no casual or impromptu bit of informal correspondence, but was intended as a deliberate and responsible commitment on the part of the two governments.

The entire subject was discussed at much greater length in an address delivered at the University of Toronto February 23, 1943, by Sumner Welles, Under Secretary of State. Although this was not in form and manner an authorized statement of governmental policy, it was a highly informative review of past economic relationships, present collaboration in war efforts, and objectives of post-war policy. Mr. Welles concluded his thoughtful address with hopeful prognostications. If the twenty-two democracies that occupy North, Central, and South America, of different races, languages, and origins, could achieve such a measure of peaceful and humane relationship as now exists, he felt that Europe and other quarters of the globe could in similar manner work out systems of practical cooperation. Mr. Welles characterized Western Hemisphere conditions in the following paragraph, which though ignoring many minor frictions and obvious exceptions to the rule of harmony, is well justified when comparison is made with other parts of our belligerent planet:

> We have evolved here in the New World a system of international relationships which constitutes perhaps the highest achievement in the sphere of practical international living which civilized man has so far created. From the historical standpoint it is very recent indeed, but it has grown, gradually perhaps but nevertheless steadily, throughout the period of the individual life of the democracies of the Americas. It is a system in which the smallest state is just as free to determine its own destiny as the largest state. It is a system where the smallest state feels just as secure as the largest state, because of its knowledge that its independence and integrity are a matter of vital concern to its more powerful neighbors, and because of its assurance that should its liberties be jeopardized by aggression coming from without the Western Hemisphere, its more powerful neighbors will take the action necessary to repel that danger.

The late Lord Tweedsmuir, Governor-General of Canada (know throughout the English-speaking countries as John Buchan, historian, biographer, novelist, scholar and parliamentarian) was as sincerely devoted to the doctrine of good relations between Canada and the United States as to the further cooperation of North America with Great Britain. He was fond of quoting Dr. Johnson's dictum that a man should keep his friendships in constant repair; and in an address on Canada and the United States (1937) he declared that "just as in private life friendship is a thing which must be cultivated if it is to endure, so between nations there must be a continuous effort towards a better comprehension." He applied this thought to the future of Canadian-American relations.

Chapter XIV

HOW WE ANNEXED HAWAII AND BOUGHT THE PHILIPPINES

In the background of our particular interests in the Pacific, as distinguished from those general interests of trade and commerce that pertain to our two-ocean frontage, are the annexation by the United States of the Hawaiian Islands in 1898 and the assumption of responsibility for the Philippine Archipelago in the following year by virtue of the treaty with Spain. The present chapter summarizes the facts regarding the Americanization of Hawaii, and deals at greater length with the story of our experience in the Philippines.

Mistakes of an exceedingly unfortunate character were made by our government in dealing with General Aguinaldo and the Filipino insurrection that he led. Aguinaldo's movement had been suppressed, and he had accepted willing banishment before Admiral Dewey's victory over the Spanish navy. Taking advice from our consular officers in China, Dewey had brought Aguinaldo back to Manila. During the half-year that intervened before the Spanish-American treaty was signed, the insurgents were fighting the Spaniards, while an American army at Manila was awaiting final instructions.

There followed our war with Aguinaldo, and many difficult adjustments as American commissioners endeavored to bring about a regime of civil order, justice in local and general administration, and progress in agriculture, education and health services.

The issue of imperialism in our presidential election of 1900 forced the American people to consider the nature and object of our new trans-Pacific undertakings. The McKinley-Roosevelt ticket prevailed, along with a determination to do a good job in the Philippines for the welfare of the people, without committing the United States to a policy of colonialism in any manner akin to the exploitation of the Philippines for several centuries by the Spaniards.

For many years past the Filipino leaders have desired independence, and the United States had established a fully autonomous government under a Filipino president. There had been no delay in our full withdrawal, except that which was thought necessary for the safety of the Filipino people, in view of revolutionary conditions in China and aggressive movements by Japan.

Following the attack on Pearl Harbor, and the heroic defense of Manila and Bataan, by Filipinos and Americans under General MacArthur, the liberation of the Philippine Archipelago and the future security of its people became recognized objects of American policy in the present war.

WHEN the Japanese began their war against the United States by a surprise attack upon our principal naval base in the Pacific, the shock was felt as keenly throughout the United States as if an enemy had entered the Golden Gate or the inner harbor of New York. It was not merely that the Hawaiian Islands constituted a strategic outpost in the Pacific. This indeed was true; and our naval authorities had long regarded it from that standpoint almost exclusively. But, only less importantly, it was felt that the island group—with its inviting climate and its unique experiment of inter-racial equality and democratic self-government—belonged as essentially to the United States as if it were just off the mainland shores, whereas it is actually more than twenty-five hundred miles distant from California.

The Hawaiian people experienced their greatest social changes more than a hundred years ago, when from a semi-civilized, feudal condition they adopted American standards of morality, religion, and community life. It was perhaps an unprecedented transition, in the rapidity of its accomplishment. Their new type of civilization was attributed to the zeal of American missionaries and teachers. Sons of the American pioneers led in developing the resources of the islands, especially their agricultural wealth. Their more than sixty-five hundred square miles of land area made them incomparably more suitable for economic and social utilization than any other of the numerous clusters of Polynesian Islands, although others could be used for way stations by navies or merchantmen. In the early Nineties of the last century the civilized elements—having been suppressed for a time—recovered control and deposed a reactionary heathen regime. They established a local republic which became almost at once a model of good government.

This Republic of Hawaii sought annexation to the United States, and President Harrison, approving the project, sent a treaty to the Senate for ratification toward the end of his term. It had not been acted upon, however, when President Cleveland again entered the White House in March, 1893, and he withdrew the treaty in order to make an investigation on his own account. An attempt to restore the so-called native Queen (Liliuokalani) was a failure, and President Cleveland duly recognized the Hawaiian Republic, under President Sanford B. Dole. It was not until the summer of 1898, however, when our Navy was making full and free use of the Pearl Harbor as a necessary station in the war against Spain, that the question of annexation was brought to the front again. Both houses of Congress supported the proposal, and on August 12 of that year Hawaii became a part of the United States. When it was organized as a Territory two years later, Sanford B. Dole was appointed Governor.

Regardless of the unusual situation caused by the greatest variety of population elements to be found anywhere in the world, the position of Hawaii as a part of the United States for forty-five years (since its incorporation in 1898) has been as firm and unquestioned as that of Vermont. When the Japanese attack was made, there were few Americans who remembered the fact that the islands were comparatively recent acquisitions, or regarded them as part of the so-called "expansion policy of 1898." The missionaries had Americanized and Utopianized them long before their final annexation.

Dewey's victory at Manila had occurred on May 1st. Pending the conclusion of a treaty with Spain, our naval forces were on duty in the harbor of Manila, and the American army was arriving in some force for an indefinite period of occupation. Our armed vessels and our transports were making as free and unrestricted use of Hawaii as if we had owned the islands for half a century. They were actually proclaimed a part of the United States on the same day, August 12, 1898, as the signing of the peace protocol that ended our war with Spain.

II.

This protocol may be regarded as a model document in the history of international conflicts and their termination. There had come about in Europe an urgent desire that the war should be brought to an end. As I wrote at that time: "Even those powers whose conduct had seemed to be slightly unfriendly to the United States were urgent in behalf of peace, for the very reason that every successive American victory was adding to the international prestige of the so-called 'Yankees,' while at the same time the Yankee elasticity of mind was rapidly accommodating itself to the idea of unexpected and far-reaching responsibilities in regions where the continental nations themselves had their own secret designs."

There were good relations at that time between France and Spain; and the French Ambassador at Washington was representing Spanish interests after the severance of diplomatic relations between Washington and Madrid. The French government had observed strict and commendable neutrality during the war, and a French statesman who had come to Washington with a background of wide experience, arranged with our Secretary of State the preliminary terms of peace. This notable personality was M. Jules Cambon. He had brought to Washington the prestige of a brilliant and successful career under difficult circumstances as a colonial administrator in Algiers and a promoter of French interests in Tunis.

The entire protocol was not made public at once, perhaps to spare Spanish feelings. Six points, however, were given immediate publicity as a general summary of the protocol. The third point derives its significance chiefly from events that are to occur in the further course of the present war. Rather, perhaps, it will have its chief meaning in the adjustments that will be made when Eastern Asia and the insular sovereignties enter upon new experiences under terms of peace that are as yet unpredictable. This preliminary agreement of 1898 simply stated (point 3) that "the United States will occupy and hold the city, bay, and harbor of Manila pending the conclusion of a treaty of peace which shall determine the control, disposition, and government of the Philippines." Thus in August, 1898, our government expected to remain in control at Manila for a time that could not be fixed in advance. On the part of the American public at large there was no thought of a protracted occupation of that trans-Pacific archipelago, and no dream of its acquisition as an American "possession."

At the time when the Newlands resolution favoring the annexation of Hawaii was adopted in the summer of 1898, and perhaps two months before the armistice and protocol that ended the Spanish-American war, I made the following comment in the course of much presentation of facts and arguments:

> The Hawaiian Islands have for a great many years been under the virtual protection of the United States, and we have acquired a title to the best harbor in the islands as a coaling station. A variety of reasons, racial and commercial, local and international, has made it highly desirable for the islands themselves that they should be placed under the flag of the

United States. Most people in this country who possess a sense of the moral fitness of things have been of the opinion that we should either let the Hawaiian Islands alone, relinquishing all peculiar claims of every character, or else that we should allow them the very reasonable privilege of floating our flag and relying upon us for a secure political future.

It was, after all, a question of stable equilibrium; and various events of the past six years—culminating in our open and frank use of the Hawaiian Islands in the present war as a naval base, totally regardless of Hawaiian obligations of neutrality toward Spain—have made annexation simply inevitable. Our war with Spain is a serious business, carried on in the presence of great nations that know their own minds and are dead in earnest. Circumstances have compelled us to go to the Philippines and are going to keep us there for some time to come. We cannot manage our Philippine business without the use of Hawaii as an intermediate station. In addition to this fact of our present war necessity, is the further fact that Hawaii had wished to be taken, while no other country was raising the slightest objection.

Even in that last decade of the nineteenth century, when wars between two belligerents were undertaken with avowals of a limited purpose—while the rest of the world observed the principles of neutrality with more or less perfect adherence to them—no one could foresee the nature or extent of the results. A conflict that had been entered upon to secure a single local objective might end surprisingly, and change the course of history in some remote quarter of the globe. Thus we began the war against Spain with no purpose either expressed or hidden except the liberation of Cuba, and this was undertaken, as we declared, for the best interests of all who were concerned.

This object was accomplished swiftly and dramatically, to the astonishment of European governments. But Spain was left almost totally deprived of sea power, and therefore could not have maintained her position in the Far Pacific. This would have been the case even if she had been able to cope with the Filipino rebellion led by Aguinaldo. The activities of that patriotic leader had begun some years earlier, but had ceased under Spanish promises to institute reforms in the Philippine government, and to make certain payments to Aguinaldo for ending the insurrection. He accepted exile with the understanding that he would go to Singapore or Java and await the dawn of a new era at Manila. But the promises of reform were not kept by the Spanish governor, and personal agreements with Aguinaldo were disregarded. The

Filipino leader returned, accordingly, under Admiral Dewey's auspices, to arouse his followers against the stranded Spanish soldiery remaining in the great island of Luzon.

III.

Having ended all possible danger of Spanish attack upon Hawaii or upon California, Admiral Dewey might have withdrawn his fleet from Manila Harbor soon after his victory of May 1, with no appreciable danger to the United States. This was the course that many Americans thought desirable at the time. A friend and neighbor of mine, of wide influence although not in official life, wrote to President McKinley with cogent arguments against sending troops to undertake the occupation of Manila. This preceded the protocol of August 12. Very few Americans could be found at that time who had ever visited the Philippine Islands. The public at large in this country had not known where those islands were situated until after Dewey's victory. It is probable that far more Americans in 1942 knew about the mandated division of Papua, and the location of the Solomon Islands, as the Japanese swept southward to menace Australia, than their parents knew about the Philippines in the early days of 1898.

Nevertheless, with little public understanding about the situation in the Philippines, our army under President McKinley's direction was massing troops at San Francisco and was sending convoyed transports in relays across the Pacific until our land forces at Manila numbered about twenty thousand men in the aggregate. Under the terms of the August protocol, war had ceased and there were three distinct armies at or near Manila waiting anxiously for final news of the peace negotiations at Paris. The first of these armies were the Spanish troops—who had not, like some of those in Cuba, been evacuated and sent home even before a treaty was signed. It may be assumed that the officers in the Philippines expected to remain, and had no thought of fighting the Americans, but supposed they would have to resume war with the Filipino rebels. The second and third of the waiting armies were the Americans and the large body of Aguinaldo's native troops.

Meanwhile, the interval of more than half a year between

Dewey's victory and the signing of the peace treaty had begun to make the American people conscious of the prospect that Spain would not be able to keep the Philippines, and that the establishment of order might necessitate American occupation for an indefinite period. When it was found that the peace commissioners at Paris (five Americans and five Spaniards) had agreed that the United States would have to assume permanent responsibility at Manila and throughout the archipelago, there was dismay in the minds of many thoughtful and prudent Americans. Yet the bargain was accepted cheerfully by the great majority.[1]

Our commissioners were men of experience and good judgment, and they had kept in touch with President McKinley

[1] In view of our present activities in the Pacific, and our prospective concern with various insular and Asiatic affairs, it is important that we should be well-informed about the circumstances under which we acquired political spheres of authority beyond our own Pacific coast line. The most searching and complete account of our diplomatic and political history as regards the Pacific at the end of the Spanish-American War, is contained in a book by Professor Julius W. Pratt. It is entitled *Expansionists of 1898: The Acquisition of Hawaii and the Spanish Islands.* The volume was published in 1936, in the series resulting from annual lecture courses at the Johns Hopkins University on American diplomatic history.

After experiences that gave him a wide range of knowledge of American life and sentiment—including a number of years as instructor in history at the Naval Academy (Annapolis), Dr. Pratt became professor of American history in the University of Buffalo. His studies of the development of American foreign policy are always objective, and they are exhaustive in research without lacking the touch of human interest. Referring to the author of the present volume, Professor Pratt remarks:

> "A civilian who fully shared Mahan's enthusiasm for expansion was Albert Shaw, editor of the *Review of Reviews.* From May, 1897, to February 1898, the editorial pages of that magazine played frequently upon the importance of annexing Hawaii, constructing a canal, and acquiring or controlling key islands in the Caribbean—all as means toward the eventual domination of the Pacific, which was to be 'the theater of great events in the coming century.'"

It is true that I had for a number of years favored the acquisition of the Hawaiian islands for explicit reasons that seemed to admit of no desirable alternative. Following Dewey's victory at Manilla, however, I had hoped that it might be possible for us to withdraw from the Philippines after the completion of the treaty with Spain. I did not approve of the initial movement to send troops from San Francisco, believing that Dewey's force of seamen and marines could keep order at Manila. I was at that time aware of the intense interest of the Japanese in the political status of the Philippines, and knew that they were hoping that Philippine independence could be established, under some sort of friendly protectorate in which Great Britain might join Japan and the United States. With the lapse of months, however, it seemed inevitable that the United States must assume control, although at no time during the past forty-five years have I believed that the Philippine archipelago should be held permanently as an American territory or possession, on the same footing as Alaska and Hawaii.

throughout the weeks of negotiation. There was no evidence of an imperialistic spirit on the part of the Administration, or of the Senate in ratifying the treaty. There was probably a greater degree of self-confidence in the national mood than the circumstances justified, although it was not a jingo mood or a vainglorious one. At the opening of the year 1899 I reviewed the achievements of the previous year with an optimism that was fairly typical of prevailing opinion. I may quote a few paragraphs from many pages that I wrote surveying conditions throughout the world:

The year 1898 is to be characterized as one that has witnessed the accomplishment of many things and that has provided several magnificent chapters in the history of progress toward the firm establishment of peace and order among the nations. Nothing could be more mistaken than to suppose that the principal exhibitions of armed force that the world has seen in 1898 have made for the triumph of brute force over justice and right. On the contrary, the English-speaking men who have in 1898 opened the Nile, made Khartoum accessible once more, and brought the Soudan into relations with the outside world, have performed a most noble and humane task for civilization and peace. The empire of the Kalipha meant the sword and the torch as the chief business of life. The men who had destroyed Edhem Pasha's army and had afterward murdered Gordon at Khartoum had spread devastation throughout a vast region, destroying the lives of millions of men, women, and children. With much bloodshed, it is true, but with as little as possible, General Kitchener has annihilated that evil dominion of the Kalipha, while leaving every Mohammedan in the Soudan as free as are the Mohammedans in India in their customs and religious observances.

No less praiseworthy than the splendid missionary work of Kitchener and his men has been the execution by the people of the United States of a righteous judgment against Spain's attempt to continue by brute force to exercise sovereignty in colonial possessions where the inhabitants had rebelled for good cause and where it had been demonstrated that those inhabitants could be subdued only by extermination. If we could have induced Spain to withdraw without our resort to compulsion, it would have been very fortunate. But since Spanish statesmanship saw no way to yield except after some show of resistance, it was only merciful to Spain that we should have sent our ships and our troops. It would have been still kinder to Spain, as one looks back upon the course of the past three years, if we had acted considerably sooner. As matters stand, we have rendered very substantial service to the people resident in the Spanish West Indies and to all legitimate commercial interests in any manner affected, while we have also performed for Spain an amputation that was absolutely required by the existing conditions.

The swift success of our aggressive policy has left the whole world in a far more stable position than we found it at the opening of the year. The annexation of Hawaii has given that interesting group of islands a settled status, and our assumption of responsibility for the Philippines will speedily bring about a vastly improved situation in that populous archipelago. We ought to have no serious difficulty in assisting the Cubans to restore order throughout the island and to maintain fairly efficient institutions under republican forms. The wisest men in Spain are venturing to express somewhat boldly the relief that they feel in the wholesome chastening that has come to them in the painful year of 1898. This view has been taken by business men especially, and prevailed in the conference of Spanish chambers of commerce that has met at Saragossa.

The heroism of Americans and Filipinos fighting together under General Douglas MacArthur's leadership will doubtless prove to have been a turning-point in the history of the vast regions of the Pacific beyond Hawaii. American authority will not settle the future problems of Eastern Asia; but the United States will influence conclusions regarding island groups, especially the Philippine archipelago. Just why we accepted responsibility for the Philippines in 1898, and what record we have made there in somewhat less than half a century, ought to be well understood, because the facts furnish backgrounds upon which future policies will be based.

IV.

It is desirable that the present generation should not be led astray as it attempts to characterize and judge American leaders of half a century ago. There linger some faint echoes of partisan controversies that have a tendency to prejudice the thinking of many citizens who desire to judge historical situations upon their merits. President McKinley was not an imperialist, nor were any of the five American members of the peace commission who sat at Paris.

It happened that the Spanish War occurred during a term of Republican administration. But Democrats, especially those of the South and West, were even more urgent in advocating and supporting the use of armed force than were the Republicans themselves. The occupation of Manila occurred as an incident of that war. Perhaps there should have been forethought about Spain's future position in the Pacific, but at Washington there was none whatever. Naval authorities in Europe regarded Spanish sea-power as decidedly superior to that of the United States. Planning at Washington, so far as the Pacific was involved, had been limited to the necessity of protecting our West Coast.

Congress had avowed its determination not to annex Cuba, but, rather, to aid the Cubans in establishing a republic of their own. It had not occurred to a single member of Congress to propose a self-denying ordinance in advance, as regarded political control of the Philippines in case of a conclusive victory over Spain's fleet in the Pacific. But the completeness of Dewey's victory had created an obvious predicament, and this occurred long weeks before the destruction at Santiago of Spain's Atlantic fleet, and the armistice of August. The full implications of the affair in Manila harbor were not as well understood by the American press and our intelligent public as by the Spanish authorities. The conditions and possible alternatives had to be examined by our peace commissioners at Paris; and through our diplomatic representatives in Europe these commissioners were made aware of an international situation which could not well be disregarded.

It would help our understanding of the realities of that critical situation if we should try to make generous allowances, and see things at their best rather than at their worst. Our peace commissioners were soon made aware of a situation that was exceedingly difficult and complex. Spanish rule had been established throughout the islands in the early period of European discovery. Manila had been made the Spanish colonial capital in 1571. The work of the Spanish missionaries had been thorough, and for the greater part the islands had been Christianized. But three centuries had created no such thing as a homogeneous racial type. Several principal languages persisted and various minor ones. While the underlying racial strain is Malay, the dominant element in the island of Luzon indicates a mixture of Spanish and Malay blood. These typical Filipinos of the chief island derive their culture in certain aspects from the long centuries of unprogressive Spanish domination.

The younger Filipino leaders, however, became sufficiently aware of modern history, as the nineteenth century advanced, to grow restless under corrupt and backward-looking colonial administration. They resented the medieval methods of the religious orders, which had become even wealthier and more oppressive than the greedy civilian tax-gatherers. A growing demand for independence had taken the form of an armed insurrection under the leadership of Emilio Aguinaldo as early as 1896. With no international obstacles to interfere with communication between the home country and the islands, the Spaniards were able to reinforce their troops and to suppress the uprising.

As I have stated in a previous paragraph, Admiral Dewey had been made aware of these conditions, and had been admonished by the American and British consuls at Hong Kong, among other advisers, to encourage the independence movement, and to lend Aguinaldo a helping hand.

Our older citizens can remember the wave of enthusiasm that swept across the United States with the first news of Dewey's naval victory. We were absorbed in the gratifying evidence of the prowess of our new navy. But we were not at that time made fully aware of the effect of this naval engagement upon the Filipino mind and spirit. It was hailed as a miraculous day of deliverance. The native population no longer feared the cruelty of their age-long oppressors. Aguinaldo's army was recruited with unprecedented rapidity. Many of the troops enrolled in the Spanish regiments were native Filipinos, and these deserted by hundreds or even by thousands to join the army that was to win independence and launch the Filipino Republic.

Although there was long-range sympathy between the contemporary uprisings in Cuba and the Philippines during the three-year period 1895-8, there was only superficial similarity between the two situations. The Cuban independence movement had the complete moral support of the Latin-American republics, so that the intervention of the United States aroused no appreciable suspicion or jealousy. Congress had made sure of this attitude by giving a definite pledge in advance regarding Cuba's self-determined future. Spain had much European sympathy in her Cuban predicament, but no practical help. The alternatives were simple: Spain would hold Cuba on some terms, or else lose it altogether. In short, the situation was not complicated, from an international standpoint.

As regards the future of the Philippines, on the contrary, there was no advance promise by Congress, and no consideration on the part of the press or the public until after Dewey's victory, and after the swift resurgence of the independence movement.

Thus it was not long before cross-purposes began to appear. It was not, however, until the announcement of the treaty terms that the dissatisfaction of the native movement under Aguinaldo's leadership assumed a menacing form.

Within a month after it was known that Spain had transferred her interest in the Philippines to the United States, I made certain comments that were in accord with prevailing American opinion in January, 1899. The views of the peace commissioners, and also those of President McKinley and the majorities in both Houses of Congress, were fairly reflected in my statements. It is now desirable to recall the tone of American sentiment at the end of the last century, because it bears upon all that has followed in four decades since the United States assumed authority in the Philippines. Accordingly I quote herewith from those observations:

Certain of our consuls in Chinese ports, and others, both American and English, probably made a mistake of judgment in advising Admiral Dewey to take Aguinaldo back to the Philippines and in encouraging the insurgents to build up an army and set up the pretense of a civil government with Aguinaldo at its head. These insurgents represent the most highly civilized fraction of the complex Philippine population, but they by no means stand for any great numerical share of the inhabitants. It is desirable to conciliate them and to obtain their cooperation in developing the best possible regime of justice and order throughout the archipelago. It is to be feared that the personal ambitions of half a dozen men, and chiefly of Aguinaldo himself, have been standing in the way of the real interests of the islands.

Nevertheless, we Americans must try to put ourselves in the places of the Philippine insurgents in order to understand something of their point of view. Aguinaldo has had a very remarkable career, as our character sketch of him, published elsewhere and written by one who knows him personally, will suffice to show. If we should withdraw, Aguinaldo would find it absolutely impossible to establish and maintain an independent Philippine government. A great archipelago cannot be held together without ships. It will be the American policy, as a matter of course, to develop practical home rule in the Philippines just as fast as it can be instituted; and it is to be hoped that the natives of ability like Aguinaldo may see the advantage of doing what the leading Cubans are now doing—namely, giving their valuable services to the American military government in order the more quickly to render military rule unnecessary.

The situation at Iloilo last month was an exceedingly anxious one. The insurgents had occupied the city when the Spaniards evacuated, and were not disposed to allow their possession to be surrendered to the American naval and military expedition that General Otis and Admiral Dewey had sent down from Manila. It is to be borne in mind, however, that many of the alarmist dispatches that appeared in our newspapers had come by way of Madrid and other continental points and were entirely false. It is to be believed that the Philippine insurgents will at an early day accept the new order of things. Our Government has the strongest assurances from Berlin that there is no truth whatever in the reports that the insurgent attitude at Iloilo had been secretly encouraged by Germany.

In the foregoing comments I alluded to an article that I was publishing upon the career of Aguinaldo. Extraordinary experiences had developed a personality and a gift of leadership that entitled him to rank with the most remarkable contemporary figures of his period. The well-informed contributor of that article gives a sympathetic account of the manner in which an obscure boy, half Spanish and half Malay, had gained early education in the Pontifical University of Manila, and had afterwards sought naval and military experience in China, consciously preparing himself for the independence movement of which he became foremost leader after the murder of Jose Rizal (whose name is cherished by Philippine patriots, even as Russians cherish that of Lenin). The article in question includes Aguinaldo's own characterizations of Spanish government as he knew it. I make no apology for giving space to the following quotation, from a statement made at Hong Kong by Aguinaldo himself to an American naval officer, as we were soon to attack the Spanish fleet:

> There will be a war between your country and Spain, and in that war you can do the greatest deed in history by putting an end to Castilian tyranny in my native land. We are not ferocious savages. On the contrary, we are unspeakably patient and docile. That we have risen from time to time is no sign of bloodthirstiness on our part, but merely of manhood resenting wrongs which it is no longer able to endure. You Americans revolted for nothing at all compared with what we have suffered. Mexico and the Spanish republics rose in rebellion and swept the Spaniard into the sea, and all their sufferings together would not equal that which occurs every day in the Philippines. We are supposed to be living under laws and civilization of the nineteenth century, but we are really living under the practices of the Middle Ages.
>
> A man can be arrested in Manila, plunged into jail, and kept there twenty years without ever having a hearing or even knowing the complaint upon which he was arrested. There is no means in the legal system there of having a prompt hearing or of finding out what the charge is. The

right to obtain evidence by torture is exercised by military, civil, and ecclesiastical tribunals. To this right there is no limitation, nor is the luckless witness or defendant permitted to have a surgeon, a counsel, a friend, or even a bystander to be present during the operation. As administered in the Philippines one man in every ten dies under the torture, and nothing is ever heard of him again.

It would be unfortunate to forget or belittle the character of the independence movement. In the interval between Dewey's victory of May 1 and the news of the treaty that reached the Philippines by way of Hong Kong more than half a year later, intense warfare had been waged between Spaniards and Filipinos. Aguinaldo had organized his men throughout Luzon and had managed to acquire a supply of war material for equipping guerrilla bands. It was said that he had captured not less than fifteen thousand Spanish soldiers while our American troops were inactive, waiting after the armistice of August to know the results of the treaty-making at Paris.

V.

The extent to which American consular officials, and officers of our navy and army, had encouraged Aguinaldo in the belief that we were expecting to support his independent republic will always remain a matter of uncertainty. There was, doubtless, an unfortunate misunderstanding. We must bear in mind that although the Filipinos were people of mixed races and all grades of culture from high civilization to savagery, the independence leadership was intelligent. Before he knew anything about the annexation for which the treaty provided, Aguinaldo had told General Anderson that he knew the American Constitution by heart, and that it contained no provision that would justify our holding the Philippines under colonial government or acquiring them as a possession.

He made it plain to his intimate American friend, Consul-General Wardman at Hong Kong, that he realized the immense difficulties of establishing a liberal and just government; but he believed that no foreign nation could accomplish it, and that the Filipinos would somehow have to work it out for themselves. He was incomparably more familiar with the situation throughout the archipelago, with savage tribes on some of the islands and with the great body of Mohammedan Moros in southern areas, than were all the American authorities taken together. Concluding the character sketch our author wrote:

> Aguinaldo's difficulties are increased by the jealousy of ambitious colleagues and by the greed of the unscrupulous and grasping. Despite his power, he knows that he may be put away tomorrow by a combination of enemies and rivals. Neither is his problem cleared by the attitude of the United States. He keeps himself well informed upon the government proceedings at Washington, and sees himself denounced by a Senator one day and glorified by another Senator the next. He reads propositions to annex, to form a protectorate, to cede to other powers, to give back to Spain, to establish a native republic. If the average American is puzzled by the superb imbecility of some of his Congressmen, how much more is a poor Filipino whose ideas of government have been derived from the contemplation of Spanish rule, of which the mainsprings are falsehood and fraud, corruption and extortion. That Aguinaldo has not done as well as might have been possibly done may be admitted; but he has done as well as he could. He has done better than any one possibly believed a year ago, and he has shown the world that the Filipino is capable of that self-control upon which all good government must be based.

When Aguinaldo in 1896 had accepted Spanish promises of government reforms and had withdrawn temporarily from the islands, he was a young man, aged perhaps twenty-six years. I published a group photograph of him with his chief associates, about twenty-five in number, all of them youthful with alert and intelligent faces. It may be argued—as we review that situation in the light of ample subsequent experience—that a native republic under those leaders could not have succeeded, even if it had entered upon its career in a world of benevolent well-wishers. Aguinaldo himself did not know how it could be accomplished in the face of internal difficulties. What these young Filipinos could not understand, however, was our appalling freedom of speech in the United States, and the processes of discussion through which American public opinion attempts to inform itself, as the government at Washington fumbles strangely while it tries to discover a sound basis upon which to frame its policy.

Our peace commissioners were at work in a European atmosphere. They were spending about five months in close contact with five representative Spanish gentlemen, of whose wounded pride they were constantly aware. Perhaps no settlement between opposing governments at the end of a war (in which one side had been overwhelmingly victorious) was ever considered with greater courtesy and dignity, or with more constant effort to deal justly with the main facts of a situation that could not be compromised. The Spaniards were assured that their large interests—governmental and military, private and pecuniary, and also ecclesiastical—would not have ruthless treatment. As in the case of Cuba, the evacuation of Spanish troops in the Pacific would be carried out under American auspices, with full consideration.

It seems regrettable that the commissioners at Paris failed to realize the nature of the new difficulties that had been created in the Islands, even while they were arriving at conclusions. In the case of Cuba the United States had intervened avowedly to support and stabilize an independence movement. In the Philippines, on the contrary, American influence had helped to foment an independence movement that was non-existent when Dewey reached Manila harbor and won his spectacular victory. The peace negotiators were seemingly unmindful of Aguinaldo's *new* war. The American representatives at Hong Kong and Manila were apparently supporting Aguinaldo's movement. The government at Washington was doing nothing to clarify the confused and dangerous situation. It seems, as we look back upon it, to have been not a comedy but a tragedy of errors.

There might not be any disagreement, at this late day, over the statement that it was a blunder of the first magnitude to have encouraged the insurrectionary movement. The only explanation lies in a careful study of the sequence of significant dates. A quarter of a year had intervened between Dewey's victory and the truce that ended the war in Cuba. Four months more were added to the period of uncertainty, if we count the time between the protocol of August 12 and the peace agreement in December.

If the peace commissioners did not attach due importance to the independence movement, we must believe that it was in part because they were made so anxiously aware of certain international complications—which may or may not have been as serious as they appeared to be. The British authorities, for example (acting through our ambassadors at London and Paris), were urging the American commissioners to consider what might happen if the United States should withdraw and leave the desirable but disorganized archipelago to its fate. Much had been made of a naval incident at Manila as Dewey's fleet was clearing for action. A German commander was said to have assumed a menacing position, while an English cruiser lined up to support Dewey as against the German. The incident might have had no real importance, but it seemed to support well-known facts.

The British had been established at Hong Kong for more than half a century, and the control of the Philippine Islands was regarded as a matter of vital consequence to British interests. It was known that Germany was ambitious to acquire colonies and strong bases in the Pacific and on the Asiatic Coast. If the United States had withdrawn promptly, Germany would without delay have undertaken to negotiate an agreement with Spain. On some terms, the Germans would have sought to gain control of the Philippines.

VI.

Although the British were more directly occupied at that time with German aims and intrigues, there was another situation—not less difficult to deal with—of which the commissioners at Paris were probably aware. Japan's bolder schemes of conquest were not then unfolded; but her designs in respect to the Philippines were not wholly concealed. While Americans had been encouraging the Cuban insurrection, and making it easy for the patriot leaders to obtain arms and supplies, the Japanese had been promoting the Philippine insurrection. It had not occurred to the particular group of Japanese leaders who were then thinking in terms of conquest and empire that the United States could have any possible interest in the Philippines.

Relations between the United States and Japan at that time were of the most friendly character. Japanese agents had been sent to the United States to study the course of the Cuban movement, and I well remember conversing with them about it in New York. They were in cheerful mood, and talked freely enough about their interest in the expulsion of Spain from the Pacific. They seemed to take it for granted that the United States would be content to acquire dominance in the West Indies and the Caribbean region.

They did not actually disclose plans for Japanese conquest, but gave the impression that an independent Philippine government would soon come under the protecting auspices of Japan. Furthermore, it did not occur to them that the United States might not look favorably upon a development of that kind. To what extent Aguinaldo had been financed and provided with supplies by the Japanese, I have no information. But I know that their agents who came to the United States gave me to understand that they were lending material support to the independence cause. Certainly the Japanese would have resented any attempt by England or Germany to control the destiny of those islands, whether as protectorates or as colonial possessions.

The peace commissioners gave themselves time and opportunity to analyze the international situation, and to exclude one solution after another. (1) They had first to decide that it was too late to reform Spanish methods. No terms could be found upon which Spanish dominion could be retained. (2) The Japanese would not have tolerated a bargain between Spain and Germany. (3) Without a strong and friendly guiding hand, a Philippine republic could not have taken its place in the family of nations. Brought down to the last analysis, the one solution seemed to be a transfer of Spanish authority to the United States. If the word had been in use, it might have been called a *mandate*. This was the one immediate decision that could be accepted by Spain, Germany, France, England, Japan, and China without producing open discord.

The attempt at Washington to amend the treaty by providing for "temporary occupation" rather than full control of the Philippines was defeated for reasons of common sense and plain logic. The treaty was, in form, a settlement with Spain alone. It would have been fruitless to covenant with the dispossessed Spaniards that we would also soon dispossess ourselves. Regardless of bewilderment and diverse opinions, there was the most complete agreement in the United States that whether we were in authority for a longer or a shorter time, the welfare of the inhabitants must be the first consideration, and international stability the second. There was never afterwards any disagreement on either of those points, although many differences in matters of greater or less import arose from time to time in subsequent years.

In the early weeks of the year 1899 it was reported that our military and naval forces occupying Manila amounted to forty-one thousand men. The Filipinos had by that time a remarkably well-organized and well-supplied military force under Aguinaldo's lead that was almost if not quite equal in numbers to the American army. It becomes necessary to remind readers who would grasp essential facts that the further sequence of dates had become of vital importance. The treaty (signed on December 10, 1898) having been submitted to the Senate, was referred to the Foreign Relations Committee and reported favorably on January 11. Thereupon the Senate continued a discussion, largely theoretical, with no limits fixed upon debate.

A high-minded Massachusetts Senator led in opposing ratification. He was doubtless unaware of the ceaseless activity of an anti-American propaganda system that was spreading false news and scandalous rumors day by day throughout every district and village of the great island of Luzon. It was without avail to explain that ratification of the treaty had no bearing whatever upon the future political control of the Philippines. The debate went on and on, while the situation at Manila was nearing the point of explosion. Ratification actually occurred early in February. President McKinley's signature made the Treaty effective on the tenth. This was the tenth month after Aguinaldo had been brought back to the Philippines by the American navy, in order to resist the Spaniards and organize his provisional republic.

The delay at Washington had become extremely embarassing to our commanding officers who were waiting at Manila. Aguinaldo claimed, with unanswerable logic, that the armistice of August had no binding character, and that no treaty could have status as public law until it had been ratified. It would be impossible to determine what agencies were most responsible for the intense bitterness of the anti-American crusade that was spreading—not only by word of mouth but with millions of leaflets and pamphlets distributed among the people of the great northern island, most of whom could read and write.

When the vote on the treaty was finally reached, fifty-seven Senators supported it and twenty-seven were opposed. Since ratification required a two-thirds vote, a shift of two Senators from the affirmative to the negative would have defeated the treaty. Such a defeat would have intensified difficulties in all directions, and it would have created a chaotic situation in the Philippines. In view of what might have happened if there had been much further delay, it may have been for the best that Aguinaldo himself, losing patience and under pressure from his followers, broke the deadlock at Manila just before the Senate voted to ratify.

Action, even though tragic, often relieves suspense and puts an end to useless verbal controversy. Aguinaldo gave our forces at Manila something to do by precipitating an attack upon them that was as unexpected as the Japanese attack at Pearl Harbor more than forty years later although better resisted. So far as his immediate aims and ambitions were concerned, they were at once destroyed by this action. From my account of it at the time I will quote two paragraphs:

The army of Philippine insurgents, under the command of Aguinaldo and his coterie of native leaders, had precipitated a night attack upon the American forces in possession of Manila. Far from being off their guard and unprepared, the American troops faced the emergency with a coolness, promptness, and aggressive vigor that the assailants were wholly unable to resist. This conflict began late on the night of Saturday, the 4th. Not only was Maj. Gen. Elwell S. Otis, with his brigade commanders, in perfect readiness for action, but Admiral Dewey was equally prepared to render most effective aid. It was necessary, of course, for the ships to wait until daylight Sunday morning; but as soon as possible after dawn the navy began a firing of deadly accuracy into the trenches of the insurgent army. In this business the monitor *Monadnock* was especially active, and the other vessels engaged were the cruiser *Charleston*, the gunboat *Concord*, and two gunboats that had been captured from the Spaniards, and now had real gunners on board.

The rout of the insurgents was complete, and it was reported on Monday that the number of Filipinos killed, wounded, and taken prisoners would probably amount to 4,000; while about 50 American officers and men had been killed and about three times as many wounded. The total strength of the Filipinos under arms in the neighborhood of Manila was estimated at about 30,000, of whom some 20,000 are supposed to have engaged in battle. The men of the Eighth Army Corps under General Otis who participated in the fighting numbered about 13,000. Considerable masses of insurgent troops reintrenched themselves at points lying several miles out of Manila, and the American army was obliged to follow up the main engagement of Saturday and Sunday by battles which, if they had occurred otherwise than as subsidiary to so large an engagement, would have been deemed of no little importance. The upshot of the matter was that the insurgents, although fighting with intelligence and bravery, were wholly unable at any point to make a successful stand against the American soldiers, even though our troops were in much smaller numbers; and thus within a week the much-vaunted army of Aguinaldo had been thoroughly defeated, totally demoralized, and virtually dissipated and scattered. It had no resource left but guerilla fighting from swamps and hills.

Everyone in the United States agreed that this collision was deplorable. But at worst it ended uncertainties and forced upon the United States the outlines of a fairly definite policy. Nothing could be done in the Philippines until a reign of law and order had been established. Aguinaldo's young men could not have accomplished that preliminary task. There had been much sympathy with the aspirations of these young patriots, and it was a sorrowful thing to have met them in battle. But illusions were removed, and it was clearly perceived that the United States had assumed responsibilities across the Pacific that could not be fulfilled in a holiday mood. The shock had chastened the American spirit, and the floods of futile talk were abated. We had now to prove to ourselves, to the Filipinos, and to the world at large that we could meet an unexpected test of our sincerity and our principles.

There was no hope for Aguinaldo's further resistance, although in fact he took to the hills with guerrilla followers and was not captured until 1901. It was widely believed in Asia and also in Europe that if the United States had withdrawn from Manila—having refused to assume any task of authority in the Philippines—the naval forces of other powers would at once have seized parts of the archipelago if not the whole of it, and confusion would have reigned.

The only escape from such a situation that Germany or Japan would recognize as valid was the transfer to the United States by Spain of a title that had international recognition. Such a title, in the nature of the case, could be held by the United States only in trusteeship for the Filipino people. It was not desirable, from the standpoint of the islands themselves, or from that of international peace and order, that this rich though undeveloped island group—which had been held together for three centuries—should be torn apart and seized piece-meal by rival empires whether European or Asiatic.

If Aguinaldo had come to America for a part of his earlier training, he would have discovered that no political element in the United States sought domination over peoples inhabiting other lands. It is to his credit that a month after his capture he took the oath of allegiance to the United States, and soon learned the truth about American purposes and policies.

VII.

We were approaching another presidential campaign, and McKinley was to be nominated for a second term in 1900 without Republican opposition. Bryan's hold upon the national and state organization of the Democratic party, regardless of his defeat in 1896, was strong enough to make him its candidate for a second time. The Free Silver plank, which had formed the principal issue in the previous election, retained its place in the platform of 1900; but the candidate chose to waive or minimize the question of monetary standards, and to challenge the Republicans upon the issue of "imperialism." In the voting of November, President McKinley carried twenty-eight states with 292 votes in the electoral college, and William J. Bryan carried seventeen states with 155 electoral votes.

To single out some matter of external policy and use it as a football in the game of party politics is not a wise proceeding. The processes of self-government in a nation of free speech like ours, with rival parties contending for control, are never marked by the emphasis of under-statement. Fortunately we have reason to hope that patriotism will always rise above partisanship in emergencies. With the minority party so alertly on guard, and with full freedom of press and platform, the country will survive regardless of the shifting of balance from one party to the other in a close election.

Mr. Bryan's arguments against imperialism echoed and elaborated those abstract views that the amiable Senator from Massachusetts had expounded in the previous year, as unwittingly he had wrought mischief by delaying the ratification of the treaty. When the election of 1900 turned upon that same issue, the Massachusetts Senator preferred to support President McKinley. Thus he accepted a situation that no theoretical disquisitions, however impressive, could have altered, unless to make it worse. In 1898 the eloquent Nebraskan had not only advocated the war with Spain, but had shown his belief in it as just and necessary by raising in his state a regiment of volunteers of which he was appointed Colonel. When his arguments were brought down to earth, they were not consistent. We had entered upon a shocking and disastrous course of imperialistic adventure by assuming authority in the Philippines, but were justified in occupying Cuba.

It may suffice to say that there was no intention on either side to present the issues in a false light. I knew the leaders of both parties well, including of course both W. J. Bryan and Theodore Roosevelt, who had been placed on the ticket with McKinley and was making speaking tours across the country. If Bryan had won in the close election of 1896, we would not have avoided the Spanish War. I am sure that he never so claimed. Nor would we have escaped strange predicaments in the Pacific.

When in his campaign of 1900 Bryan was obliged to answer practical questions, he adopted the theory that we might retain Manila Bay as a coaling and naval station, but otherwise cease to concern ourselves about the Archipelago and its millions of inhabitants. If he had been elected, he would have taken office in March, 1901. He would then have found that the Philippine Commission, with William Howard Taft as its President, had been doing its best for an entire year to bring the people of the Islands under an orderly and modern civil administration.

Mr. Taft had left his place as a United States Circuit Judge to undertake this difficult task across the broad Pacific. Could Mr. Bryan have been so little appreciative of the great public service rendered by Judge Taft as to have recalled him? I prefer to answer the question in the negative. President McKinley on July 4, 1901, made Taft the first American Governor-General of the Philippines, and he held that position for almost three years.

In 1902 Mr. Taft was sent to Rome by President Roosevelt in order to confer with Pope Leo XIII regarding the extensive agricultural lands held by the Dominican and other religious orders. Their retention of vast Philippine estates, upon which many thousands of humble agricultural workers lived as laborers or rent-paying tenants, might have been likened to the condition that prevailed in England in the time of Henry VIII. But whereas in England—and later, in Revolutionary France—the monasteries were suppressed and their estates confiscated, it was the American plan to find an equitable solution; and this was done through Mr. Taft's legal ability and his broad-minded sense of justice.

Elihu Root, who had been Secretary of War in McKinley's Cabinet, remained in that office under President Roosevelt until

1904 when Mr. Taft succeeded him. During the early years of our so-called "insular" policies—having to do with Cuba, Puerto Rico, and the Philippines—Mr. Root was the constructive genius who framed the governing systems, in close accord with President Roosevelt and Mr. Taft, and with intelligent support in Congress. While upholding necessary authority on the part of the United States, these statesmen were single-mindedly devoted to the welfare of the insular peoples, and were looking forward to the time when they could safely undertake complete self-government. General Leonard Wood, having served as military governor of Cuba with notable success, was sent to the Philippines to succeed Mr. Taft as Governor-General when the Cuban Republic had been duly established. No better choice could have been made in view of General Wood's medical, military, and administrative experiences and aptitudes.

I shall not undertake to summarize our American experiment of full forty years since Mr. Taft, as civil administrator, welcomed Filipino cooperation and addressed himself to the task of gaining the confidence of the people. One change, which came without delay, was a magical transformation in judicial procedure, as the protection of law was extended to the humblest individual. Schools and public health administration followed the establishment of civil order. Communities were trained in local self-government, while Filipino citizens were brought into the central government as rapidly as possible.

For many years past the Filipino leaders have desired independence and full sovereignty for their island realm, and American public opinion has never discouraged their aspirations. The delays that have postponed the consummation of independence have been caused by circumstances best understood by the native leaders themselves. In 1934, however, an independence act was passed at Washington and confirmed by the Philippine Legislature. It established a native government under an elected President, and set up the so-called "Commonwealth of the Philippines."

A certain measure of oversight on the part of the United States was to be retained until 1946. The new constitution had been accepted throughout the major islands, including those occupied chiefly by Mohammedans, who continued to live in accordance with their own local customs. The admission of Philippine products to the United States duty-free had resulted in a great expansion of trade, and the outlook for peace and prosperity was seemingly unclouded.

When in 1936 General Douglas MacArthur retired as Chief of Staff of the United States Army, he was sent as military adviser to the Philippine government, at the request of President Quézon. That he had accomplished excellent results in training an army was proved to the world by the heroic resistance of his native soldiers after the attack of the Japanese on December 8, 1941. This chapter ends with our recognition (in 1943) of the undisputed fact that the entire Archipelago is under Japanese exploitation. Predictions would be presumptuous; but there can be no reason for hesitancy in giving voice to deliberate intentions. When General MacArthur left the Philippines under order to assume command in Australia, he gave assurance to the people that he expected to return.

Through many vicissitudes, and with countless errors in matters of detail, the government of the United States has conducted itself creditably in its trusteeship of the Islands. As history records major changes, forty years is not a long time. Our armed forces and our civil authorities alike, are fully agreed in the purpose to re-establish the Commonwealth of the Philippines, in full and independent control by the Filipino people. Their status at the end of the war will have the full and generous recognition of the United Nations. This will vindicate the good faith of the American people during almost half a century of effort.

Also, it will have international bearings of no slight significance in times to come, even as our occupation of the islands in 1898 was in basis—although not in any announced expression—a mandate from the civilized world to undertake a piece of administrative and supervisory work for the general good. It is a part of the faith of the American people in the triumph of good causes that its well-ordered work for civilization in the far Pacific shall not be in vain, even though tested by fire.

Chapter XV

JAPAN, CHINA, AND AMERICAN CONCERN WITH THE FAR EAST

A chapter on conditions in the great countries of the Far East, and our relations to them, recites fragments of past history, comments upon present conditions, and makes allusion to revolutionary changes in oriental states of mind and political outlook.

India is cited as a great sub-continent regarding the political future of which all the world has a right to be concerned. The trends of British policy since the period, almost forty years ago, when John Morley was Secretary for India have been consistent with social and economic progress. They have been preparing the way for full self-government, and a status of independence.

The American flag as an emblem of authority in the Philippines had been universally recognized since the end of the nineteenth century. In like manner there had been assurance that the new Commonwealth of the Philippines would be received as a member of the family of nations, with good will on all sides and without menace from any quarter.

The present war in the Pacific is waged by the United States first in self-defense, second in fulfillment of its moral guarantees to the Filipinos, and third in friendliness to China as a member of the group of United Nations, this also being consistent with our own essential strategies.

The remarkable capacities of the Chinese are recognized, and their new purpose to achieve liberty and create efficient peace-time institutions is regarded as promising well for the future of Asia. Economic cooperation rests upon promises that cannot be disregarded.

The danger of racial prejudice, fanned into flames by widespread propaganda, is illustrated in an account of the Boxer Rebellion which the Japanese and Americans with four European governments suppressed by a joint expedition to Peking in the year 1900.

The rapid rise of Japan to a leading place among the most enterprising and powerful of modern nations had received much encouragement and praise from the United States. In earlier years Japan had looked to America for justice, when European powers were less considerate. The present Japanese program turns largely upon an intensive racial propaganda throughout Asia, in an endeavor to detach China, India, Burma, and other trans-Pacific nations from confidence in the sincerity and fair-mindedness of the United Nations.

THIS chapter will be concerned with some aspects of the confused and changing pattern of relationships in Eastern Asia and the island realms of the Pacific. Our citizens of the Coastal States look with deep concern toward the ocean expanses, while millions in China, India, the Philippines, Indonesia and the Antipodes strain their eyes as they gaze outward with even greater anxiety, hoping for support and relief from America and her Allies.

We must know well, however, that we cannot supply a blueprint for a new order in Eastern Asia, or for idyllic conditions in archipelagos, or safety in island dominions. Even if we could produce such a design it would be little else than a tender of good will aided by such intelligence as might be invoked.

That we could never prevail upon the Asiatic peoples (including those of the Islands) to seek peace and pursue it under threat of our displeasure, or under our discipline as a military, naval and aerial police authority, is too obvious to be discussed.

There can be no hope for prolonged peace in Asia and the regions of the Pacific except through a recognition of mutual interest, and an appeal to all that is best in the ancient philosophies of a civilization much older than that of Europe. It may not be easy for the present-day custodians of European empires (or certain of their spokesmen) to face the truths of recent history and to change habitual points of view about their role in Asia and the South Seas. Yet the war itself will have reduced their arrogance—if any still remains—to the vanishing point. In a world of free inquiry it is as permissible for an American to investigate and report upon the political status of India as to study the history of ancient empires or to devote himself to astronomical research. The British are learning to welcome serious and open-minded study of their methods and achievements in colonial administration. The truth is that for a long time past the mission of England in India has been that of monitor and guide—of umpire between discordant elements.

It is when we institute comparisons that we can answer fairly the question whether or not the British regime has been one of tyranny and rapacity or of social advancement. Even in the days when Edmund Burke added immortal chapters to the stately prose of forensic literature, his indictment of the career of Warren Hastings found conclusive response. If the British East India Company had been guilty of errors, it was even then beginning to reconstruct a national unit from the shattered and demoralized fragments of the Mogul Empire. We can understand the Anglo-Indian problems better because of our own trans-Pacific experience. We could not wholly surrender our authority in the Philippines until forty years had elapsed. Then, before our withdrawal was technically complete, an aggressive conqueror pounced upon the islands. England (as our Philippine experts know) has not hitherto been able to withdraw from India because of conditions both within and without.

British colonial policies as regards India are determined by the Prime Minister and Cabinet in London, while administered by the Viceroy through instructions from the office of Secretary of State for India. John Morley held the position of Secretary for India from 1905 to 1910. (During that time he was raised to the peerage in 1908, as Viscount Morley of Blackburn). He continued to occupy a place of great influence in the Cabinet until the beginning of the war in 1914. It was my privilege to know him throughout that period, having made his acquaintance twenty years earlier, before he left literary and editorial pursuits to enter Parliament.

If any man in the first decade of the present century could be said to have been the actual ruler of India, that man was Morley. He admitted it freely in conversations with me. No man of Indian birth and native aspirations could have been more truly devoted to the welfare of the inhabitants of that Asiatic empire than this Liberal Englishman, who selected Viceroys and made decisions. He was consistent in his opposition to the jingo school of imperialism, but he was too wise a statesman to have favored England's withdrawal from India abruptly or by impetuous renunciation.

In order to judge intelligently of the British position in India with its historical background, it is essential to discover the tendencies of a transition toward self-government both in localities and throughout large areas. Under altered circumstances, the people of India might have had occasion since 1941 to regret the absence of the guiding hand of Britain, with its spirit of freedom and justice, while they experienced the ruthlessness of Japanese domination. The retention of British authority in India during the twentieth century has had no motives that will not bear the test of scrutiny by those who believe that peoples everywhere are entitled to self-ordered liberty.

British rule could not henceforth be maintained for purposes of British trade monopoly, for India is now highly industrialized, makes her own protective tariffs, trades freely with the world, and is in a better financial and budgetary position than any other large country. There has come to pass a relationship that Anglo-Indian statesmanship must develop and perfect for the best interests of a people who are many times as numerous as those of Great Britain. When India in the near future decides for herself upon the constitutional form of her national government, she will have to undertake internal tasks of great complexity. To uphold central authority and keep the peace within her boundaries will absorb the attention of all her leaders. It will be necessary for her to rely upon the good will of Asiatic, European, and American powers for security from external assault. Such a consummation is no longer a fanciful dream or a " fairy tale," in Mr. Churchill's deprecatory phrase, but a reality within grasp if the United Nations win the present war.

Such a political culmination—seemingly desirable as we view it from a distance—must be conditioned in large part upon the definite choice of alternatives by Indian leaders in the existing emergency. The best future of their country requires their full cooperation with the United Nations. Regardless of credit or prestige, and in spite of admitted aggressions in the past, India's future, if a fortunate one, will rest upon foundations laid by British administrators, and upon what they have accomplished in political and social fields of administration.

Several years ago a titled Englishman who was willing to be regarded as his country's chief advocate and exponent of the League of Nations, was received in the United States as a distinguished visitor. In New York he addressed a group whose meetings are not reported and whose membership includes men of the highest rank as authorities in the field of foreign relations. The visitor paid glowing tribute to past and current movements for the settlement of international disputes by arbitration and legal methods, rather than by domination and force.

In the question period that followed his address he was asked whether he would favor the submission of certain pending differences between England and India to the Hague Tribunal or to some form of arbitration. His Lordship flustered, stammered, and made painful efforts to restrain his visible anger. At length he declared in a frigid tone, intended to silence the questioner, that such matters were strictly " within the framework of the British Empire " and concerned no one else. There was a painful pause and the subject was dropped, with an unpleasant sense of embarrassment throughout the room.

There can, of course, be no future organization for world peace if such questions as that of self-government for India are not regarded as of universal interest. No empire henceforth can be a law unto itself. This visitor was simply unprepared to do justice to himself or to his cause. He was hiding his light under a bushel, to use a Scriptural phrase. He was actually as fair-minded and sincere as Morley himself, but shuddered at the thought of discussing the Empire with outsiders. He did not have the grace or tact to set forth the simple fact that the question was not pertinent, because the problems of government in India were not then of a kind that an international court of justice could decide.

II.

As for the status of the Philippines, it had never been a question simply between Spain and America, nor was it afterwards one solely between the Filipino leaders and the United States. From 1898 until the present time it has always, in reality, been subject to international approval or disapproval. We supposed that we had sufficient reason to understand, as we encouraged the set-up of the Commonwealth of the Philippines, that we were proceeding with the approval and good will of Japan, Russia, China, the British and Dutch Indies, Australia, New Zealand, French Indo-China, and as many other governments as had consuls or representatives at Manila.

President Quézon and his associates were intelligent men, who believed that their Commonwealth under its liberal constitution would be welcomed and respected by Asiatic nations. The Filipino leaders thought themselves entitled to the approval of Spanish-speaking American Republics, because of a common cultural heritage. They counted upon the benevolent attitude of the Vatican, because of the preponderance of Roman Catholics in their new

Commonwealth. As we look to the future it would seem essential that the community of nations should agree to uphold this well-considered status, and to give the Philippines a secure place in the reorganized system of world relationships.

War makes many unpredictable changes, but also it intensifies loyalties. Thus the Chinese people, whose racial existence and superior civilization have had a longer record than that of any other nation, have hitherto lived as families and communities without the intense degree of loyalty to institutions of central government that has been the distinguishing trait of the Japanese. Through the ages the Chinese have prevailed over enemies by sheer racial persistence and capacity to absorb.

The inertia of the largest, most industrious, and most highly civilized mass of people of a definite racial character that the world ever knew, has baffled one invasion after another during many long centuries. But the shocks produced by contacts with the occidental world have at last awakened in China a new national consciousness, and have stimulated a loyalty that must result in strong political institutions. This awakening of the Chinese people is not to prove an ephemeral condition, nor is it altogether due to the present war. One incident has followed another during the past half-century, as a result of which China has at last been shaken out of a condition of relative passivity, and she is preparing to take her proper place as the foremost nation of Asia [1]

The Chinese are a pacific race by nature and philosophy, whose interests have always centered in family life and in the local communities of densely peopled agricultural provinces. Having

[1] In September, 1943, it was announced that Generalissimo Chiang Kai-shek had been made President of the Chinese Republic, which had been founded upon the overthrow of the Manchu dynasty, and the revolution inspired by Sun-Yat-Sen in 1911. During recent years China has been governed by the Nationalist party (the Kuomintang) led by Chiang Kai-shek.

It is now promised that, within one year after the expulsion of the Japanese and the end of the war, there will be promulgated a new Constitution, providing for a central government in which all elements and parties (including the Communists) will be given proportionate representation.

The new Constitution will also provide for a system of provincial governments, somewhat resembling our American states. Within the provinces there will be democratic forms of local government, in districts, towns and villages. To give this symmetrical plan of popular government a full measure of stability and success will take time, perhaps many years. But friends of China who are best informed, like Mr. Lattimore, have faith in the political outlook, and believe that responsible and stable civil government on a popular basis is possible in China.

had no hostile designs upon other nations, they have not until lately entertained such conceptions as that of the armed totalitarian state. But they have been compelled to learn the art of war, because modern methods have so completely changed the nature of warfare, and so intensified its deadliness, that mere superiority in numbers is no longer a safe reliance. They have had to learn to fight with modern weapons; and in the relative lack of industries that could be converted to munition-making, they have been compelled to use their amazing ingenuity in creating utensils for guerrilla warfare. With by far the greatest available man-power in the world, and with prowess no longer doubtful, China has only awaited airplanes and material supplies from the United Nations to turn the scales and expel the Japanese invaders.

European governments seeking Chinese trade pursued courses during the nineteenth century that present-day historians would not attempt to justify. They were exploiting China to the utmost of their ability, finding excuses in corrupt or inefficient governments of the Chinese Provinces, and in the lack of responsible control by the central government at Peking. Toward the end of the century these occidental powers were well advanced in their scheme to divide China into so-called "spheres of influence." John Hay as McKinley's Secretary of State was concentrating his efforts upon a policy that was called the "Open Door in China," which was opposed to these exclusive spheres of economic control, and sought to uphold the political authority of the Chinese government and equality of rights for merchant nations in all the "treaty ports."

There had, however, come into existence certain powerful secret societies bitterly resentful of foreign influences, and they were fostered by the Dowager Empress who was opposed to all modern reforms. Favored by such reactionary sentiments there occurred what was known as the Boxer Rebellion, which took the form of sudden and violent attack upon all foreigners, especially missionaries. Many were massacred; but most of them fled to Peking where, in the summer of 1900, they were in great peril. An international army of rescue was quickly improvised and it included contingents of British, French, Russian, American, German, and Japanese troops. In that expedition American and Japanese were in especially cordial cooperation.

The situation existing at that time can be understood only by those familiar with the course of events in the Far East, or by students who have taken the trouble to inform themselves. In the thick of that conflict a dispatch in the name of the Emperor of China was sent to the Emperor of Japan appealing for assistance to restore order and peace, under Japan's "powerful guidance." This appeal was made in a telegram dated July 3, 1900, of which the following paragraph is the essential part:

> From the general trend of events in the world, We are persuaded that the East and West confront each other; and that Your Majesty's country and Ours are the only Powers that maintain their ground in the East. It is not China alone which is made the object of the ambitious longings of the Powers that assert their strength in the West. Should China fail to hold her own, We are afraid that Your Majesty's country might also find the situation untenable. The interests of the two countries are therefore linked together, and We venture to hope that Your Majesty may find it possible to set aside for the present questions of minor importance and make common cause with Us in the maintenance of Our general interests. China is at the present moment so completely occupied in conducting military operations for the suppression of the insurgents, that it is impossible for her to take proper measures for averting the dangers from outside and for bringing the complication to a successful termination. We are therefore constrained to rely on the support of that country which like Our own dominions forms part of Asia.

The Japanese reply dated ten days later summarized the alarming situation that had resulted from China's inability to suppress the insurgents and to protect foreign diplomats, the minister of a certain power having been murdered. This Japanese reply included the following passage:

> We need not remind Your Majesty of the fact that under International Law diplomatic agents are entitled to the highest respect and that their person is inviolable. Any offense against their person is therefore a direct contravention of International Law, and it is not necessary to point out the extreme gravity of the responsibility that would be incurred when the offense consists in their murder.
>
> If Your Majesty's Government earnestly suppresses the insurgents and rescues the foreign Representatives, their suites, and other foreigners, We trust the difficulties of the situation might not prove insurmountable. We wish Your Majesty to understand that the suppression of the insurgents and the rescue of the foreign Representatives are duties which Your Majesty owes no less to Your Own country than to the other nations of the world, a duty the fulfillment of which does not admit of the least delay

or hesitation. Since last month the Powers have dispatched large forces to Tientsin, and Japan has likewise found it necessary to send her troops. In taking this step the object kept in view has been to suppress the insurgents and to rescue the diplomatic Representatives and other foreigners. Beyond that the Powers have no ulterior motive.

In conclusion, the reply sent in the name of his imperial Japanese majesty expressed feelings of cordial friendship for China, and further assurance was given in the following sentence:

If Your Majesty's Government, therefore, at once suppress the insurrection and actually rescue the foreign Representatives, Japan will be prepared to use her influence, in eventual negotiations between Your country and foreign nations, with a view to conserve the interests of Your Empire.

In consequence of her proximity and her military efficiency there was an impression in Japan that the European powers were expecting her to take the lion's share in putting down the Chinese rebellion and restoring order. It could not be known at that time how extensive and costly the task might prove to be. Far from seeking the opportunity, however, the Japanese were openly resentful of the idea that they ought to incur the risk and the pecuniary sacrifice that would be involved in protecting Occidental interests throughout the Chinese empire. They fought their war with China in 1894, largely to convince themselves and the world of their military and naval efficiency; and even at this time (1900) they were conscious of the approach of their war with Russia, which actually occurred in 1904-5.

Japan assumed no position of priority or leadership in the relief of Peking and the defeat of the insurgents, but did her share. As I remember the circumstances, the American and Japanese were more exemplary in their conduct after the fall of Peking than the Germans and some other of the contingents of foreign soldiery who looted the Chinese palaces and carried home much booty.

Among scores of articles on China and the Far East that I published in that critical time was one by Sir Robert Hart, the trusted Englishman who had then for forty-five years served officially in China, most of that time at the head of the Customs Service. Sir Robert regarded the Boxer movement as the outburst in action of an instinctive kind of feeling—unofficial and purely voluntary, but " patriotic in origin, justifiable in its fundamental idea, and in point of fact the outcome of either foreign advice or the study of foreign methods." Revolutions usually take violent forms, but they grow out of a cumulative sense of injustice. The missionaries and the diplomats were not personally at fault, and their rescue by combined international forces was a necessary step.

Sir Robert had made innumerable financial statements and reports, but had seldom expressed himself in language addressed to the public opinion of the world at large. As the best-informed foreigner in the Far East, his views were much quoted at the time, especially as he lashed out with honest wrath and indignation against the faults of western nations in their treatment of the Chinese. It is possible that Sir Robert had in mind the fact of more recent German encroachments, not less than earlier ones by other powers. When he penned the following warning it is to be remembered that the Boxer Rebellion had not been suppressed, and that China was actually at war with all the so-called treaty powers:

> Twenty millions or more of Boxers, armed, drilled, disciplined, and animated by patriotic—if mistaken—motives will make residence in China impossible for foreigners; will take back from foreigners everything foreigners have taken from China; will pay off old grudges with interest, and will carry the Chinese flag and Chinese arms into many a place that even fancy will not suggest today—thus preparing for the future upheavals and disasters never even dreamed of. In fifty years' time there will be millions of Boxers in serried ranks and war's panoply at the call of the Chinese Government; there is not the slightest doubt of that! And if the Chinese Government continues to exist, it will encourage—and it will be quite right to encourage, uphold, and develop this national Chinese movement; it bodes no good for the rest of the world, but China will be acting within its right, and will carry through the national programme!

III.

In some respects Sir Robert Hart's predictions have been realized. The Chinese people have been aroused to the pitch of national consciousness and self-assertion that he foresaw. Moreover, in 1943 more than twenty-five million soldiers have had drill and discipline, though not armed for war with a sufficient supply of modern weapons. The Chinese government, to employ Sir Robert's phraseology, "encourages, upholds and develops" this nationalistic movement. However, he would not say that the Chinese national program "bodes no good for the rest of the world." This awe-inspiring development of national spirit, although primarily exhibited in defense against Japan's formidable invasion, is in accord with the purpose of the United Nations to establish peace and justice in the world.

Regardless of great impending changes, we may rest assured that the Chinese and other Eastern peoples will not devote their future efforts to the satisfaction of war-time animosities. The present war is only one of a series of struggles for balance and adjustment in the Far East. As we have seen, China was attacked by Japan in 1894. In the settlement of 1895 Japan acquired the important island of Formosa. Our war with Spain in 1898 brought us recognition as a world power, gave us the Philippines with Guam as a way station, and made us a neighbor of both China and Japan. Two years later in 1900 China was in the throes of an anti-foreign rebellion, and was technically at war with six leading powers: four European, one American, one Asiatic.

In the course of that brief but serious conflict, China appealed to Japan for understanding and aid—urging the view that Eastern powers should stand together against Occidental intruders, and ignoring her defeat by Japan only six years earlier, and her losses and sacrifices in that war. Japan's brilliantly conducted duel with Russia was begun in 1904 and was concluded in the following year, with a treaty negotiated at Portsmouth, New Hampshire, under President Theodore Roosevelt's mediation. It gave Japan valuable footholds on the continent and high prestige everywhere as a world power. She was not only considered a formidable rival of European powers on land and sea but was praised as among the foremost—if not the very first—in exemplifying ethical principles in warfare as well as the applied arts. Her sanitary standards in the care of her armed forces had admittedly set the world a new record.

There was no ill will on the part of the best public opinion in America and Europe towards the people of Russia, but undoubtedly there was greater sympathy with the Japanese people and government in their conduct of the war of 1904 than with the Russian authorities. Great political reforms were instituted in Russia in consequence of that war, while Japan made immediate territorial gains on the mainland, and soon afterwards annexed Korea without fighting and without international protest.

As early as 1902 Great Britain had formed an alliance with

Japan. It did not involve the British in the Russian war, but it protected Japan against simultaneous attack from any other quarter. This alliance added prestige to Japan's new position, and made her less resentful of the American decision to hold the Philippines.

It was Britain's all-prevailing diplomacy that had cleared obstacles away and established the United States at Manila; and the Anglo-Japanese alliance, following so soon after, gave promise of harmony in the Pacific and on the coasts of Asia. Peace in the Pacific seemed to find a guaranty in the aggregate of sea-power resulting from this treaty of 1902, and at that time it was regarded as altogether compatible with American interests. It was intended to put some check upon the restless acquisitiveness of Germany in the Far East, although it could not have been thought to afford much comfort to China.

Among other evidences of their determination to extend commercial activities in that ill-governed and (in coastal provinces) over-populated Celestial Empire, the English in 1898 had acquired a foothold on the north coast of the Shantung peninsula under a ninety-nine year lease. The Germans had at once acquired a lease on Kiaochow Bay, creating a modern administrative center and setting out to develop and control the great Shantung Province, with its thirty million inhabitants.

The French, not to be outdone in the pious work of European encroachment, had been adding from time to time to what is known as French Indo-China; and they also in 1898 acquired under leasehold a convenient slice of Chinese territory. It was added to their Laos Province of about 90,000 square miles, rounding out a total area of French Indo-China that exceeded 280,000 square miles, with a population of 25,000,000. (By way of comparison, France has a European area of nearly 213,000 square miles, and had a population in 1936 of 41,900,000.)

When Sir Robert Hart, as an honest friend of China, voiced his indignation in 1900 and called the Boxer frenzy against the " foreign devils " nothing more than a natural phenomenon, these latest German, British, and French activities were simply the more recent of the inpositions upon the Chinese in their military weakness that disturbed his European conscience. The missionaries returned after the undiscriminating rage had subsided, and their friendly endeavors took form increasingly in the establishment of colleges and universities, the promotion of public health, the provision of facilities for training native physicians and surgeons, and other useful directions that were welcomed by Chinese leaders.

As something more substantial than a friendly gesture, the United States had refused to retain any part of its share of the $320,000,000 that China was compelled to pay as an indemnity after the Boxer Rebellion. A sum of fifty million dollars or more was set aside by the United States to make possible the education of an increasing number of young Chinese men and women in the United States.

IV.

There had been no serious friction of any kind between America and China, although the treatment of the Chinese on our Pacific Coast had become a subject of heated discussion in this country. The Chinese people are natural colonizers, and they are able to meet economic competition wherever they find themselves. They were brought to California in very large numbers when common labor was needed for railroad building. Afterwards labor unions turned against them, and there were race riots, especially in California. The agitation was ended by the enactment at Washington of the Chinese Exclusion Act of 1882.

Afterwards Japanese immigrants came in considerable numbers, and again the agitation against Asiatic labor created disturbing incidents in our Pacific Coast states. The Japanese government made this situation a matter of diplomatic protest, and it was dealt with tactfully by President Roosevelt and his Secretary of State Elihu Root. It was proposed at Tokio to restrict the flow of coolies or laborers to America by refusal to issue passports. This formed the basis of what was known as a "gentleman's agreement"—observed with fidelity by the Japanese government.

Everything possible was done in that period upon the part of our administration at Washington to show respect for Japan and good will for the Japanese people; but the tide of immigration was firmly checked. I remember that in the year 1908, when invited to make an address at the University of Virginia, I discussed the race problems of the United States in view of the forgotten fact that we had then arrived at the centenary of the abolition of the slave trade. A twenty-year period had been allowed in the Constitution as adopted in 1788, after which

African slaves should not be imported into the United States. I reviewed the Southern race problem from the standpoint of forced immigration (slavery in any case being a transient phase), and treated the law that took effect in 1808 as an Exclusion Act.

But for that prohibition (as I explained) the Negro population of the South would certainly have been far greater than it actually was in 1860. The Exclusion Act of 1808 probably changed the racial destiny of several Southern states. In like manner, beyond any reasonable doubt, our Pacific Coast states would have had a predominance of Asiatic people—after the example of Hawaii—but for the Chinese Exclusion Act and the later agreement with Japan. My address made no appeal for the white race as having inherent claims; but it pointed out the difficulties that a new country like ours—most of which had been scantily occupied by hardy pioneers within memory of people living in 1908—would have encountered if an Asiatic race problem had assumed large proportions. For many years we received European immigrants at our Eastern ports by the million. If we had extended the same unrestricted welcome to the Chinese and Japanese, those thrifty and skilful workers would soon have occupied all of the country between the ocean and the Rocky Mountains.

The ease with which the Chinese can be mobilized as colonizers was illustrated by the rapidity with which thirty millions of them—chiefly farm workers—made their homes in Manchuria, a great part of them within a single generation. The pretext for the Russo-Japanese war was the occupation of Manchuria by Russian troops at the time of the Boxer Rebellion. The Japanese had previously sought to control Manchuria; and the accomplishment of their purpose some twenty-five years later was in fulfillment of an object that they had never abandoned.

Mr. Owen Lattimore, who is our highest authority upon political and economic conditions in China and in little-known Asiatic regions that lie beyond, has given us clarifying pictures of the industrialized China that is in the making. With transportation facilities, heavy industry will desert Shanghai and the agricultural provinces of the alluvial coastal regions, where population is dense and where farming is more highly intensified than anywhere else. Resources of coal and iron are in upland regions of the West and South that are not now over-populated. Ample employment will be found for millions of migrants in the great southwest

Province of Yunnan, which Mr. Lattimore calls "the pivot of southeast Asia."

I shall not attempt to summarize Mr. Lattimore's descriptions of present-day China, or his forecasting of vast changes that are impending. But I will make two quotations from a recent article by this much-travelled American who has recently served as a political adviser of the Chinese government.[2] First, as regards economic changes:

> An attraction has been created for the eventual shifting of surplus population from eastern China to the underpopulated southwest. The basic lines of a system of rapid bulk transportation have been so laid out that they will develop immense new territories. The emphasis of industrial demand is more on skilled labor than on cheap labor. At the same time agriculture, being without a surplus of cheap labor, will be under pressure of a kind that encourages modernization and the mechanization of farming—something that had barely begun to take place in eastern China.

The second quotation from Mr. Lattimore's article has to do with fundamental politics:

> Today, there is in Asia not an adult man or woman, not an adolescent child, who does not know what freedom is. If these people are not either given the freedom which is as much their birthright as ours, or guaranteed a future freedom on terms that are specific, patently genuine, and above suspicion of political juggling, they will look to China. They will understand even better than we do the significance of the fact that China has both emancipated itself from a hundred years of Western imperialism and resisted successfully in war the imperialism of Japan. From the hinterlands that actually touch the Yunnan frontier, there will be direct and open appeals to the Chinese. How the Chinese might respond to such appeals would not be likely to depend on whether they were intent on expanding their frontiers; but it would be very likely to depend on whether they felt that their frontiers were being hemmed in by a renascent imperialism of the Western Powers.

[2] Mr. Owen Lattimore, after many years of residence in China, extensive travels, and researches in Asiatic history and political institutions, became Director of the Walter Hines Page School of International Relations at the Johns Hopkins University in 1936. He had written important volumes on Manchuria, Turkestan, Tartary, Mongolia and the Frontiers of China, and had gained an international reputation as an authority on the interior expanses of the Asiatic continent. In 1941 he was one of General Chiang-Kai-shek's political advisers at Chung-king. The quotations in this chapter are from an article by Mr. Lattimore in *Foreign Affairs* (1943), published by the Council on Foreign Relations.

It is not believed by such authorities as Mr. Lattimore that the Chinese will be actuated in the appreciable future by an ambitious policy of imperialism, although circumstances might force them to assume a leadership to which they do not now aspire. Upon that point Mr. Lattimore quotes a statement by Generalissimo Chiang Kai-Shek:

> Having herself been a victim of exploitation, China has infinite sympathy for the submerged nations of Asia, and towards them China feels she has only responsibilities—not rights. We repudiate the idea of leadership of Asia because the Fuehrer principle has been synonymous with domination and exploitation, precisely as the [Japanese] East Asia co-prosperity sphere has stood for a race of mythical supermen lording over grovelling subject races.

American relations with China have been clouded by the fact that we were continuing to supply Japan with essential war materials during long years after her invasion of China from the north and her later attack upon Shanghai. We were assisting her in the development of her munition industry and were promoting the expansion of her air force, which under American patronage had become second only to that of Germany. All this, of course, was not due to cold-blooded or sinister designs at Washington, but simply to the lack of firm policies and statesmanlike precautions.

V.

When the war assumed global proportions, and Japan's bold plans of aggression were associated with those of Germany and the Axis, our abrupt curtailment of certain trade activities gave the signal for war. However mistaken or negligent our Far Eastern policies might have been, they were never malign. We were engaged—in a halting and dilatory fashion—in the slow process of extricating ourselves from the responsibilities we had assumed more than forty years earlier in the Philippines. We were not consciously abetting Japan's policies of imperial conquest. It might be enough to say that we were merely exhibiting incompetency as regards Far Eastern matters, whether insular or continental.

These remarks are not intended to reflect upon the Harding-Coolidge-Hoover period of Republican administration, nor upon the three-term period of Democratic control under Franklin D. Roosevelt. The American people have always had the kind of government that they chose and deserved. No one is likely to argue that our people at large have not been content with their heritage of a goodly land. They have not been tempted to seek imperial adventures, since the rounding out of their domain almost a hundred years ago. If certain of the so-called "expansionists of 1898" had been infected with the virus of imperialism, Mr. Bryan's campaign of 1900 served an educational purpose. It compelled the Republicans to renounce all thought of controlling alien peoples and territories for our own advantage. We were not in the Far East as one of the rival empire-grabbing powers of the Occident.

To be wise in matters of public policy is an important thing, and to be ignorant or foolish is not praiseworthy. But genuine good will may atone for "invincible ignorance" in government circles, and may prove a better shield of defense than astuteness in policies. American officialdom will not be asked to supply any pattern for the stabilization of the Far East. But the friendliness of the American people themselves, and the sincerity of their desire for freedom, justice, and peace, whether in Europe or in Asia, may serve some valuable ends because it inspires confidence.

The goodwill of Americans towards the Chinese people in their heroic efforts to expel the invaders and to redeem their national heritage is too evident to need proof. As the war progresses further, it might be discovered that America needed the cooperation of China not less than the Chinese have needed our material support. We must assume that the United Nations can defeat Japan, although the task may prove the most difficult one in all the history of warfare. After that, a settlement of some kind will come; and the United States will at least seek an opportunity to be heard and to be helpful.

It is indeed difficult to concentrate full national energy upon waging a desperate war, and at the same time to think philosophically about the future. Yet there must be some effort to consider what lies beyond. Those who can think in historic terms know that Germany will not be eliminated from Europe, and that Japan will not be forever negligible, as one measures future time. There will be Asiatic adjustments in which China and Russia will perhaps play the more influential roles, but the islanders of Japan will certainly have their place, just as the islanders of Britain will have part in all future European settlements.

It will be useful to remember that no country is made up of political and social groups who always think and feel in unison, although parties may be suppressed in the stress of war. There was once a peace party in Japan, even as there was a pre-Hitler peace party in Germany. The Japanese war lords gained control, and dazzled their fellow-countrymen by showing what miracles could be accomplished by unrestrained force and the denial of human rights. The thorough defeat of such aggression is necessary for the welfare of Japan itself, hardly less than for that of the many occupied and victimized areas.

A proper settlement will not at once convert the hate and wrath of injured peoples to a belief in the repentance and good faith of the aggressor. But past history proves that anger does subside, and that hatred—which is an unpleasant emotion—is not, as some persons assert, a duty to be passed on to posterity. Warring nations must sometime learn how to live together again in the same world, even cherishing the common hope that permanent peace and friendship are possible.

I am disposed to call attention to a unique expression of international sentiment, made as recently as the year 1915. The Japanese, still in alliance with England, entered the First World War in 1914 without reluctance. They were not expected to lend assistance to England and France on the European fronts; but their navy could serve a useful purpose in the Pacific. In March of that year, however—some three or four months before the outbreak of the great war—a number of the leading statesmen, scholars, and business men of Japan joined in the publication of a volume that they called *Japan's Message to America.* Each contributor expressed himself in his own way; but they were alike in their assurances of unshakable regard and good will. It was a book of sentiment; but most of its authors were men of culture, estimable character, and wide knowledge of the world.

Shortly after the appearance of that volume in its English version, Japan was dispossessing the Germans in the Province of Shantung, and was helping to patrol the Pacific in the interest of Great Britain and her allies. The United States was not to enter the war until almost three years later; but there was general sympathy in this country with the course that Japan had pursued. Germany had bought from Spain the island groups north of the Equator that had been left undisturbed by the Spanish-American treaty. Japan lost no time in expelling the Germans, and taking control of those archipelagoes.

In 1915, under the auspices of the Japan Society of New York, a volume was prepared and published under the title *America to Japan.* It was intended as a cordial response to the Japanese message of the same year. More than fifty Americans contributed to this volume, each man expressing himself in accordance with his own feelings and impulses. As a sub-title it was called " A Symposium of Papers by Representative Citizens of the United States on the Relations between Japan and America and on the Common Interests of the Two Countries."

Among public men whose statements appeared were Theodore Roosevelt; William Jennings Bryan; Elihu Root; Francis B. Loomis (who had been Assistant Secretary of State, and was conversant with Far East diplomacy); George W. Wickersham (who had been Attorney-General of the United States, and always much concerned with foreign relations), and Dean C. Worcester (who had been connected with Philippine administration for fifteen years). Among college presidents who contributed were Nicholas Murray Butler, Charles W. Eliot, David Starr Jordan, Benjamin Ide Wheeler, Harry Pratt Judson. Some of the most impressive statements were made by business men, among them Elbert H. Gary of the Steel Corporation and Charles A. Coffin of the General Electric Company.

Mr. Coffin's message of several pages could not have been excelled in its tribute to what he described as the ideals and moral qualities for which Japan had long been distinguished. I quote two brief paragraphs from his extended message, because they are typical of the volume as a whole:

> Japan's unsurpassed valor on land and sea in the Russian war won no greater laurels than her chivalrous treatment of her prisoners of that war. By contributing for the sufferers of the San Francisco earthquake, from her then depleted resources, a larger amount than all the other nations of the world combined, apart from the United States, she demonstrated the spontaneous sympathy of a great-hearted and magnanimous people.
>
> Let Japan continue in the practice of those virtues which have brought her to her present high estate. Let her persist by every honorable endeavor to maintain peace with all the world. Let her hold to her ancient attributes of chivalry, kindness to strangers, love of children and flowers, sincere friendships, and simplicity of living. Let her keep even the scales of justice and shun unworthy ambitions.

President Eliot's statement disclosed his knowledge of Far Eastern affairs, and especially commended Japan's participation in the World War. Dr. David Starr Jordan remarked: "I have been in many nations and among many peoples and I have never found any form of race hatred that was natural to the people." He proceeded to denounce the "War System descended from medieval Europe," declaring it to be "weakened by commerce, culture, and internationalism, intensified and sharpened to its final doom by science, and now moving toward its death." He expressed the sage hope that "with the well-earned victory of the present war, Japan will suffer as few as possible of victory's inevitable evils."

Theodore Roosevelt's message was brief, but every word of it was significant, and I quote it herewith:

> Few things are more important to the future progress of the world than the heartiest good will and a complete understanding between the Empire of Japan and the Republic of the United States. Japan made her entry into the circle of the great advanced civilized nations of modern times only fifty years ago. Her progress has been astounding. The lessons that the American people can and ought to learn from her are numerous and of the highest importance. Nothing is more important to the future of all the civilized communities that border on the great Pacific Ocean than that the United States and Japan should work hand in hand for the development of mankind on the basis of national self-respect and mutuality of respect. I speak for every thoughtful American when I express my earnest desire for the future well-being of Japan.

Scores of sympathetic passages from publicists, diplomats, and men of experience and judgment might be cited, but one or two more will suffice. Dr. Hamilton Holt opened his paper with the following sentence: "If the Pacific Ocean is to be the theater of the world's future civilization—and the Great War in Europe is helping to bring this about—then there are no two nations on the face of the earth which should be better friends than Japan and the United States." This message from Dr. Holt, entitled "World Unity," also included the following reference: "The volume from our Japanese friends contains among others a very remarkable article by Count Okuma, Japan's sage and premier. The most significant sentence in that article, it seems to me, is the following: 'It is Japan's mission to harmonize the Eastern and Western civilization in order to help bring about the unification of the world.'"

Dr. Butler's message of several pages ended with a paragraph that is typical of views and methods promoted by the Carnegie Peace Foundation of which he has been the guiding spirit for many years:

> The world is ruled in last resort by its public opinion. Wise and just public opinion rests in turn upon instruction and education. The exchange of ideas, the international visits of leading personalities, the acquaintance by one people with the literature, art, and science of another, the development of international trade and commerce, are the steps by which to promote the acquisition and the spread of the international mind. Armed with the international mind rather than with huge navies and with great armies, a civilized people is equipped to march in the front rank of those who advance the cause of humanity throughout the world.

My own contribution to the sheaf of papers was among the longer ones, and I shall reprint it, not by reason of special knowledge or wisdom on my part, but because it took the form of a statement of historical facts that is in keeping with my purposes in this volume.

VI.

TREATY THRALDOM AND RELEASE (ALBERT SHAW, 1915)

America has desired, among the nations, friendship, good will, and mutual help in advancing the cause of human welfare. In the progress of Japan, Americans have felt a pleasure and a pride that have been tangible enough to be a real element in our country's consciousness of its neighbors and of the world in which we live. There come points of strain and misunderstanding in the foreign as well as the domestic policies of all governments. It is fortunate, therefore, if between nations there has been the habit of mutual trust, admiration, and good will, and if there has been laid an historical foundation of confidence due to relations of a generous nature.

It is now more than sixty years since the first treaty was signed between the United States and Japan. It is hard for present-day Americans to realize the great extent of their ocean shipping, and the vast number of their vessels engaged in the whaling trade, in the period from 1840 to 1860. Hundreds of American ships were liable to find themselves at one time or another off the northern coasts of Japan. Occasionally a wreck occurred, and it was experience with the shipwrecked sailors that led up to Commodore Perry's expedition in 1853. The Japanese of all classes had been kind to such unfortunates. Commodore Perry's treaty of 1854 related in particular to shipwrecks and the treatment of sailors.

Two ports were opened, involving incidental business but not providing for commerce or encouraging it. But the fates were preparing Japan for her new era, and her interest in the things of the outside world was destined to develop rapidly. It was in 1856 that Townsend Harris went to Japan as the consul-general from the United States. He secured the signature of a new treaty in 1857, granting Americans many rights and privileges in Japan; but it was not until the following year that he persuaded the conservative authorities to make the important Treaty of 1858 granting commercial intercourse.

This American treaty was soon followed by treaties with European countries, and so Japan entered upon her modern international career. Foreigners were, however, restricted to specified areas adjacent to the opened seaports, and it was under many limitations that they were accorded the privilege of consular jurisdiction,—that is to say, the right was accorded to foreign consuls in the specified seaports to act as judges in cases involving persons of their own nationality.

Having had no foreign commerce, Japan had not developed a revenue system of which duties on imports formed an essential part. It was therefore understandable that the historic treaty negotiated by Townsend Harris should have included an agreement as to the rates to be paid upon American wares which were now for the first time to be brought into the commerce of Japan.

Consular jurisdiction was the established European and American custom in Turkey, Egypt, China, and other parts of the world which did not have systems of law that were similar in principle to those of Western nations. Such arrangements are not humiliating as a temporary expedient if they are made terminable after a given date or upon due notice.

Neither was Mr. Townsend Harris's arrangement of 15 per cent, as the customs duties rate, unsuitable as the beginning of a system. Our government very properly agreed that Japan should collect a duty of 35 per cent upon alcoholic liquors, and 20 per cent upon some other articles. It was also recorded that "the President of the United States, at the request of the Japanese Government, will act as a frinedly mediator in such matters of difference as may arise between the Government of Japan and any European Power."

But Europe in that period was more commercial and ruthless in its attitude towards the Orient than friendly or considerate. In the period from 1861 to 1863 there were internal troubles in Japan, due to reactionary influences and to discord between the respective supporters of the dual systems of government then existing, that of the Emperor and that of the Shogunate. And, mixed up with this domestic discord was a strong anti-foreign feeling that resulted in certain incidents of technical affront rather than serious damage to several foreign governments. The United States was involved in her own great domestic struggle, and England led the European Powers in compelling Japan to make adjustments and reparation.

Commodore Perry's fleet had several years earlier visited Japan with overtures of peace and friendship. A far more powerful British fleet appeared, and bombarded Japanese cities on pretexts of offense too slight to Englishmen to justify in retrospect. One Englishman had been killed for having gone where he had no right to be. An unfortunate anti-foreign port officer had fired, without doing any harm, upon the flags of France, Holland, and the United States. Nothing whatever was due to England, or to the other three countries, except an expression of regret and a salute to the flags, which Japan would have given with all good will. But, not content with an unnecessary bombardment, the four foreign governments demanded the payment by Japan of an indemnity of $3,000,000, to be divided among them.

It was further intimated, however, that if Japan would open up additional ports, and would permit the foreign treaty powers to push their wares into Japan by paying a nominal duty of 5 per cent or less, the $3,000,000 of indemnity would be remitted. Japan was forced to yield. The general level of duties, as fixed by the American, Townsend Harris, at 15 per cent, was reduced by the now dominant European diplomats to 5 per cent. And this included the duty on foreign intoxicating liquors, which under the American lead had been placed at 35 per cent.

Japan was now beginning to be a commercial country, and this compulsion by outside governments to accept a merely nominal rate of import dues was equivalent to the payment of a large indemnity every year until Japan could recover her freedom. Worst of all, having punished Japan by bombardment, and then by the cutting down of her tariff rates, the four concerted governments still exacted payment of the $3,000,000 indemnity, of which one quarter was to come to the treasury of the United States.

Let it be remembered, as a token of the historical friendship between the United States and Japan, that America did not take the leading part in forcing down the customs rate to 5 per cent; was not active in the demand of an indemnity, and, finally, that America paid back to Japan the entire sum of three-quarters of a million dollars. So far as we are aware, Great Britain, France, and the Netherlands have always retained their shares of this unfair exaction. I have no thought of reflecting upon the policies of these European governments. They then believed that international statesmanship must adopt the policy of consulting one's own interest and taking what one could get. I am glad to believe that the American Government has more often been actuated by the principles and motives that govern private relations among just and considerate men, although we too have made errors, and I do not wish to overlook them.

My own interest in the position and progress of Japan, which is merely typical of the feeling that has long prevailed in America, began in my early youth; and therefore I did not fail to note with sympathy, during a period of years culminating in 1894, the efforts of Japan, aided by the United States, to secure her release and her rights of sovereignty. In that dark period of our own Civil War, the Powers that were subjecting Japan to pressure were not very friendly to the United States. Soon after our own recovery, however, from domestic strife and its immediate consequences, Japan was assured of our readiness to enter at the earliest possible moment upon new arrangements, that would give her back an unimpaired sovereign right over her own sources of revenue, and would relieve her from any humiliation due to the fact of alien jurisdiction on her soil.

It was manifestly impossible for Japan to impose a high rate of duty upon American goods while continuing to admit European goods at a merely nominal rate. A new policy must obviously have general application. America was always willing and ready to abrogate the treaties in Japan's favor. Europe was not willing, and so the matter stood for more than twenty years. Meanwhile, the United States led the way in signing a postal treaty and bringing Japan into the international postal union. And, again, the United States led in the making of an extradition treaty with Japan, upon terms of perfect reciprocity.

As an American journalist and student of international affairs, I had taken the ground that Japan ought to denounce the commercial treaties, assuming full rights over her tariff rates after a declared date, while of course giving ample notice as to the ending of consular jurisdiction. It was with this belief that I came to the editorship of the *American Review of Reviews* in 1891. I am glad to find that I put into the very first number of that periodical, twenty-four years ago, the following words:

When the Emperor's "golden rule" is more commonly observed, the ordinary relations between great nations and small ones will be radically improved. What act of neighborly kindness ought America not to perform towards Japan, whenever occasion offers? It is to be hoped that the Japanese Government may in the early future have occasion to erect a mammoth monument in memory of the staunch friendship of the United States in helping to secure a revision of the commercial treaties under which Europe is throttling Japan.

There was no criticism of our home Government at Washington in what we American friends of Japan were writing and saying in those days, because we all knew that our Government had given its full consent to Japan long before, and was ready at any moment to sign a treaty—which indeed had already been written—or to acknowledge Japan's right on due notice to declare the treaties null and void.

In the summer of 1894, Japan's pent-up energies burst forth. Her practical relationships to Korea seemed more important than China's titular and traditional relationships. The war was regrettable. Possibly if the European Powers, joining America, had come forward promptly, offering generous and unselfish friendship to Japan, including the granting of simple justice in the matter of the treaties, there could have been mediation with careful and permanent adjustment of all questions relating to Korea, and to Japan's interests on the Asiatic continent. Such a solution in the spring of 1894 might not only have prevented one war, but it would probably have saved Japan from two others, each of which grew out of the results of the first.

In the course of a few swift weeks in 1894 Japan was recognized as a naval and military power henceforth to be reckoned with. The Rosebery Cabinet was now ready to abrogate the treaties, and the United States signed the Treaty of 1894, to go into effect after five years. Other nations more or less grudgingly followed the course adopted by Great Britain and the United States.

Thirty years ago, two little Japanese villages showed great kindness to a number of shipwrecked American sailors. The United States Government showed recognition by awarding gold medals to certain individuals and a sum of several thousand dollars to the villagers as a whole. The money was invested for the permanent benefit of the village schools. The villagers themselves erected a monument, upon which they inscribed the circumstances in full detail. The concluding language of the inscription, as translated, is as follows:

> Therefore, we, the people of these villages, acting in harmony, erect this monument and inscribe thereon all these facts, together with the following verse which we dedicate to posterity in immortal commemoration of the goodness of the United States Government:
>
> The principle of loving our neighbor
> Is a very important matter.
> Our Emperor made this Golden Rule;
> We act in accordance with it.
> We must help each other in calamity,
> For Sympathy is the law of nature.
> Our act was humble, but its reward was great
> So, perceiving the spirit of the Giver,
> We accept this gift forever
> And dedicate it to the education of our children.

These lines, so simple and sincere as they are, express such confidence and good will as two great countries can maintain through generations to come, if their governments will but act at all times in response to the best feeling of their citizens. I do not believe that the American people cherish any aims or projects that are contrary at any point to the welfare, progress, and dignity of Japan.

The Monroe Doctrine, as applied to conditions in our own hemisphere, has not meant aggrandizement for ourselves but a protecting interest in the development of a series of younger and weaker nations until such time as there could be no danger of their being humiliated or injured from without. Towards every other country in the Western Hemisphere the people of the United States have no attitude except one of good will and of sincere desire for their peace and prosperity.

Many Japanese scholars and statesmen understand well the problems of our American development. I was intimately associated with Dr. Shosuke Sato when, some thirty years ago, he made his noteworthy study of the public land system by virtue of which the people of the United States were spread from the Alleghanies across the Mississippi Valley, and on to the Pacific Coast. Your scholars, of whom Dr. Sato is a type, know with what pain and hardship we have pioneered our way across this North American continent, subduing the wilderness and creating our present national entity. Almost everything that we have done has been accomplished by us in this period since Commodore Perry made us acquainted with Japan.

Broadly speaking, countries that aspire to a great future must have a definite, unified nationality, with harmony of institutions and of language and customs. This had been previously achieved by Japan, as the great foundation upon which to build her recent progress and her great future. Germany had her unity of language and race, upon which to erect her modern political structure and her international position. But we in America, although with a British beginning, are even now trying to create a blended, distinct nationality out of many elements, of widely different origin.

Our Japanese friends, with their wonderful solidarity of nationhood, reaching a long ways into the past, must be patient and generous towards our seething and struggling population, as the process goes on of trying to bring unity of life and consistency of high aim into the America that is yet to be. I have long believed that in the nature of things the mutual friendship between the American and Japanese governments ought, without any formal bonds of alliance, to be quite as strong and unshakable as that between any other two governments in the world.

Neither should entertain the remotest thought of doing the other injury, and both should stand for peace and justice, in a world which ought henceforth to discard war and hatred among nations and races. National ideals may still find room, even though they sacrifice something on behalf of a still higher realizable ideal,—that of cooperation, good neighborhood, and common humanity.

VII.

Our religious leaders are concerning themselves with the problems of future peace, and are showing some difference of opinion regarding the necessity of hatred as an impelling motive in the prosecution of a successful war. Having hated to conclusive ends, they will turn from the Old Testament to the New, and preach the gentler doctrine of loving one's enemies. A different approach to post-war problems is more encouraging. Belligerency, under the law of nations, is a legal and political status, but not a private and personal one. With belligerency ended, a wholesome public opinion may gain ascendency, even in countries so frightfully infected by the poison of false national ambitions as Germany and Japan.

Those who have been responsible in our day for appalling crimes against humanity are more guilty than Attila or Jenghiz Khan, because they have lived in an enlightened age, and have defied all the moral gains of civilization. The only basis for the "Co-prosperity" that Japan professes to desire in the East is goodwill and voluntary cooperation by all nations and races on both sides of the Pacific. The Japanese people have capacities that should give them a share in the world's prospects of a beneficent future. This cannot be realized, however, until they renounce the false policies of the past quarter-century, and allow themselves to be guided by the concepts and principles for which they were praised in 1915 by many Americans who knew their history and set value upon their qualities.

We may well regret the long train of events that has seemed to emphasize racial differences in the Pacific theatre of the present war. The furious Boxer uprising in China was based upon antiforeign propaganda, directed chiefly against Europeans and their encroachments. The Japanese, with intense national and racial pride, have relied even more upon propaganda against the American and European nations, as composed chiefly of the Caucasian or white race, than upon their advantages for war-making of preparation and proximity.

Along with a supply of war materials for the aid and relief of China, it is hardly less important that we should use every possible means to prove that it is our desire and purpose to live on equal terms with the Chinese Republic in a future world of personal, national, and racial equality. Educated Chinese are aware of their full welcome in America, and understand the history and circumstances of the competition between standards of living that led to the Exclusion Act as applied to Chinese laborers. That Act should be repealed, not as effecting any appreciable change in immigration volume or character, but as a token of understanding and good will, and to counteract Japanese propaganda.

In the light of history it will become clear enough that in the present war we are fighting Japan in self-defense. We have acquired and populated a certain domain that includes our Pacific Coast states, and also Alaska and Hawaii. We do not seek, whether by force or by peaceful means, to add any more territory to our national domain. But national sentiment is unified and unyielding in the determination to keep and protect what we have. Japan's objectives have undoubtedly included conquest of some parts of our home domain.

Also, in the international sense, our flag has rightfully belonged in the Philippine Archipelago, and our fully announced plans of withdrawal had been based upon world-wide assurances that the Commonwealth of the Philippines, with full sovereign rights, and with accredited membership in the family of nations, would be immune from attack. Beside our prime duty of self-defense, therefore, we have taken it upon ourselves as a moral obligation to see that the Philippine republic is secure in its right of independence; and in that war objective we have the support of the United Nations.

Wholly compatible with these two objects is our desire to aid the Chinese people in their effort to regain control of their own territory and resources. This friendly motive actually exists, although our cooperation with China is also a part of the war strategy that is essential to the accomplishment of our first two objectives. We expect to do business on equal terms with a reorganized China, asking no economic advantages that are not reciprocated.

We are aware that vast changes are impending in Asia, based largely upon improved transportation projects; and perchance the Asiatic people may wish to employ some of our American engineers and construction experts who will be looking for new jobs when the war is ended. But Americans will not entertain the view that the Chinese, or other Asiatic peoples, are in any manner to be supervised or to be held in leading strings by Americans or Europeans. They must " police " themselves, and adjust their own boundary lines by neighborly agreements.

The volume to which I have previously referred, containing messages by thirty-five Japanese leaders, was intended to inform Americans regarding the conception entertained in Japan of that country's mission to the world. No nation has ever revealed its sense of a great destiny with such self-conscious avowals as those expressed by Japan's chief spokesmen in the period of the First World War. Japanese life was in process of fermentation, absorbing everything that could be learned in the West, in order to demonstrate the fact that " mankind is a one and indivisible whole, that the yellow race is not inferior to the white, and that all the races should cooperate in perfect harmony for the development of the world's civilization." So wrote the Viscount Kaneko; and he added, " We have obtained a voice in the Parliament of Man at the cost of blood and money; we must use that new right to good purpose."

This distinguished jurist—a graduate of the Harvard Law School and an experienced authority in international affairs—was a warm friend of America. He could not have thought that Japanese ambition would lead to a perverted sense of racial rivalry, and a determination to conquer the world in order to disprove European ideas of race superiority. It was a strange inconsistency that led the Japanese to join the Germans in an alliance for war aggression, while fully aware that Germany was the only country in which the doctrine of racial superiority had been accepted as a basis upon which the supreme law of might and conquest had been predicated.

It is true, meanwhile, that in America as in most countries, justice to groups and classes—including racial minorities— must begin at home. The ideals of freedom have become world-wide and must be upheld as universal concepts; but the application of these principles, to be successful in concrete reality, must be localized. They must be asserted in our thousands of communities, as we regulate the daily affairs of common men.

Chapter XVI

NAVAL COMPETITION AND THE WASHINGTON CONFERENCE

The Atlantic Charter, when considered at first as a pious expression of friendly regard for the human race on the part of Messrs. Churchill and Roosevelt, seemed little more than a series of platitudes, not as strikingly expressed as Jefferson's Declaration of Independence. But when this creed was studied, and men began to take it literally, pledges of profound importance were found in it that the world meant to see fulfilled.

These pledges were confirmed on January 1, 1942, when they were included in a larger statement, signed by twenty-six members of the United-Nations group, with the expectation of additional signatures. One of the promises provides that the peace to be made "should enable all men to traverse the high seas and oceans without hindrance."

Assurances of "sea-freedom" took prominence when the cause of the United Nations became so dangerously hampered by the destructive use of submarines in the Atlantic. One of the greatest mistakes of the policies adopted in 1919 was the failure to ordain and secure the abolition of submarines.

President Wilson believed that naval disarmament was to proceed rapidly, but he relied too much upon general ideas. Nothing illustrated more strikingly the fallacies and imperfections of the Versailles Treaty than its construction on plans which required the maintenance of a great French conscript army and of an expanded British navy.

Since there was slight prospect of general disarmament, Mr. Wilson continued to advocate a large American navy for our own defense, and especially as a contribution toward the maintenance of freedom of the seas for all lawful purposes. There resulted a competition in naval building; and to deal with that situation, and also with the problems of the Pacific, the Naval Conference of 1921 was invited to meet at Washington by President Harding.

The arrangements were carried out by the Secretary of State, the Hon. Charles E. Hughes. The Conference had one notable result, namely an agreement upon naval equality as a principle between Great Britain and the United States. This agreement was an important transitional step in the history of Anglo-American relations.

The same conference drafted the nine-power treaty which guaranteed the independence and territorial integrity of China. If the Washington conference was not conclusive as regards the matters that came before it, it was at least more efficient than had been expected. The Conference exhibited in its spirit and in its open and straightforward methods the typical American policy of reasonableness and good will in foreign relations.

IN the declaration of principles known as the Atlantic Charter promulgated by President Roosevelt and Prime Minister Churchill August 14, 1941, the larger aims of their countries are set forth in a series of eight numbered paragraphs. Each expression is in accordance with enlightened public opinion, and will assuredly be brought to the test of concrete application if the United Nations are completely victorious.

The fourth point declares that the two signers, on behalf of their Governments, will endeavor "to further the enjoyment by all states great or small, victor or vanquished, of access on equal terms to the trade and to the raw materials of the world which are needed for their economic prosperity."

The sixth point asserts that "after the final destruction of the Nazi tyranny they hope to see established a peace which will afford to all nations the means of dwelling in safety within their own boundaries, and which will afford assurance that all the men in all the lands may live out their lives in freedom from fear and want."

The seventh point—which I propose to discuss with some references to past experience, and with some unusual proposals for the future—declares: "Such a peace should enable all men to traverse the high seas and oceans without hindrance."

The eighth point is not so tersely expressed, but I think it well to quote it in full: "Eighth, they believe that all of the nations of the world, for realistic as well as spiritual reasons must come to the abandonment of the use of force. Since no future peace can be maintained if land, sea or air armaments continue to be employed by nations which threaten, or may threaten, aggression outside of their frontiers, they believe, pending the establishment of a wider and permanent system of general security, that the disarmament of such nations is essential. They will likewise aid and encourage all other practicable measures which will lighten for peace-loving peoples the crushing burden of armaments."

Thus it will be seen that the Atlantic Charter contemplates the abandonment of the use of force and the ultimate relief of peace-loving peoples from the burdensome necessity of keeping up heavy armaments. But it also proposes to disarm the aggressive nations first, and to discard the physical means of enforcing peace and order, at no specified future time but as a serious promise rather than a pious hope.

When it was first proclaimed to an expectant world, the Atlantic

Charter did not make more than a casual and passing impression in any quarter. In so far as its avowals were at all explicit, they implied no sacrifices on the part of Great Britain or the United States, because neither country was seeking further aggrandizement, and because both had nothing to lose and much to gain from a world of peace, justice and security.

The United States was not then at war, but was providing for defensive island air-bases in the western Atlantic by a reciprocal arrangement with the British Government. Meanwhile, on June 21, the Germans had made their surprise attack on Russia; and the European war had entered its new and colossal phases in the East, as German armies were speeding across the Ukraine and threatening Moscow.

Fifty-seven days had elapsed between the attack upon Russia and the promulgation of the Atlantic Charter. The document seemed utterly remote from the harsh realities of the summer of 1941, and it was mildly disparaged as a tissue of platitudes. It gained only secondary attention from a press that was publishing startling news of German victories day by day. France had been crushed; Germany was in control of the continental shore-line from Norway to Spain; England—lacking superiority of guns and airplanes—was still fighting alone, and still fearing invasion, while making painful recovery from the disaster of Dunkerque, that had occurred in the previous year (May 30, 1940).

In less than four months after the President and the Prime Minister had met at sea and drafted their " visionary " pronunciamento, came our own disaster at Pearl Harbor; and—presto—we were at war all over the world with inadequate preparation. The Atlantic Charter had faded from memory in the din and the confusion of our defensive undertakings, as if it had been written with what is known as " evanescent ink."

On January 1, 1942, however, there came a supplementary declaration, signed by the United Nations, embodying the program of purposes and principles set forth in the Atlantic Charter and giving pledges pertaining to the war itself. The earlier document had now assumed a character of reality, and had come down from sky to earth, as a vital program not to be by-passed or evaded. It had taken form as the most impressive and important statement of world objects and of means for their attainment ever made in the records of mankind. Its only rival was Woodrow Wilson's

"Fourteen Points," which had never (one may venture to say) been whole-heartedly accepted by the nations concerned, although incorporated in the Armistice agreement.

The signatory governments "being convinced that complete victory over their enemies is essential to defend life, liberty, independence and religious freedom," pledged themselves to employ their full resources in the war, to cooperate with each other, and not to make a separate armistice or peace with the enemies. As issued officially, on January 1, 1942, it was entitled: "A Joint Declaration by the United States of America, The United Kingdom of Great Britain and Northern Ireland, The Union of Soviet Socialist Republics, China, Australia, Belgium, Canada, Costa Rica, Cuba, Czechoslovakia, Dominican Republic, El Salvador, Greece, Guatemala, Haiti, Honduras, India, Luxembourg, Netherlands, New Zealand, Nicaragua, Norway, Panama, Poland, South Africa, Yugoslavia."

It will be noted that Russia, China, and India are included among the nations which had then agreed to the Atlantic Charter and to collective war action. The last clause of this document stated that: "The foregoing declaration may be adhered to by other nations which are, or which may be, rendering material assistance and contributions in the struggle for victory over Hitlerism." This provided for the adherence of Brazil, Mexico, and other of the larger Latin-American republics.

As we entered the summer of 1943 the United Nations had been gaining superiority in naval tonnage and air force, and Germany with her allies had lost her earlier initiative and was on the defensive, while still controlling almost all of Europe. But with five hundred submarines, operating chiefly in the Atlantic, the destruction of ships under American and allied flags had been at the rate of almost or quite a million tons a month. It reminded me of what I have long regarded as one of the most appalling of all the mistakes of the Allied nations in conference at Paris in 1919: their failure to abolish at once and for all time the use of the submarine as a naval type.

It is true that there may have been reliance placed upon the implied assurance given to Germany that general naval reduction, if not full disarmament at sea, would follow the destruction of the German fleet. But it would have been reasonable to give that understanding some definite and precise formulation in the peace treaty, not merely to console the Germans but also to protect Great Britain and her allies, looking to the future.

President Wilson in the course of the war had declared repeatedly not merely that the German method of submarine attack upon merchant ships without warning was not to be tolerated, but that the submarine itself should be outlawed. In the naval appropriation bill of 1915, some time before we had entered the war, Congress had inserted clauses which were intended to express certain broad American principles that were traditional and were entertained without dispute. Since those clauses were repeated in naval bills in several successive years and adopted with full accord, I think it well to quote from the bill as follows:

> It is hereby declared to be the policy of the United States to adjust and settle its international disputes through mediation or arbitration to the end that war may be honorably avoided. It looks with apprehension and disfavor upon a general increase of armament throughout the world, but it realizes that no single nation can disarm and that without a common agreement upon the subject every considerable power must maintain a relative standing in military strength. In view of the premises, the President is authorized and requested to invite at an appropriate time, not later than the close of the war in Europe, all the great Governments of the world to send representatives to a conference which shall be charged with the duty of formulating a plan for a court of arbitration or other tribunal to which disputed questions between nations shall be referred for adjustment and peaceful settlement, and to consider the question of disarmament and submit their recommendations to their respective Governments for approval.

On his return from Europe, in speeches advocating the ratification of the Versailles Treaty, President Wilson referred repeatedly to the foregoing expression of American policy, and he insisted that Congress should be satisfied with the functions assigned to the League of Nations. He reminded his audience that Congress had further instructed the President to cancel the naval building program authorized by the bill of 1915, or as much of it as he thought wise in the circumstances, in case of a general agreement relating to naval disarmament.

II.

Mr. Wilson was of the opinion in 1919 that the acceptance of the Versailles Treaty by the United States Senate would somehow be followed by naval disarmament. This might indeed have been possible; but nothing in the subsequent proceedings at Geneva or elsewhere would seem to support that anticipation. The treaty was specific in allowing Germany to maintain an army limited to one hundred thousand men for the maintenance of internal authority. But no explicit promises were made in the treaty that the conquerors would also take measures of disarmament.

The fourth in the list of Wilson's original points upon which the Armistice was afterwards based was in the following language: "Adequate guarantees given and taken that national armaments shall be reduced to the lowest points consistent with domestic safety." This meant reduction on both sides. Wilson envisaged a Europe with such freedom from the fear of strife across boundary lines as prevailed in the United States and Canada. Article 8 of the League of Nations recognized that the "maintenance of peace required the reduction of national armaments to the lowest point consistent with national safety," and declared that the Council of the League—"taking account of the geographical situation and circumstances of each state—shall formulate plans for such reduction for the consideration and action of the several governments."

But this was altogether evasive and meaningless. Each country admitted to membership in the League would decide for itself, while Germany and her allies were disarmed indefinitely. Mr. Simonds remarks that failure of the peace arrangements began at this point, and he continues as follows: "For by the same peace treaties which established the League there were imposed upon the defeated nations territorial changes, financial burdens and unilateral disarmament provisions which were inequitable and therefore intolerable. Because they were helpless, the vanquished countries were compelled to ratify these treaties but, from the start, they did not disguise their resolution to procure revision by peaceful means if possible but by force if necessary."

Having failed to obtain guarantees of security from Great Britain and the United States, France considered it necessary not only to maintain a large army and an attitude of watchful distrust toward Germany, but also thought that it enhanced her future safety to militarize the new so-called Succession States, Czechoslovakia and Poland particularly.

The British, who had less occasion to fear the revival of German aggression, believed that Germany could be placated by revising the Treaty of Versailles to make it less odious in the German mind. France could not abandon the idea of the permanent coercion of Germany, and the British in turn could not even think of seeking to enforce their different view by virtual coercion of France. Thus the situation was deadlocked, and France continued to rely upon conscript armies, while England, more than ever, trusted to her warships—including submarines.

Even if nothing could be done to interfere with the encirclement of Germany by land forces, something certainly could have been done, regardless of the League of Nations, to deal with certain phases of naval armament. Many people must wonder—finding no satisfactory explanation to dispel their bewilderment—why sumbarines as instruments of warfare were not abolished by universal consent in the conference of Allies that drew up the Versailles document, before the Germans were asked to sign on the dotted line.

Great Britain was dependent in the First World War for much more than half of her food supply, and for a great part of her raw materials, upon imports by water from North America, South America, Asia, Africa, and the Antipodes. Yet in 1916 and '17 her very existence was menaced by Germany's successful and destructive use of submarines in the sinking of thousands of cargo ships. In a previous chapter I have mentioned Mr. Herbert Hoover's return from England in April, 1917, with grim and alarming facts regarding the submarine warfare that had not been revealed to our government. His recital made so deep an impression upon my mind, as I heard it on the day of his return, that I could never again think of the submarine otherwise than as a diabolical instrumentality that would surely be abolished by the eager consent of all nations at the earliest moment after the end of that First World War.

On shipboard in the last year of the war, in the midst of a large convoy of grotesquely camouflaged vessels that carried a full division of American troops to Europe, we were constantly reminded of the submarine danger. We were never allowed to be without our lifebelts. Black-outs were strictly enforced at night. Boat-drill was a matter of daily discipline. Our ships meandered through strange waters, far from the usual sea-lanes. In London we became acquainted with Admiral Sims, who had assumed a position of prominence as foremost representative in Europe of our naval interests.

Ambassador Page had fallen ill from the over-strain of his wartime services, and Ambassador John W. Davis had not yet assumed his duties as Mr. Page's successor. Admiral Sims was the American most in evidence, and he agreed to tell us what he knew about submarines if our group of visiting American journalists would submit questions in advance, and would arrange for an evening of confidential discussion. The Rt. Hon. Arthur J. Balfour, then head of the Foreign Office, having learned of our engagement with this American naval authority, asked if he might also be present, and thus we had two eminent official guests at our dinner. Admiral Sims had studied the limitations as well as the dangers of submarine warfare, and knew as much as any American or Englishman about methods by which the menace could be met or reduced.

At the conclusion of a remarkable discussion of the topic in all its phases by our frank and sturdy master of naval strategy and tactics, Mr. Balfour took the floor. In a graceful speech he reminded us of his own recent experience at the head of the British naval department, and then proceeded to tell us that he had gained more information from Admiral Sims, during the two or three hours of that evening's presentation of facts and conclusions, than he had acquired in all his previous experience.

This incident might seem irrelevant—a mere bit of personal reminiscence—but for the impression it made upon my mind. It intensified the feeling, derived from Mr. Hoover's narration of the previous year, that there could be no remedy for the submarine menace but to outlaw it as essentialy an illegal instrument of warfare. I had seen hundreds of young American soldiers in base hospitals, as they were brought from the front in terrible agony as a result of the use of poison gas by the German army. Although war itself (as we hoped) would be outlawed at some future time, international law had already pronounced against the use of gas, against the bombing of hospitals and non-militarized places, and against practices known as bacteriological warfare. I thought that the submarine, in warfare on the seas, like poison gas in land fighting, should be abolished without waiting for the era of perpetual peace that Victor Hugo and Tennyson had predicted.

This conviction led me further to a consideration of naval warfare, and the rights of all people to use the high seas for peaceful objects. People within their own national domains have rights that they do not assert outside of their own boundaries. But to whom should be assigned the authority to rule the seas? This domination had at times been assumed by Great Britain, not so much in the spirit of usurpation as in that of sober responsibility. But the scepter of Neptune belongs by right to no single maritime power; and nothing is more demonstrable than the need of a collective control of the seas, under a code of maritime law, for the welfare of all nations, regardless of their naval strength.

In another chapter I shall discuss the League of Nations in theory and practice, and the bearing of the decision of the United States to abstain from official membership in the Geneva organization. In the present chapter I am concerned with a specific topic of higher consequence to the world at large than any other—and one which required the most immediate and uncompromising treatment. Yet the League avoided that topic, for reasons of its own structural impotence.

With all its defects, the League was indeed a good international training-school for men from small countries, who were taking equal part in the discussions of the Assembly. Forty-one nations were represented at the first meeting of the Assembly, which opened November 15, 1920, and remained in session for more than a month. But the statesmen from these small countries did not have to wait for a second or a third annual meeting to discover that when tested in practice the League did not respond to Mr. Wilson's dream. They discovered promptly that in all policies of major concern the League was firmly controlled by the permanent members of its Council.

No editor could have been more well-disposed toward the League than I had been; and I was willing to have it accepted at Washington either with or without the explanatory reservations that the Senate regarded as necessary. But at the conclusion of the very first Geneva session I was impelled by the facts to make the following observations relating to the power of the League Council:

England, France, Italy and Japan can, together, sway any issue of the old world, and influence any in the new. But it sits in secret; it failed Poland when attacked by Russia. Each of these four powers has followed an individual and selfish policy, France in aid to Poland, Italy in the Adriatic, England in Mesopotamia and Persia, and Japan in Eastern Siberia. Each has gained, but all collectively have lost the chance of a world leadership along constitutional lines. The Assembly has forty-one powers in its membership, no one of which, except the Big Four, can alone influence the world's destiny except through the Assembly. They have taken their work seriously and it has held the center of the world's stage.

I proceeded to show how and why the principle of the equality of nations great and small had come into existence only as a matter of diplomatic courtesy; and that it was, palpably, nothing more than a legal fiction when the great powers regarded their interests as vitally concerned. In whatever related to armament and disarmament, world opinion could not assert itself through the League, for the simple reason that its machinery was designed to prevent such an assertion. The so-called "Covenant," in its twenty-six numbered articles as adopted and incorporated in the Treaty of Versailles, was not wholly responsive to the ideas and purposes of President Wilson. Some at least of his aims had been rendered ineffective by European statesmen who were not thinking of world harmony as a primary object, but rather of their own national interest in maintaining the *status quo*.

Whereas four powers that had shaped the Versailles Treaty for their own ends were dominating the League Council, the Assembly could be controlled by fifteen Latin-American states which had no navies and virtually no armies, when acting in conjunction with six small European states similarly lacking in defensive strength. The small powers, controlling the Assembly, would have demobilized France, reduced the British navy to a fraction of its strength, and brought at once into League membership the defeated powers—Germany, Austria, Hungary, Bulgaria and Turkey. But the Council's mastery at Geneva was quietly exhibited, and the Assembly could do nothing but accept the fact of its inferior position. A ferment had followed the shaping of the new political map of Europe and the Near East, and the Assembly was, of course, too eager for immediate results.

Thus it soon became evident to close and impartial observers of the Geneva scene that the League could never in practice carry out any of the objects or purposes relating to limitation of armaments that were set forth in the six clauses of the League's Article VIII.

In my pages of editorial comment relating to that first session of the League I find the following allusion to the naval situation, as uninfluenced by the Assembly and left undisturbed by the Council:

> The lesser powers of the world once had effective armies and navies. The British fleet destroyed the Danish navy in 1801 because it was large enough to be dangerous, and Campbell made much of the "Battle of the Baltic." Only five countries have effective fleets today. The lesser powers were too wise to take extreme steps. Each country was left free to act or not in enforcing the blockade to be imposed on recalcitrant powers. Disarmament was left to future action and discussion. Japan flatly declared that it could not disarm unless the United States did, though the army and navy with which Japan crushed China was organized when this country had an army of 27,500 men and a fleet too small to cope with Japan's. The Island Empire armed long before the United States.

While deferring further discussion of our relation to the League, I may pause to remark at this point simply that those who have learned to think of it as a matter of controversy between our two political parties, or to narrow it still further by turning it upon Senator Lodge's antipathy to President Wilson or *vice versa*, have not only a scanty acquaintance with the facts but also a perverted and mischievous view of them. If there was any dereliction that impartial historians at some future time may uncover, it was not attributable to President Wilson or any other American. It was the European exigencies, with which Mr. Wilson and his delegates at Paris were unable to contend, that befogged the issue.

III.

The Treaty of Versailles was framed in its essentials by the European allies under the leadership of Great Britain and France. They were concerned with the maintenance of their empires, and they regarded the League of Nations as an instrumentality that could be used by them to maintain or even enhance the power they had secured by the defeat and disarmament of Germany. Thus the differences between President Wilson and Senator Lodge were too slight to be considered, when brought into contrast with the differences between undisputed American views of peace and disarmament and those of the dominant European powers (with Japan included as at that time a military and naval ally of Great Britain).

Although President Wilson was impatient of the Senate's delay, the Treaty would have been ratified with a majority far in excess of the necessary two-thirds of the Senators if he had been willing to defer somewhat to their judgment. The Senators were proceeding conscientiously, and not in a partisan spirit, to adopt—along with the Treaty but not as a part of it—certain explanatory statements that were miscalled " reservations." Such statesmen as Mr. Root, Mr. Taft, and Mr. Hughes, who were internationalists in full sympathy with President Wilson's ideals and aims, saw no harm in the Senate's scruples. But the President, knowing the faults and errors of the Versailles Treaty apart from the League, was trusting to Geneva to rectify them. He was afraid that the Senate's explanatory statements might cause endless trouble and delay in Europe, and weaken the League's prestige and authority at the outset.

Mr. Wilson preferred to test public opinion in the forth-coming presidential election; and James M. Cox and Franklin D. Roosevelt on the Democratic ticket of 1920 made a gallant campaign in support of his position. I was inclined to share their views, because I could see no reason for believing that our ratification of a treaty that Europe had accepted could injure any American interest. The so-called " reservations " seemed to me merely to recite what was implied and self-evident. But the overwhelming victory of the Republican ticket might have been taken as favoring a still more effective organization for peace, rather than a rejection of long-time American ideals and doctrines. This view could have been derived from Senator Harding's expressions before and after his election as President. But more importantly, it was sustained by his appointment of Mr. Hughes and Mr. Hoover to the most influential places in the Cabinet.

Neither of these two men had ever been narrow partisans. Neither of them had been isolationists. Both had favored, conspicuously, some plan of united effort on the part of all nations for political, economic, and moral cooperation. As a jurist, Mr. Hughes represented the development of international law and the substitution of courts and tribunals for the menace of arms. Mr. Hoover was the world's foremost exponent of economic progress through the expansion of commerce, and of social advancement through cooperative measures for international health, and for relief in times of famine or other emergencies too drastic for local remedy.

The new administration did not conceive of this country as having changed its attitude of good will towards the nations with whose governments we had been cooperating in the war. In many matters affecting our return to normal conditions, we could act for ourselves. There were other matters, however, about which it was necessary to proceed in consultation with foreign governments. The most pressing of these was the subject of naval armament, which the League of Nations had shown its inability to face, on any plan whatsoever.

I shall proceed to comment upon the Washington Naval Conference, which was one of the first undertakings of the Harding administration. But to understand the circumstances a preliminary statement is requisite. Early in 1916, a year before we entered the war, President Wilson had made a series of speeches on what was called his "Western Preparedness Tour." While the Eastern states were already convinced of the need for an enlarged army and a great expansion of the navy, people beyond the Mississippi had yet to be awakened, in Mr. Wilson's opinion. In a speech at Kansas City he praised our small navy for its quality, but dwelt upon the great sweep of our coastlines; and then he asked this question: "Do you think that a Navy that ranks only fourth in the world in force is enough to defend the coasts and make secure the territory of a great continent like this?"

He disclaimed the wish to have either an army or a navy as an object of national pride. But he proceeded with the following statement of what was to amount to a five-year building program:

> It is the arm of force which must lie back of every sovereignty in the world, and the Navy of the United States must now be as rapidly as possible brought to a state of efficiency and of numerical strength which will make it practically impregnable to the navies of the world. The fighting force of the Navy now is splendid, and I should expect very great achievements from the fine officers and trained men that constitute it, but it is not big enough; it is not numerous enough; it is incomplete. It must be completed, and what the present administration is proposing is that we limit the number of years to five within which we shall complete a definite program which will make that Navy adequate for the defense of both coasts.

An army can be expanded quickly, as was shown in 1917-18 when four million men were trained. But a naval program—at least in times past—required years rather than months for fulfillment. We were reducing the navy personnel as rapidly as possible before the end of the Wilson administration; but the building of battleships and other naval types was going forward, and the early completion of the program, already authorized by Congress, was expected to give us the greatest navy in the world, soon after the opening of a new presidential term.

The Hon. Josephus Daniels of North Carolina was Secretary of the Navy through the eight years of Mr. Wilson's two terms, and the Hon. Franklin D. Roosevelt of New York was Assistant Secretary for more than seven years, retiring only when he was nominated for the Vice Presidency in 1920. Their conduct of naval affairs was creditable to the country and they had fully supported the policy of naval expansion. Commenting at the end of the year 1919 upon the Department's annual report, I wrote the following paragraph:

> Secretary Daniels tells of the Navy's work in helping to bring the soldiers home—a very brilliant record in every way. He describes also breaking up of naval bases in France, Great Britain and the Azores, and here again the record is one of efficiency. We had soon reduced the man power of the Navy from 500,000 to 132,000, not including several hundred thousand Naval Reserves released from active duty. Mr. Daniels declares that the Navy has not lost sight of the future, and that its symmetry is unimpaired. Our naval strength is now next to that of Great Britain and far beyond that of any third power. The Secretary holds as firmly to naval aviation as Mr. Baker does to military aviation. He tells also the brilliant story of sweeping up the 50,000 mines that our Navy had planted in the North Sea. The sentiment of the country, insofar as we understand it, is in favor of a skeletonized Army reduced to the lowest possible limit of safety and of expenditure. The personnel of almost 4,000,000 men, highly trained in the war period, will be available in any emergency for at least a dozen years to come. We need to maintain military material, and to introduce gradually some system of training. The Navy, for some years to come, should be supported without hesitation upon a very large scale, this being our most necessary means of security and protection in a turbulent world.

With our prompt shrinkage of the army to a mere skeleton, and reduction of naval personnel by three-fourths, the great naval program almost completed in the shipyards did not seem consistent with any symmetrical scheme of disarmament. President Harding in an address to Congress in April (a few weeks after his inauguration) had said: "We are ready to cooperate with other nations to approximate disarmament, but merest prudence forbids that we disarm alone." He had then expressed his purpose to call an international conference to consider the limitation of armaments.

IV.

This, however, in view of obvious facts, could refer only to the problem of competitive Navies. The proposal met with favor in both houses of Congress, and the subject was discussed in the press and on the platform throughout the country. Meanwhile, the project was in the stage of official negotiation through diplomatic agencies. Since the views I expressed in 1921 are those that I have always held, I will quote certain extracts from my comments made while the proposed naval conference was a current topic:

> The one sphere in which a properly conceived League of Nations could have been of most obvious service was the sphere of things strictly extra-national. The high seas in the nature of the case cannot belong to separate nations, either in whole or in part. They are the world's common possession, for common and equal use. They can be rendered safe for everybody by international cooperation. The completion and acceptance of a code of maritime international law is the first step to be taken. This would mean the substitution of law for force on the high seas, and its logical sequel must be the abolition of naval warfare. The principle to be adopted, therefore, is that of cooperation in maintaining the free and proper use of the seas for commerce and travel. The United States has no more right to conceive of being supreme on the sea, by virtue of having the largest navy, than has any other power a right to make such an improper and fallacious claim. There must be an abandonment of the idea that nations may go out upon the common seas to destroy each other's commerce, and to claim as a duelling ground the domain that belongs to peaceful peoples for beneficial purposes.

I called attention to the fact that on June 10 the French Chamber of Deputies had adopted a bill providing for the immediate construction of sixty-six new vessels, more than half of them submarines. If we in the United States could ill afford to maintain an immense naval establishment, it was obvious that other governments were far less able than ours to meet the cost of naval competition. In view of actual conditions affecting debts, credits, and commerce, we were indirectly paying a great part of the armament bills of other countries. In consequence I reached the conclusion that "if we desire to perpetuate this harmful system of competition in armaments, particularly at sea, we can find no more certain way of producing such a result than by cutting down our own program of national defense and accepting a certain rank—whether first, second, third, or fourth—by agreement with a few other nations on the false theory that some nations have an inherent right to exercise more power at sea than other nations."

My argument proceeded as follows:

> Until, then, the world is ready to accept a plan by which the seas may be made safe for the ships and the commerce of all nations alike, it would be merely silly to talk about the abolition of force and the coming reign of law. Disarmament on land is a very difficult and complex affair at best, and under existing circumstances it is not feasible. Naval disarmament is a different question, calling for separate treatment. It was the argument of Senator Poindexter that the only way by which the United States could be effectively influential in maintaining peace, and in bringing about a permanent reduction of armaments upon a reasonable plan, was by providing that the United States should be—not greater in naval strength than any other country, but not inferior to any. Far from containing a menace this doctrine is, of all others, the best single guarantee of world peace that exists anywhere at the present time.
>
> The British and American navies in cooperation—and with complete abandonment of the ridiculous theory that they are latently hostile to one another and are maintained because of underlying distrust or enmity—could easily enforce the precepts of maritime international law. But, in order to serve the cause of peace, these navies would have to be maintained on the new theory that they were not designed to promote nationalistic or imperial aggrandizement, but to insure universal peace and to enforce justice. This would mean the acceptance in good faith of a system of judicature, together with the acceptance of a code of international law.
>
> With cooperation established and competition abandoned, disarmament could proceed rapidly. If national ambitions are to dominate, or if instincts of fear, distrust, or racial pride are to prevail, we must continue to maintain great armaments and watch the horizons for signs of trouble. There are different ways by which the principle of cooperation may be put into practice; but the important thing is to adopt the principle. This idea ought to appeal strongly to the statesmen now assembled in London from the British Dominions.

The allusion in the preceding sentence related to a gathering in which statesmen from Canada, Australia, South Africa, New Zealand and Newfoundland, with representatives from India and other parts of the British Empire, were endeavoring to deal with various problems affecting the British realms. The Dominions had been allowed to have their seats at the so-called "peace table" at Paris, and had also been accorded individual and equal membership in the League of Nations. South Africa and Australia were not hesitant in expressing the hope that Great Britain would not renew the ten-year alliance with Japan that was renewed in 1912 and was therefore about to expire.

It is highly instructive to open volumes of periodicals printed in 1921 and the following year, to see how discerning were some of the discussions of the Far Eastern situation that accompanied or preceded the Washington naval conference. This historic gathering began its sessions on Armistice Day (November 11, 1921) with the delegates assembled in the amphitheatre at Arlington to hear an address by the President.

Careful preparations had been made not only for the dignified and appropriate setting of the conference, but also for the achievement of serious and salutary undertakings. Its general objectives were twofold: first, to limit competitive navies by agreement; second, to bring some semblance of stability into Far Eastern affairs. It was even then perceived that the most striking change in world conditions, apart from the defeat of Germany and the cessation of major warfare in Europe, was the phenomenal rise of Japan in naval strength.

England's far-flung empire called for naval squadrons in all the seas. America, obviously, needed a two-ocean navy. Japan—with aims that were concentrated, although extensive and not wholly disclosed—had already gained a one-ocean predominance in the western half of the Pacific. Under the mandate system, invented at Paris seemingly as a cloak for imperial ambitions, Japan had been accorded full control of thousands of islands grouped in archipelagoes of the Pacific north of the Equator. She had even asserted claims as against the United States to the tiny island of Yap, which we had been using with prior rights as a cable station.

There was a little comprehended situation in the Far East that was described with penetrating analysis by Mr. Frank Simonds under the title "The Far Eastern Question and America." I published it in the issue of my *Review* for November. Mr. Simonds always thought it better to be realistic and truthful than to be blandly complimentary or merely optimistic. Japan had already acquired a position, in the opinion of Mr. Simonds, which did not promise well for the future of peace. "Japan's military forces, her political agents, and her diplomatists, control the Chinese situation. They raise Chinese factions against Chinese factions, promote disorder, and then intervene to restore order."

Mr. Simonds proceeded with a stern and disquieting kind of logic that reads today as if he had written his article twenty years later to the very month. Let me quote two paragraphs relating to Japan's policies with regard to China:

> Obviously the thing is a farce unless we mean to bring the whole situation back to a sound basis, unless we mean to put our force behind the principles of Chinese independence and Siberian freedom. We are going to invite the Japanese to abandon their policy of the past few years, to get out of China politically and militarily, or we are merely going to have a dangerous discussion leading nowhere but promoting bad feeling everywhere. And if Japan says "no" and means it, what are we going to do? And if she says "yes" and doesn't mean it—which has been her historic course in similar situations—what are we going to do about it?
>
> If the object of the Conference is to arrive at mere verbal statements, another Lansing-Ishii agreement, all is simple. But the American people have unmistakably had their attention fixed upon Far Eastern affairs and expect something different. For them the conference is for the purpose of insuring equality in the East. It will fail not merely if such equality is not obtained in language, but also if it does not result in practice; and they will eventually demand that their government give force to the words written at Washington in 1921, if such shall be written.

The last section of Mr. Simonds' extended article was called "A Warning." It asserted that Japan would not have come to Washington in 1914 to confer upon the Far East. Seven years had elapsed, and we had demonstrated a new capacity for world affairs. We had shown how formidably and speedily we could act, in a war emergency, and Japan could respect such facts. Said Mr. Simonds:

> Whatever idea there was in Japan, even in chauvinistic quarters, before 1918 of an aggressive war, an attack upon the Philippines or upon the Pacific Coast, that conception has gone, with the general staff plans of operations, into the scrap basket. Japan has not abandoned her own dream, her own conception of supremacy in the Far East. At most she has only considered the limitations which the new state of affairs placed upon her ineluctably.

Still having Japan in mind, Mr. Simonds concluded his article with the following paragraph:

> The gravest danger now, as I see it, is that we shall one day be surprised by war, as Britain was surprised in July and August, 1914, despite all the danger signals which from Tangier to Agadir had lightened the European horizon. And we shall be surprised if we continue to neglect the obvious necessity of appreciating the Japanese point of view, instead of merely iterating and reiterating the merit and the wisdom of our own. Moreover —a fact which Geneva appreciated, if Washington did not—the surprise will all be American, for the world already expects the clash.

I might devote several pages to the membership of the Conference, and the different points of view with which the foreign delegations arrived on the scene. Contemporary descriptions, however, are readily available, and a brief summary will suffice for my present purpose. The four American delegates were Secretary Hughes, Mr. Elihu Root, and Senators Oscar Underwood and Henry Cabot Lodge. Associated with them was an advisory committee of twenty-one members, widely representative of American opinion.

Our delegates had spent many weeks prior to the gathering in close and continuous study of the situations they were to meet, and the policies they would support. They were in full agreement, and were determined to uphold large and comprehensive measures rather than a proposal or two that might restrict naval expenditures for a few years, and thus save the tax-payers of several countries a billion dollars more or less. The British Prime Minister Mr. Lloyd George could not arrive at the opening because of pending negotiations with Ireland that set up the Free State; and Mr. Balfour was acting head of an Empire delegation that included the Prime Ministers of Canada, Australia, and New Zealand. The French delegation included Premier Briand and the eloquent Viviani.

Japan's delegates were brilliant men who exhibited throughout the Conference a most affable and cooperative spirit, which did not conceal from the Chinese delegates and many of the journalists of the world—who were present in large numbers—those ultimate Japanese ambitions which could await opportunity without any change of heart or mind. The Italian delegation was intent upon claiming equality with France, while members from Belgium,

Holland and Portugal were on hand to represent colonial interests of their respective nations in the "regions of the Pacific."

The Japanese delegates were aware when they came that the alliance with Great Britain would not be renewed, and that the British were proposing to make Singapore the most impregnable fortress of the Southern Pacific. Writing for my December number, Mr. Simonds was more optimistic than usual. He recognized a change of mood that affected the principal delegates and their large accompanying groups of official advisers. Also in the give-and-take, "off-the-record" comments of the foreign journalists, many of whom Mr. Simonds had known in Europe, the tendency to scoff had changed to something like enthusiasm.

V.

There had been no loss of time in announcing a concrete program. At the very first business session on November 12, Mr. Hughes (who was made permanent chairman of the Conference) made definite proposals that at once gave promise that the gathering would achieve important results. The American chairman, attaching primary importance to the question of competition in naval programs, declared: "There is only one adequate way out, and that is to end it now." Stating alternatives, he argued that existing programs should be sacrificed regardless of nominal losses. Taking the tonnage of capital ships as a measure of the relative strength of navies, he proposed that there should be no further construction of these large armored vessels for ten years.

Beyond that, he was prepared to submit a concrete plan that would affect immediately the British Empire, Japan, and the United States. To summarize four points that he specified, capital-ship building programs would be abandoned; further reduction would be made through scrapping of certain ships; there would be relative regard for existing naval strength, and (with capital ship tonnage as the measurement of strength) there would be prescribed "a proportionate allowance of auxiliary combatant craft." Further details, as Mr. Hughes applied his principles to precise situations, astonished the delegates, because such frankness in a matter of major international concern was a wholly novel experience to all of them.

Setting forth just what the United States had done toward carrying out the program of 1916 (that called for ten new battleships and six battle cruisers) Mr. Hughes proposed to scrap all these capital ships in various stages of construction, with several completed and others far advanced. Fifteen were to be scrapped, having a total tonnage if completed of 618,000 tons. Next, all the older battleships except two were to be scrapped. These were fifteen in number, with a tonnage of 227,740 tons. The question of disarmament had never been approached before with any such boldness of challenge.

Mr. Hughes did not wait for Great Britain and Japan to suggest what they had to offer in turn, but made proposals in the case of each that he regarded as " fairly commensurate with this action on the part of the United States." The British program as he set it forth in detail was not quite as drastic as that offered on behalf of his own Government. Our completed program would have given us a decided naval superiority; and we did not desire anything more than equality with British sea power.

Japan was asked to abandon a program of eight battleships and battle cruisers that she had adopted but not yet begun to construct. In addition, certain vessels in course of construction were to be scrapped, besides a number of older ones. "Thus under this plan," said Mr. Hughes, " there will be immediately destroyed, of the Navies of the three powers, sixty-six capital fighting ships, built and building, with a total tonnage of 1,878,043."

Of the three navies an aggregate of fifty capital ships would remain at the end of three months, after sixty-six had been destroyed. There were to be no replacements for ten years, and the purpose of the agreement, looking to the future, was to hold the maximum of capital ship tonnage to a limit of 500,000 tons for the United States, the same tonnage for Great Britain, and 300,000 tons for Japan. This became known as the " 5-5-3 " formula.

There was much more in technical detail that I shall not attempt to summarize. Mr. Hughes and his associates had prepared their plan with thoroughness, with constant aid from the Navy's best qualified experts, and from the office of the Secretary of the Navy. The liaison official between the Naval authorities and our delegates was the Assistant Secretary, Theodore Roosevelt, Jr., of whose efficiency Mr. Root spoke to me in the highest terms. His father had been Assistant Secretary of the Navy prior to the war with Spain, and his kinsman Franklin D. Roosevelt had served in the same capacity during the World War.

Mr. Frank Simonds, Mr. H. G. Wells, and other American, British, and European journalists regarded this stunning attack upon the existing trends of naval competition as what might in later parlance be spoken of as an irresistible " blitzkrieg." They did not hesitate to remind us that it seemed like a planned effort to turn attention from the European to the Asiatic situation. Taken together with the termination of the Anglo-Japanese alliance, and the British proposal to erect the world's most formidable naval base at Singapore, these journalists (notably Mr. Wells and Mr. Simonds) felt that Japan was put at a relative disadvantage. While the plan of naval reduction had all the precision of a blueprint drawn to scale, there were other objectives of the Conference that could not be dealt with in the same mathematical fashion.

There were opposing points of view among the Japanese statesmen at home, and there were widely varying opinions about Japan and the Far East in the United States. As against Europe and America, Japan had claimed a preeminence of interest in China; and this had been acknowledged during President Wilson's administration in an agreement signed by our Secretary of State, Mr. Robert Lansing, and Viscount Ishii. This distinguished " elder statesman " of Japan had negotiated the so-called " gentleman's agreement " with Secretary Root in 1907 relating to Japanese immigration, and continued in posts of high authority for many years afterward.

The second thrilling scene at the Conference was that in which the place of prominence was assumed by the Rt. Hon. Arthur J. Balfour. On behalf of Great Britain he accepted the principle of naval equality between the British Empire and the United States. This gentleman—who carried the air of a scholarly amateur and divided his leisure time between writing abstract essays in the field of philosophy and his favorite game of tennis—was also a shrewd and hard-headed politician, who had been trained for the Premiership by his uncle, Lord Salisbury. I had heard him on many occasions including the period, more than thirty years earlier, when he was called " Bloody Balfour " by his Irish enemies whose Land War he opposed, as Irish Secretary.

Perhaps on no other occasion in his long public career had Mr. Balfour risen to what seemed so memorable an opportunity. His manner was rather hesitant and informal, in contrast with the vigorous and incisive oratory of Mr. Hughes. But he well knew that the whole world was awaiting his deliverance, and that it would be regarded as a turning-point in history. Although his manner seemed so casual, every word was carefully chosen; and his deliberate acceptance for his country of a status of naval equality with the United States was hailed with enthusiasm among peace-loving people throughout the world. Mr. Balfour returned from the Conference to accept a peerage; and as first Earl of Balfour he became leader of the Tories in the House of Lords.

It was pointed out at the time that the Washington agreement in its spirit was an application, on the broad scale of the seven seas, of the Anglo-American principle of 1814 relating to the Great Lakes. Many other things were agreed upon during the weeks of the Washington Conference besides the capital-ship ratio, some of which did not survive to justify the hopes and expectations with which they were launched. France and Italy were not satisfied with the relatively low tonnage assigned to them. The British delegates urged the abolition of submarines, but the French with their small defensive force would not accede to that proposal. The five powers did, however, adopt a treaty applying to submarines the rules of naval warfare that related to surface ships. The use of poison gas in warfare was prohibited.

Great Britain, Japan, and the United States agreed to maintain the *status quo* as regards naval bases and fortifications in the Western Pacific. This restricted further strengthening of the American position in Manila Bay. Also, it was a reminder to Japan that under the mandate no fortifications whatsoever were allowable in the vast archipelagoes that had been acquired by her in the distribution of war spoils at Paris.

There was drafted and signed the so-called Nine Power Treaty, that guaranteed the independence and territorial integrity of China. But as Mr. Simonds pointed out, there had already been great encroachments upon what were formerly recognized as domains of the Chinese Empire, and this treaty avoided geographical definitions. Among these other agreements was one between China and Japan that returned the province of Shantung, which Japan had occupied upon the expulsion of the Germans at the beginning of the war. To make this easier for Japan, the British also sacrificed their Shantung interests.

The Conference adjourned without having dealt with the

problem of relative strength in categories of cruisers, destroyers and submarines. After much haggling and disagreement among the naval experts of the five countries concerned, and after more than one futile conference, the United States, Great Britain and Japan compromised their differences in 1930, with the theory of general equality still controlling the two leading navies, while Japan's relative position was somewhat improved. Since the main purpose of the Washington Conference had been to eliminate competition, it was not quite creditable that the experts should have haggled for almost ten years over the manner in which tonnage was to be distributed between heavy cruisers and light ones. The British naval authorities continued to argue—not in bad temper but with dogged insistence—that naval equality on the part of the United States was a purely theoretical attitude, while naval superiority on the part of Great Britain was for many reasons a practical necessity.

VI.

The technical and harmless differences about a cruiser agreement only served to point the more plainly to the historic surrender, voiced by Mr. Balfour, of all that insular pride and prejudice with which it had been claimed, from the time of Queen Elizabeth, that Brittannia ruled the waves. In the larger sense it was no surrender. On the contrary, it meant in future emergencies a doubling of Britain's naval strength. Three and a half years earlier I had been on board of English and American battleships cooperating to patrol the North Sea. Admiral Rodman's fine American squadron was serving willingly and gallantly under the British Naval Command.

At the conclusion of the Conference, I wrote an editorial review which was meant to express what seemed to me the spirit of a noble effort to promote human welfare. I shall conclude this chapter with extended quotation of some of those paragraphs:

> The Washington Conference, in order that its value may be justly appraised, should be considered in its entirety. There must be taken into account (1) the circumstances under which the Conference was convened, (2) the particular questions which were considered, (3) the specific settlements that have resulted, and (4) the broader bearings both of the methods employed and of the decisions reached. Considering the magnitude of the issues presented and the diversity of interests that had to be

harmonized, the work of the Conference has moved with a rapidity that was wholly unexpected in any quarter previous to the actual opening of the sessions on November 12.

If one should start from idealistic premises and consider the net results of the Conference as expressed in definite agreements, it would be possible to regard the outcome as disappointing. As compared with the nominal plans and specifications of a paper constitution for the ending of all war and for the government of the world, the agreements of the Washington Conference might seem to be meager and rather unsatisfactory. On the other hand, there were many practical persons who were not expecting anything excepting some temporary restriction of naval expenditure for the slight relief of taxpayers. These skeptics have been surprised, and are now quite enthusiastic. They declare the Conference a notable success.

So greatly, indeed, have the achievements of the Conference exceeded all the expectations of these critical and experienced observers that they are perhaps in danger of being unduly enthusiastic over it. Many of them are applauding it as having pointed out true paths that may lead to a world of peace and order, thus saving the remnants of our civilization, and opening before the twentieth century a good prospect for the rebuilding of a devastated world. It would seem as if the hard-headed realists—the diplomatists, politicians, military men, and seasoned journalists—had become generous, sentimental, and hopeful in the friendly atmosphere of this Conference, while those who have been accounted the apostles of internationalism have shown a slight tendency to be fault-finding and unhappy.

The truth is that both realists and idealists have earned the right to claim shares in the achievements of the Conference. The methods have been those of the realist, and the Conference has taken every step carefully and upon solid, ascertainable ground. But if the methods are those of diplomacy and of practical negotiation, the atmosphere has been that of human brotherhood; and, in its wider and deeper interpretations, the work of the Conference has been wholly in accord with the aims of the idealists.

For example, the idealists say, with obvious truth, that naval warfare ought to cease altogether, that competing navies are absurd as well as dangerous, and that the common seas ought to be protected for the proper use and service of mankind by a maritime force of international character, with battleships totally abolished, and (of course) with such devices as submarines rendered wholly unnecessary. Proposals that the high seas ought to be neutralized and that they ought to be protected through some common arrangement are so reasonable, when considered as a matter of theory or of doctrine, that not very many people nowadays would care to argue otherwise.

If, indeed, our Government had demanded in advance the acceptance of this doctrine as a part of the price of our naval services to the Allies and of our shipbuilding efforts of 1918, there could have been no possible denial of so reasonable a proposal. We should have seen not merely the sinking of the surrendered German battleships, but a subsequent scrapping of all navies, with the retention of a sufficient number of destroyers to constitute an international maritime police. We did not, however, propose the "freedom of the seas" doctrine [in 1918] until it was too late to insist upon it; and, although from some points of view it was the most practical and important of all the Fourteen Points, we were obliged to withdraw it in order to secure an armistice otherwise based upon American principles.

What could have been done for naval disarmament quite easily in the early part of 1918, could not be done in November of that year; and much less could it be done in the peace-making Conference at Paris. President Wilson came home with a fixed determination that if the United States was not to promote the cause of disarmament and peace through the mutual guarantees of a League of Nations, we would have to proceed to support our principles, as well as to defend our interests, by creating as rapidly as possible a navy that should be not merely *one* of the strongest, but decidedly the most powerful in the world.

This demand of the Wilson Administration upon Congress and the country was made at a time when the British Government was proclaiming, with equal earnestness and determination, the continued and permanent policy of supremacy for the British fleet. Up to that time, the British Government had not wavered in its purpose to build ships in maintenance of its two-power policy. That is to say, the British navy must either be twice as powerful as the navy next in rank, or else at least as powerful as the second and third navies combined.

The Japanese, furthermore — having by virtue of circumstances been enabled to increase their financial resources, their military and naval power, and their hold upon Eastern Asia during the war period — were now entering upon a policy of naval expansion that was intended to make them decidedly stronger in the Pacific (taking into account their strategic locations) than any other power. Their naval strength would probably in the future have been concentrated in a type of marine monster beyond the present capacity of the Panama Canal, so that the United States would not have been able in case of trouble to bring super-dreadnoughts from the Atlantic Fleet to the aid of our ships in the Pacific.

British interests in Asia were so complicated that the Japanese felt secure in the belief that Great Britain would be obliged to renew the Anglo-Japanese Alliance. While this alliance would probably not have brought the British fleet into direct action against the United States if we had been engaged in war with Japan, it was evident enough that, with the alliance maintained and renewed, the danger of strife in the Pacific would be increased rather than diminished—unless, indeed, the United States should practically abandon what had hitherto been regarded as American interests and American responsibilities in the Pacific and Far East.

Such were the situations that our Government was facing last year; and Secretary Daniels, with President Wilson's approval, did not hesitate to ask Congress to support a ship-building program that would in due time have made the American navy stronger than the British, while leaving Japan far in the rear. It was admitted everywhere that, in a competition for naval prestige and power, the United States was foremost in command of money, materials, shipyards, and labor, and could soon take first rank.

All other interested governments were anxiously studying the signs at Washington to see if the proposed naval policy would have Republican as well as Democratic support. It soon became apparent that foreign policy as directed by President Harding and Secretary Hughes was of a most friendly and pacific quality, but that it was even more firm and more definite than had been the foreign policies of the Wilson Administration during its last year. The Republican Administration was very anxious to reduce public expenditures. It had no desire to participate in a competitive armament race. It was willing, however, to spend as much money as might be found necessary to defend the peace of the United States and to protect American interests.

The Republican Administration saw only two ways to keep the United States secure from being dragged into war. One was an international agreement to stop competitive arming, which also provided for settling questions in dispute; and the other was to make such abundant preparation in advance that no nation under any pretext would involve itself in war with us without having been willing to try all possible methods of peaceful settlement of disputes. It is necessary to have in mind these considerations in order to understand the difficulties and dangers that confronted governments when President Harding invited Great Britain and Japan to study the international problems of the Far East and the Pacific. It was a happy decision at Washington to give the Conference a broader character by inviting France and Italy to participate, with China as vitally concerned, and with Holland and Belgium not merely as having colonial interests, but also as representing highly civilized members of the family of nations not engaged in naval competition and deeply interested in peace by agreement.

There are times when to yield is to conquer. Judged by the highest tests of statesmanship and diplomacy, Great Britain won enduring praise for herself, and made an almost measureless contribution to the future harmonizing of the world, when she abandoned the position she has held since the days of Queen Elizabeth, and cordially adopted the proposal that the American navy should be as strong as the British. The people of the British Islands, and those of the British Dominions, have made no mistake in accepting this profound change in their naval policy.

Mr. Balfour, as head of the British delegation, in endorsing the Hughes program at the second open session of the Conference, painted an eloquent picture of the British Empire, with its dependence upon ocean transportation and its defensive needs. It is a high order of statesmanship that is able to look all the facts in the face and to make a decision that might seem to involve a sacrifice, whether of power or of prestige. As a matter of fact, this decision will bring to the British people and their associated countries a succession of substantial benefits.

Where competition ends, cooperation almost inevitably begins. If Secretary Hughes had proclaimed the end of naval warfare and the internationalization of the high seas, he would have been regarded as a visionary and a doctrinaire, and he would have failed. The burden of naval supremacy was too great henceforth for the British, and it would have been in many ways most unfortunate for us if we had felt ourselves compelled to assume that burden. However, for the American and British governments to accept the principle of naval equality is equivalent to declaring before the whole world that Great Britain and the United States, in further development of the principles of 1814, are not going to make war upon one another, either in the present century or in those to follow.

Gradually this Anglo-American accord will be made the basis of an association for the regulation of maritime affairs, with a still further limitation of naval armaments. The United States abandoned a prospective position of naval leadership, and the British in turn abandoned an actual leadership, having behind it the tradition and the experience of centuries.

The British Government, fully supporting its delegates at Washington, acted in accordance with the clear sentiment of the British people, as expressed in many ways, notably through the brilliant work of the Conference correspondents of British newspapers, and through the strong endorsement of British editors at home, regardless of political partisanship. At no other point had British national opinion been so sensitive as at this one point of naval policy. To accept whole-heartedly the doctrine that Uncle Sam's navy is to be as strong as John Bull's navy is for the British people to say that the fundamental dogma in their new creed is that of harmony and cooperation with the people of the United States. They believe that the American people will be just, generous and gallant in all real emergencies.

There is no intention whatever on the part of either of these two governments to try to get the better of the other in the development of new forms of naval equipment. It may be true that battleships are becoming obsolete, and that vessels equipped to carry bombing airplanes are to be regarded by the technical authorities as henceforth more important. But neither of the two governments has any notion of taking advantage of the other through the development of new kinds of machinery for wielding sea power. Their intentions are pacific and cooperative. They will unite to make naval holidays permanent.

My readers should understand that the foregoing pages, written by me in January 1922 at the conclusion of the Conference, are not here reprinted merely in assertion of personal views, or to justify my own interpretations and forecasts. As it happens, the views I set forth at that time are not only in accord with what has happened in the further development of Anglo-American relations, but they expound the logical basis upon which the navies of the two countries might henceforth act together. Without danger of serious friction, they could unitedly assert the lawful doctrine of the freedom of the seas, as common rights were challenged by Germans in the Atlantic, and by Japanese in the Pacific.

As regards Mr. Balfour personally, his services at Washington should now be recalled, because of their exhibition of high statesmanship. (1) His agreement with Mr. Hughes regarding naval limitations has had far-reaching effects. (2) It is to his credit that he made so strong and persistent an effort to secure the total abolition of the submarine as a naval type. He would have succeeded, but for the undeviating insistence of the French delegates, who regarded their country's interests as otherwise neglected and imperilled. It may be remarked, however, that without some international organization to assure an effective enforcement of treaties, the aggressive nations would not have hesitated to disregard agreements, and the Battle of the Atlantic would perhaps not have been averted.

The termination of the Anglo-Japanese Alliance in 1922 was an international event of the utmost consequence. For more than twenty years Mr. Balfour had given constant attention to the complexities of Far Eastern politics. More than any other British statesman, he had favored and upheld the alliance with Japan. He had believed that the security of the British Empire lay in encouraging rather than opposing Japanese enterprises and policies. But the statesmen of Australia, New Zealand, South Africa and Canada were now opposing a renewal of the alliance with Japan for another ten-year period.

As originally formed in 1902, the alliance would have drawn the British Navy into war against the United States, if Japan had launched an attack upon this country. With the alliance terms afterwards modified, Great Britain would have stood upon the sidelines as a benevolent neutral, in the case of an assault upon our West Coast that most Far East experts regarded as probable.

Even in face of that prospect, Mr. Balfour was reluctant to annul the Treaty. He yielded, only to the more far-reaching views of American and Dominion statesmen, still hoping somehow to make Japan reasonably happy in Anglo-American company. The Japanese would not, however, have reciprocated Balfour's good-will, and might even have struck at Singapore before they made their attack upon Pearl Harbor. The correspondence between Mr. Balfour and Sir Charles Eliot, who was then British Ambassador at Tokyo, throws much light upon conditions that were affected by the treaties relating to the Far East, as they were adopted at Washington after three months of most careful study, under the joint leadership of Mr. Hughes and Mr. Balfour, who reached agreements upon every critical subject.

The following chapter makes departure from the general plan of this book, because it ventures into the field of international proposals for the future. Yet I think it is justified as a logical sequel to my account of the Washington Conference; and it is offered as a contribution to one phase of the still nebulous program for a future of global understanding and secure peace.

CHAPTER XVII

SHALL WE CREATE A GOVERNMENT OF SEAS AND ISLANDS?

"Freedom of the seas" is a phrase that expresses a doctrine of international law, but does not attach itself to any method or system ever yet devised for giving the doctrine reality in practice. At different times in the past particular nations have asserted authority over one area or another of the indivisible oceans, but the principle of *mare clausum* was long ago discarded and its particular applications were nullified. The indivisible seas are not susceptible of lawful control by any national sovereignty.

British naval and maritime authorities, assuming that President Wilson had in mind a collective or international arrangement for securing freedom of the seas, accepted the Fourteen Points with reservations as regards that one proposal, although they did not deny the abstract doctrine. Mr. Wilson returned from Paris to advocate a predominant American navy. There followed in the first year of the next administration the Washington Naval Conference, that fixed ratios on the principle of Anglo-American equality. This did not meet the fundamental problem, but in removing certain obstacles it prepared the way for a logical solution.

At the end of the present war (if the United Nations prevail) the United States and Great Britain will have great superiority in naval power, probably also in air power. But they will not take upon themselves the burden of permanent sea patrol in order to make the oceans secure for all the world.

In the present chapter I have proposed that a true government of the seas should be provided, with an appropriate constituency of maritime nations, and that it should be given sovereign powers. It would act upon its own initiative in such a way as to relieve all other governments of the necessity of maintaining navies.

When the mandated archipelagoes of the Pacific are taken from Japanese control, they will have to come under permanent international oversight. It is suggested in this chapter that the proposed Government of the Seas should also be entrusted with the control of these archipelagoes. From time to time other islands or strategic points, as this sovereignty of the seven seas gives evidence of its capacity, could be assigned to its jurisdiction, and it could pay its way with a revenue derived from a small tax upon insular commerce, after it had lived through initial stages.

IN wartime, throughout the ages, treaties have been cast aside, and constitutions and laws have been suspended. The god of battle takes control, and the nations submit either willingly or under duress. Three things seem possible, looking to the dawn of peace, as temperaments and habits of mind affect different groups.

First is the group who fear that democratic liberties will not be recovered. Second are those who see visions and believe that nations and peoples will start afresh. They hope to achieve the Four Freedoms of President Roosevelt, with the annexed freedoms of Vice-President Wallace. They hail the opportunity to throw off the shackles of an unequal and conservative past. Third are those others, most numerous perhaps, who are determined not only to resist change, but to lay hold upon what they once had and to yield nothing of the old landmarks.

There is some reasonableness in each of these three standpoints. Individual liberty and democratic freedom will have to fight back against governmental autocracy and regimentations. Forward-looking men are right in resolving that a better world must emerge from the horrors and sufferings of the war. Those who still value traditions and past achievements are also justified in holding that a brand new world is not going to be brought to the Garden-of-Eden stage in some new seven-day miracle of transformation.

We should indeed be in a sorry plight if we did not think our civilization was worth salvaging. Also we should be unhappy pessimists if we did not realize that to save it we must vastly improve it. Foundations have been laid in the past, and the purpose of the war is to keep them and to better the super-structure. These, however, are mere generalities of little pertinence unless we propose to give them concrete meaning. The object of this chapter is to apply them to the naval conditions that now exist, and those that may confront us when we reach the end of the war.

If the United Nations hold to their avowed purpose, the defeat of Germany will remove forever the submarine menace from Atlantic and European waters. Japan's conceptions have been much bolder, more far-reaching, believably more dangerous, than those of the German militarists and their accepted expositor Herr Hitler. But Japan's vast empire can be held together only by sea-power, accompanied by superiority in the air.

There have been differences of view about the fundamentals

of American strategy as applied to the war in the Pacific. No American is to be denied the right to have opinions upon a matter of such vital consequence. But questions of strategy do not touch principles, and these are not in dispute. The supremacy of Japanese sea-power in the Pacific would disturb the peace and welfare not merely of a few nations but of all peoples in both hemispheres, as well as those in island homes from the Aleutians to the Antipodes. We must assume that the United Nations will succeed in breaking Japanese control over peoples who do not welcome it. Full support of China will hasten the day of liberation; but this fact also is obvious and not in dispute.

One thing, however, can be said without hesitation. It is this: The more clearly we face the possible alternatives, as we contemplate conditions to be met after Japan's supremacy collapses, the better qualified we shall be to accomplish the main object. Our own maritime strength has been widely scattered, while that of Japan in the years 1942–3 has been concentrated, and directed with superior strategy. This is not said to discredit our own efforts or achievements. We have not been a nation relying mainly upon sea-power or foreign trade. Speaking relatively, our maritime strength was at the maximum a hundred and thirty years ago as we finished the naval war of 1812. Japan as an island empire has dreamt by night of naval supremacy in the Pacific, and has worked by day to make the dreams come true, and this for half a century or more.

For a long time without realizing the danger of such a course, we were encouraging Japan's ambitions and assisting them in material ways, while neglecting our own defenses on the Western Coast. Just as England and France underestimated the strength and persistence of Germany's motives, we in America failed to understand the depth and scope of Japanese ambitions, and also Japan's capacity to carry out her amazing program.

The democracies should have been sufficiently warned; for the danger signals were numerous and alarming. Yet Japan, for all her advantages at the outset will soon have lost the initiative. Her sea-power will be reduced to inferiority by attrition. Her ill-gotten gains of empire will fall apart like ropes of sand, because they can be held together only by ships and aircraft. There will be no strong navies at the end of the present war, except those of the United States and Great Britain. These will have been developed to meet exigencies as they arise, and will have acted in cooperation to support the common cause.

In the United States there is a prevailing public opinion in favor of what has been called a "policing" of the world by the United Nations, organized in some fashion to meet the earlier American conception of a so-called "League to Enforce Peace." It is to be remarked, however, that democratic nations will police themselves; and that the more immediate question to be answered has to do with the seas and their control. During the present war, for the first time, there is whole-hearted acceptance of the doctrine that the seas are a common possession, and must henceforth be so regarded in practice no less than in theory.

Navigation of the air has had a compelling part in giving world-wide character to the present war; but its most important effect—already recognized—is in the realm of the human mind. School-books have taught children that the earth is round; but the average person, while preferring not to contradict the circumnavigators, has never really believed it. The maps have projected the continents and separate countries as parts of a flat world. The oceans have been treated as separate bodies of water, also flat and level, except as disturbed by tides and rippling waves. The navigators of the sixteenth century compelled the heads of church and state to accept the dictum that the earth is round and revolves about the sun, but that belief made its way slowly among common men.

It has taken the airplane, as it roars over sea and land in the terrific crisis of the Second World War, to change popular conceptions of geography. The seas as well as the lands are the theatre of this universal conflict. The atmosphere is an unbroken medium surrounding the globe. Long-distance air routes do not have to follow sea lanes. Alaska and Greenland become important for long-flight purposes. The new study of geography requires the use of terrestrial globes for the comprehension of a war that has established an important American base in Australia, half-way around the world.

II.

It is not only this new conception of the facts of physical geography that affects the minds of people in all continents. Above all, it is the bearing of physical and economic facts upon post-war relationships, among the peoples of different races and nations, that is the subject of anxious concern. Mr. Wendell L. Willkie—with a mind open to new impressions—made a tour which took him to the Middle East, to Russia, to Central Asia and China, and came home to write a book under the title "One World." He returned with a message to America from the peoples of the East. This was a much more comprehensive message than that which came from Japan to America in 1915. Japan had intended to dominate Asia and the islands of the Pacific, for the good of all concerned. But the great peoples of Continental Asia now wish to govern themselves. They have no intention to be controlled from without, whether by the autocratic power of Japan or by the benevolent and patronizing intervention of the British Empire aided by the United States.

The peoples of the East, says Mr. Willkie, "want us to join them in creating a new society of independent nations, free alike of the economic injustices of the West and the political malpractices of the East." Mr. Willkie writes with the fervor of a man who has heard voices and has had a revelation like that of the Apostle Paul. He comes forward as a champion of the whole human race. It is simply a part of his feeling that we now live in "One World," and that we are bound to do something about it. Mr. Willkie ends his book with these sentences:

> Our allies in the East know that we intend to pour out our resources in this war. But they expect us now—not after the war—to use the enormous power of our giving to promote liberty and justice. Other peoples, not yet fighting, are waiting no less eagerly for us to accept the most challenging opportunity of all history—the chance to help create a new society in which men and women the world around can live and grow invigorated by independence and freedom.

For convenience, we continue to use old names for particular parts of the indivisible ocean that covers about seventy-two per cent (practically three-quarters) of the surface of the globe. If the nations who occupy the twenty-eight per cent—that of the land areas—will govern themselves on democratic principles with economic freedom and doors open to world trade, they will not desire to take by force anything that does not belong to them, or to quarrel with their neighbors. They can and will unite upon methods for keeping the peace along their borders. But the vast expanse of salt water which has hitherto been without a government can no longer remain in that condition.

Obviously, the code of maritime international law must be rewritten and greatly developed to meet new conditions. It must be universally accepted, because the high seas do not belong for purposes of domination to countries that happen to have large navies. When President Wilson first announced his so-called "Fourteen Points" as a platform of principles upon which to end the First World War and to establish a lasting peace, he cleared the way (in his first clause) by demanding open and honest diplomacy and condemning hidden understandings between nations. His second point was phrased as follows:

"Absolute freedom of navigation upon the seas, outside territorial waters, alike in peace and in war, except as the seas may be closed in whole or in part by international action for the enforcement of international covenants."

Mr. Wilson had in mind an international system for regulating all that related to the use of the seas. Attempts had been made to codify maritime international law, but nothing of the kind had been adopted before war occurred in 1914. The British government, for its own reasons, would not promise in 1914 to act in accordance with the terms of the Declaration of London which had provided the main outlines of such a code. Also, at the end of the war the Armistice terms had been modified by the Allies, and Wilson's proposal that the oceans be brought under international control—which would have meant the end of naval warfare—was not included as part of the armistice agreement.

At the end of the present war a certain state of facts will have resulted, if the United Nations hold to the principles of the Atlantic Charter and their compact of January 1942. Germany and Italy will be left without their U-boats and their armed surface ships. The remnants of the French fleet will be small. British naval and air power will be in control of the Mediterranean, and Russia will command the Black Sea and its outlets to the Mediterranean. As regards the broad oceans, it is probable that the British and American fleets will so greatly predominate that for a time they will have to accept the responsibility for securing to all nations the freedom that President Wilson contemplated.

But this arrangement could only be temporary. Mr. Willkie would agree that the human race must control its own oceans, outside of territorial coast-line limits. What kind of international plan could be devised for setting up what I prefer to call a *government of the seas?* In discussing that subject I shall proceed by a method of exclusion.

First, I would exclude the idea of a kind of "police" or "patrol" system, relying principally upon Anglo-American sea-power under mandate from the United Nations, and subsidized by proportionate contributions. The one enduring and triumphant achievement of the Washington Conference (about which I have written at length in the preceding chapter) was the plan that ended naval competition between Great Britain and the United States, and that prepared the way for full cooperation. This was a forward-looking agreement that has served well its deeper purpose. It was in fact a preparatory step, in anticipation of the world war that was to begin with the rise of the Nazis and the encroachments of Japan. However, that scaffolding has no place in the architecture of a permanent project for ocean control. There will be no further suggestion of security at sea by virtue of an arrangement for assigning tonnage quotas to different national governments.

During the years of friction over relative types of cruisers, and over tonnage of destroyers and submarines, I entertained certain ideas that I ventured to discuss from time to time with different Englishmen who held positions of influence. I suggested that the sea-faring powers hold a conference to complete a code of maritime law. Upon their adoption of the code, it was my further proposal that the British Navy should undertake the policing of the seas, while all other navies—including the American and Japanese—should be completely withdrawn and scrapped. This idea made exception of vessels needed for revenue and coast-guard purposes, and also of ships that might be required to round out the British fleet for its new purposes.

A suitably constituted advisory board, appointed by international agreement, was a detail of the plan; and the British fleet would perform its duties in accord with provisions of the maritime code, which would be revised at stated periods. This plan, of course, contemplated the complete abolition of naval warfare. The British fleet (adjusted from time to time to the needs of a maritime police service, as might be disclosed by experience) would not burden the British Exchequer, because the cost of maintenance and operation would be apportioned upon equitable principles among the commercial and sea-faring nations.

It is true that I never gave wide publicity to the foregoing proposal. I had attended the Washington Conference, and was acquainted with many political and naval officials who were (either openly or behind the scenes) endeavoring to extend to lesser naval types the ratio agreed upon for capital ships. The British experts haggled, as if the United States had been a recent enemy or was likely to become one in the near future. They even objected to a change of gun-levels in the reconditioning of old American cruisers.

Throughout the world they stood on guard at their posts of duty. With their loyal, obdurate, inelastic minds, these splendid men had been trained from early youth to believe that every advance of the British Empire must be held immutably. To that end they had pledged their lives and their sacred honor. They could not adapt their thinking to the principle that "the greater includes the less." Lord Balfour, whose philosophic mind could grasp broad conceptions, knew that the Washington agreement meant mutual helpfulness. The minutiae of adjustment, that worried the naval experts for another decade, meant nothing at all to men like Balfour and Hughes, or to Hoover and Ramsay MacDonald. Neither could such technical details signify much to men like Admiral Sims and Admiral Rodman, who knew that we had nothing to fear from the minor adaptations of the British Navy to meet its supposed needs at remote places.

What they could see was that France—reduced to the low point in capital ships — was determined to perpetuate the submarine monstrosity. Also, they could see that Japan was improving the opportunity to gain each year in relative naval strength, improving her shipyards and preparing to repudiate the 5-5-3 ratio. They could see, also, that the Germans, under cover, were preparing to dominate the Atlantic by outbuilding the French submarine fleet, five to one.

In all my talks with Englishmen on the dangers that were looming up before us—with no plan whatsoever for the security of sea-borne commerce, or for protection against the use of the seas by nations preparing to adopt the black flag of piracy—I never found one who would entertain for a moment the plan that I proposed. Nor could I find one who would suggest any alternative arrangement.

They were always polite, but tight-lipped and evidently somewhat disturbed in their minds. They had never accepted the idea that Britannia was not henceforth to rule the waves. They thought that American equality was a myth—a form of words with nothing behind it. They did not call me impertinent, but in their manner there was something that implied resentment. Like just so many Casabiancas on their burning decks, with an Empire at stake, they could be faithful unto death. They would hearken to no siren call, bidding them to leave their posts.

British backbone is an indispensable asset; but doggedness and self-reliance on the part of one nation will not solve the problems of an anxious world. President Wilson had a more intelligent outlook than British or French leaders twenty-five years ago, and also a more disinterested one by far. But he could not gain acceptance for his principles in Europe, and there was no quality visible in the United States that resembled British stubbornness or backbone, to uphold American standpoints.

The third world war will not be far below the horizon if American principles are compromised again, as they were in 1918–19. Realizing the failure of his proposals for world control of the seas, Mr. Wilson came back from Paris to advocate the plan of American naval superiority. This was partly for our own security, but chiefly to uphold ideals of world peace. In this chapter, however, I am dealing solely with what is to be the key problem, namely, the *government of the seas*. Because we have needed warships, and have been better able to build them than any other of the United Nations, it is probable that our navy at the beginning of 1944 will be stronger in most categories than any other, whether friend or foe. But who would think of such an accident of circumstances as a continuing arrangement, suited to our own future needs, or to those of the world at large?

At the end of the present war the nations of America and Asia (including Russia) will be looking forward to an immense increase of sea-going commerce. Great Britain also entertains such hopes, but is too close to the desperate plight of all the nations of continental Europe to be greatly cheered by bouyant expectations. It must be plain to all thoughtful persons, and therefore to be assumed without argument, that the English-speaking world regards itself as committed to a program of complete and generous cooperation. This program had made substantial beginnings before Pearl Harbor. It had risen to a stage suggestive of tentative federation in 1942–3. That there shall be Anglo-American mutuality of helpfulness, rather than obstructive economic rivalry in times to come, is the purpose of enlightened men and women.

III.

This will demand free and unmolested use of the seas; but any plan envisaging permanent control of the world's waterways and the atmosphere above them by an Anglo-American affiliation, would look backward rather than forward. People numbering 200,000,000 in widely scattered domains will not set up the rule of the seas that belongs to 2,000,000,000 people having equality of right and interest.

Neither can the seas be ruled henceforth by an international agreement regulating the size of navies. Any national sovereign on the high seas is but a private person. Where law and order prevail, private persons do not go about carrying weapons whether exposed or concealed. Nations, as such, should not be allowed to go armed at sea. The Washington Conference system, apart from its effect upon the rivalry of the two foremost naval powers, was chiefly valuable for the demonstration it gave of the complete futility of a plan that left the high seas without any government or control, while it told particular nations that they must not use their own judgments in deciding upon the amount and character of their armed strength outside of their own jurisdictions.

Disarmament on land does not imply the abolition of local, state, and national police forces. Neither does disarmament at sea imply the absence of a system for maintaining peace and order. But such a system will not be derived either logically or equitably from the circumstance that certain commercial countries now have large navies, while others have not. Norwegian shipping has the same right of security as British, and the same thing can be said of other flags at sea, including the Greek and the Italian. Protection at sea will have to be a joint enterprise. Furthermore, it will have to take the form of a positive government, regulating the use of the oceans not in any arbitrary or tyrannical way, but with no object whatsoever except to secure order and freedom.

There are many thoughtful persons, believing in the necessity of world organization, who are inclined to think that the League of Nations affords the best starting-point. They would change the character of the League in important ways, transferring to it all armaments alike of defeated and victorious nations. I will not comment at this point upon the problems of a league or a superstate. I will seek, rather, to mark a distinction that has not been kept sufficiently in mind by authors of certain proposals for world government. Concrete statements are more readily understood than those that are couched in abstract or logical terms, and the American mind will instinctively inquire how we are to be affected in the every-day sense.

Let us begin, then, with the Western Hemisphere and its peoples. These self-governing nations are not only endeavoring to live on terms of friendship with one another, but are trying to settle every question that arises between them on principles of amity and justice. If democratic concepts were alike prevalent in the Eastern Hemisphere, the Americas might live at peace without feeling the need of a so-called world government. But our republics would all agree that while they can control their relations with one another, they cannot exercise any form of jurisdiction over the seas. They cannot say that European submarines shall not interfere with their secure use of the Caribbean and the ocean lanes between North and South America. The Monroe Doctrine does not bear upon such questions.

Those writers who would rebuild the League of Nations and confer upon it the power to enforce peace, do not refer to the ungoverned and indivisible seas as a distinct subject. I have never supposed for a moment that Geneva would be abandoned as a focus of world opinion. I am confident that it will be maintained as a clearing-house for many matters of common concern—especially matters affecting the peoples of Europe. I should not be easily convinced, however, that the Geneva society of nations could be made to function effectively as a legislative and executive body capable of exercising control over the seas.

Temporary control was changing month by month in 1943, as one belligerent group or the other gained or retained superiority. The Allied Nations were recovering control of the Mediterranean, while the Battle of the Atlantic was still raging as the German submarines hunted down Allied shipping in ferocious "wolf-packs." Japan was still in virtually unassailed control of the Western Pacific. With undaunted purpose the United Nations were struggling to gain mastery of all the seas. Once gained, they would not relinquish it immediately to a League of Nations in which Japan and Germany were to have equal place, as some authorities have recommended on grounds of logical consistency.

I shall not proceed further by the rule of exclusion. It would seem necessary to think of sea power as a distinct problem, and to regard the oceans as requiring a government of their own. Even if the power of Germany were broken in the near future and the Atlantic ocean were made relatively safe, the war on the Pacific would still have to be fought to a finish.

The supreme struggle against Japan for superiority on the sea and in the skies above the expanses of ocean would require all the resources of the United Nations; and without the help of Russia the Anglo-American combination would encounter many disadvantages, and meet with unwelcome surprises, before achieving the victory that awaits them. It will be fortunate for the United States and Great Britain, and for the stability of trans-Pacific conditions, if that victory is fully recognized, when it comes, as due to the indispensable cooperation of Russia and China.

The colonial system as expanded twenty-five years ago by the bargaining process of "mandates," has had more or less to do with those incitements that gave the present war its world-wide character. To understand and accept this fact is not to condone German or Japanese aggressions. The British, French, and Dutch colonial administrations were the very acme of benevolence and good government when compared with the programs and methods of Germany and Japan. Already they have been enslaving both civilized and semi-civilized peoples.

But it will not be a felicitous outcome of the current struggle if the victory of the United Nations is regarded by any large element of world opinion as intended to perpetuate colonialism. Systems of protectorates, crown colonies, dependencies and satellite states pertaining to individual European countries, whether England, France, Holland or Belgium, will have to be reconstructed. Certainly the American people would not be so reckless as to demand the liquidation of those systems through sacrifice of private rights when avoidable, or through ill-considered transfers of political authority. At best, there will be careful transitions. At worst, there will be unblushing reversion to imperialism, or an outburst of misguided and bloody revolution, such as that of Haiti at the end of the eighteenth century. American Abolitionists gloried in Haiti's realistic adoption of the principles of the French revolution. But that impoverished island was in the hands of blood-thirsty tyrants for much of the nineteenth century, and their rule was tempered only by assassination.

It has been said with some truth by political authorities in Washington and London that post-war details cannot be submitted to public opinion in advance of victory. It is well known, however, that exiled rulers have been occupying themselves with these questions, and it is natural that they should not think in terms of abdication or relinquishment. Who would say that they do not deserve both sympathy for the present plight of their peoples and also a hearing for what they seek to regain? I am not arguing against their plans that contemplate recovery of possessions in distant seas, when their freedom at home is first assured. It is merely suggested that, without any real loss, their colonial interests might be merged under some larger formula.

IV.

For, it should now be admitted, when I have referred to the need of a government for the oceans I have had in mind something much more extensive and complicated than control of navigation, with the suppression of separate and competing navies. These objects alone would, indeed, justify a distinct international administration. But, to be concrete rather than to generalize, we must ask ourselves what is to become of the island archipelagoes north of the equator that were assigned to Japan under the mandate project agreed upon at Paris in 1919?

Some of these vast groups of coral islands had been previously acquired by Germany, as that country was casting about so feverishly for an empire in rivalry with England's. Japan was under pledges not to fortify those mandated islands, and the League of Nations was charged with the duty of seeing that they were not fortified, and that they were kept open to all nations on equal terms for trade and intercourse.

But the Japanese violated all these conditions, and the League of Nations was without means of enforcing them, even if it had shown much concern. The most ingenious and extensive system of naval bases and air bases ever devised or contemplated has been established there by the Japanese. Those islands dot the

Pacific for thousands of miles, and they are held in dastardly and treacherous defiance of the civilized world. When the United Nations at length have gained naval and air superiority in the Pacific, Japanese control will wither and die like the leaves and branches of a tree after the trunk is girdled.

These islands will never be returned to the custody of Japan. They will not become American, British, Chinese or Russian. Neither will any authority centered at Geneva be capable of giving them the oversight that their scattered native populations and their commerce will require. It is not, then, a government of the seas alone that seems to be required, but an administration of the affairs of the common seas that will at the same time exercise authority, in the joint interest of all nations, over these archipelagoes recovered from Japan. But should it not also have supervision over various other groups, or insular areas, where self-government in the larger sense cannot be established?

The war is global; and victory on the side of the United Nations will not be divisible by percentages, whether in honorable mention or in distribution of awards. At present under international law most of Europe belongs to Germany by right of conquest and occupation. The Philippines, Malaya, Java and Sumatra, and much else in the Pacific, belong to Japan by the same title of conquest and retention. If the Japanese Empire goes down in defeat, the reconquered colonial entities will belong by right of conquest to the United Nations. Previous titles will have validity only as the United Nations choose to recognize them.

Might it not be better for Holland if the United Nations should not only expel Japan from the Dutch Indies but continue to give them security, while also controlling certain external relationships? Such questions might also be asked regarding mandated areas that were assigned to Australia and New Zealand. These inquiries look to the long future, and relate to the larger aspects of security. Internal administration might well be kept distinct (in the Dutch Indies, for instance) from external relations. It might be objected that such a plan as I am outlining would be difficult to round out, to organize, and to put into effect. This would be admitted without argument, but with the passing remark that to carry on a world war involves difficulties at least a thousand times greater.

The fatal defect of the settlements at Paris in 1919 lay in the fact that the real difficulties were not squarely faced. The Allied governments seemed to be sacrificing the larger good for unsatisfying messes of pottage. The victory that made possible this short-sighted policy was not won by England or France or the United States, but by joint efforts. After Russia withdrew and made a separate peace, the United States intervened to turn the scales. If the Germans had won they would not only have kept their former colonies but would have controlled all of Africa, from Suez to Cape Colony. American intervention alone prevented that result.

The mandate system was not the product of statesmanlike consideration at Paris in 1919. It was in consequence of a series of secret treaties that had been made early in the European war, chiefly by Czarist Russia, France and Great Britain. This network of secret compacts was extended later, to provide inducements by virtue of which these Allies were able to outbid Germany in the diplomatic contest for Italy's support. South Africa was reluctant to enter the war, but consented by reason of the arrangement made by Generals Smuts and Botha in accordance with which the Union of South Africa was to acquire and keep the large adjacent area of German Southwest Africa.

Japan became a belligerent with alacrity, on the assurance of her British ally that she could take and hold that part of the Chinese province of Shantung that the Germans had acquired by lease in 1898. Also Japan was given a free hand in driving the Germans from archipelagoes north of the equator, an exploit afterwards confirmed by League of Nations mandate. These things had been arranged before the United States entered the war, and without official report to our government. They became known to the world only when the Second Russian Revolution gave power to Lenin and his party. Having made peace with Germany, they published the secret agreements—as they happened to find them when they overhauled the archives of the late Czarist government.

It was in the opening weeks of 1918, when we had been in the war eight months, that the nature of these commitments became generally known in the United States. Mr. Balfour's war mission had been in Washington for some time, and had returned to England. It was afterwards asserted that Mr. Balfour had made President Wilson fully conversant with these plans for distributing German and Turkish domains. However, in an extended conversation with President Wilson, in which he talked to me with the frankness of long-time private friendship, he assured me that he had not been so informed by Mr. Balfour. In view of the complete change of conditions, with Russia out and America in the war, I urged Mr. Wilson to consult the British ambassador without publicity, and suggest the immediate abrogation of those agreements by consent of the Allied governments.

We were then sending 300,000 men each month to France. The war was to turn upon our reinforcement of the French and British armies. The Germans were transferring great forces from the Russian to the Western front. A request from Mr. Wilson at that time could not have been refused. In the early weeks of 1918 the secret treaties had no value in the world market. They could be cleared away in forty-eight hours, if weighed against the need of American war support. Mr. Wilson's denunciation of those secret treaties was in language so unrestrained that it would violate confidence to quote his remarks, although I remember them well. Theodore Roosevelt in like circumstances would have acted without hesitation, and the British authorities with French concurrence would assuredly have agreed without demur, knowing that the compacts had lost validity through a complete change in the circumstances that had given rise to them.

Those circumstances, fairly considered in their sequences, were understandable in view of the history of European alliances. But all American parents, like myself, were entitled to know what kind of a victory their sons were helping to win. The bargain pledges had indeed lost value in January 1918, but they might gain high levels in the peace-making market, when the Germans were disarmed at the end of the year. Mr. Wilson was angry, but could not take the bull by the horns. Such bold informality was repugnant to his sense of good manners. He went to Paris and found these agreements dominating the methods of territorial readjustment.

It would be purely speculative to insist that abrogation of the treaties would greatly have affected results at Paris. Claims would have been revived and probably allowed. The mandates did not result in changes for the worse, as regards the inhabitants of most of the mandated areas. (The foregoing remark does not refer to Japan, but to the German, Austrian and Turkish Empires). Germany in defeat could not expect rewards, and was not leniently treated. Turkey was the better for relief from out-moded suzerainties.

I am indulging in reflection, rather than in argument or criticism. Mr. Wilson and the American delegates were not well satisfied with the treaty arrangements as a whole, but their efforts had not been futile. The President was relying upon the League of Nations to rectify injustices or errors of judgment, as these should become manifest.

But the League of Nations was so constructed that its momentum tended to support rather than to correct mistakes. The world had arrived at a certain stage of human experience, but it had not reached the goal of secure peace. It is time, learning from the past, to find better ways to adapt means to ends. There is nothing sinister in the expressed designs of any member of the group of United Nations now fighting for liberty, justice, and escape from war. Nothing in these pages has any purpose except that of laying emphasis upon the word " united," when we refer to the contest now raging, and to the bewildering problems that must follow victory.

V.

It is hard to persuade men to entertain the idea that peace is anything more than the temporary absence of war. Peace is so valuable that to lose it through neglect after it is won is merely to show us the dangers of nationalistic rivalry. The government of the seas and of island groups, together with the control of such other matters of *common concern* as are affected with a maritime interest, should exist in its own right when once established. A code of maritime international law should be so developed in a world conference as to include a Statute providing for such an administration. This statute should be in the nature of a constitution. It should provide for a representative body of the highest character, that would resemble in some respects the British House of Commons. An executive organization should bear the same relation to this assembly that the British Cabinet bears to Parliament.

Such a government as I have in mind would be neither a superstate nor a subsidiary one. It would simply be a sovereignty in its own name and right, like the United States or Russia or Great Britain. It would not borrow its fleet, on a lend-lease plan, from other governments. It would own its ships and airplanes, and employ such naval and aviation personnel as it might find needful through experience of patrol work. Neither should it derive all of its financial support from other sovereignties. It should have its own assets as soon as possible, and its own sources of revenue. A small tax levied upon commerce could be so adjusted as to suffice for the maintenance of the ocean patrol. It would maintain quarantine and health services for the islands under its custody.

This government of the seas would exercise jurisdiction from various regional centers. The British Colonial Office in conjunction with the Admiralty could envisage the set-up of such an administrative mechanism, and furnish preliminary blueprints with ready knowledge and few headaches. If such an administration were organized in reliance upon the support and goodwill of mankind at large, it would apply literally the principles of the Roosevelt-Churchill Charter. It would show some grasp of the conceptions that Mr. Willkie sets forth, with such ardor and freshness of appeal, in the report of his flight of 31,000 miles around the world.

Why should not President Roosevelt and Mr. Churchill, in due time, be ready to make over to the United Nations—as they undertake a government of seas and islands—those insular air bases obtained on a 99-year lease by the United States in exchange for a half a hundred old destroyers? Surviving destroyers, along with the air bases, might be vested in the common enterprise.

Many recent writers in advocating various plans for world government have been on common ground in one proposal that they all regard as fundamental. They hold that nations must yield some of their present sovereign powers to the "federation of mankind." In legal theory this would follow the analogy of a government formed like that of the United States. The suggestion that I have made, however, avoids any such transfer of powers or functions. This is for the reason that the international law doctrine of the Freedom of the Open Sea was well established more than a hundred years ago after long centuries of dispute. It is agreed that no strictly national sovereignty has rights of ocean jurisdiction beyond a coast-line margin.

In his valuable textbook entitled *The Essentials of International Public Law*, Professor Amos R. Hershey, after summarizing the attempts by different nations to maintain authority over portions of the sea, reaches the following conclusion: "It may therefore now be regarded as a universally accepted rule of International Law that the open sea is free for the common use of all nations. Being practically insusceptible of effective occupation, it cannot be appropriated by any sovereignty or subjected to any jurisdiction; being indispensable for free intercourse, more particularly as an international highway, it is free and common to all. It is not so much *res nullius* as *res communis omnium*."

Accepting the foregoing statement as wholly true in its negations, an affirmative doctrine is implied. Nothing in the general theory of the freedom of the seas, or in the many maritime regulations existent by agreement or common consent, would preclude any part of the scheme that I have outlined. Naval disarmament, in any case, would have to come about through the decision of a conference. It would simply carry the policies of the Washington Naval Conference to the logical end of full reduction. It would substitute collective security at sea for rival and uncontrollable navies. There could be no sacrifice of national jurisdiction where none exists, and no loss of sovereignty.

Difficulties are so numerous—some of them so obvious—that I have no thought of listing them or of offering solutions. To many minds, no form of international progress is possible when stated in practical terms. Any endeavor to set up a trustworthy mechanism of maritime government has to face the delicate task of providing for the equitable representation of a world constituency. No one would consider the League of Nations plan, of equal membership by nations great and small. Nor would anyone be likely to propose that membership of such an assembly, responsible for governing the seas and islands, should be in the ratio of populations. China and India should be fairly represented; but if—on the basis of sheer numbers—they were to claim more representation in a world parliament governing the seas than all other commercial nations put together, the plan would die before it was born.

The world will not cease to change; and some parts of it during the next half-century will be more concerned with internal problems than with such questions as the control of the seas. There could, of course, be no lasting kind of authoritative union of nations or peoples if it were not generous in its inception and just in its development. Underlying all such projects must be a high moral sense of human welfare, and freedom from prejudice and narrow localism. We must presuppose those broad understandings that inform what Dr. Butler has always called "the international mind."

I have previously referred to an address at Cleveland in which I elaborated the conception of world citizenship. In this country the same individual could at the same time be an active citizen of his community, of his state, and of the nation. I remember a period when Dr. Butler himself, always with high ideals, was active in the local politics of New York City, in the concerns of New York State, and in all the national affairs of politics and government. He was serving his university, and also speaking throughout the country on behalf of educational progress. All these interests were part of one consistent program. He could also direct the Carnegie Peace Foundation, holding a place in the front rank of so-called internationalists.

In the broad conceptions of a world organized for peace, President Wilson represented the views entertained today by thousands of men in our seats of learning, in the churches, the professions, in every occupation and calling. The important thing in providing for a government of the common seas is to have its personnel composed of men who can think in terms of the higher world citizenship.

Evidently, problems of apportionment will not be solved by any census figures or mathematical formulas. Initial arrangements would be somewhat arbitrary; and compromise would follow as plans became mature. It is only too easy to drift along after a great war, with domestic readjustments throwing one nation after another into political upheavals and economic convulsions. It was while America and the peace-loving world were preoccupied with agricultural depressions, financial crises, droughts, dust storms, booms, panics, and the turmoil of political partisanship (as in France and the United States) that Germany, Italy, and Japan were preparing for their great adventures. It should have been evident that war on a greater scale than ever was approaching, and that it could be only slightly delayed by concessions and appeasements. Yet a disorganized world could not rise to meet the predicament.

To put the seas under the vigilant control of a well-established world authority would go far toward providing a policy of insurance against a third world war. The United States and Great Britain might assume the initiative, and the world might accord them a position of joint leadership in such an undertaking. In creating this safeguard against piracy, men would remember that the merchant ships of all honest nations would have been swept from the seas before the end of the year 1943, if almost superhuman efforts had not been made to replace losses with new construction.

With air as well as water transportation to be considered, some form of active and efficient administration of maritime interests has become imperative, and it will have to be unified and collectively supported. World changes have made this need far more pressing and insistent than in President Wilson's time, or in the decade of controversy over naval ratios. Nothing would be gained by disparaging past efforts to provide security for private and public interests. Their relative failures have served a good purpose in pointing the way toward bolder and more far-reaching programs.

Chapter XVIII

MR. WILSON AND THE LEAGUE OF NATIONS IN RETROSPECT

Since its activities are in abeyance, and it is commonly regarded as defunct, it seems to be a suitable time to deal reminiscently with the League of Nations. What of its origins, its merits in actual experience, and its failure in the sterner tests?

The League was not proposed by Mr. Wilson as an original idea or a scheme of his own invention. It had been widely discussed in the United States for several years before the peace conclave of 1919, especially through the activities of the League to Enforce Peace, of which ex-President Taft was the head.

Mr. Wilson, by reason of the fact that he was President and had turned the war scales in favor of the Allies, had become the most influential personage in the world. He had cherished the ideal of collective security ever since his student days, and he found opportunity to embody that principle first in the Armistice terms and afterwards in the Peace Treaties.

England and France did not espouse the American view, either of war settlement or of peace maintenance. The Covenant of the League, in those articles that concerned its effectiveness for future war prevention, was devised to protect the advantage of the *status quo* for European victors. In brief, the League as constructed was not exactly the League that lay in Wilson's mind. His thought was of a League that could revise the treaties as their faults were exposed, and that could improve its own efficiency from time to time.

It was President Wilson's misfortune that in conducting negotiations at close range through long weeks at Paris he sacrificed much of his European prestige. Furthermore, in his absence from Washington his political influence at home had become seriously impaired. I have relied in this chapter to a considerable extent upon comments that I made at the time in the *Review of Reviews.* I held the view that the realities of our adherence to a League of Nations did not lie in our acceptance or rejection of certain forms of words, but in the recent fact of our military cooperation on a vast scale.

From 1917 until the present time, through almost countless minor acts and through the most conclusive major forms of cooperation in the military sense, we have proved that the United States has been actually a member of a League that undertakes to maintain peace and will help to enforce it as a legal process if necessary.

It was to be regretted that Mr. Wilson's mind at certain times clung so inflexibly to certain forms of words. The reservations insisted upon by a majority of Senators would not have invalidated the Covenant of the League of Nations in any fundamental respect.

The League, however inadequate, came into being as an institution, and the end of the Second World War will undoubtedly find it resuming its functions at Geneva. It may be regarded as certain in advance that the United States will cooperate with it on some terms, from which all misunderstandings will have been cleared away.

THE League of Nations, as became obvious to everyone, could carry on certain useful functions in peace time, but could not of itself exercise restraining power in serious cases of aggression. Thus its prestige began to suffer as skies grew clouded, with Japan seizing Manchuria, with Germany repudiating the Versailles Treaty and flouting the League, and with Italy entering upon the conquest of Ethiopia, seizing Albania and menacing Greece, while both Axis governments trespassed on the rights of the people of Spain. Geneva had become a focus and a store-house of world intelligence, and a laboratory of internationalism. As a peacetime institution, the League of Nations was making a justifiable record.

When the war clouds grew dark, and the gathering storm broke in full fury on September 3, 1939, the League of Nations was neither a place of refuge nor an operative agency. It was no more effective against the hurricane than Mr. Chamberlain's umbrella, of Munich fame. Thus it was assumed, too readily I believe, that the League of Nations was defunct, discredited, and discarded by common consent.

There was published in 1939, immediately after the outbreak of the Second World War, a small but highly authoritative volume on the *Foreign Policy of Great Britain from 1918 to September 1939.* It has a preface by the Rt. Hon. Viscount Halifax, who was Secretary of State for Foreign Affairs at the time, and was about to proceed to Washington as Ambassador to fill the place made vacant by the death of Lord Lothian. Referring to the author of the book, Professor E. H. Carr, Lord Halifax says that he "was for some years a member of the Foreign Office, where he distinguished himself not only by sound learning and political understanding, but also in administrative ability . . . He is an eminently suitable person to survey the history of British foreign policy in recent years."

I think it desirable to quote this endorsement by the Ambassador at Washington because the present chapter will concern itself with the League of Nations, and a trustworthy source of British opinion on that subject has evident value, looking to post-war conditions. Mr. Carr concludes his chapter on the League with the following paragraph:

> The League of Nations is now in eclipse. In the events leading up to the outbreak of War in September 1939, the machinery of the League was not brought into operation, or even seriously thought of. Not a country in the world has allowed its attitude to be influenced in the minutest degree by its membership of the League or by its obligation under the Covenant. The League had proved its worth as a valuable focus of international activities of a social, technical and humanitarian character and as a clearing-house for some minor international disputes. Its revival in some form at the end of the present War seems not improbable. But care will have to be taken not to repeat the mistakes which were committed in 1919 and which led to so rapid and complete a collapse of the great hopes built upon it.

Nations individually and also in collective groups must go forward as they can, impelled by the forces of their history and their experience. Mr. Chamberlain's conciliatory attitude was not craven or unworthy. It was a consequence of previous British policies. Realizing deeply the tragic implications of war, he thought that, with the lapse of twenty years since the Armistice, Germany might well be freed from the restrictions of the Versailles Treaty. He was aware that the League could not act with authority for the simple reason that its machinery had been so devised as to leave Great Britain in the practical position of Europe's arbiter.

Mr. Chamberlain's diplomacy was approved in 1938 by British and American public opinion. The attack upon Poland a year later broke the promise that the German Chancellor had given to the Prime Minister and his French colleagues. They were representing the nations that stood for peace, order, and justice, and in this category the peoples of North and South America were included. When Hitler cast aside that promise with defiance and without pretext, England was inevitably at war, in partnership with France. I was visiting in the British Isles at that time, heard Mr. Chamberlain's voice on September 3, respected his courageous verdict, and realized that we had never in fact escaped from the commitments of our participation in the First World War.

We had set forth in 1917 upon an undertaking that had been

left incomplete, partly through mismanagement but chiefly through confusion of minds, and through the tedious, wayward processes of history. We were living in relative contentment in 1939, believing that our American civilization rested upon an efficient political structure, and above all that its future was assured because of the reliance of a well-disciplined population upon the further growth of the democratic process for the improvement of social conditions. Taking the Western Hemisphere as a whole, there were wide diversities of political and economic status. Yet Pan-Americanism was on constant guard, bringing moral pressure to bear at points of danger, and achieving an unprecedented goal in the current fact that no American republic was proposing to obtain what belonged to a neighbor by use of force.

There were remnants of European empires on our side of the Atlantic, but they were tolerated in the West Indies and on the northern coast of South America with no feeling of irritation. This was to be explained on two grounds—first because after the emancipation of Cuba they were no longer out of accord with the American system. Second, they were not coveted, because they had little appreciable value for any American republic. The principal business of the Western-Hemisphere nations lay in the further intensive cultivation of law and order in their respective domains, and mutual confidence and good will in their relations with each other. If only wars could have been limited, and the oceans could have provided us with permanent safeguards or quarantines against disorders in Europe or Asia, we might have thought with less concern about a world-wide peace society formed by universal consent.

Perchance for another half century we would have clung to our own ideas of democracy and federation, and continued to promote harmony in the Western Hemisphere on the expanded formulas of Jefferson and Monroe, with the aid of Latin-America's brilliant legal authorities. But invention and industry had created new instruments of war. The oceans were no longer barriers affording us security. Geographical isolation had failed us in a crisis. We could no longer crawl back into our shell and be safe. For better or worse, our dream of safety through doors closed and locked did not correspond to reality. We were shaken out of isolation, as truly as Japan's privacy was disturbed when Perry broke into that sequestered hermitage.

The standard schoolbook lessons in American history had taught us that our doctrine of isolation rested after all upon nothing but the sense of our ability to make defensive use of military power. We had fought two earlier wars with England, had luckily escaped a third in 1846, had been challenged by a British ultimatum in 1861, had engaged in a two-ocean war with Spain in 1898, and had fought an unpleasant war with the Filipinos in pursuance of our " right by conquest " to protect them and shower blessings upon them. We had joined Japan and other powers in a campaign to crush the Boxer Rebellion in China. In short, for a stay-at-home, isolated people, we had had several contacts with a troubled trans-oceanic world before we joined England and France in 1917.

II.

I entertain a great respect for the breadth of view and the foresight of those American citizens who were touring the country almost thirty years ago to bring public opinion to the support of their movement for a " League to Enforce Peace." Popular history heretofore has occupied itself largely with the annals of warfare. There will come a time when efforts to promote peace will have more prominence in the story of civilization. When that time comes, as undoubtedly it will, the genesis of the League of Nations will have its appropriate chapters, and there will be no apologies necessary for the early sponsors of that noble effort.

It took a long time to build the Gothic cathedrals of Europe during the centuries that we call the Age of Faith. In most instances there were changes of ground plan and also of superstructure and architectural detail, before the great edifice was completed. The League of Nations, as projected in the Covenant that formed a part of the Versailles Treaty, was the imperfect embodiment of a great conception. The ideas underlying it were those of philosophers and statesmen and humanists whose tentative proposals have come down through long centuries. Beginnings were made from time to time, although no permanent and continuing agency of the nations had ever come into existence until the League began to function at Geneva, after the general ratification of the Versailles Treaty.

Even the Congress of Vienna in 1815 may be said to have made a fragmentary contribution to the edifice of world peace. In one of the chapters of his valuable work on the Peace Conference at The Hague, held in 1899, my friend the late Frederick W. Holls, having referred to earlier conferences after great European wars and also to that of Berlin in 1878, continued in the following vein:

> All of the other gatherings above mentioned also had the object of affording guarantees for as permanent a peace as seemed possible at the time, and this is notably true of the Congress of Vienna, held at the close of the Napoleonic convulsion. That Congress, it should be remembered, fixed the general outlines of the boundaries between European nationalities in a manner which has scarcely been disturbed, the one important exception being the annexation of Alsace-Lorraine to the German Empire. The problem following the fixing of these general lines was that of national consolidation under the freest possible institutions and the struggle for this object fills the history of the sixty years immediately following that historic gathering. When national unity and liberty had been gained by Germany and Italy, the most of Europe was able to contemplate what certainly seems to be a stable equilibrium of international relations; and this equilibrium is only slightly affected by the shifting of the Franco-German frontier on the Vosges and the Rhine. The more immediate and historic causes of friction having thus been removed, no insuperable obstacle remained to a federation of the civilized Powers, definitely organized for purposes of international justice. The time had come to make the expression "International Law" a reality, instead of the cover for a miscellaneous collection of moral precepts and rules of intercourse.

I shall refer in the concluding chapter to the first Hague Conference, and to the second one that followed eight years later. Their primary object was to give international law a more definite character, and to provide a permanent tribunal for the handling of disputes. This tribunal, which was actually created and given a permanent place of meeting at the capital of Holland, was designed as a part of that international peace foundation which is to be as permanent and real—if we continue to use the architectural analogy—as some early fragment of the sub-structure of a great cathedral.

After the outbreak of the war in 1914, thoughtful men everywhere began to consider bringing nations together in a League, to promote their common concerns, and to seek with constant vigilance to prevent wars by dealing with their incipient causes. Such projects were more openly discussed in the United States before 1917 because, although the war was brought home to us in many ways, we were not engaged in it and were at liberty to express ourselves. There were peace societies in the United States of long standing and undoubted usefulness. There was the Carnegie Endowment for International Peace, established in 1910 with Elihu Root as president of a board of trustees made up of American citizens of great influence, and with Dr. Nicholas Murray Butler as the most energetic member of its executive committee. Its elaborate organization extended to Great Britain, France, and other European countries, and through more than a third of a century President Butler has maintained his official connection with it, succeeding Elihu Root as its directing head.

In that same year, 1910, the World Peace Foundation was organized at Boston by Edwin Ginn, a prosperous publisher of textbooks, who provided an endowment for it, its object being to promote peace, justice and good will among nations, principally through educational methods. In no other country were there so many men and women who gave studious thought to the problems of war and peace as in the United States.

The most definite movement, however, was that of the "League to Enforce Peace." It set forth to promote a plan for organizing the world against war, and was publicly launched at Independence hall, Philadelphia, June 17, 1915. This meeting had been preceded by conferences of an informal kind, the results of which had emboldened the initiators to organize in a public way. Theodore Marburg of Baltimore and Hamilton Holt of New York were the moving spirits at the outset, and they had no difficulty in discovering that men of wider official experience, as well as thoughtful citizens everywhere, could be readily persauded to support their general views and aims. Mr. Marburg had been a Johns Hopkins student in my early period there, and afterwards studied at Oxford, Paris, and Heidelberg, and had recently served as the United States Minister at Brussels. He could afford to give time and thought to the advancement of public causes in which he believed.

Mr. Marburg was in correspondence with Lord Bryce and other Englishmen, and with officials of several European countries. Hamilton Holt of New York, who was a much younger man, was at that time editor and owner of *The Independent*; and with great energy and wide acquaintance he could secure the attention of the press and make broad appeals to public opinion on behalf of a cause to which he was fully committed.

At the Philadelphia meeting William Howard Taft was made president of the new organization; and this choice—together with Mr. Taft's whole-hearted acceptance of the position and his full cooperation with his associates—gave the movement both prominence and good standing at once. As Cabinet member and President, Mr. Taft had encountered an extraordinary range of foreign problems, which had taken him to the West Indies, South America, Europe, and the Far East. He had previously served on the Federal bench, and was to become Chief Justice after an interval as law professor at Yale. As his study of the subject progressed, Mr. Taft's belief in the League of Nations as an instrumentality grew stronger, and he did not share the objections that led, four years later, to the defeat of the Versailles Treaty at Washington through lack of the necessary two-thirds vote of approval by the Senate.

Among the books that require fresh study as the United Nations are going forward from a war basis to some kind of collective peace-time association, are the two large volumes by Theodore Marburg entitled *Development of the League of Nations Idea.* They were published in 1932, and are made up largely of documentary material and correspondence. Mr. Marburg's efforts were indefatigable, and had a wide international range. He was not pursuing his subject in the rarified atmosphere of abstract thought, but was dealing at all times with actual conditions, and as a widely informed person.

In a letter of September 1914 to President Wilson, written from Europe and relating to the invasion of Belgium, Mr. Marburg expressed himself with such clarity and force that his views are as pertinent today as twenty-nine years ago. He remarks: "Germany is not and has not for years been amenable to reason. There is no reasoning with mad dogs and now only force will answer. Germany must be beaten to her knees to stem this flow of barbarism, to free the German masses themselves from the grip of the bureaucracy and ruthless military class and to arrest militarism itself."

Even at that early stage of the war, in view of our commitment to the doctrine of neutrality at the Hague Conference, Mr. Marburg thought we might find cause "to depart from our traditional policy and to lend our fleet to the cause of England and her allies." Three years later our fleet was actually in the North Sea, operating in conjunction with the British. Further in this message to President Wilson, Mr. Marburg asked a question and answered it in the following terms: "Are we not again at a turning point in history? What we have witnessed is as nothing compared with what is to come if Germany wins out. And America will not only share the added burden which will be placed on the shoulders of all nations but will be opened to the dangers of actual attack by men of boundless ambition and inhuman callousness."

The volumes to which I am referring are not confined to a record of efforts in the United States to arrive at some agreement regarding the character and scope of the proposed League. Studies in this field were going forward in England, France, the Netherlands, Switzerland, Italy, and elsewhere. In 1918, before the end of the war, Mr. Marburg's conferences at home and abroad had made him undoubtedly the best informed man in the world regarding the tentative plans and proposals that were taking form for a post-war League of Nations. Residing in Baltimore, and a trustee of the Johns Hopkins University, he was invited by the Academic Council to give a lecture before members of the University on "Plans for Permanent Peace." He was asked to examine in this lecture "all the proposals which have been put forward by statesmen or important publicists for the realization of better international order after the war."

The material out of which Mr. Marburg could have compiled a dozen lectures is contained in the volumes that were prepared for the press eleven years ago, under the editorial supervision of the late Dr. John H. Latané of the Johns Hopkins University. Professor Latané himself had become a distinguished authority in the field of diplomatic history, and his preparation of the Marburg volumes for the press was the last of many services in the field of his chosen labors as research scholar, teacher, and author. In his introduction to the Marburg volumes, Dr. Latané remarks:

> The most important event in the history of the movement was President Wilson's address at the meeting of the League to Enforce Peace at Washington, May 27, 1916. There was great enthusiasm among the members of the League when it was announced that the President of the United States had accepted the invitation to address them and still greater enthusiasm when he endorsed the general principles of their program, although he avoided the use of the word "enforce" and spoke of "an universal association of nations." President Wilson was the first statesman of the world in office to give official approval to the idea, and from this time he was the leading advocate of a League of Nations.

The address to which Dr. Latané referred was made by President Wilson at a public meeting of the League held in Washington on May 27, 1916. This was almost a year before we entered the war, and about three years before President Wilson sponsored the Covenant of the League of Nations and secured its acceptance by the allied governments in their peace conference at Paris.

III.

That speech in my opinion is as well-balanced an expression of Mr. Wilson's views as he ever made in public. Its statement of underlying convictions is persuasive, and at no point controversial. The speech as a whole, although it was an extemporaneous utterance, was an example of Mr. Wilson's remarkable ability to clothe his thoughts in words as he faced an audience. After his return from Paris, when seeking to convince the country of our duty to accept the specific form of League arrangement embodied in the Versailles Treaty, his speeches—especially on the Western tour—had no parallel, in all the history of comparable efforts, for their cogency and eloquence. But I should prefer to quote from the intimate and friendly speech at Washington in 1916 as most typical of Mr. Wilson's thought as he considered the state of the world.

He was speaking in general terms, and trying to express views that represented American opinion as we were observing the war from our standpoint of neutrality. He declared that when the war came to an end, we should be "as much concerned as the nations at war to see peace assume an aspect of permanence, . . . [and] bring some assurance that peace and war shall always hereafter be reckoned part of the common interest of mankind." He continued as follows: "We are participants, whether we would or not, in the life of the world. The interests of all nations are our own also. We are partners with the rest. What affects mankind is inevitably our affair as well as the affairs of the nations of Europe and Asia."

I am quoting several detached extracts from that address, because they represent so clearly the trend of his thought. Mr. Wilson was not "improvising life-long convictions" on the spur of the moment merely because he had agreed to make a speech. He had held these views for more than thirty years; and probably every college president and every publicist of influence in America would have agreed at that time to everything the President said. Five extracts which follow are typical of the speech as a whole:

> Only when the great nations of the world have reached some sort of agreement as to what they hold to be fundamental to their common interest, and as to some feasible method of acting in concert when any nation or group of nations seeks to disturb those fundamental things, can we feel that civilization is at last in a way of justifying its existence and claiming to be fully established. It is clear that nations must in the future be governed by the same high code of honor that we demand of individuals. . . .
>
> Repeated utterances of the leading statesmen of most of the great nations now engaged in war have made it plain that their thought has come to this, that the principle of public right must henceforth take precedence over the individual interests of particular nations, and that the nations of the world must in some way band themselves together to see that that right prevails as against any sort of selfish aggression; that henceforth alliance must not be set up against alliance, understanding against understanding, but that there must be a common agreement for a common object, and that at the heart of that common object must lie the inviolable rights of people and of mankind. The nations of the world have become each other's neighbors. It is to their interest that they should understand each other. In order that they may understand each other, it is imperative that they should agree to cooperate in a common cause, and that they should so act that the guiding principle of that common cause shall be even-handed and impartial justice. . . .
>
> This is undoubtedly the thought of America. This is what we ourselves will say when there comes proper occasion to say it. In the dealings of nations with one another arbitrary force must be rejected and we must move forward to the thought of the modern world, the thought of which peace is the very atmosphere. That thought constitutes a chief part of the passionate conviction of America. . . .
>
> So sincerely do we believe in these things that I am sure that I speak the mind and wish of the people of America when I say that the United States is willing to become a partner in any feasible association of nations formed in order to realize these objects and make them secure against violation. . . .
>
> I feel that the world is even now upon the eve of a great consummation, when some common force will be brought into existence which shall safeguard right as the first and most fundamental interest of all peoples and all governments, when coercion shall be summoned not to the service of political ambition or selfish hostility, but to the service of a common order, a common justice, and a common peace. God grant that the dawn

of that day of frank dealing and of settled peace, concord, and cooperation may be near at hand.

Now that we are thinking again of some union of nations for peace maintenance—a union more ambitious in strength and scope than the League of Nations, if we are to follow the current blueprints—we should do well to consider again with open minds the experiences of 1919 and the following year.

In any group made up of older and younger citizens who revert to the League of Nations as a topic of discussion, there is likely to be agreement on only one point. It will be taken for granted that the League was a failure, that it will not come out of its coma, and that neither its framework, its machinery nor its assets, is likely to be salvaged for future purposes. Although I regard this commonly accepted supposition as ill-founded and mistaken, I am not mentioning it in order to refute it. Rather, I am concerned about the numerous points upon which one discovers widely differing opinions.

Controversy reached a high level of strain and excitement during the long months when the Versailles Treaty was under debate in the Senate. The League of Nations became the football of party politics, and older citizens who took sides in 1920 have a tendency to cherish their collection of antipathies and prejudices, rather than to remember impartially—what is always more tedious and humdrum—the objective facts. They personify the struggle between the Democratic President and the Republican Senators, and do not like to re-open a judgment that they have held for almost a quarter of a century. Younger citizens, as a rule, while trying to think sincerely and without bias, have either studied the subject too meagerly, or else have accepted one censorious view that upholds Wilson as a martyr, or the opposing censorious view that has become traditional in some quarters.

Mr. Wilson's part in the transaction can be stated briefly, although it would justify elaboration. I shall hope to summarize it fairly, without much detail. I have quoted from the 1916 speech to refute an impression among young citizens that the League of Nations idea was some kind of secret or confidential proposal that Wilson took to Paris in a guarded brief-case, and sprung upon the statesmen of Europe as an American surprise. The Germans had agreed to the Armistice on terms which included a League of Nations, and all the Allies had previously accepted it.

It was not a surprise package in any quarter. In his speech on "The War Aims and Peace Terms of the United States" before a joint session of Congress on January 8, 1918 (this speech including the formulated Fourteen Points), the President enunciated his League doctrine as the last of the series and its climax, in the following language: "A general association of nations must be formed under specific covenants for the purpose of affording mutual guarantees of political independence and territorial integrity to great and small states alike."

The so-called "Covenant" of the League was not devised in its precise details by Mr. Wilson. Upon his insistence, however, it was made an essential part of the peace treaty with Germany, although the English delegates would have preferred to have it adopted as a separate arrangement. Quite apart from the League plan, there were many things in the Treaty that might call for future revision; and it was Mr. Wilson's hope that the League would from time to time deal with questions as they arose. This theory of the League's functions was strictly Wilsonian.

The treaty which Germany was compelled to sign established a general European status that was especially advantageous to France and Great Britain, and supposedly beneficial to the new states that were called into being (Poland, Czechoslovakia, and the others). The League was so constituted that while the Assembly was a *talking* body, and a meeting place for all the small countries, the Council was an *acting* group which Great Britain and France expected to dominate. Nothing whatever could be done by the League, even if fifty countries in the Assembly favored some action, if a single member of the Council objected.

To state contrasting ideas in a sentence, Wilson desired a League that could remedy injustices and mistakes, while France and Great Britain, desiring to maintain the *status quo*, wished to have a veto power which either of them could use in self-interest. Wilson himself was a man of legal training, and he had made a life study of comparative constitutional systems. He could not, therefore, have been unaware of the manner in which Lord Robert Cecil and General Smuts had put their British impress upon the Covenant of the League at vital points. The document as formulated was not obscure or ambiguous, and it was exactly what the men at the "Peace Table" chose to make it. Mr. Wilson did not regard it as disappointing and unacceptable.

But Wilson was thinking of peace at long range, and of universal justice as vindicated by American intervention; while Europe was thinking of short-range conditions, and of security during the painful effort to re-establish life on a normal basis in a devastated continent. If the League were once set at work, thought our President, it would in due time become conscious of its own defects, and would be remedied both in representative structure and in practical applications. It would acquire capacity to deal with questions arising from the drastic terms of settlement with Germany and Austria, and from the operation of a system of mandates.

IV.

A mid-term Congressional election had occurred in the first week of November 1918, and Mr. Wilson had made a personal appeal to the country to return a Democratic majority in order to assure the support of his international policies. Whether or not this appeal affected the election results, it was sharply criticized. The war was still raging, and with two million Americans fighting under General Pershing in France, our share in the effort of the Allied nations had no partisan character. As it happened, the election resulted in Republican majorities in both House and Senate. The election occurred on the 5th day of November, and the war ended on the 11th with the Armistice agreement.

Germany's associates were Austria, Bulgaria, and Turkey; and their military collapse, one after another, during thirty-six days from September 29 to November 4 left the German army in retreat, and with no further hope of victory. Thus the war ended a year earlier than had been generally expected in America and England. On Armistice Day, November 11, Mr. Wilson appeared before Congress to read the terms upon which the war had ceased, the German authorities having accepted and signed the document presented to them by Marshal Foch on the authority of the Supreme War Council.

In his remarks that followed his reading of the extended Armistice document, with its many military and naval clauses, the President returned to his favorite theme: "The great nations which associated themselves to destroy it [German militarism] have now definitely united in the common purpose to set up such a peace as will satisfy the longing of the whole world for disinterested justice, embodied in settlements which are based upon something much better and much more lasting than the selfish competitive interests of powerful states. There is no longer conjecture as to the objects the victors have in mind. They have a mind in the matter, not only, but a heart also. Their avowed and concerted purpose is to satisfy and protect the weak as well as to accord their just rights to the strong."

It was not a long speech, but it was replete with sentences typical of the Wilsonian ideals. For example: "To conquer with arms is to make only a temporary conquest; to conquer the world by earning its esteem is to make permanent conquest." He thought that the allied nations, having won their military victory, were "about to make conquest of the world by the sheer power of example and a friendly helpfulness." This speech ended with the most optimistic expressions regarding the peoples "who have just come out from under the yoke of arbitrary government, and who are now coming at last into their freedom."

He ended his discourse on a note of complete confidence that the German people (and those of Austria-Hungary and Bulgaria) "would set their own affairs in order, and would choose the way of self-control and peaceful accommodation." The war was gloriously ended. We were ready to forgive our enemies, and believe with the President that the Golden Rule would have sway henceforth, and that peace would reign on earth as in heaven.

The country's elation was in fact—and naturally enough—inspired by the thought that our army would be rapidly demobilized, and the troops would be brought home from France. There was no expression of cynicism regarding the President's belief that war had somehow transformed the spirit of such rivals as France and Germany. Americans in general believed in world harmony, and in the value of generous dealings with defeated foes, although more immediate things were on their minds. It was assumed that the German people would be glad to repudiate militarism and take their places in a free, democratic Europe, under the watchful care of a League of Nations.

But American enthusiasm was not definitely centered upon President Wilson as the sole exponent of American ideas. Although party feeling subsides quickly after an American election, the political machines run their campaigns on such issues as they can stir up; and Mr. Wilson's appeal to the voters of America on October 24 was what the campaign orators termed a "boomerang." He was taking the exact tone of a British Prime Minister and Cabinet who appeal to the country for a vote of confidence. This tone might have been appropriate when a President seeks re-election, as Wilson sought it in 1916. But once elected, in our theory of government the President is leader of the nation rather than of a party, and is not expected to tell the voters whom they should send to Congress. Mr. Wilson had always favored the English Parliamentary system, as I had known from many hours of discussion with him.

He was an excellent chief magistrate, and he had always been—as I had also reason to know—remarkably free from narrow party prejudice. He had a Cabinet of broad-minded, patriotic men who were as free from mere partisan bias, in conducting their respective branches of the executive government, as could have been possible in the circumstances. These men—certainly the majority of them—did not approve of Mr. Wilson's address of October 24 which began with the following paragraph:

> *My Fellow Countrymen:* The Congressional elections are at hand. They occur in the most critical period our country has ever faced or is likely to face in our time. If you have approved of my leadership and wish me to continue to be your unembarrassed spokesman in affairs at home and abroad, I earnestly beg that you will express yourselves unmistakably to that effect by returning a Democratic majority to both the Senate and the House of Representatives.

Not to extend quotations, it is enough to say that Mr. Wilson proceeded through a number of paragraphs to expound his theory of an undivided and personal leadership that must not be impaired by the assertion of any discordant judgment of its own on the part of Congress. "Unity of command is as necessary now in civil action as it is upon the field of battle." He did not mean to be autocratic, but since he believed that he was standing as the exponent of American public opinion at a critical time, he regarded a non-coöperating Congress as harmfully obstructive. The following paragraph was as distasteful to Republicans as any other part of the address:

> The return of a Republican majority to either house of Congress would, moreover, be interpretative on the other side of the water as a repudiation of my leadership. Spokesmen of the Republican patry are urging you to

elect a Republican Congress in order to back up and support the President, but, even if they should in this impose upon some credulous voters on this side of the water, they would impose on no one on the other side. It is well understood there as well as here that Republican leaders desire not so much to support the President as to control him.

Let no one suppose that Mr. Wilson's state of mind, as disclosed in this address to his fellow countrymen, should be attributed solely to egotism, or to a theory regarding the nature of our division of authority between the law-making body and the executive. We were approaching the close of the war, and Mr. Wilson was to remain in the Presidential office until March 4, 1921. Less than half of his second term had elapsed, and a little more than two years and four months remained. Under our system of fixed terms, it would devolve upon him to take the initiative in negotiating peace treaties. He thought that the election of a Republican Congress would discredit him abroad, and therefore weaken American influence.

In this Mr. Wilson was sincere, but mistaken. When the man power and resources of a great country are subjected to the hazards of war, major parties work together in essential things even if they differ in points of detail. In England a coalition cabinet was formed in 1914, and in the course of the war Mr. Asquith's leadership was overthrown and a reorganized coalition supported Mr. Lloyd George. In the United States, Republicans and Democrats joined in the support of war measures in Congress, and the Congressional elections merely showed approval of the Republican leaders for their support of the nation's policies.

Europe was too much absorbed in the disturbing situations that beset every country from Scotland to Turkey to have thought of the American election as perhaps harmful to Mr. Wilson's prestige. Few people across the Atlantic were aware that there had been an election here, and those who knew about it (like Mr. Lloyd George) were merely confirmed once more in the sound view that our fixed four-year term gives the American President an enviably firm seat, regardless of Congressional changes.

There are a few, perhaps, who think that the course of history was altered by the Republican victory of 1918, which had a bearing upon the failure of the United States to accept the Versailles Treaty and to become a member of the League of Nations. Not pausing to consider that view, I will proceed with a convenient summary of a few facts and dates. The expiring Congress met for its last session at the beginning of December, and the President informed it of his purpose to go to Paris. The announcement came at the end of a very long annual message. Explaining at some length the reasons for his unprecedented journey, he concluded with the following sentence: "I shall make my absence as brief as possible, and shall hope to return with the happy assurance that it has been possible to translate into action the great ideals for which America has striven." The President sailed two days later (December 4).

If every Congressional district in the country had responded affirmatively to the President's appeal in the November election, he could not have been received with greater enthusiasm in Europe than he met on his arrival. He was honored in France, was fêted at many places in England, addressed the Italian parliament, and was made an honorary citizen of Rome. He was tendered a banquet by King George in Buckingham Palace, and an official reception in the Guildhall by the Lord Mayor of London and British officialdom.

These are the barest allusions to a personal tribute of ardent welcome in three great European countries that has had no parallel in the records of mankind. Mr. Wilson's speeches were graceful and appropriate, and he recognized the fact that he was appearing as the representative of America, and that the acclaim was for the American people and the recent services of their army and navy.

In his address at the Sorbonne, when receiving an honorary degree from the University of Paris, Mr. Wilson declared his conception of the League of Nations to be "that it shall operate as the organized moral force of men throughout the world, and that whenever or wherever wrong and aggression are planned or contemplated, this searching light of conscience will be turned upon them." That he was more intent upon moral consciousness than upon organized force becomes evident to the reader of his European addresses and dissertations.

He was especially happy when he found himself in the atmosphere of universities, as he declared at the University of Turin where he remarked: "So soon as I entered the quadrangle and heard the voices of the students, it seemed to me as if the greater part of my life had come back to me." He dwelt in the Italian speeches upon the ideals of justice and right as the only source of permanent peace. In one of the Italian speeches he said: "We go to Paris to conclude a peace. It is your duty to continue it. We can only make the large conclusions. You constantly transact the details which constitute the processes of the life of nations."

V.

The appearance of President Wilson had lifted the spirits of men and women throughout Europe. All countries had suffered inexpressibly. Plain men everywhere, whether citizens of the allied countries or the central powers, were hoping for settlements that would give assurance of a new era of comity and friendliness among all nations. Mr. Wilson had spent his first four weeks on European soil to good purpose. He might well have greeted the peace conference at its opening session on January 18, and then returned to his official duties at Washington. He would have been able to follow the proceedings with closer attention and with more accurate perspective if he had chosen to have America represented by delegates in whom the whole American people, regardless of party, would have full confidence.

President McKinley had chosen that course when the treaty with Spain had been negotiated at Paris in 1899. For the purposes of this peace conclave at Paris in 1919, the two trans-Atlantic cable systems were merged under government control; and Mr. Wilson at Washington—constantly informed by his own trustworthy agents at Paris—could have dominated the conference. It happened that several of the men most competent to represent the United States were Republicans, although they were entirely free from partisan bias in all that affected international relations. Mr. Taft was president of the League to Enforce Peace, and was as fully committed as any man in the world to the principles that Wilson expounded so eloquently. Hon. Elihu Root cherished the same ideals, had no personal ambitions, and was our most experienced negotiator in the field of foreign affairs. Mr. Wilson for personal reasons would not have preferred to appoint Theodore Roosevelt, who had made an address at Oslo in 1910 strongly advocating a league of nations, and who had been the recipient of the Nobel Peace Prize.

Nor would he have considered the appointment of Senator Lodge, although this Massachusetts "scholar in politics" was to be chairman of the committee on foreign relations when the new Congress assembled. There were Democratic senators who would have represented his views at Paris with full competence, though the Republicans—certainly Taft and Root—were better known and more expert in the field of foreign affairs. The four delegates actually selected by Mr. Wilson were Colonel Edward M. House of Texas, Mr. Robert Lansing (who had become Secretary of State by promotion after the withdrawal of William Jennings Bryan from the Cabinet), Mr. Henry White, an experienced career diplomat, and General Tasker H. Bliss.

Every president in times of critical importance acts in accordance with his own conceptions of the office. Mr. Wilson conceived of himeslf as a prime minister, and proposed to conduct peace negotiations at Paris in his own person, with the prime ministers of Great Britain, France, and Italy as the other chief members of the conference. If he had taken the traditional view of his official position, he would have chosen a different group of delegates. Commenting upon his selections at the time, I referred to the four American delegates as follows:

> Mr. Lansing is versed in all subjects of international law and diplomacy, and thoroughly acquainted with the problems of the war period. Colonel House has been the President's most trusted personal adviser, is widely acquainted with public men at home and abroad, and has during the past year given his whole time and attention to the questions that must follow the end of the war, being assisted in his studies by a corps of experts. General Tasker Bliss has been abroad since we entered the war, and has been our military representative in the Inter-Allied conferences at Versailles. His great intelligence, fine judgment, and recent experience qualify him for membership in the Peace Conference. Mr. Henry White was for many years in the diplomatic service, holding the highest posts at several capitals, and is greatly esteemed and respected. It is now known that their premiers, foreign ministers and military chiefs will represent the Allied countries.

Mr. Wilson surrounded himself with a large group of American economists and other specialists, who had already qualified themselves to act with European experts at Paris in the study of various parts of the reconstruction program. I might reproduce many passages from my comments upon the situation with which we had to deal at the end of the war, but I will quote several paragraphs written in December and published in the *Review of Reviews* for January, 1919.

In order to keep the sequence of dates in mind it should be stated that the President remained in Europe for two months (from December 13 to February 13) when he came back to the United States to be present at the close of the session of Congress on March 4, after which he returned to Paris with little delay. On January 18 he had spoken at the opening session of the Peace Conference, and had nominated the French Premier, M. Clemenceau, as permanent chairman. The paragraphs to which I have alluded as published in the *Review of Reviews* for January 1919 are as follows:

In the working out of principles, the best results come through the clear recognition of actualities. We shall do well, therefore, if we turn away from theories at this historic juncture and try to find upon what concrete foundation the prospect of future peace rests. When the United States entered the war in the spring of 1917 we declared in this *Review* that our country had then and there joined a league to enforce peace. We set forth the view that the very fact of our joining the Allies had so enlarged the issues involved as to change the character of the war and to make it "a war to end war" and to establish permanent security against the menace of aggression. Future peace does not rest upon any paper scheme or project for a league of nations, but upon the united effort that has now brought about the peace which began on November 11.

Gradually, through the years to come, there may grow out of this joining of hands in the Great War an elaborate system for the improvement of international law, the settling of disputes, and above all for the administrative conduct of certain large and responsible tasks such as the government of equatorial Africa. But a mere project of a League of Nations, written out as a theory and apart from the concrete facts, would not of itself give peace and security to the world, even though at first it were unanimously adopted. The Constitution of the United States with its Supreme Court and with the Army and Navy of the Union did not of itself avail to hold together the sisterhood of sovereign States. The thing that finally welded us into our firm American union was the intense conviction of the need and the value of that union, on the part of a major group of the States—a group so intrinsically strong that it was able when the test came to establish its principles and to cause them finally and completely to be accepted.

Whatever may be the nominal form of a League of Nations, as adopted by the master minds of the Peace Conference now assembling at Versailles, the underlying facts are the important thing to observe, not the mere phrase "League of Nations," or the language that may clothe the accepted scheme. The Hague treaties looked like a long movement towards international harmony and agreement; but they fell apart when Germany and her allies challenged the "balance of power," and undertook to secure the dominance of Europe and Asia, which would have meant, in the end, the dominance of the world.

The essential fact today is the complete disappearance of that system heretofore known in Europe as the balance of power. Germany, Austria, and Russia, in their former character as great military systems and as dynastic Empires—with their policies uncontrolled by the will of the people—have forever disappeared. Upon the ruins of the old system there has arisen a new power, capable of controlling the destinies of the world. This new power consists of the combination for international purposes of Great Britain, France, Italy, the United States, and Japan.

If this combination holds together in generous goodwill, and in adherence to the high aims which these nations have professed and vindicated, there will still remain many perplexing problems to be dealt with; but there will be no further danger, for a long time to come, of war on a large scale. The best mode of approach, therefore, to the so-called League of Nations is to start with the existing facts, and then to think through them into the improvements that can be made to grow out of them. This way of proceeding will lead us to a better understanding of several points that need clearing up.

Take, for instance, the question of the United States and its old-time tradition against "entangling alliances." It is true we entered the war without a written alliance with England or France or Italy. But no written treaties could have made more real or powerful the alliance that was actually entered into, and that still exists. A closer cooperation between great nations never went into effect than that between the government of the United States and the governments of Great Britain and France. Sending a drafted army of more than two million men, gathered from every neighborhood of the Union, across a wide ocean, and then putting them under the absolute command—along with the armies of three other great nations—of a General-in-Chief and his staff, constitutes an alliance more sweeping and profound than any that the world has ever known before.

This great military fact of alliance has been, and still is, visible to all men; but other facts and evidences of alliances have been less apparent to the onlooker. These have had to do with the union of credit and financial strength among the Allies, by means of which the resources of the greater part of the world have been massed and effectively pooled for the attainment of the desired results. Behind the scenes there have been inter-Allied boards to apportion maritime tonnage, boards accumulating and distributing foodstuffs, boards giving common effectiveness to munition supplies and so on, in amazing extent and variety.

When one lays aside mere words and legal distinctions, and looks at hard facts, there is little left to be said about alliances. With hundreds of thousands of Americans at this moment encamped as an occupying army along the Rhine, it would be the height of absurdity to pretend that we are not concerning ourselves in the liveliest possible way in the adjustment of European affairs. Then comes the question, so much discussed in the newspapers last month, of the future of navies and the control of the seas. Here again the solution becomes simple enough if we proceed from the place where we actually are, rather than from some imaginary place.

The existing alliance is for the suppression of disorder and the maintenance of justice and the freedom of self-governing communities. This will require the abandonment of the militaristic methods that have kept Europe an armed camp for the past generation or two. Germany will have no need to rebuild the military machine that has now been broken. France may gradually relieve herself of the financial burden of a military regime that was essentially defensive. The peace of the world at large is going to require for some time to come a naval control and authority that can protect passages such as the Straits of Gibraltar, the Suez Canal, the Dardanelles and Bosphorus, and the entrance to the Baltic, and that can render swift aid in emergencies throughout the world. The German fleet is surrendered, Austria is no longer existent as a naval power, and there remain in full and undisputed control the fleets of the Allied powers, namely, those of Great Britain, the United States, Japan, France, and Italy.

Thus, nations have only to agree upon policies in furtherance of the great aims for which their sons have fought, suffered and died. That they will agree upon such permanent policies, we have not the slightest doubt. They will certainly agree not to quarrel among themselves, but to settle all differences by friendly and legal methods. They cannot and will not use either naval or land power against one another. This being the case, it could not in the smallest degree endanger the well-being of France or that of the United States, if Great Britain, having vastly the largest ocean-going commerce, and having governmental responsibilities widely separated by great expanses of water, should expect to maintain her large navy.

This navy cannot be used for the well-being of the diverse parts of the British Empire without at the same time maintaining conditions beneficial to France, Japan, the smaller neutral powers like Holland, and also to the United States. Our own country in its policy of developing the American Navy has never thought of possessing a sea-power that would in any way be detrimental to the safety of Canada, Mexico, or the South American republics. On the contrary, Uncle Sam's Navy has behind it the doctrine that it is an agency for the secure and peaceful development of every part of the Western Hemisphere, each country being at full liberty to work out its own political and economic future.

In like manner there is back of the British Navy no scheme for aggression, or for taking advantage of countries with smaller navies or with none at all. It is clearly perceived in England that naval power is henceforth to be held and exercised as a trust on behalf of the enlightened public opinion of the world. After the transient presence in England of more than a million young American soldiers, and after the long sojourn in British waters of American battleships, and numerous destroyers, serving gallantly and even brilliantly under the higher authorities of the British Navy, it has become inconceivable to the British mind that the sea power of the British Empire should ever be used to the detriment of the people of the United States.

That being the case, it should be clearly understood in this country that British statesmen and naval authorities, when talking about the future, are merely proceeding from the present facts. They are not thinking in terms of conflicting or competing navies. It will be discovered in the near future that neither England nor the United States will wish to bear the financial burdens of a larger navy than may appear to be required by safety and prudence.

VI.

I have given space to a reproduction of the foregoing comments not only because they had pertinence as the Paris conference began to consider the tasks that lay before it, but chiefly because they seem to me to have some continuing application, and a bearing upon much that has happened in the quarter-century since January 1919. Mr. Wilson had made a contribution to the future of the world union for justice and peace, and it was unquestionably important. Nevertheless, it had little or nothing to do with the exact and detailed provisions of the document known as the "Covenant of the League of Nations."

American aims and ideals were set forth by the President as we entered the war, and again as we finished it, and he carried those American views to Europe and upheld them to the best of his ability. This broad expression of the doctrine of right and justice in the affairs of nations was Mr. Wilson's real service. He grew so intent upon the incorporation of his League plan in a treaty that provided for the reconstruction of Europe and the disposal of German colonies and Turkish domains that at length he seemed to attach more importance to words than to major facts. On January 25th, a week after the opening of the conference, he had initiated the discussion of the League of Nations in a speech that set forth his logical theory. The conference (he declared) had to make present settlements, and also had to provide for the future peace of the world. Many of the present settlements would need subsequent reconsideration, and the League should be charged with this responsibility.

"Settlements may be temporary," (he continued) "but the action of the nations in the interests of peace and justice must be permanent. We can set up permanent processes. We may not be able to set up permanent decisions." Therefore he believed that the League of Nations must have continuity. "It should be the eye of the nations to keep watch upon the common interest, an eye that does not slumber, an eye that is everywhere watchful and attentive." It was a rhetorical speech, but clear in its purport. This was the "keystone of the whole program which expressed our purposes and ideals in this war, and which the associated nations have accepted as the basis of the settlement." He thought that if our delegation returned to the United States without having made every effort to realize this program "we should return to meet the merited scorn of our fellow-citizens."

About three weeks later, on February 14, 1919, Mr. Wilson reported a League of Nations text which had been agreed upon with unanimity by a commission of which he was chairman. Representatives of fourteen nations had been members of this commission, these comprising the United States, Great Britain, France, Italy, Japan, Belgium, Brazil, China, Czechoslovakia, Greece, Poland, Portugal, Roumania, and Serbia. Having read the document, Mr. Wilson discussed it in an intelligent and highly optimistic speech. It was on the following day that he set sail for the United States in order to be at Washington during the closing days of the Sixty-fifth Congress.

With high noon of March 4 ending the need of his immediate presence at Washington, and marking the exact middle point of his second term, Mr. Wilson later in the day addressed a great meeting in New York, as he was to sail for Europe again within a few hours. Mr. Taft presided at the New York meeting, and his address preceded that of Mr. Wilson. The President declared that he was happy to associate himself with Mr. Taft in the great cause which was the theme of both addresses. Referring to his predecessor in the Presidency, Mr. Wilson said: "He has displayed an elevation of view and devotion to public duty which is beyond praise, and I am the more happy because this means that this is not a party issue. No party has a right to appropriate this issue, and no party will in the long run dare oppose it."

Having satisfied himself that American ideals were accepted by the great mass of people throughout Europe, and having launched his League of Nations with remarkable concurrence of view, it would have been fortunate on many accounts if Mr. Wilson had then resumed his place in the White House, and had sent Mr. Taft to Paris as chairman of our American delegation. The conference was settling down to difficult problems having to do with the rearrangement of the greater part of the Austro-Hungarian Empire, and with other controversial questions—geographical, political and economic. There was a dispute between Italy and Yugoslavia relating to the control of the port of Fiume; and Mr. Wilson so deeply offended the Italian delegates by his championship of Yugoslavia that they withdrew from the peace conference.

Mr. Wilson was aided, perhaps, by too many zealous young American experts, whose theories of a map of Europe reconstructed on racial lines—with a seaport or a corridor for each new political entity—were convincing enough, if only they were found acceptable to those most immediately concerned. Only five years later, in 1924, Fiume was annexed to Italy.

It is not my purpose to recite in further detail the story of the peace conference, although I am satisfied that the more essential facts have faded from the memories of older citizens, while the younger generation of Americans has been content to ignore them. Since this chapter relates principally to the League of Nations, it may be noted that on April 28 a revised text was submitted, which Mr. Wilson explained minutely. The Swiss city of Geneva was reported as the seat of the League, and in various details the Covenant was made more explicit and satisfactory in its drafting.

Some of the more useful functions of the League were added to Article XXIII, these relating to the just treatment of aborigines, prevention of the traffic in opium, abolition of the white slave traffic, and concern for the prevention and control of disease. A new Article mentioned the Red Cross as one of the voluntary organizations to be sponsored in its international character by the members of the League.

Responding to a notice that the delegates of the Allied countries, about eighty in number, were ready to receive the German delegates, there was an impressive ceremonial at Versailles on May 7. The Germans were given time to consider the treaty that had been drawn up without their participation. Naturally, they did not like the treaty, but finally they signed it under protest.

Some parts of the treaty were not justified in the light of subsequent experience; but—considered as a settlement made at the end of a terrible world war—it was in most respects a complex of arrangements and provisions that showed more intelligence, and a more pervasive sense of justice, than was to have been expected. American influence had been exerted unselfishly and in good faith. Mr. Lansing wrote a book soon afterwards that indicated disappointment on the part of the four American delegates with some of the decisions of the Conference, but they all signed the treaty with Mr. Wilson. It was my opinion at the time, which I expressed explicitly and with care, that the settlement left the Germans in a fortunate position.

Meanwhile, our new Congress with Republicans in control of both branches had been called in special session to consider appropriation bills and revenue measures. Mr. Wilson transmitted his message by cable on May 20, as the session began. Every aspect of the war settlement had been under constant discussion in the press, on the platform, in every schoolhouse and at every cross-roads grocery. The League of Nations had become a bone of contention throughout the United States, and controversies were taking party lines.

On June 28th, Mr. Wilson sent a cablegram from Paris which was made public at Washington, and addressed to his "fellow countrymen." It announced the fact that the treaty of peace had been signed, and it eulogized the achievement in several hundred words of sanguine interpretation. The cablegram ended as follows: "It [the treaty] furnishes guarantees such as were never given or even contemplated for the fair treatment of all who labour at the daily tasks of the world. It is for this reason that I have spoken of it as a great charter for a new order of affairs. There is ground here for deep satisfaction, universal reassurance, and confident hope."

The President had been seriously ill in Paris (it was the year of a deadly influenza epidemic), and in spite of many disheartening circumstances he was elated in May because he felt that his mission had attained a reasonable success. Alas, the peoples of Europe were already sinking into the mire of post-war disillusionments, and cared too little about the League. The whole Italian nation was bitterly alienated, and regarded Wilson as its personal enemy. A writer in the *Revue de Deux Mondes* tried to assure the French people that they were not justified in their extreme revulsion of feeling toward the American President.

John Maynard Keynes (now Lord Keynes), who represented the British Treasury at the peace conference, wrote a famous book in 1919 called *Economic Consequences of the Peace* that was so unpleasant in its allusions to Mr. Wilson that his language had to be modified in the American edition. The President had withdrawn his confidence from Colonel House, and Secretary Lansing was obliged to resign a few months later. Yet the President had seen his self-appointed task through to the end. With the treaty signed, and the assurance that the League of Nations would be set up at Geneva at the opening of 1920, he was eager to return and build up a supporting public opinion at home. Whatever his critics may have thought, he had not sought popularity. He had sacrificed himself for what he believed to be the greatest of American ideals.

As I am endeavoring to show throughout this book, from the first chapter to the last, the League was conceived in full accord with the American spirit of cooperative good-will. During the war and following it, Americans had given $100,000,000 for Near East Relief. They had made large provision for Serbian Relief and Child Welfare, and they had shown their sense of human brotherhood in many other distant fields. The Rockefeller Foundation had promoted public-health administration in South America, and medical education in China.

The Rockefeller agencies are generous, but never impulsive in their selection of objectives. When Mr. John D. Rockefeller Jr. some years ago made a personal gift of $2,000,000 for the new Library of the League of Nations at Geneva, he was exemplifying the American wish and purpose to uphold the League in its proven capacity for usefulness. The further grants of the Rockefeller Foundation, aggregating more than $2,400,000, as contributions to the League in support of its various activities, have given the practical endorsement of careful and intelligent stewards of philanthropic funds to a society of nations that is destined to live on, and to function permanently at Geneva.

Chapter XIX

REJECTED AT WASHINGTON, THE LEAGUE FOUND AMERICAN SUPPORT

Returning from Paris in July to lay the peace treaty before Congress and the country, Mr. Wilson did not find his own enthusiasm widely prevalent. There were clashes of opinion regarding the nature and extent of American obligations under the Covenant of the League.

The Republican leaders of the Senate were ready to ratify the treaty if at the same time they could express, in the form of a memorandum of reservations, the inability of the American government to join in collective war proceedings (to protect one country or another against aggression) without Congressional approval in the particular case.

President Wilson was not only opposed to these Senatorial exceptions to certain articles of the Covenant, but would not allow the treaty to be ratified unless enough Senators took his views to defeat the reservations. The consequence was that the United States ultimately made peace with Germany without becoming a member of the League of Nations in the official sense. Meanwhile European governments had ratified the treaty and launched the League, although, in every such acceptance of the League Constitution, the American Senate's reservations were actually implied.

Regardless of our non-membership, I soon discovered at Geneva that Americans were among the foremost supporters of the League, and that our government's cooperative spirit was always in evidence. Americans supervised the methods of German reparations payment, and served the League in various capacities.

As an outgrowth of experience in the First World War, Great Britain's foreign policies were radically changed in fundamental character. By dominating the seas with a navy twice as powerful as that of any other country, and by playing through skillful diplomacy upon the varying shifts of balanced power in European alliances, Great Britain had formerly held the position of sole umpire in world affairs. The new British policy was based upon cooperation with the United States.

This change was definitely formulated in the agreements of the Washington Naval Conference (1921–22) and the new policy has been followed both in theory and in practice for more than twenty years. Anglo-American collaboration will not seek to control the post-war world, but may take the leading place in upholding the principles of the Atlantic Charter.

The present chapter is concluded with a discussion of the so-called Hoover-Stimson policies, as regards Japanese encroachments in Manchuria and complications in Europe. We were not complacent, but abstained from interventions.

WHEN Mr. Wilson landed at New York on July 8, 1919, he made a brief informal speech that revealed the depth of his feeling for his own country and his confident belief that America would not, "in this day of new-born liberty all over the world, fail to extend her hand of support and assistance to those who have been made free." He had been welcomed by the Governor at a meeting in Carnegie Hall, and he concluded his response with the following sentences:

> The Governor has spoken of a great task ended. Yes, the formulation of the peace is ended, but it creates only a new task just begun. I believe that if you will study the peace you will see that it is a just peace and a peace which, if it can be preserved, will save the world from unnecessary bloodshed. And now the great task is to preserve it. I have come back with my heart full of enthusiasm for throwing everything that I can, by way of influence or action, in with you to see that the peace is preserved—that when the long reckoning comes men may look back upon this generation of America and say: "They were true to the vision which they saw at their birth."

Two days later the President made an elaborate address to the Senate presenting the peace treaty and expounding his philosophy of America's new position in the world. I think it worth while to quote a paragraph from that address:

> It was not an accident or a matter of sudden choice that we are no longer isolated and devoted to a policy which has only our own interest and advantage for its object. It was our duty to go in, if we were indeed the champions of liberty and of right. We answered to the call of duty in a way so spirited, so utterly without thought of what we spent of blood or treasure, so effective, so worthy of the admiration of true men everywhere, so wrought out of the stuff of all that was heroic, that the whole world saw at last, in the flesh, in noble action, a great ideal asserted and vindicated, by a nation they had deemed material and now found to be compact of the spiritual forces that must free men of every nation from every unworthy bondage. It is thus that a new role and a new responsibility have come to this great nation that we honor and which we would all wish to lift to yet higher levels of service and achievement.

The Senators had not been made familiar in advance with the text of the treaty, although hundreds of Americans in subordinate positions at Paris had been fully acquainted with it, and many copies of it were under lock and key in the Department of State.

Since the Senate under our Constitution shares with the President the responsibility for international agreements, it would have been fortunate if leading Senators of both parties had been called upon earlier to spend some time at Paris in the atmosphere of the world conclave.

On the part of the critics of the treaty the Senate debate seemed legalistic and theoretical, rather than fully appreciative of realities. After the discussion had continued until October, Senator Knox, Senator Borah and others were wholly convinced that there lurked in the Covenant of the League certain dangers to the United States that must be removed by unambiguous reservations. I remarked at that time:

> It was a very difficult thing to formulate the great treaty of Versailles, and doubtless the experience of the future years will show that many mistakes were made; but we are quite frank in expressing the opinion that our Senators have not shown us very much that is vitally wrong. Mr. Root, Mr. Taft and Mr. Hughes, as wise and judicious Republican leaders, made some suggestions in the late winter or early spring that were heeded at Paris, and that to some extent at least were actually embodied in the existing treaty.
>
> If the document were ratified as it stands, it would not be amiss to seek modifications from time to time in the future. The League of Nations is simply an arrangement for organizing the governments of the world for the purpose of preventing the evils and dangers of militarism, for the perfection of international law, and for the establishment of justice among the nations and the protection of the rights of weaker peoples. This part of the treaty is the tentative framework of a world constitution. It can be amended from time to time just as our Federal Constitution has been amended. It will be remembered that our Constitution was adopted upon the implied understanding that a series of amendments would soon be adopted to meet the demands of certain States. Such amendments, it will be borne in mind, followed very promptly after the Constitution went into effect.

The Foreign Relations Committee, having held the treaty for two months of constant study, reported it to the full Senate. The Republican members of the Committee made a majority report (through Senator Lodge as chairman) recommending ratification with certain reservations. The Democratic members presented a minority report through Senator Hitchcock of Nebraska, favoring the adoption of the treaty exactly as presented by President Wilson, but not declining to allow certain interpretative expressions which would not be deemed a part of the treaty itself.

It is not easy, except perhaps for a few men who were active in France during that period—among these being General Pershing, General Dawes, Mr. Hoover, Mr. Thomas Lamont—to recall with full knowledge and vivid memory the appalling confusion and distress that prevailed in Europe during the months after the Armistice. Mr. Wilson thought that the prompt ratification of the treaty, and the establishment of the League of Nations as a going concern, and as a body capable of dealing with scores or even hundreds of new problems of adjustment, would give assurance to the world. Germany had been disarmed, but not conquered in spirit. Germans were hoping for disagreement among the Allies; and Mr. Wilson felt that our disapproval of the treaty would reopen European questions all along the line. We had been involved in issues of European political geography that we could not avoid in the circumstances. To ratify the treaty was to help stabilize these difficult changes.

Obviously, it would have been much easier for Mr. Wilson and the American delegation to side-step these boundary controversies altogether; but, as it happened, the Americans were in a disinterested position, and their services on boundary commissions were for that very reason insisted upon. Surely Americans could have had no motive in disappointing the Italians in a detail like the control of Fiume or points on the Dalmatian coast of the Adriatic. But the United States, having participated in the war, was obliged to take part in the Peace Conference that followed; and, just as our agency in the ending of the war had been conclusive, so our participation in the Peace Conference was bound to be conspicuous and vital.

As I remarked at the time:

> It would be unfair to Senators to deny that the Republican debate has upon the whole been very able as well as patriotic, although it has seemed to us not to have a true sense of proportion and to have unduly emphasized some details while failing to recognize that the treaty as a whole lies in the necessary line of that cooperation which was involved in the victory over Germany. The victory itself was on behalf of the rights of peoples great and small to be protected against military conquest. The victory was not to be regarded as an event, but as a continuing condition. International peace must henceforth be the object of active organization and constant vigilance.

The British, French, and other Allied governments showed no eager haste to ratify the treaty, although there was no hesitation elsewhere that could be attributed in the slightest degree to the questions about the League of Nations that absorbed American attention. Europe was concerned with reparations, boundary lines, disarmament, mandates, food, unemployment, loans, debts, revolutionary disorders, and the whole bitter aftermath of a war that had lasted more than four years. Foreign statesmen, wondering about the deadlock in the United States, found that senators were chiefly apprehensive about the employment of force in case of some future aggression.

The proposed "reservations" (which were not embodied in the text of the treaty, but were a memorandum merely expressing the views of the majority of the Senate) explained that in any situation calling for the use of our navy or army, our constitutional methods would have to be followed. This, however, was obviously true of all other governments. If the League of Nations had been supplied with an army and navy of its own, the case would have been different.

Having followed the long controversy as carefully and as impartially as could have been asked by either side, I came to the conclusion that the Senate might have ratified the treaty (after having debated it frankly) without creating misunderstanding at home or abroad. On the other hand, it was clear to my mind that Mr. Wilson might well have instructed his Senatorial following to come to such an agreement as they could with the Republican majority, and ratify the treaty.

However, the President would not consent to any compromise. He had often remarked to friends that he had a "one-track mind," and he would not use conciliatory methods. He believed that an appeal to the country would result in such a pressure of public opinion upon the Senate that his Republican opponents would be discredited. Against the advice of friends who feared that he lacked the physical strength for such an ordeal, he entered upon a nation-wide speaking tour that began at Columbus, Ohio, on September 4, and that included forty major addresses in seventeen states among which were all those of the Far West and Pacific Coast. Having spoken at Pueblo, Colorado, on the 25th, he became ill on his train and returned to Washington.

The speeches were wholly unlike those of an ordinary electoral campaign, for all of them were devoted to the exposition of an unprecedented international situation, with American ideals as the central theme. The sole purpose of the twenty-two-day tour was to convince the public that the treaty ought to be ratified, and that the reservations of the Republican senators were unnecessary. The speeches failed, however, to prove that the reservations could do any practical harm.

The President's illness proved serious, and its protracted character contributed to the further delay in disposing of the treaty, as well as to the transaction of other public business. Meanwhile, Viscount Grey of Fallodon (formerly Sir Edward Grey, who had been head of the Foreign Office for a number of years) had come to Washington as temporary Ambassador to succeed the Earl of Reading. Mr. Wilson's illness made it impossible for him to present his credentials, but he remained for several months, improving the opportunity to study our situation thoroughly, and becoming acquainted with many public men of both parties. Lord Grey returned to England in January (1920) to confer with his government, and soon afterwards an extended letter by him appeared in the *London Times*, which was promptly republished throughout the United States. I commented as follows:

> In this letter Lord Grey undertook to enlighten the British public as to the nature of the reservations adopted by the Republican majority in the Senate, and he made it quite clear that he regarded the reservations not only as reasonable from the American standpoint, but as in no way detrimental to Great Britain or the other members of the League of Nations. In our analysis of the reservations in the December number of the *Review* we explained that in any case arising in the future the British or French governments would of necessity act with the sanction of parliament. Most of the Lodge reservations merely recognize the principle that the United States also, like these foreign countries, will, in cases involving the exercise of war powers, act through the legislative as well as the executive part of the Government. A considerable portion of Lord Grey's letter was devoted to making this same explanation. The effect was immediate.

II.

This letter, as we were advised at the time, had been approved by the British Cabinet and shown in advance to the French Government. It was made clear that the European Allies found no reason to object to the Lodge reservations, and would be glad to have the treaty ratified whether with or without the accompanying memorandum. Following this letter of Lord Grey's, which had made a sensation in political circles, a new debate began in the middle of February with good prospects that enough Democrats would act with the Republican majority to ratify the treaty on Mr. Lodge's terms. Senator Hitchcock, in charge of the Wilson forces, admitted frankly that Lord Grey had previously told him that England did not object to the reservations.

To consider this controversy in further detail would be tedious, although many things that were said and done have a quality of pertinence today as we wonder, again, how we may avoid the pitfalls of partisanship in dealing with the aftermath of another world war. The final vote came on March 19, with 49 senators voting for the treaty, and 35 against it. It failed of ratification because of the lack of seven more affirmative votes to constitute the necessary two-thirds majority. These additional votes would have been readily forthcoming if such action had been favored by Mr. Wilson.

We were to hold a Presidential election in November, and both parties were already making plans for their conventions. President Wilson proposed that the election take the form of a referendum upon the League issue from his particular standpoint, but this idea was not accepted by party leaders in general. Mr. Cox as Democratic nominee stood upon firm ground in advocating the view that the United States should still enter the League. Such a course might have been pursued at any time, especially after the Republicans won a conclusive victory at the polls, because the implications of the Lodge doctrine had already been accepted at home and abroad. The long debate had become tiresome because it had lost its practical character.

We had entered the war in 1917 in acceptance of views and doctrines that had committed us in advance to a permanent association of free nations. We had expected when the Armistice came, and when the peace plans were taking form, to continue our active cooperation with the victorious governments.

It is reasonable, therefore, to inquire whether in reality we had drifted away from our ideals and had refused to live up to the promises we had made to ourselves and to the world. The Republican victory at the polls in November was sweeping, decisive and convincing as respects national opinion. In commenting upon the verdict of the voters I remarked:

> It is purely a matter of conjecture whether or not the Democrats lost votes as a result of their campaign efforts and arguments. It is proper to say, however, that the attempt to shape the League of Nations issue in such a manner that the Democratic party might be set in direct opposition to the Republican party, as nobler in spirit and more faithful to humanity in its views on our international relationships, was a dire failure.

There had been very few actual opponents of the Versailles Treaty in the Senate. The majority vote favoring ratification had been composed of Republicans with a few Democrats. Their affirmative vote carried with it the approval of the Lodge reservations. Those voting against ratification were in favor of the treaty, but were upholding Mr. Wilson's leadership. The country was not repudiating the ideals that President Wilson had expressed more fully than anyone else. Mr. Harding had voted twice for the Versailles Treaty, and on the eve of the election he telegraphed a statement to a college magazine at Grinnell, Iowa, from which I quote a passage:

> The Versailles settlement is so closely interwoven with the entire settlement of the world that I believe we should preserve everything useful that has been written into that treaty. An Association of Nations for the purposes of conference and with a court possessing jurisdiction over justiciable questions would, I am confident, be accepted by the civilized world. Many European statesmen have expressed this same view. The British Premier has declared that the League Covenant could be changed for the better. We of the Republican party entertain the same opinion and hope to be able, while saving the useful parts of the Versailles accomplishment, to build upon and improve upon them.
>
> Assuredly we have no intention to repudiate the world's ardent aspirations for peace. European leaders of state seem agreed that America can best lead in this effort at reconstruction, and I feel that for us to fail them would be to evade a plain duty. Viscount Grey and others have even suggested that the United States be entrusted to draft a plan for a reorganized Association of Nations. To accomplish that would be a great service to the world, and I hope America may be able to do its full share.

Two years had elapsed since the Armistice was signed. We were beginning to realize that the territorial reconstruction of Europe was not producing contentment and stability, and that Article X of the League Covenant (this being the article most severely scrutinized in the United States) seemed to imply unlimited obligations. The secret treaties had never been abrogated by the Allied governments; but the boundary changes of Europe were worked out without any reference to secret treaties since they were not comprehended in them. American influence was well exerted in drawing eleven thousand miles of new European frontiers. German colonies were "mandated" under League of Nations supervision.

Article X of the League Covenant had been so drafted as to create an unlimited obligation on the part of members to maintain — as a whole and in detail — all this network of reconstructed political geography. England, France, and Japan could not complain, because they were beneficiaries of the new system. They would not, however, have felt themselves impelled to use force in a given instance without having considered the case upon its merits. The United States had accepted no territory, and had refused to claim any share in war indemnities. Yet having been foremost in advocating the League of Nations, this country could not well have taken a leading place in the Council at Geneva without upholding the Covenant in all its parts.

It was for this reason that statesmen of Mr. Root's caliber, carefully analyzing Article X, thought that we should not be acting with good conscience if we did not indicate our unwillingness to be bound by it in given cases without specific action by Congress. Article X reads as follows:

"The Members of the League undertake to respect and preserve as against external aggression the territorial integrity and existing political independence of all Members of the League. In case of any such aggression or in case of any threat or danger of such aggression the Council shall advise upon the means by which this obligation shall be fulfilled."

As time had elapsed, it became increasingly evident to thoughtful Americans that their ideals had not dominated European minds when final form was given to certain articles of the League Covenant. European governments were not intending to disarm, or to relinquish national or imperial advantages. They were merely looking upon the League of Nations as an additional source of strength and security, as they pursued their respective policies. The vast majority of people in the United States, however, still believed in the maintenance of peace through collective agreements, and had by no means turned their faces away from Geneva in antagonism to the League.

In his statement to the *Grinnell Review*, Mr. Harding on the eve of his election had said:

> The Republican party earnestly wishes to perform for the cause of world peace the very service that the world wishes performed. It desires to help in every possible way. But it will never surrender our national heritage of complete national freedom and self-determination.

My own comments, after the election, included the following forecast which was in undoubted accord with the views of a majority of thoughtful Americans:

> There will come a time when the League will not only protect small nations in their essential rights as against powerful neighbors, but when no single country will be powerful enough to defy the opinion of the world as expressed through the League, or to run the risk of being outlawed. There must be no lowering of aims or relinquishment of ideals. It is as feasible a thing to have a League of Nations and international peace as it is to have a confederation of entities like our forty-eight States. But, while it is feasible, it is by no means easy; and it cannot be accomplished by a group of diplomats sitting around a table. Imperialism must be superseded, and a series of nations must emerge, each of which for vital purposes of its own security must insist upon an association of civilized peoples.
>
> The League of Nations formulated at Paris was in many respects fundamentally wrong. It was carefully framed to protect and preserve the domination of certain interests. It is true that the combined power of the Allies must persist until the world is reconstructed. It follows that an actual and real League of Nations cannot assume its full sway by moral authority, until the reconstruction period has been lived through. There is high value, then, in the ideals of the League advocates; and there is also hard sense and truth in some of the criticisms of the American opponents of the League Covenant as it now stands. It becomes necessary now to find an irreducible minimum of agreement. This minimum will suffice for the present.
>
> The opinion of the country is clarifying rapidly, and it would not be so difficult as some people suppose for Senators Knox, Borah, and Johnson to agree upon a program with Republicans like Mr. Root and Mr. Taft, or with Democrats like ex-Secretary Lansing and Colonel House. The President-elect will doubtless be as ready to confer freely with these two eminent Democratic members of the American peace delegation as with any of his Senatorial colleagues or his Republican supporters. We should not try to go beyond the steps which our country can freely and willingly agree to take.

President Harding, Secretary Hughes, and Secretary Hoover took no active steps in 1921, as the new administration assumed its responsibilities, to enter the existing League of Nations or to secure a revision of the Covenant. American objections had not been so much concerned with immediate problems as with general and future contingencies, and our adherence to the League was not a matter of urgency. Canada and other neighboring American countries were members, and we were indirectly represented at Geneva by the Dominion and by fellow-members of the Pan-American Union. The new governments of Europe—Poland, Czechoslovakia, Yugoslavia, as well as the young republics on the Baltic shore—were all sending their legations to Washington, where they were soon to feel more at home than in any other capital. Isolation was practically impossible for the United States.

There was great economic distress in Europe, and the United States was loaning money freely to the governments of countries great and small with which to buy American food and other supplies. Excepting for the exclusion of Germany and her recent Allies and the absence of our own country, there were no gaps in the rounded membership of the League of Nations.

III.

When ten jurists of international standing had met at The Hague in 1920 to draw up the "Statute of the Permanent Court of International Justice," otherwise known as the World Court Protocol, Elihu Root was the American member of that Committee. The Court was to be affiliated with the League of Nations. Presidents Harding, Coolidge, Hoover, and F. D. Roosevelt in succession, together with their Secretaries of State, urged the Senate to agree to our official endorsement of the Protocol of the Court; but it never became possible to secure the necessary two-thirds vote. Yet the World Court was established promptly, and distinguished American jurists one after another had seats as members of this high judicial body at The Hague.[1]

[1] An American professor, Manley O. Hudson, is the foremost authority on the World Court, of which he has been a member for several years. He has published (1943) under the auspices of the Carnegie Endowment for International Peace an authoritative work entitled *The Permanent Court of International Justice 1920–1942*. Judge Hudson, at the beginning of the League's activities at Geneva, was a member of its Secretariat; and he is typical of the many American political and legal experts who have been associated with the League of Nations and with various efforts for peace-keeping, during the past quarter-century.

We were not destined to enter the League of Nations "by the back door" or in any round-about manner, yet it might have been asserted that Washington was henceforth to be even nearer the center of world affairs than the pleasant Swiss city on the shore of Lake Geneva. With almost no delay, the Harding administration was facing the serious situation arising from naval competition. Nothing in the twenty-year history of the League of Nations could compare in importance with the Naval Conference at Washington, an account of which I have given in a previous chapter.

In September of each year the Assembly of the League held its annual session, and Geneva became a meeting-place for delegations from all parts of the world. The staff of permanent officials had adapted themselves to their expanding range of duties, and when I visited Geneva in September, 1924, to observe the organization in annual session, I found a loyal and capable body of men and women serving under the League's Secretary-General, Sir James Eric Drummond. Besides the delegates and their advisers and attendants from half a hundred countries, there were many visitors in Geneva, anxious to obtain tickets that would admit them to the galleries of the large Assembly Hall, or to the small meetings where seven or eight members of the Council sat together like judges of a high tribunal.

As a class, the visitors were not casual tourists. They were concerned about particular matters that were pending, or their presence indicated an approval of the general idea of a world society. To my surprise, I found that more than half of the visitors in Geneva at that time were Americans. Among them I encountered my friend the Hon. George W. Wickersham, prominent New York lawyer, who had been Attorney-General in Taft's administration and was one of our most public-spirited citizens. Others were there who had been connected with the large body of American experts and advisers at the peace conference. Mr. James McDonald, active head of the Foreign Policy Association, was among those who were studying the League in all its methods and activities.

I happened to be present at a meeting of the Council when the late Jeremiah Smith, Jr. made a report upon financial conditions in Hungary. This brilliant Boston lawyer and Harvard Fellow had served as an officer in the A. E. F. and was afterwards counsel to our Treasury Department and an adviser on financial questions at the peace conference. The dismemberment of Hungary and the distress caused by extreme currency inflation had reduced that once-prosperous Danubian country to a state of almost hopeless misery. Mr. Smith had been appointed Commissioner-General of the League of Nations for Hungary; and as a man of good will and a financial wizard, he had been sent to Budapest to re establish currency and credit. His oversight of Hungarian finance continued for two or three years.

Although Mr. Smith was taking no credit to himself, the report that he made (as I listened with close attention) gave me a new sense of the value, to a world in political chaos and economic collapse, of timely help from a disinterested citizen of a solvent country who was an expert and who spoke and acted with authority. An American lady, whose husband was also an eminent financier, turned to me and remarked as Jeremiah Smith concluded his report: "We must take this religiously." His services to Hungary were those of a man who was recognized as having saved the unhappy country from a condition too extreme for self-help. He gave this aid at personal sacrifice; but he thought of it as a "good Samaritan" kind of job, and refused to take any compensation, although a grateful government at Budapest sought to reward him in some way.

Mr. Hoover had administered relief to starving millions in that same spirit of willing service, and he could name many Americans who, like Jeremiah Smith, gave time and effort, through at least a dozen years, in cooperation with the League.

After some direct knowledge of the League and its work, I encountered an individual who said to me (reproachfully, as it seemed) that the United States had failed of its duty in declining to become a member of the League. I replied with some emphasis that the United States was the *only* member of the League! One does not have to explain or defend a paradoxical remark of that kind. In the official sense, Japan was a member of the League and the United States was not a member. But during the entire period—almost two decades—of the League's activities, the United States government was cooperating loyally with the League in all its general projects for world betterment, while Japan was using its membership in the League as a cloak for deliberately-studied policies of encroachment.

Among the most difficult of the tasks committed to the League was the supervision of the collection and payment by the new German government of the heavy indemnities and reparations exacted on behalf of the European Allies. At points of serious deadlock, necessitating readjustments of method or amount of payment, the Reparations Commission found American advice and judgment their best recourse. Thus the "Dawes Plan" (for which Gen. Charles G. Dawes of Chicago was sponsor) was in due time followed by the "Young Plan" (recognizing the financial and diplomatic talents of Mr. Owen D. Young of New York. When the Bank for International Payments was established on the Rhine at Basle, Switzerland, an American banker was engaged to organize and manage it. These are a few typical illustrations of American collaboration. Volumes will yet be written, in addition to much already in print, to present and review the nature and scope of American activities in support of the League of Nations.

Speaking from unusual and varied experience, in a time of turmoil and change throughout the world, Secretary Hughes once expressed to me a somewhat changed attitude regarding the advantages and disadvantages of our non-membership in the League. No one could doubt his devotion to the cause of international peace, and to all feasible methods of cooperation. But he had come to the conclusion that we—although outside the Geneva organization—could cooperate efficiently in various matters of importance both with the League and also with its various members. And he thought that our influence might be less, rather than greater, if we were officially at Geneva and were dragged, in spite of ourselves, into one European controversy after another in the capacity of an impartial umpire.

There were various activities, such as the suppression of the trade in narcotics, in which our initiative was even more insistent than that of the League. Our present Ambassador at London, John G. Winant, was director of the International Labor Office at Geneva, and had served there for several years, when in September 1939 the League's activities were suspended. Many reports and documents would supply evidence of cooperation on the part of the United States, whether directly or indirectly, with the League of Nations in the exercise of its useful peacetime functions.

In 1940 there appeared a volume by Professor William Starr Myers of Princeton entitled *The Foreign Policies of Herbert Hoover 1929–1933*. Mr. Myers observes that no man had ever occupied the Presidency with such a previous intimate acquaintance and experience with foreign peoples and their governments as Mr. Hoover. I have mentioned in a previous chapter the nature and extent of his international activities during the First World War; and as Secretary of Commerec (1922–28) he had taken a leading part during the Harding and Coolidge administrations in all that concerned our foreign relations.

The Naval Conference of 1922 had established a principle, and the scrapping of many great ships had impressed the world. England had adopted a new theory of world policy. Throughout most of the nineteenth century Britain had regarded herself as dominant on the seas, and as entitled to interfere almost anywhere when a forlorn cause needed a champion. Mr. Carr gives us the picture, in a few pages of frank and straightforward admission, of Britain's relative decline in capacity to make effective the government's declarations, protests, warnings, resolutions, and tentative courses of action. British relations with the United States had come to assume a different character from those with other foreign countries. This trustworthy exponent of his country's foreign policies expresses the changed position in the following paragraph:

> Behind the rivalry with the United States, there was a deep-seated feeling of a community of vital interests between the two nations. This feeling, intensified by cooperation in the War, made the Washington Naval Treaty seem a natural development of British policy. Its implication was that war with the United States had become unthinkable; for Britain, with her day-to-day dependence on imports and her long and vital lines of communication, could not possibly face war with a naval Power as strong as herself. The two-Power standard of the pre-War period had been replaced, as the corner-stone of British policy, by the one-Power standard *plus* perpetual peace with the United States.

Having in mind, undoubtedly, the situation in September 1939, Mr. Carr proceeds as follows: "Not only can Britain never contemplate war with the United States, but she could never contemplate any war with a first-class Power in which she could not count on the benevolent neutrality of the United States." That the British Government was assured in advance of American support "short of war" in 1939 was the general opinion throughout Great Britain. It was not only believed in official circles, but was expressed everywhere by private citizens—the small shopkeeper or the man in the street, as I discovered for myself during the weeks of late summer that preceded the war.

Mr. Baldwin as Prime Minister had said in 1934: "Never, so long as I have any responsibility for governing this country, will I sanction the British Navy being used for a naval blockade until I know what the United States of America are going to do." And Mr. Baldwin's successors were undoubtedly of the same mind.

It is not so easy, however, to translate a broad principle into the details of application. The Washington Conference had left its work incomplete. The agreement upon the 5-5-3 formula had been applied only to capital ships. Naval parity could not be obtained in fact, however, until the agreement had been extended to cruisers, submarines and destroyers. As President, Mr. Hoover took the lead in trying to complete the work of the Washington Conference. He had the sincere cooperation of Prime Minister Ramsay MacDonald, but while he encountered bitter opposition in the United States from certain ship-building interests and opponents of naval disarmament, Mr. MacDonald also had to contend with the traditional view, still cherished in naval circles, that Britain would never relinquish supremacy on the seas.

President Coolidge had attempted in 1927 to secure a further naval agreement, but a Conference at Geneva had failed to accomplish anything. Mr. Hoover undertook to prepare the ground carefully, negotiating personally with Prime Minister MacDonald who visited him at Washington, and having the full cooperation of Secretary Stimson and our Ambassador at London who was then General Charles G. Dawes. Principles were established first, and both countries renounced the idea of naval competition, accepted the doctrine of parity, and were alike in hoping that some reduction might be secured in the practical settlement. The complete account of the London Conference of 1930 is to be found in Professor Myers' chapter on naval limitation.

Agreements were worked out in this London Conference, but there were serious reasons to fear that the necessary two-thirds vote in the Senate could not be secured. President Hoover submitted the treaty to that ratifying body on May 1, 1930, but on

July 3 the Senate completed its session leaving the treaty in suspense, and not expecting to convene again until November or December. Yet Mr. Hoover was resolute. Using his constitutional prerogative, he convened the Senate in special session four days later, presenting a special message in which he summarized the agreement itself, and strongly defended the principle of armament limitation by agreement. Ratification, he declared would "translate an emotion deep in the hearts of millions of men and women into a practical fact of government and international relations. It would renew again the faith of the world in the moral forces of good will and patient negotiation as against the blind forces of suspicion and competitive armament."

The treaty was ratified on July 21 by a vote of 58 to 9, which was a remarkable result in view of bold propaganda against it and bureaucratic naval influences that were less open. One reason for this achievement was the practical wisdom used by Mr. Hoover in the appointment of delegates to the London Conference. Senators David A. Reed and Joseph T. Robinson, respectively Republican and Democratic leaders of the Senate, were members of the delegation at London. Their cogent arguments before the Senate Foreign Relations Committee had secured a favorable report.

IV.

In a letter to Prime Minister Ramsay MacDonald written at that time, President Hoover remarked: "The world makes its progress in short steps, and always by compromise; it is disheartening at times, but the main thing is to keep the light ahead."

President Hoover and Prime Minister MacDonald had taken the Kellogg-Briand Peace Pact "not only as a declaration of good intention but also as a positive obligation to direct national policy in accordance with its pledge." They had issued a joint statement to that effect in October 1929. Among the fifty-five countries that had signed this peace pact were China and Russia. But during the summer of that year 1929, these two great powers were engaged in a controversy that concerned Manchuria. Mr. Hoover and Mr. Stimson, citing the nine-power treaty of 1921 which guaranteed the independence of China, took the lead in bringing diplomatic pressure to bear upon the Russian and Chinese governments, with fortunate results. Their hostile forces were withdrawn. They signed an agreement, and the Kellogg Pact was (as it seemed) vindicated in a significant instance.

It was two years later, in September 1931, that the military forces of Japan invaded Manchuria and an international situation arose at once that affected the peace of the world and that could not be ignored either by the League of Nations or our government at Washington. There was nothing but moral force behind the Kellogg-Briand Pact and the nine-power treaty, but the plain duty was before our government to protest strongly, and to invite other nations to join us in some form of disapproval. China brought the situation before the Council of the League of Nations, and that body undertook to investigate and report.

President Hoover and Secretary Stimson were acting on lines parallel with those of the League, but perhaps with more energy. On January 7, 1932, the Department of State informed China and Japan that it would not recognize any situation brought about by force, in disregard of the obligations of the Kellogg-Briand Pact. That meant in plain words that our government would never recognize Japan's control of Manchuria.

Secretary Stimson was prepared to adopt economic sanctions against Japan, but Mr. Hoover felt strongly that any action of that kind, in view of the state of opinion in Japan, would have led to further aggressions and to war in which the United States would probably be involved. Mr. Stimson accepted the President's judgment, and the doctrine of non-recognition was announced as an administration policy. Japan had entered upon a program of aggression that was not affected by protests from Washington or Geneva; and toward the end of January an attack was made upon Shanghai. Perhaps we should have taken stronger measures, but our government at that time sought only to protect American interests by reinforcing our Hawaiian and Philippine bases and by sending our Asiatic squadron to Shanghai.

Mr. Stimson had served as Secretary of War in the latter part of the Taft administration and had been Governor-General of the Philippine Islands from 1927 until 1929. He left Manila to become Secretary of State in the Hoover Cabinet for four years (1929–1933). Some years later he was to enter President F. D. Roosevelt's Cabinet as Secretary of War, but could not be regarded as accountable for the policy that maintained unrestricted trade relations with Japan, and supplied that country with large quantities of war material until a few months before the surprise attack at Pearl Harbor.

It is enough to say with regard to the Hoover-Stimson policy of 1932 that the United States could not have been induced at that time to engage in war with Japan merely on account of an obscure and complicated situation in Manchuria. Mr. Hoover himself, while strongly opposed to Japanese aggressions, had outlined (in a paper that he read to the Cabinet) the kind of plausible argument that Japan might have made in justification.

Meanwhile, a tidal wave of financial panic and bank failure, starting in Austria and Eastern Europe, had spread westward and across the Atlantic. Mr. Hoover had a good financial head, and I think it fair to say that he did everything in his power to mitigate the situation. But banks were failing by the thousand, and a Congress that had been organized by the opposing party could not be persuaded to confer emergency powers upon the President, or to cooperate in any practical way to meet the disastrous situation. A party "swing of the pendulum" was indicated as wholly probable; and in November Franklin D. Roosevelt was elected President. Professor Myers in his concluding chapter on the foreign policies of Herbert Hoover, gives the following summary:

> In his drive for peace Hoover was constant and energetic. His practical accomplishments were: (a) reversal of the Wilson policies of intervention in Latin-American States; (b) withdrawal of all occupations by our marines and the consequent building of good will in the Western Hemisphere; (c) treaties further limiting the three leading navies of the world, an extension of the Hughes capital-ship limitations, to include cruisers, destroyers, and submarines. He urged economic cooperation with other governments.
>
> Hoover rightly opposed all entanglements in Europe and Asia and refused to engage in economic sanctions against other governments. When he left office three great negotiations were under way making for peace. These were concerned with the World Land Disarmament Conference, the World Economic Conference, and the extension of naval limitations.

The further discussions of land disarmament were futile, because of menacing situations. Japan had withdrawn from the League, and had flouted a series of treaties. In Europe, moreover, there was uneasiness as Hitler was coming into power, prepared to cast aside the Locarno agreements of 1925, that Foreign Minister Austen Chamberlain had signed with Foreign Minister

Briand and Foreign Minister Stresemann. But although nothing could be done about rival armaments, the appalling demoralization in the fields of production, trade, and standards of value required remedies that no single nation could apply.

The proposals for a World Economic Conference had been approved at Geneva, and in the summer of 1932 a conference at Lausanne had set about the formulation of programs. The League of Nations was placed in charge of preparations, and the conference was to be held at London in the following summer. The American delegation represented the new Roosevelt administration. Sixty-seven nations were invited to participate, and sixty-six were present. The absentee was of such minor importance that I cannot remember it, although I was in London at the time and in possession of all the official reports and records of the Conference. Daily bulletins for the convenience of the delegates, and of the hundreds of accredited journalists from all parts of the world, gave lists of members, committee assignments, synopses of speeches, and all pertinent data.

My final chapter includes a general description that I wrote at the time of this Monetary and Economic Conference, although I have never, hitherto, made any public use of it. This account seems to me appropriate for my present purposes, because that Conference was the last—and in some aspects the greatest—of all modern efforts to bring the nations of the world together in friendly discussion for purposes of vital importance. Germany and Russia, Japan and China, Italy and Greece were all represented by delegations of their ablest public men, and there was no line drawn between former enemies.

My account of the conference is that of a steadfast and undaunted believer in world cooperation; and although I write this chapter while a Second World War is raging, my general points of view have not changed. I believe no less firmly now than ten years ago, when I wrote of the London Conference, in the necessity—and also in the certainty—of future international arrangements to deal with problems of economic supply and distribution, and to stabilize monetary standards of value.

Chapter XX

ECONOMIC COOPERATION IMPERATIVE—THE WORLD CONFERENCE OF 1933

THE most casual reader will have discovered that this book has not deviated greatly from its promise at the outset to deal chiefly with things that have been accomplished hitherto—things that are quite certain to remain as contributions to the world's future stability. Although it has not been my purpose to forecast new forms or patterns of international relationship, I have no thoughts but those of good will for many attempts already made to outline such projects.

On all sides it is agreed that there should be timely foresight in planning for conditions that must be met immediately, when aggression — passing more or less rapidly through the stages of desperate defence — will at length have collapsed, as it must.

There will be hunger riots and political chaos in many places. For several years the shocks of ill-disciplined peace-time may be almost as violent as those of war. Social and political recovery in occupied European countries will be a slow and painful process. It will require international supervision. Public-health measures, and systematic efforts to produce and distribute food, will be quite as essential for some time to come as international agencies to furnish police protection.

These immediate post-war tasks will be the more difficult, because in the United States we will also have to provide for the return of armies and the demobilization of war industries. Public and private efforts must afford re-employment for at least thirty million persons. Through long periods of the world's history there were no such abrupt transitions from war to peace and *vice versa.* Armed conflicts were local and limited, and armies were relatively small and of professional character. What our English friends call "all-out" war can be endured only for a brief term of years. Thus, with all the difficulties of the transition to normal life, we know that peace is worth whatever it may cost, and that it can be established.

After the first strains of readjustment, the world will have to face a series of economic problems of permanent character. These will call for the application of broad principles, and the suppression of those devices of economic nationalism that followed the First World War, and that bore some causative relation to the present conflict.

The attempt to meet many of these problems in the world Monetary and Economic Conference at London ten years ago seems to me so instructive, as it bears upon conditions that will have to be faced after the end of the present conflict, that I am reproducing herewith an unpublished memorandum that I wrote at the conclusion of that conference.

(THE LONDON MONETARY AND ECONOMIC CONFERENCE: AN ACCOUNT WRITTEN IN 1933)

In the summer of 1933 there was assembled in London a "Monetary and Economic Conference" representing all the nations of the earth. Every Government had sent as Delegates men who were in positions of authority at their own capitals. In most cases these principal members of the Conference were accompanied by economists and technical experts, all of them well regarded in their own countries, and many of them of international reputation. His Majesty, King George V, inaugurating the Conference in person, declared this to be "the first time in history that any Sovereign has presided at the opening of a Conference of all the nations of the world."

The Conference had been called by the League of Nations, which had prepared its agenda after much consultation. But the League did not assume to control its organization, or to restrict its proceedings. "Without the League and without the ideals of the League," said the King, "I doubt whether this great meeting could ever have taken place. I welcome no less cordially the representatives of those States who are not members of the League; I recognize the spirit of helpful cooperation which has brought them to join in these discussions."

It was both unusual and felicitous that the King's address, which was typically brief, should have included some sentences spoken in French for the benefit of many delegates who were not familiar with English. Addressing them as "Messieurs les Delegues," he said that it was with a feeling of profound emotion that he saw around him this august assembly, which seemed so vast, but which represented a conception infinitely greater: the hopes and the vision of the entire world.

Continuing, he said: "The world finds itself in a state of disquietude; and for you, gentlemen, who begin today the work of restoration, the task is heavy. It can be achieved only by force of good will and sincere cooperation." Resuming his address in English, his Majesty declared that "all nations are suffering from a common ill," and he appealed to the assembly "to cooperate for the sake of the ultimate good of the whole world." There followed these significant sentences, well worthy of an occasion so unusual and so inspiring, and fit to stand as the short but complete creed of a New Era:

"It cannot be beyond the power of man so to use the vast resources of the world as to ensure the material progress of civilization. No diminution in those resources had taken place. On the contrary, discovery, invention and organization have multiplied their possibilities to such an extent that abundance of production has itself created new problems. And together with this amazing material progress there has come a new recognition of the interdependence of nations and of the value of collaboration between them. Now is the opportunity to harness this new consciousness of common interests to the service of mankind."

The British Prime Minister, the Rt. Hon. Ramsay MacDonald, as President of the Conference, made the principal opening speech. "Sixty-seven Governments have been invited," said Mr. MacDonald, "ten who are not members of the League of Nations, and the importance attached to our purpose is recognized by the fact that practically every Government invited has accepted the invitation. There is a greater authority gathered in this hall today than has perhaps ever been brought under one roof in the world's history."

Mr. MacDonald presented a startling picture of recent economic decline in normal vitality. He pointed to the closed factories, limited employment, and reduced standards of living that had brought some States to the verge of bankruptcy, and inflicted upon others recurring budgets that could not be balanced. The vigor of the human life of the world, so greatly dependent upon the machinery of international commerce, had been sapped to such an extent that "the world is being driven upon a state of things which may well bring it face to face once again with a time in which life revolts against hardship, and the gains of the past are swept away by the forces of despair."

Making comparisons over a three-year period, Mr. MacDonald found that the production of raw materials had fallen 30 per cent, and the exchange between town and country had been tragically limited. National income had fallen seriously everywhere—in some countries by 40 and 50 per cent. The Prime Minister further summarized the alarming situation in the following terms:

"The general crisis, accentuated by restrictions, by tariffs, quota, exchange-control, has reduced international trade between 1929 and 1932 to less than three-quarters in volume, exchanging at about half the price.

The gold standard has had to be deserted more generally than has been the case in time of peace since it was erected into the international measure of exchange, and inevitably, irrespective of fiscal policy and of forms of government, unemployment has mounted up until the world figure issued by the International Labor Office has reached 30,000,000."

Extreme nationalism, in the Prime Minister's view, while seeming to offer some temporary relief could only add to the general stagnation of world trade, and so intensify the influences which increase our troubles. "No one," said he, "who has surveyed the facts and watched their progress, can doubt for a moment that the experiences of the last few years have proved that a purely national economic policy in this modern world is one which, by impoverishing other nations, impoverishes those who pursue it. No nation can permanently enrich itself at the expense of others. Mutual enrichment is the condition of individual enrichment.

"Nationalism in the sphere of *politics* may be essential to human freedom; self-sufficient nationalism in *economics* is the death knell of advancing prosperity. The nearer we can make the world an economic unit, the better it will be for each nation. In any event, international cooperation is our best way to national recovery; and the nation which looks after itself in an international frame of mind will not only lead the world in enlightenment, but in well being."

These were impressive remarks; and as delivered in Mr. MacDonald's fervent oratorical manner, they thrilled the distinguished audience. Concluding that part of his speech, he added, "We are here, therefore, to pursue the better course of international agreement."

Among other observations made by the eminent Prime Minister was the following: "Statesmanship today will be judged by what it devises to dispel the stern realities of the present and anticipate the requirements of the future." He noted the intricacy of the Conference program, which included subjects upon which views had hitherto been irreconcilable. Yet he held that there could be no delay, and that rapidity of agreement was essential to success.

Since in point of fact rapidity of agreement was impossible—as became evident after a few weeks of serious effort on the part of many committees—the world was inclined to accept Mr. MacDonald's test, and to pronounce the Conference a failure because it could not provide an international money standard, agree upon sweeping tariff reductions, or bring the production of basic commodities to an agreed balance with market demands, while assigning to each particular country its exact quota of particular imports and of particular exports.

It would have been better, perhaps, if Mr. MacDonald had told the Delegates at the outset that the assemblage itself was a thing of great promise; and that there should be patience in view of what must be a slow process of gradual agreement upon experiments in the concrete problems of commerce and exchange.

The King was more profound, in his assurance of a future that can in due time be realized, than was the Prime Minister in his sanguine appeal for immediate results.

Hundreds of leaders were brought together from the ends of the earth. Experts elucidated problems of monetary gold and silver, of currency and exchange. They laid foundations for future measures that will save the world from dire catastrophes.

Furthermore, personal contact and frank discussion help to strengthen those methods and habits of intercourse and discussion that are destined to liberate us all from surviving dangers of appeal to arms. The Conference did not afford conclusive evidence that the millennium had dawned in dazzling refulgence. But it was not a failure by any reasonable test. Where it seemed to some observers to have been most discouraging in what they termed its futile and barren effort to achieve practical results, it may in time—as I think it will—prove to have been of exceptional value in clearing the way.

The "great States" had sent as delegates men holding the highest offices of Government, especially their ministers of finance, commerce, and agriculture. But the "small States" were not treated as of inferior right or influence; and they sent their most representative statesmen and men of affairs.

In the reformed world of intercourse and cooperation, there will have to be much further study given to the question of units for purposes of international representation. Whether continuous bodies like the League of Nations, or occasional world gatherings like the Economic Conference, are to furnish the starting point for a revised plan, it is obvious that Abyssinia, Liberia, Iraq, and Haiti will not have equal voice as sovereign units with the great nations that are also now reckoned as single entities when the world is assembled to consult or to ordain.

But adjustments as between large nations and small ones will come in due time, when the further development of international institutions has brought such questions into practical importance. To thoughtful minds, that time is not far remote, in view of the experience that has been provided by the League of Nations, as it has operated, under the disadvantage of grave structural defects.

Meanwhile, the actual governing of the world in the new period is not by League or by administrative machinery, but rather by public opinion. Hitherto, for many generations, the world has been dominated by major powers. Great States have justified conquest and over-rule on the ground of their superiority. Public opinion is a new force that sweeps across boundary lines. It is the enemy of brute force and ruthless tyranny. It comes to the support of small states that are suffering injustice, and it refuses to ignore the conduct of great states that are oppressing minorities within their own jurisdictions.

We are passing through a period of change that is full of contradictions and that often confuses the student of affairs, while it brings anxiety and pain, if not disheartenment, to idealists in all countries. But the old order was deeply entrenched. It was not ready to yield up its system of authority and privilege, except by degrees and by grudging concessions.

In these circumstances it was a great triumph for the new influences—demanding world-wide freedom of expression—to bring small sovereignties into contact with the so-called major powers, on terms of equality for purposes of argument and consultation. The Economic Conference provided a forum upon which the attention of the entire world was concentrated. The farmers of Canada, represented by their Prime Minister, Mr. Bennett, were in special conference with Argentina, Russia, Australia, and the United States upon the marketing of surplus wheat; and the experts of Italy, Germany, France, and Great Britain were at hand to explain their agricultural tariffs, and their policies aimed at the increase of wheat production at home, the raising of farm prices, and the reduction in quantity of imported breadstuffs. This was not a trivial matter. On the contrary, it was of vital importance to the well-being of millions of people in many countries.

Difficult problems having to do with the position of silver in India and in many other countries were discussed through long weeks in committees made up of statesmen and economic experts from all parts of the world. Never before had so much statistical information been brought to bear upon questions of currency, exchange, and standards of value as in this London Conference. There will be agreements in the future, toward which these London discussions were essential as preliminaries.

Cuba and other sugar-producing countries were placed in position at London to deal with sugar as an international problem, and this could be said as regards other important commodities.

The mere statement that sixty-six governments were represented at the Conference, ten of which were not members of the League of Nations, was a reminder of political changes of deep historic significance. Half a dozen of these states had once been parts of the Turkish Empire, and could not have appeared in their own right, previous to events within the memory of elder statesmen. Rearrangements following the Great War had given autonomy and full sovereignty to a number of new European States.

Out of the British Empire as formerly constituted there had evolved, by agreement and consent with no outside pressure or interference, a group of sister states enjoying full autonomy, and with no status of inferiority as regards their international position. These members of the so-called British Commonwealth of Nations were present in the London Conference, each being as independent of restraint and as free to determine its own course as was the mother country herself, namely, the "United Kingdom of Great Britain and *Northern* Ireland," as now officially designated.

The story of each one of these new self-governing entities, if fully told, must include long chapters of modern history that would bring many other countries and peoples into the narration. Poland was appearing in her own right. Egypt had come to London as an independent State. Finland was on hand in the dignified assertion of her ancient liberties. Belgium was present in restored security. These and many other existing examples of untrammeled statehood are now safe in the sanction of a new world of justice, in which the common sentiment of mankind becomes the best protection for the rights of unoffending nations. This simple fact is enough to stimulate the historical imagination of all those who cherish the hopes of an established reign of peace and order throughout the Continents, and over the ocean expanses.

II.

To return to the scene of that Conference of 1933—apart from its impressiveness as a peaceful gathering for consultation of all the nations of the earth—what was regarded as its most urgent objective? Undoubtedly it was the need of standardized and stable kinds of money, or media of exchange. The economic life of the world had become a matter of common concern. Trade could not be carried on by a primitive system of barter. Credit and value had to be expressed in terms of money. Monetary nationalism had run riot.

An increasing number of nations, both great and small, might indeed eke out a bare existence, but could not enjoy either prosperity or safety without external trade. But the movements of commerce require accounting, book-keeping, banking facilities, all in terms of money. When the purchasing power of money was changing as rapidly as in Germany in 1923 and '24, the real value of the mark at the food shops varied notably from day to day. I was in Germany in 1924 when it cost me *two thousand million* marks to buy coffee and rolls for breakfast. When that inflated currency was wiped out, and the attempt was made to put values on a sound basis, the inflated paper was redeemed on a scale of about five hundred million to one.

The ruble in Russia had gone through a similar experience of inflation. The sky was the limit. A cousin of mine, George E. White, President of an American college in Turkey, had occasion to visit the Russian Caucasus on some errand of mercy, and wrote to me that for the first and only time in his life he had found himself a millionaire. It is not for me to dwell upon the havoc that had been produced in the world by monetary nationalism, in an age when internationalism prevailed in the commercial world, and when it was essential to fix world standards for purposes of exchange and as measures of value.

Tariffs were a subject of heart-to-heart discussion in that London Conference. For example, the Chinese delegates complained that a change in the British tariff on eggs in powdered form was making millions of people unhappy in that Asiatic country of small farmers and low incomes. Countries of wheat production were in serious discussion with countries of wheat consumption, in an endeavor to find the best manner in which to recognize the law of supply and demand.

Mr. Cordell Hull, our dignified Secretary of State, as Chairman of the American delegation, was a respected figure in this London Conference; and he sought earnestly to find ways and means to harmonize the political interests of the United States with those of Europe, especially as affected by conditions of trade and commerce. The Hon. James M. Cox as head of the strictly economic section of our delegation, was in a similar mood of accommodation.

If an agreement could have been reached upon some monetary formula, the Conference would have been pronounced a brilliant success. For some reason, never made fully apparent either at home or abroad, President Franklin D. Roosevelt, at the very moment when the hopes of the Conference seemed to observers to be brightest and its spirit most fraternal, sent word to London that a special emissary representing his views was on his way to London. Professor Raymond Moley, who had for a time been the chief spokesman of the New Deal, was in Mr. Roosevelt's confidence and was serving conveniently as an Assistant Secretary of State. London was almost literally breathless with suspense as it waited for the arrival of Mr. Moley. The message was one of negation. The United States was unable at that time to join other nations in an agreement regarding currency and monetary standards.

Inasmuch as I was in London observing the Conference with hopeful interest, I can testify to the dismay that was wrought by this refusal to cooperate. After some days, the Conference adjourned. Its despondent mood was in evidence, but it did not break up in disorder, confusion, or bitterness. The hope was expressed that after a brief period, perhaps two or three years, this same Conference would be called in session again presumably by the United States, to hear reports of committees, and perhaps to find the acceptable formula for a universal monetary system. Committees charged with various phases or topics of economic interest were not disbanded, but were to continue their explorations. They were now aware that it would take time to find working solutions of various problems affecting international commerce.

History must and will move at its own tempo. Mankind has to learn things the hard way. The Conference of 1933 demonstrated the fact that the nations could come together in a spirit of goodwill to consider the welfare of a thousand million people and many more. Cooperation will come, regardless of the exact framework of world organization. The United States will not be able to pursue its future economic course in isolation, nor will any other national entity, whether great or small. The London Conference of ten years ago set up another conspicuous and still visible signpost, which stands as a symbol. International conferences to deal with economic questions that are international in their nature have begun again in 1943. Admittedly these questions are complicated and difficult; but when they are properly solved, we shall have arrived at the reasonable certainty of peace for future generations.

The United States Secretary of State, the Hon. Cordell Hull, had been accorded the foremost position of honor and prominence at the London Conference, and his prepared address of June 14 at an opening Plenary Session deserves high rank at a document in the history of economic internationalism. It would be difficult to find a better statement than Mr. Hull made, on that occasion, of the vital importance of world commerce and of the harm that had been wrought during previous years by national restrictions. In his first paragraph Mr. Hull declared that "the success or failure of this Conference will mean the success or failure of statesmanship everywhere, and a failure at this crucial time would long be conspicuous in history."

He advocated in that speech the policy of reciprocal trade agreements that he set in motion at Washington on his return from London,—a policy that Congress authorized in 1934 and again at three-year intervals, the last endorsement of the policy occurring in 1943. Mr. Hull, Mr. Cox, and their associates advocated practical middle courses, knowing that more than sixty nations could not at once so transform their nationalistic policies as to unite upon a program of universal and unrestricted freedom of trade. It was hoped, however, that a method could be found to give monetary systems a sound basis, with some reliable and permanent ratios of exchange. Having outlined what should be done, Mr. Hull concluded his address with the following sentences:

> The nations which sent us here are interested above all else in peace and prosperity, and the prerequisites of either is a wise readjustment of economic policies. Economic conflicts, with some exceptions, are the most serious and the most permanent of all the dangers which are likely to threaten the peace of the world. Let this great Conference, therefore, proceed to the herculean task of promoting and establishing economic peace, which is the fundamental basis of all peace.

III.

As the Conference was about to adjourn *sine die*, President Roosevelt sent a cablegram to Prime Minister MacDonald which I regard as important enough to deserve quotation in full:

> Before the recess of the Conference I want you to know of my sincere admiration and respect for your courage and your patience as its presiding officer. I feel that because of it the nations of the world can continue to discuss mutual problems with frankness and without rancor. Results are not always measured in terms of formal agreements. They can come equally from the free presentation of each nation's difficulties and each nation's methods to meet its individual needs. We in the United States understand the problems of other nations better today than before the Conference met and we trust that the other nations will in the same spirit of good will view our American policies which are aimed to overcome an unprecedented economic situation at home.
>
> Such interchange, especially if it results in full discussion of all problems and not a few only, makes progress more and not less possible in the future.
>
> That is why I do not regard the Economic Conference as a failure. Largely because of your tact and perseverance the larger and more permanent problems will continue to be analyzed and discussed. You recognize with me that new adjustments are necessary to meet world and national conditions which have never existed before in history. You can count on our continued efforts towards world rehabilitation because we are con-

vinced that a continuation of the work of the World Economic Conference will result in practical good in many fields of joint endeavor.

This message did not lift the drooping spirits of delegates who were leaving their London hotels, having come from places far and near in the vain hope that the Conference could at once do for their countries, by some magic of cooperation, what they could not do for themselves. But President Roosevelt had not meant to dash cold water upon such warmth of premature enthusiasm. This conference had been the most ambitious achievement of the League of Nations, and it had been valuable even in its seeming failure.

At the last Plenary Session on July 27, Mr. Hull made a concluding address which opened with allusions to the difficult circumstances that had impeded the progress of the Conference, and which proceeded as follows:

> It is inevitable in the light of these extremely complicated conditions that the Conference, having reached a few important agreements and concluded a thorough appraisal and understanding of the problems presented, would find it necessary to recess. Time must be afforded for some of these difficulties to be ironed out and for the nations further to broaden their economic plans and policies so as to coordinate them on a gradually increasing scale with the program of international cooperation which this Conference is undertaking to promulgate.

Not to quote further from the body of this able speech, which had no notes of apology or anti-climax, I will recall Mr. Hull's concluding words. They expressed the American spirit, in accordance with which certain members of our delegation were remaining in Europe to continue work upon the special committees to which they had been assigned. Said this forthright Tennessean to the statesmen of all lands, who were not soon to meet again in peaceful conference:

> The duty and responsibility of the Conference are well known to us, as they are to every intelligent citizen on the planet. I pray that each of us may be given the light clearly to see and fully to understand. We cannot falter. We will not quit. We have begun and we will go on.

When Mr. Hull spoke the final word at London in these terse, prophetic declarations, he could not have foreseen the rough experience that lay ahead. Yet he knew that in the very nature of things we would go on. Nine years later almost to the day, Mr. Hull made an address over a radio network in which he characterized the present conflict as "a life and death struggle for the preservation of our freedom, our homes, our very existence." Advocating future cooperative action under common agreement, Mr. Hull declared:

> Such cooperative action is already under way. Twenty-eight United Nations have proclaimed their adherence to a program of principles and purposes by which mankind may advance toward higher standards of national and international conduct. That program is embodied in the Declaration made on August 14, 1941, by President Roosevelt and Prime Minister Churchill, now known as the Atlantic Charter. The pledge of the Atlantic Charter is of a system which will give every nation, large or small, a greater assurance of stable peace, greater opportunity for the realization of its aspirations to freedom, and greater facilities for material advancement.

III.

Just how the nations of the world will proceed, in their recognition of common rights and duties, I do not know. Nor shall I attempt to make predictions. It is reasonable to believe that cooperation in the war effort, upon principles set forth in United-Nation pledges, may be followed by some successful efforts to complete the work of the London Economic Conference.

There are two impelling reasons for the resuscitation of the League of Nations. The more obvious one is the fact that it has a suitable habitat, unimpaired material facilities, and availability for a wide range of functions concerning which no one will question its capacity for usefulness.[1] The less obvious but more important reason for re-shaping the League of Nations into a serviceable organ of future international cooperation lies in the fact that its defects of structure have been so fully exposed and demonstrated that they can be remedied. Men who represent Mr. Wilson's spirit and purpose could revamp the Covenant, make it responsive to actual conditions, and give it a truly representative character.

[1] No sensible person could find arguments for the abandonment of Geneva as a focus for activities of an international character, at the end of the present war. The investment of millions in the League's new buildings and facilities by John D. Rockefeller personally, and by the Rockefeller Foundation, are evidence of America's actual, though unofficial, adherence to the world organization.

There are practical considerations that should impel the United States to take the leading place in making the League of Nations a worthy instrument of world service. The late Lord Lothian, Ambassador at Washington until his sudden death in December 1940, had made many speeches pointing out the imperfections of the Covenant of the League, and Professor Carr whose book is commended by the successor of Lord Lothian, devotes a chapter to the proof of his statement that "the League of Nations was ultimately wrecked by the fundamental discrepancy between its two functions." Mr. Wilson had proposed it as an arrangement to keep the peace, while Great Britain and France had actually shaped it to keep the *status quo*, or, as Professor Carr puts it, to serve as a "bulwark of the British Empire."

It was not the League's fault that it had no power to do what its disinterested projectors hoped for it. It could not revise its own framework, and it could not revise the peace treaties. Yet it became a valuable agency; and with a reformed constitution—acceptable to Russia, China, and India as well as to the English-speaking world and to the freedom-loving states of Europe and Latin-America—it can become a clearing-house of activities for economic and social progress, capable of winning the justified approval of liberal-minded people everywhere.

IV.

It would seem to me a great mistake to think lightly of the International Peace Conferences that were held at The Hague in 1899 and 1907, or to assume that, because Holland has had to endure such cruel wrongs and indignities in this Second World War, it will not become once more a focus of international interest, and a center for the administration of justice in disputes between nations. The so-called Palace of Peace at The Hague, begun in 1907 and completed in 1913, was built with money given by Mr. Andrew Carnegie. It was to provide a court house and library for the permanent court of arbitration that was established under a general treaty of 1899, signed at the first Hague Conference.

At least twenty countries cooperated in providing materials, furnishings, or decorations for this symbolic structure. When the Permanent Court of International Justice was formed at the end of the First World War, it became an occupant of this Hague building. The first of the two conferences was called by the Czar Nicholas, and it made great advances in international law while also providing a permanent tribunal for arbitration. The second Hague Conference was called by President Theodore Roosevelt, who afterwards transferred the initiative to the Czar and the Queen of Holland. Forty-four states were represented, and among other things the conference ruled against the use of force for the recovery of debts. There were important treaties relating to wartime practices, all of which Germany and Japan have disregarded, although they were parties to the agreements.

The future of peace and war in the world must for a time—perhaps a long time—be conditioned upon the sheer balance in war power between the United Nations and the Axis group. We believe that the democratic spirit will prevail, and that the aggressive autocracies will be overwhelmingly defeated. The transition from United-Nations authority to normal conditions of peace will be gradual. Relief and rehabilitation will become a universal task. My own proposals for a government of the oceans and the islands may gain consideration when the Anglo-American fleets can safely afford to merge themselves in a permanent arrangement.

Learning to apply the principles of self-government and federation will absorb the energies of the half-hundred Soviet Republics of Russia. The reconstructed republic of China will perhaps have to face a century of domestic difficulties. The puzzling but not insoluble problems that the people of India must work out for themselves will require little except good will and fair play from Europe and America.

With no desire to gloss over any faults or mistakes of American policy, it is my belief that our forefathers set us upon right courses, and that we have followed the light with approximate consistency. Henceforth we shall proceed, not by reversals of policy or change of convictions, but by dealing with issues as they arise, in the spirit of our traditions and ideals.

There are so many interests that require collective consideration that few wise and thoughtful persons deny the need of united agencies in some form that is authoritative and continuous. But more fundamental than any machinery of world government is (1) the purpose of men to be at peace, (2) the methods of intelligent democracy, and (3) the removal where possible of causes that provoke bad feeling and incite trespass by armed forces of one country upon the domain of another.

The failure to provide for a powerful union of states at the end of the First World War has not been the sole cause of the present conflict, but it has been a contributing factor. It might indeed be said that if nations were contented and prosperous within their own bounds, they would not make war upon their neighbors, and powerful international organization would not be necessary. An argument of this kind, however, could be disposed of by carrying it to its ultimate conclusions.

Thus it might be asserted that if our states were peaceful and neighborly, maintaining freedom of trade and intercourse with one another, they could fare well without a federal government, and save themselves much expense and disputation. We should have forty-eight small nations, respecting boundary lines and living as good neighbors, without a federal government that seems always trying to usurp authority beyond the limit of its delegated functions.

But our early experience—and our later, not less—has clearly demonstrated the fact that there must be political union and a central government for many good reasons beside that of defense on sea and land. If a higher federation, bringing nations and continents together, were formed by common consent, its constructive services would soon prove of great value to the world, apart from what is often called the "police" function.

We have learned that the United States Army is not needed on any large scale to keep the people of the United States from rebelling against their own institutions. For a few years after the War between the States federal troops were maintained in the South to uphold the new amendments of the Constitution. A brief ten-years' experience led the dominant party to abandon that policy.

Democratic freedom along with schools, churches, newspapers and all the other instruments and agencies of community life makes for social stability. If we have arrived at certain average conditions that are endurable although far from perfect, with freedom on the part of majorities to improve conditions as they see their way, while minorities are respected, further progress can be made through moral incentives and through educational and economic advantages.

If we attempt to survey world conditions, country by country or region by region, at once we confront different degrees of democratic freedom, of popular enlightenment and of social advancement. We may look across the border at our Canadian neighbors. Their confederacy is much younger than ours, and its racial and economic contrasts are greater. Yet no federal army under control at Ottawa is needed to maintain order in this northern half of our continent, with its four thousand miles of international boundary separating it from our republic. With several million inhabitants of French race and speech, the Dominion fears no race conflict, and has no reason to wish that all Canadians spoke the same language and read the same newspapers. All things in this world are relative: so we may call Canada a stable and contented nation.

With their history of conquest by a European power, the native Indian races of Mexico—who had long ago attained a civilization of their own that lifted them far above the status of primitive tribes—have had four centuries of difficult experience. They have been gradually adjusting themselves to the conditions of modern life, and adapting principles of democracy and economic independence to their confused racial and traditional backgrounds.

Mexicans lived far below a reasonable subsistence standard in the long period when President Diaz controlled them by his ubiquitous force of military police. Then they strove to assert their right to freedom and opportunity by following one revolutionary leader after another. With liberty achieved, with farms for peons, and with schools for their children, the Mexicans will become a great people to be cherished as desirable neighbors.

It is this process of freedom and advancement in their own home-setting, for those whom Lincoln called the "common people," that will make possible a successful form of international association. It will require constant effort and vigilance to supersede spasmodic and occasional efforts to harmonize nations, and to maintain world civilization as one strong and continuing fabric.

The present war period has already added much to our knowledge of the interesting and terrifying world in which we live; and it is to be expected that when peace is established it will be upon terms widely different from those of 1919. It will have a more comprehensive scope, not so didactic and prim, and more tolerant because less narrow-minded. Union lies in the conceptions and purposes of well-disposed men; and this union of minds will create its own institutions.

APPENDIX A

PRESIDENT WILSON'S FOURTEEN POINTS

In an address before the Congress at Washington, meeting in joint session on January 8, 1918, President Wilson stated the war aims and peace terms of the United States. This was at the mid-point of our nineteen months of war activity. It was in the preparation of this address that Mr. Wilson had formulated what has since been known as his "Fourteen Points." The paragraphs of this address that immediately preceded the peace program (embodied in the fourteen numbered declarations) are presented herewith, and are followed at once by the so-called "Wilson Program for Peace":

"We entered this war because violations of right had occurred which touched us to the quick and made the life of our own people impossible unless they were corrected and the world secure once for all against their recurrence.

"What we demand in this war, therefore, is nothing peculiar to ourselves. It is that the world be made fit and safe to live in; and particularly that it be made safe for every peace-loving nation which, like our own, wishes to live its own life, determine its own institutions, be assured of justice and fair dealing by the other peoples of the world as against force and selfish aggression.

"All the peoples of the world are in effect partners in this interest, and for our own part we see very clearly that unless justice be done to others it will not be done to us. The program of the world's peace, therefore, is our program; and that program, the only possible program, as we see it, is this:

"1. Open covenants of peace, openly arrived at, after which there shall be no private international understandings of any kind but diplomacy shall proceed always frankly and in the public view.

"2. Absolute freedom of navigation upon the seas, outside territorial waters, alike in peace and in war, except as the seas may be closed in whole or in part by international action for the enforcement of international covenants.

"3. The removal, so far as possible, of all economic barriers and the establishment of an equality of trade conditions among all the nations consenting to the peace and associating themselves for its maintenance.

"4. Adequate guarantees given and taken that national armaments will be reduced to the lowest points consistent with domestic safety.

"5. A free, open-minded, and absolutely impartial adjustment of all colonial claims, based upon a strict observance of the principle that in determining all such questions of sovereignty the interests of the populations concerned must have equal weight with the equitable claims of the government whose title is to be determined.

"6. The evacuation of all Russian territory and such a settlement of all questions affecting Russia as will secure the best and freest cooperation of the other nations of the world in obtaining for her an unhampered and unembarrassed opportunity for the independent determination of her own political development and national policy and assure her of a sincere welcome into the society of free nations under institutions of her own choosing; and, more than a welcome, assistance also of every kind that she may need and may herself desire. The treatment accorded Russia by her sister nations in the months to come will be the acid test of their good will, of their comprehension of her needs as distinguished from their own interests, and of their intelligent and unselfish sympathy.

"7. Belgium, the whole world will agree, must be evacuated and restored, without any attempt to limit the sovereignty which she enjoys in common with all other free nations. No other single act will serve as this will serve to restore confidence among the nations in the laws which they have themselves set and determined for the government of their relations with one another. Without this healing act the whole structure and validity of international law is forever impaired.

"8. All French territory should be freed and the invaded portions restored, and the wrong done to France by Prussia in 1871 in the matter of Alsace-Lorraine, which has unsettled the peace of the world for nearly fifty years, should be righted, in order that peace may once more be made secure in the interest of all.

"9. A readjustment of the frontiers of Italy should be effected along clearly recognizable lines of nationality.

"10. The peoples of Austria-Hungary, whose place among the nations we wish to see safeguarded and assured, should be accorded the freest opportunity of autonomous development.

"11. Rumania, Serbia, and Montenegro should be evacuated; occupied territories restored; Serbia accorded free and secure access to the sea; and the relations of the several Balkan states to one another determined by friendly counsel along historically established lines of allegiance and nationality; and international guarantees of the political and economic independence and territorial integrity of the several Balkan states should be entered into.

"12. The Turkish portions of the present Ottoman Empire should be assured a secure sovereignty, but the other nationalities which are now under Turkish rule should be assured an undoubted security of life and an absolutely unmolested opportunity of autonomous development, and the Dardanelles should be permanently opened as a free passage to the ships and commerce of all nations under international guarantees.

"13. An independent Polish state should be erected which should include the territories inhabited by indisputably Polish populations, which should be assured a free and secure access to the sea, and whose political and economic independence and territorial integrity should be guaranteed by international covenant.

"14. A general association of nations must be formed under specific covenants for the purpose of affording mutual guarantees of political independence and territorial integrity to great and small states alike."

APPENDIX B

DECLARATION BY UNITED NATIONS JANUARY 1, 1942, WITH ATLANTIC CHARTER

DECLARATION BY UNITED NATIONS:

A JOINT DECLARATION BY THE UNITED STATES OF AMERICA, THE UNITED KINGDOM OF GREAT BRITAIN AND NORTHERN IRELAND, THE UNION OF SOVIET SOCIALIST REPUBLICS, CHINA, AUSTRALIA, BELGIUM, CANADA, COSTA RICA, CUBA, CZECHOSLOVAKIA, DOMINICAN REPUBLIC, EL SALVADOR, GREECE, GUATEMALA, HAITI, HONDURAS, INDIA, LUXEMBOURG, NETHERLANDS, NEW ZEALAND, NICARAGUA, NORWAY, PANAMA, POLAND, SOUTH AFRICA, YUGOSLAVIA.

The Governments signatory hereto,

Having subscribed to a common program of purposes and principles embodied in the Joint Declaration of the President of the United States of America and the Prime Minister of the United Kingdom of Great Britain and Northern Ireland dated August 14, 1941, known as the Atlantic Charter.

Being convinced that complete victory over their enemies is essential to defend life, liberty, independence and religious freedom, and to preserve human rights and justice in their own lands as well as in other lands, and that they are now engaged in a common struggle against savage and brutal forces seeking to subjugate the world, DECLARE:

(1) Each Government pledges itself to employ its full resources, military or economic, against those members of the Tripartite Pact and its adherents with which such government is at war.

(2) Each Government pledges itself to cooperate with the Governments signatory hereto and not to make a separate armistice or peace with the enemies.

The foregoing declaration may be adhered to by other nations which are, or which may be, rendering material assistance and contributions in the struggle for victory over Hitlerism.

Done at Washington
January First, 1942

The United States of America
by FRANKLIN D. ROOSEVELT

The United Kingdom of Great Britain
and Northern Ireland
by WINSTON S. CHURCHILL

On behalf of the Government
of the Union of Soviet Socialist Republics
MAXIM LITVINOFF
Ambassador

National Government of the Republic of China
TSE VUNG SOONG
Minister for Foreign Affairs

The Commonwealth of Australia
by R. G. CASEY

The Kingdom of Belgium
by Cte R. v. STRATEN

Canada
by LEIGHTON MCCARTHY

The Republic of Costa Rica
by LUIS FERNÁNDEZ

The Republic of Cuba
by AURELIO F. CONCHESO

Czechoslovak Republic
by V. S. HURBAN

The Dominican Republic
by J. M. TRONCOSO

The Republic of El Salvador
by C. A. ALFARO

The Kingdom of Greece
by CIMON G. DIAMANTOPOULOS

The Republic of Guatemala
by ENRIQUE LOPEZ HERRARTE

La Republique d'Haïti
par FERNAND DENNIS

The Republic of Honduras
by JULIÁN R. CÁCERES

India
by GIRJA SHANKAR BAJPAI

The Grand Duchy of Luxembourg
by HUGUES LE GALLAIS

The Kingdom of the Netherlands
by A. LOUDON

Signed on behalf of the Government of
the Dominion of New Zealand
by FRANK LANGSTONE

The Republic of Nicaragua
by LEÓN DE BAYLE

The Kingdom of Norway
by W. MUNTHE MORGENSTIERNE

The Republic of Panamá
by JAÉN GUARDIA

The Republic of Poland
by JAN CIECHANOWSKI

The Union of South Africa
by RALPH W. CLOSE

The Kingdom of Yugoslavia
by CONSTANTIN A. FOTITCH

DECLARATION OF PRINCIPLES, KNOWN AS THE ATLANTIC CHARTER, BY THE PRESIDENT OF THE UNITED STATES OF AMERICA AND THE PRIME MINISTER OF THE UNITED KINGDOM, AUGUST 14, 1941.

Joint declaration of the President of the United States of America and the Prime Minister, Mr. Churchill, representing His Majesty's Government in the United Kingdom, being met together, deem it right to make known certain common principles in the national policies of their respective countries on which they base their hopes for a better future for the world.

First, their countries seek no aggrandizement, territorial or other;

Second, they desire to see no territorial changes that do not accord with the freely expressed wishes of the peoples concerned;

Third, they respect the right of all peoples to choose the form of government under which they will live; and they wish to see sovereign rights and self-government restored to those who have been forcibly deprived of them;

Fourth, they will endeavor, with due respect for their existing obligations, to further the enjoyment by all States, great or small, victor or vanquished, of access, on equal terms, to the trade and to the raw materials of the world which are needed for their economic prosperity;

Fifth, they desire to bring about the fullest collaboration between all nations in the economic field with the object of securing, for all, improved labor standards, economic advancement and social security;

Sixth, after the final destruction of the Nazi tyranny, they hope to see established a peace which will afford to all nations the means of dwelling in safety within their own boundaries, and which will afford assurance that all the men in all the lands may live out their lives in freedom from fear and want;

Seventh, such a peace should enable all men to traverse the high seas and oceans without hindrance;

Eighth, they believe that all of the nations of the world, for realistic as well as spiritual reasons must come to the abandonment of the use of force. Since no future peace can be maintained if land, sea or air armaments continue to be employed by nations which threaten, or may threaten, aggression outside of their frontiers, they believe, pending the establishment of a wider and permanent system of general security, that the disarmament of such nations is essential. They will likewise aid and encourage all other practicable measures which will lighten for peace-loving peoples the crushing burden of armaments.

APPENDIX C

ITALY'S CHANGED STATUS AS DECLARED ON OCTOBER 13, 1943—A PATTERN FOR RECONSTRUCTION

The earlier dismissal of Mussolini by the King, with the downfall of the Fascist regime, and the announcement of a new Government headed by Marshal Badoglio, soon led to an Armistice, under terms prescribed by General Eisenhower and accepted by the Italian authorities.

Five weeks later, on October 13, 1943, there followed an Italian Declaration of War on Germany. This was accompanied by a note to General Eisenhower, and by a Proclamation to the Italian people. At the same time there was made public a joint Statement by President Roosevelt, Prime Minister Churchill and Premier Joseph Stalin acknowledging the changed status of Italy, and accepting the nation as a co-belligerent in the war against Germany.

The military aspects of this reversal of position by the Italian government were by no means unimportant. But the political bearings of the situation, as affecting Italy's internal and external relationships subsequent to the expulsion of German troops and the termination of the war, are of even greater consequence. The nation will be free to set up a constitutional democratic government, and "nothing can detract from the absolute and untrammeled right of the people of Italy" to decide on the political arrangements they may prefer.

Thus while the war was still raging, a pattern was set that might afterwards be followed in the cases of Bulgaria, Austria, Hungary and Rumania. Similar principles, evolved from Wilson's Fourteen Points and the Atlantic Charter, could be applied to the political reconstruction of some of the occupied European countries when liberated from German oppression.

A few days earlier, an announcement had been made by Generalissimo and President Chiang Kai-shek to the effect that within a few months after the defeat of Japan the people of China would be brought under a free and thoroughly democratic system of constitutional government. Repeated assurances, also, have been given to the people of India that as soon as the necessity for the present military regime has lapsed with the end of the war, they will be at liberty to set up such institutions of government as they may decide upon, with a position of full sovereignty as a member of the family of nations.

The documents relating to Italy, bearing the date of October 13, follow herewith:

NOTE TO GENERAL EISENHOWER

Marshal Badoglio communicated Italy's declaration of war against Germany to General Dwight D. Eisenhower in the following message:

I take great pleasure in informing you that His Majesty the King of Italy has declared war on Germany.

The declaration will be handed by our Ambassador in Madrid to the German Ambassador at 3 o'clock p. m. (Greenwich Time) on October 13 (today).

By this act all ties with the dreadful past are broken and my Government will be proud to be able to march with you on to the inevitable victory.

Will you be good enough, my dear General, to communicate the foregoing to the Anglo-American, Russian and other United Nations Governments?

I should also be grateful to you if you would be kind enough to inform the Italian Embassies in Ankara, in Buenos Aires and the legations in Berne, Stockholm, Dublin and Lisbon.

MARSHAL BADOGLIO'S PROCLAMATION

Immediately after Italy's declaration of war against Germany Marshal Badoglio issued the following proclamation:

Italians, with the declaration made September 8, 1943, the Government headed by me, in announcing that the Commander in Chief of the Anglo-American forces in the Mediterranean had accepted the armistice requested by us, ordered the Italian troops to remain with their arms at rest, but prepared to repel any act of violence directed at them from whatever other source it might come.

With a synchronized action, which clearly revealed an order previously given by some high authority, German troops compelled some of our units to disarm, while in most cases, they proceeded to a decisive attack against our troops.

But German arrogance and ferocity did not stop here. We had already seen some examples of their behavior in the abuses of power, robbery and violence of all kinds perpetrated in Catania while they were still our allies.

Even more savage incidents against our unarmed populations took place in Calabria, in the Puglie and in the area of Salerno.

But where the ferocity of the enemy surpassed every limit of the human imagination was Naples. The heroic population of that city, which for weeks suffered every form of torment, strongly cooperated with the Anglo-American troops in putting the hated Germans to flight.

Italians! There will not be peace in Italy as long as a single German remains upon our soil.

Shoulder to shoulder we must march forward with our friends of the United States, of Great Britain, of Russia and of all the other United Nations.

Wherever Italian troops may be, in the Balkans, Yugoslavia, Albania and in Greece, they have witnessed similar acts of aggression and cruelty and they must fight against the Germans to the last man.

The Government headed by me will shortly be completed. In order that it may constitute a true expression of democratic government in Italy, the representatives of every political party will be asked to participate.

The present arrangement will in no way impair the untrammeled right of the people of Italy to choose their own form of democratic government when peace is restored.

Italians! I inform you that His Majesty the King has given me the task of announcing today, the 13th day of October, the declaration of war against Germany.

THE ALLIED STATEMENT

The text of a joint statement by President Roosevelt, Prime Minister Churchill and Premier Joseph Stalin on the declaration of war by Italy against Germany follows:

The Governments of Great Britain, the United States and the Soviet Union acknowledge the position of the Royal Italian Government as stated by Marshal Badoglio and accept the active cooperation of the Italian nation and armed forces as a co-belligerent in the war against Germany.

The military events since September 8 and the brutal maltreatment by the Germans of the Italian population, culminating in the Italian declaration of war against Germany, have in fact made Italy a co-belligerent and the American, British and Soviet Goxernments will continue to work with the Italian Government on that basis.

The three Governments acknowledge the Italian Government's pledge to submit to the will of the Italian people after the Germans have been driven from Italy, and it is understood that nothing can detract from the absolute and untrammeled right of the people of Italy by constitutional means to decide on the democratic form of government they will eventually have.

The relationship of co-belligerency between the Governments of Italy and the United Nations Governments can not of itself affect the terms recently signed, which retain their full force and can only be adjusted by agreement between the Allied Governments in the light of the assistance which the Italian Government may be able to afford to the United Nations' cause.

APPENDIX D

JOHNS HOPKINS UNIVERSITY LECTURES ON DIPLOMATIC HISTORY

(The post-graduate department of history and political science at the Johns Hopkins University has always kept international relationships and diplomatic history at the forefront as a field of study and research. At the instance of Professor Herbert B. Adams, who was head of that department for twenty-five years (from the opening of the University in 1876 until his death in 1901), provision was made in 1898 for a course of lectures each year on some phase of American diplomatic history.

(The first and second courses were given in 1899 and 1900 by young men who greatly distinguished themselves in subsequent years as historical scholars. The following list gives names of lecturers year by year, with their subjects. Most of the lecturers prepared their material for subsequent publication, and many noteworthy and authoritative volumes were issued by the Johns Hopkins Press. All but seven in the long list that follows were issued as Johns Hopkins volumes in the series known as "Albert Shaw Lectures on Diplomatic History." This lectureship is now directed by Owen Lattimore as a feature of the Walter Hines Page School of International Relations.)

ALBERT SHAW LECTURES ON DIPLOMATIC HISTORY

1899. John H. Latané. The Diplomatic Relations of the United States and Spanish America. 1900 (out of print).

1900. James Morton Callahan. The Diplomatic History of the Southern Confederacy. 1901 (out of print).

1903. George M. Fisk. Commercial Relations of the United States and Germany. 1903 (unpublished).

1904. John W. Perrin. Diplomatic Relations of the United States During the Administration of Thomas Jefferson. 1904 (unpublished).

1905. James Alton James. Diplomatic Relations of the United States, 1793–1801. 1905 (unpublished).

1906. Jesse Siddall Reeves. American Diplomacy under Tyler and Polk. 1907 (out of print).

1907. Elbert Jay Benton. International Law and Diplomacy of the Spanish-American War. 1908.

1908. Ernest Ashton Smith. Diplomatic Negotiations Concerning the Ohio Valley, 1740–1760 (unpublished).

1909. Ephraim Douglass Adams. British Interests and Activities in Texas, 1838–1846 (out of print).

1910. Hiram Bingham. The Scots-Daren Company: An International Episode (unpublished).

1911. Charles Oscar Paullin. Diplomatic Negotiations of American Naval Officers, 1778–1883. 1912.

1912. Isaac J. Cox. The West Florida Controversy, 1798–1813. 1918.

1913. William R. Manning. Early Diplomatic Relations between the United States and Mexico. 1916.

1914. Frank A. Updike. The Diplomacy of the War of 1812. 1915 (out of print).

1915. Clarence W. Alvord. The Partition of the West in 1783: A Study in Diplomacy (unpublished).

1916. Edward Porritt. The Diplomatic History of the International Waterways between the United States and Canada from the Treaty of Washington of 1871 to the End of the Trouble over the Welland Canal in 1893 (unpublished).

1917. Payson Jackson Treat. The Early Diplomatic Relations between the United States and Japan, 1853–1865. 1917.

1921. Percy Alvin Martin. Latin America and the War. 1925.

1922. Lindsay Rogers. The Control of Diplomacy.

1923. Henry Merritt Wriston. Executive Agents in American Foreign Relations. 1929.

1926. Samuel Flagg Bemis. Pinckney's Treaty: A Study of America's Advantage from Europe's Distress, 1783–1800. 1926. Second printing 1941.

1927. Bruce Williams. State Security and the League of Nations. 1927.

1928. J. Fred Rippy. Rivalry of the United States and Great Britain over Latin-America, 1808–1830. 1929.

1929. Joseph B. Lockey. A Decade of Control of American Diplomacy.

1930. Victor Andrés Belaunde. Bolivar and the Political Thought of the Spanish-American Revolution. 1938.

1931. Charles Callan Tansill. The Purchase of the Danish West Indies. 1932.

1932. DEXTER PERKINS. The Monroe Doctrine, 1826–1867. 1933.

1933. CHARLES SEYMOUR. American Diplomacy during the World War. 1934. Second printing 1942.

1934. DEWITT C. POOLE. Democracy and Foreign Affairs.

1935. FRANK H. SIMONDS. American Foreign Policy in the Post-war Years. 1935.

1936. JULIUS W. PRATT. Expansionists of 1898. The Acquisition of Hawaii and the Spanish Islands. 1936.

1937. DEXTER PERKINS. The Monroe Doctrine, 1867–1907. 1937.

1938. ARTHUR PRESTON WHITAKER. The United States and the Independence of Latin-America, 1800–1830. 1941.

1939. WILLIAM SPENCE ROBERTSON. France and Latin-American Independence. 1939.

1940. ALBERT WEINBERG. History of American Isolationism.

1941. THOMAS A. BAILEY. The Policy of the United States toward the Neutrals, 1917–1918. 1942.

1942. WILFRID HARDY CALLCOTT. The Caribbean Policy of the United States, 1890–1920. 1942.

INDEX